Interdisciplinary Studies in Human Rights

Volume 8

Human rights are one of the normative cornerstones of contemporary international law and global governance. Due to the complexities of actual or potential violations of human rights and in light of current crises, new and interdisciplinary research is urgently needed. The series Interdisciplinary Studies in Human Rights recognizes the growing importance and necessity of interdisciplinary research in human rights. The series consists of monographs and collected volumes addressing human rights research from different disciplinary and interdisciplinary perspectives, including but not limited to philosophy, law, political science, education, and medical ethics. Its goal is to explore new and contested questions such as the extraterritorial application of human rights and their relevance for non-state actors, as well as the philosophical and theoretical foundations of human rights. The series also addresses policy questions of current interest including the human rights of migrants and refugees, LGBTI rights, and bioethics, as well as business and human rights.

The series editors are Members of the Centre for Human Rights Erlangen-Nürnberg (CHREN), an interdisciplinary research center at Friedrich-Alexander-University Erlangen-Nürnberg. The Advisory Board brings together human rights scholars from a wide range of academic disciplines and regional backgrounds. The series welcomes suggestions for publications of academic research falling into the series subject matter.

More information about this series at https://link.springer.com/bookseries/15339

Hyun Jung Lee

Discrimination Based on Sexual Orientation

Jurisprudence of the European Court of Human Rights and the Constitutional Court of Korea

Springer

Hyun Jung Lee
Public Law
Friedrich Alexander University
Erlangen, Germany

ISSN 2509-2960 ISSN 2509-2979 (electronic)
Interdisciplinary Studies in Human Rights
ISBN 978-3-030-95422-2 ISBN 978-3-030-95423-9 (eBook)
https://doi.org/10.1007/978-3-030-95423-9

This Springer imprint is published by the registered company Springer Nature Switzerland AG
The registered company address is: Gewerbestrasse 11, 6330 Cham, Switzerland

Preface

This book is based on the legal dissertation that I submitted to the Law Faculty of the University of Erlangen – Nürnberg in April 2021 under the title of "Discrimination Based on Sexual Orientation in the Jurisprudence of the European Court of Human Rights (ECtHR) and the Constitutional Court of Korea (CCK): Towards the Prohibition of Discrimination." In my dissertation, the first supervisor was Prof. Dr. Jan-Reinard Sieckmann, the second reviewer was Prof. Dr. Markus Krajewski, and the third reviewer was Prof. Dr. Laura Clérico.

I have had an academic as well as practical passion for the rights of sexual minorities for the last 10 years. Particularly, I wanted to give references to other jurisprudences including Korea where sexual minorities still suffer from discrimination. As a result of the process of fighting for democracy since 1980, the level of general human rights protection has been continuously improved in Korea. However, in some areas of human rights violation, there has been no or very little progress. One of these is discrimination based on sexual orientation. Sexual minorities are considered to be one of the most vulnerable groups who suffer from discrimination in various aspects in South Korean society.

In the jurisprudence of the European Court of Human Rights as well, there are many areas including same-sex marriage, where more protection is needed for sexual minorities. However, the level of protection is surprisingly low in South Korea even in cases where the protection is regarded as mostly provided by the ECtHR. One of those cases is criminalization of homosexual relations between consenting adults. In this work, the discrimination based on sexual orientation is criticized by means of the methods of adjudication, principles, and theories.

One of the most important methods is the principle of proportionality. It is widely used as a criterion of fairness and justice to assist in discerning the balance between the restrictions imposed and the severity of the prohibited act. And it has affected the jurisprudence of Korea as a right adjudication. Throughout this work, there is a focus on how discrimination based on sexual orientation in Korea cannot be justified and how disproportionate it is, for example, to punish homosexual relations under the

Korean military criminal law, or not to provide any legal framework to recognize same-sex relationships from the legal perspective.

Analysis of the jurisprudence of the ECtHR can certainly give implications to the development of the jurisprudence of the CCK in protecting the rights of sexual minorities in Korea. As alternative measures to foster the prohibition of discrimination based on sexual orientation in Korea, applications of the principle of non-discrimination, the principle of proportionality, legislation of anti-discrimination law, and legal philosophical implications of moral enforcement are suggested in this book.

I am particularly indebted to my supervisor, Prof. Dr. Jan-Reinard Sieckmann, not only for his critical suggestions and valuable comments regarding this work; but also, because he has trusted me, given me chances, cheered me up with confidence so that I have been able to research, teach, and grow in the law faculty of the University of Erlangen – Nürnberg since March 2016. I am sincerely grateful to his support. Without it, I could literally not have completed this work throughout all the difficulties that arose during my study.

I want to thank Prof. Dr. Laura Clérico for being my supervisor of my master's thesis, which has become the preliminary work of this book. It was the luckiest thing that happened to my academic career to be able to learn from her since fall 2015. Prof. Dr. Laura Clérico! Thank you for giving me confidence as a researcher as well as a teacher. Your passion, energy, knowledge, and warm hearts always have inspired me, and will continue to do so. You are the engaged scholar I admire, the elder sister I like, and the role model I want to follow.

I want to express my gratitude to Prof. Dr. Markus Krajewski, the second reviewer of my doctoral thesis which this book is based on, for giving me in-depth insights about human rights law through his lectures, seminars, and conferences since beginning my master's in human rights.

I want to thank my sons—Joon, Yeonsu, Eunjun, and Yoon. Thank you for being my sons and being always there for me. And I also want to thank mom, dad, and my sister Miya for believing me.

Finally, I want to dedicate this work to my husband Hyungjoon JUN. While writing this work, I had extensive conversations with him, who has written his first book of "Beyond Asiatic Perfectionism – Reflections on the legitimacy of Moral Enforcement and Hopes for Human Nature through an in-depth study on 'Asian values' and Asiatic Perfectionism (FAU University Press, 2021)" and I was greatly inspired by the philosophical considerations of where such hatred against sexual minorities come from. You are the most wonderful person I know. I love you as a good husband, I respect you as an inspiring colleague and a good researcher.

Erlangen, Germany
November 2021

Hyun Jung Lee 李賢貞

Contents

Abbreviations

AGG	The General Equal Treatment Act (AllgemeinesGleichbehandlungsgesetz)
Art.	Article
BVerfG	Federal Constitutional Court of Germany (Bundesverfassungsgericht)
CCK	The Constitutional Court of Korea
CCT	The Constitutional Court of Taiwan
CEDAW	Convention on the Elimination of All Forms of Discrimination Against Women
CESCR	UN Committee on Economic, Social and Cultural Rights
CRPD	Convention on the Rights of Persons with Disabilities
ECHR	The European Convention of Human Rights
ECtHR	The European Court of Human Rights
FRA	European Union Agency for Fundamental Rights
IACHR	The Inter-American Convention of Human Rights
IACtHR	Inter-American Court of Human Rights
ICCPR	International Covenant on Civil and Political Rights
ICESCR	International Covenant on Economic, Social and Cultural Rights
KMCL	Korean Military Criminal Law
LGBT	Lesbian, Gay, Bisexual and Transgender

Chapter 1
Introduction

One of the challenges for universal human rights today is whether morality can be enforced by law. To overcome such challenges, it is necessary to distinguish between the areas in which states must and must not intervene. In the past, many moral issues in Korea were enforced by the state based on Confucian traditions in Korea. One of the most well-known examples is criminal punishment for adultery.[1] Although a considerable amount of time has passed since it was a punishable offense, some people have still sent a petition to the administrative authority in Korea to reintroduce a law to criminalize adultery.[2] Such a belief that the state has to actively punish and enforce morality, exceeding the level of simple moral condemnation, has significantly influenced legal entitlement in Korean society. The criminalization of same-sex relations under the Korean Military Law can be understood as part of such an influence.

On the other hand, individuals' human rights are overly emphasized in certain areas such as protecting personal information in Korea. In the debate over whether to expose a criminal's face to the public or not, the majority of people participating in the discussion are actively interested in establishing the protection institutionally. They tend to agree with the protection of personal information. Nevertheless, recognition that the patriarchal culture is fading slow and there is a lack of respect for minority rights. Particularly, the rights of sexual minorities are still ignored in public debate in Korean society. This current work begins by asking about such a gap between different views in distinct areas of human rights. More importantly, the

[1] On February 26, 2015, The Constitutional Court of Korea decided the Korean criminal law Article 241 to punish adultery as imprisonment of 2 years or less as unconstitutional because it violates the right of self-determination in sexual matters and the right to privacy. (The Constitutional Court of Korea, decided on February 26, 2015, 2009 Hun-Ba 17).

[2] The petition for legislation to criminalize adultery again started on April 19, 2020 through an administrative authority and ended unsuccessfully on May 19, 2020 with 2,262 votes because the petition will only come into effect when it has a minimum of 200,000 votes (source: https://www1.president.go.kr/petitions/588152. Accessed November 30, 2021).

H. J. Lee, *Discrimination Based on Sexual Orientation*, Interdisciplinary Studies in Human Rights 8, https://doi.org/10.1007/978-3-030-95423-9_1

main questions to ask are where such a gap comes from and why it is difficult to recognize discrimination, especially in relation to sexual orientation.

I believe that such a gap in Korean society comes from the divergence in recognizing the difference between the ethical realm and the moral realm. According to *J. Habermas*, ethical deliberations refer to my/our own good life while moral viewpoints consider equal respect for each person and equal consideration for the interests of all.[3] It can be advantageous to distinguish the ethical deliberations of individuals from morals that could apply universally for all. The state can intervene in moral considerations as universal principles, but it cannot intervene in individuals' ethical deliberations. In other words, even if other individuals have different ethical deliberations from me/us, we should respect the difference and tolerate them. Why do people respond to violations concerning their own personal information but are surprisingly insensitive to all the discriminatory acts against sexual minorities in Korea? I believe that some of the reasons come from confusions between ethical deliberations and universal morals. The critical analysis of the cases throughout this work clarifies that prohibiting discrimination based on sexual orientation is considered a universal moral principle.

In South Korea, it is not recognized as discrimination to criminally punish consenting same-sex relations under military criminal law or to not legally recognize same-sex marriage. Some acts such as drug use are punished by criminal law because they are considered harmful to other people. Even if sexual minorities do not harm anyone because of their sexual orientation, people hesitate to accept and respect them. That is because people may misunderstand their individual ethical considerations as universal moral considerations. Majorities may have depended on the state to act on their uncomfortable feelings towards sexual minorities by enforcing morality—by criminalizing same-sex relations or by inaction in the case of institutionalizing same-sex marriage. However, such a misunderstanding prevents universal human rights from being able to guarantee the protection of sexual minorities.

This work does not argue that the state must be completely neutral with respect to individuals' rights and freedom. Nevertheless, states cannot intervene in criminalizing same-sex relations because other people have uncomfortable feelings towards sexual minorities; nor can states effectively intervene by being inactive in the case of institutionalizing same-sex marriage due to uncomfortable feelings of others. It is possible for a community to eventually attain universal values by guaranteeing individual freedom to those who have different values and ideas. In this work, I want to clarify the prohibition of discrimination based on sexual orientation as a universal value in pluralistic societies by critically analyzing the cases mainly in the jurisprudence of the European Court of Human Rights and the Constitutional Court of Korea.

The conflicting relationship between the role of the state and morality relates to the critical claim behind the debate whether the universality of human rights can be

[3] Habermas (1996), p. 97.

found in the extension of morality. Arguing that the validity of universal human rights emerges from a moral perspective justifies law as a sub-category of morality in that case. It is only natural that what is morally justified is applied to the law. However, the validity of legal norms is believed to justify their coercive role in reducing the various conflicts that arise in relation to the liberties of individuals. The tension between morality and law needs to exist on the prerequisite of mutual understanding that *Habermas* seeks, and can be resolved by allowing universal justification of human rights.[4] Furthermore, the principle of democracy[5] can be explained by the fact that community members make autonomous decisions and recognize each other as free and equal members.

I have reflected on the importance of this mutual understanding and recognition considering the hate directed at sexual minorities, especially in Korean society.[6] Mutual understanding means that the ability to resolve social conflicts when implementing democracy in a modern pluralistic society overcomes the limits of the moral justification of human rights. Moral discourse could give rise to conflicts because views on moral justification differ widely. However, if human rights are discussed in legal discourse, justification of human rights is less complicated and conflicts arise less compared to moral discourse.[7] This is because the law can be a mutual and cooperative relationship rather than a subordinate concept of morality. If people believe that morals take precedent over laws, then it is difficult to respect others who have different moral standards. Some people feel that homosexuality is greatly at odds with their own morals or values, leading them to discriminate against sexual minorities, or even support the criminalization of homosexuality.

Discussing discrimination based on sexual orientation with reference to individual freedom can lead to conflicts between individuals with different opinions in a pluralistic society. On the dispute over moral coercion in South Korea, the basis for those claiming that states need to impose a certain morality on others is that they view human rights as an extension of morality. If human rights are regarded as subordinate to morality, it is not easy to understand and acknowledge others, even if it is an integral part of a democratic society. If some people claim that morals take precedence over the law, relativists will reply that it would be difficult to understand

[4] Habermas (2001), p. 129.

[5] Habermas (1996), p. 110.

[6] In the first case to confirm the prohibition of same-sex marriage as a court ruling in Korea (Seoul Seo-Bu District Court, 2014 Ho-pa 1842, decided on December 6, 2016), the Court stated that there is no consensus about same-sex marriage among national people in Korean society yet. In reality, the consensus of public opinion is far from accepting legal recognition of same-sex relations.

[7] I have referred to moral norms and legal norms to justify human rights (taken from Habermas 1996, pp. 104–111). I have reflected that the discussion on discrimination based on sexual orientation faces strong resistance because people approach the issue only from moral discourse. From this perspective, human rights can be considered only as abstract rights, which do not have the power to implement themselves. Nevertheless, from the perspective of legal discourse, human rights can be considered as specific rights to be implemented. Therefore, I want to approach the right not to be discriminated based on sexual orientation as *Habermas*'s idea to view human rights not only as moral norms but also as legal norms.

other people with different moral standards. This work starts from a critical perspective on the tension of individual ethics and universal morals and the subordination of law to morality because this is one of the main reasons for such extreme hatred towards sexual minorities in Korean society. If prohibiting discrimination can be recognized as a legal right, it would be easier to understand others with different moral standards. Mutual understanding is the basis of a democratic, pluralistic society.

1.1 Aims of the Study

The study's general aim is to analyze the cases dealing with discrimination based on sexual orientation according to the types of the jurisprudence of the European Court of Human Rights (ECtHR) and the Constitutional Court of Korea (CCK). The work aims to suggest some legal considerations for prohibiting discrimination based on sexual orientation by creating an analysis from a comparative perspective. Moreover, this work will reflect on moral enforcement by states and clarify how the enforcement of morality and individual autonomy will be necessary to establish legal entitlements to prohibit discrimination based on sexual orientation. To make non-discrimination workable, this work examines the need for a general anti-discrimination law in Korea. Furthermore, legal methodological tools will be reviewed to further clarify how violations can be found in the jurisprudence of the ECtHR and the CCK.

There are three central aims in the study: analytical, critical, and normative. The *analytical* aim is to better understand the principles and theories applied in the jurisprudence of the ECtHR and the CCK dealing with discrimination based on sexual orientation. It is academically important to analyze the cases of the ECtHR and the CCK because the protection of sexual minorities is currently evolving not only in Europe, but also globally, including Korea, and the rights of sexual minorities is the most under-developed area considering the degree of democratization and the level of rights protection in Korea. Even if some of the approaches are seen as lagging,[8] the ECtHR is clearly moving in the right direction towards prohibiting discrimination based on sexual orientation to provide positive stimuli to the Constitutional Court of Korea.

The *critical* aim of this work is to examine the jurisprudence of the ECtHR and the Constitutional Court of Korea from a crucial perspective towards making the prohibition of discrimination based on sexual orientation workable. I will particularly examine the applicability of the principle of non-discrimination, the principle of proportionality, and other relevant concepts, including positive state obligations, the margin of appreciation, and the consensus argument in the case law on

[8] *E. Abrusci* discussed some of the approaches that the ECtHR adopted, such as "regional consensus" are behind the Inter-American Court of Human Rights (IACtHR) (Abrusci 2017, pp. 255–256).

non-criminalization of same-sex relations and same-sex marriage. Non-criminalization of same-sex relations is considered as the beginning of a discussion of discrimination based on sexual orientation because the protection is mostly given by the jurisprudence of the ECtHR. On the other hand, it is still criminally punishable under the Korean Military Criminal Law. Same-sex marriage is an issue where there is still no European consensus within the Member States of the Council of Europe, thus this is considered as a difficult case.[9]

The *normative* aim is to contribute to a better development of the legal methodology in discrimination based on sexual orientation. More specifically, I will suggest applying the principle of non-discrimination, and the principle of proportionality, with a better understanding of the concepts of positive state obligations, the margin of appreciation, and the consensus argument with the end goal of prohibiting discrimination based on sexual orientation in the case law of the ECtHR and the Constitutional Court of Korea.

1.2 Raising the Issue

Limiting the freedom of individuals is closely related to the role of the state. In that sense, it is a fundamental question to find out if such limitations by the state can be justified. There are different opinions on how the state should position itself. Some believe that the state must be completely neutral, and no morality can be enforced on individuals. According to these opinions, the state should merely prevent or punish the infringement of the freedom of others so that individual freedoms can be extensively protected. However, it is difficult to find situations where the state does not intervene simply because the individual does not harm others. In some cases, the state must intervene even if people do not harm others. There may be indisputable cases in which the state should intervene and punish obvious harm to others, such as assaults, thefts, or murder. On the other hand, discussion is still open as to whether states have positive obligations to intervene in cases that do no harm to others, such as drugs, euthanasia, suicide, pornography, adultery, abortion, and homosexuality.[10]

[9]The ECtHR uses consensus argument and the doctrine of margin of appreciation, especially in the case law on same-sex marriage, without providing any clear guidelines for future cases. There are many different factors to be known as determinants to affect the width of margin in the applications of the doctrine of margin of appreciation. Nevertheless, many scholars still question what the exact factors that determine the width of the margin are. Furthermore, the ECtHR has held the “consensus argument” to be particularly relevant where the cases raise “sensitive moral or ethical issues” or “complex issues, and choices of social strategy” and the case law on same-sex marriage is considered to be included there (please see Lavrysen 2016, pp. 189–190).

[10]Especially related to discrimination based on sexual orientation, I can think of the state’s positive obligation as a role to guarantee pluralism as *Lavrysen* discussed (please see Lavrysen 2016, pp. 94–98). The state has obligations not to criminally punish same-sex relations or to provide

If it is argued that the state should intervene in matters that may give others an unpleasant feeling, the breadth of the argument can be deeper and wider. My question starts here: can the state punish same-sex relations between consenting adults and intervene morally on the grounds of cultural differences or religious differences? This question is closely related to how individual human rights can be seen. As *Kant* argues, if individual autonomy is considered as residing in sole and fundamental rights that belong to all human beings just because they are human, individuals should be independent of the coercion of others.[11] If so, as long as an individual has autonomy and his/her own personality, his/her behavior and conditions are compatible with the freedom of other people based on generally accepted social rules, hindrances interfering with such actions are regarded as unjustified.[12] When the conditions above are fulfilled, it seems to be difficult to coerce a particular moral by state actions simply because such actions are "unpleasant" due to cultural and religious differences. In other words, no one can actually tell me to become happy not in my way but in their own way, or to legally force some actions or inactions just because my pursuit of happiness creates "unpleasant" feelings for other majorities in the society or the state itself.

It is not a simple matter of whether moral coercion by the state is justified or not. Certainly, in a "positive" state, the authorities have already intervened positively in so many areas of human conduct.[13] However, for such moral coercion by the state through intervention, a certain premise is needed. That is, individual autonomy should be positively guaranteed and prioritized because the idea of individual autonomy is the premise for the justification of human rights.[14] If the legal punishment of same-sex relations is considered as punishing some acts that give an "unpleasant" feeling to others, it allows the law to punish moral misconduct without any victims. Legal moralism seems to provide some legitimacy that could overly limit individual autonomy for the sake of society's public order or moral standards. In Korean society, the majority of its members state that they have unpleasant feelings when they think of same-sex relationships. Moreover, same-sex relations between consenting adults in the military are also generally understood as "abnormal" acts. The starting point of the discussion should be that "unpleasant" feelings cannot define the legal discourse.

---

legal recognition of same-sex relations to guarantee pluralism as the sexual minorities are one of the most vulnerable groups in most societies.

[11] Kant (1968), pp. 238–239.

[12] Ibid. pp. 103–104.

[13] Lavrysen (2016), p. 3.

[14] Sieckmann (2012), p. 146.

1.3 Scope of the Study

A recent important study of the methodological tools in the ECtHR case law is the *Human Rights in a Positive State* by *Laurens Lavrysen*.[15] This book provides a general introduction to develop the concept of positive obligations applied by the ECtHR. Cases of discrimination based on sexual orientation involve the state's positive obligation because not only interference but also the provision of legal recognition of same-sex relations matter when finding violations committed by the states. In this sense, *Lavrysen*'s work is relevant for my work, because it gives an extensive overview in the specific field of positive state obligations under the European Convention on Human Rights (ECHR), and *Lavrysen*'s work aims to contribute to a better development of the ECtHR's legal methodology, especially in the field of positive obligations.

However, this work will not be the same as *Lavrysen*'s work or other works dealing with methodological tools adopted by the ECtHR. The former studies' scope is limited to a problem with a specific methodology or analysis of case law in the ECtHR. For example, *Lavrysen* focused on the relationship between positive and negative state obligations under the ECHR, while *Arai-Takahashi*[16] concentrated on the margin of appreciation doctrine in the jurisprudence of the ECHR. Unlike *Lavrysen* or *Arai-Takahashi*, this work does not focus only on one specific methodological tool but on the cases related to discrimination based on sexual orientation both in the jurisprudence of the ECtHR and the Constitutional Court of Korea to prohibit discrimination mainly through the applications of more extensive methodological tools.

In this work, the scope of the cases is limited mainly to the two topics of non-criminalization of same-sex relations and same-sex marriage in the ECtHR[17] and the Constitutional Court of Korea. My justifications are as follows: firstly, there are no previous works analyzing the jurisprudence related to sexual orientation in the ECtHR and the Constitutional Court of Korea by a Korean lawyer or Korean legal scholar. There are some works[18] that analyze the U.S. Supreme court cases, but there has been no attempt to analyze the jurisprudence of the ECtHR and to explore if there are implications into the case law of the Constitutional Court of Korea. Secondly, the case law on non-criminalization of same-sex relations is the beginning of a discussion about prohibiting discrimination based on sexual orientation as the

[15] Lavrysen (2016), pp. 2–27.

[16] Arai-Takahashi (2002), pp. 2–15.

[17] *F. Edel* analyzed the extensive scope of case law of the European Court of Human Rights relating to discrimination on the grounds of sexual orientation or gender identity, and there are many topics such as parental authority and adoption, the establishment of a legal parental relationship with the partner's child, and social protection where a sufficient standard of protection is not given to sexual minorities under the ECHR (please see, Edel 2015).

[18] *Sung-Jin Ryu* is one of the Korean legal scholars who have analyzed the US Supreme Court cases about same-sex relations (please see, Ryu 2013).

right to sexual freedom. Even if the ECtHR banned criminalizing same-sex relations between consenting adults,[19] there are still many other jurisdictions where such protections are not provided, surprisingly including Korean Military Criminal Law. In that sense, it is important to carry out a case analysis of the non-criminalization of same-sex relations. Thirdly, it is important to analyze same-sex marriage cases because they are considered as hard cases in the European context as well because no European consensus exists yet.[20] As *Edel* argues, "the recognition or non-recognition of same-sex marriage is a matter left wholly to the discretion of states"[21] and the process of legal reasoning is also not very clear, which makes same-sex marriage cases under the ECtHR hard cases. Analyzing such cases to include some evolving tools under the ECtHR will provide implications for the Constitutional Court of Korea, where no constitutional case of same-sex marriage currently exists.

The main normative sources used for the present study are the judgments and decisions of the ECtHR case laws in the field of sexual orientation and same-sex

[19] European Court of Human Rights, ***DUDGEON v. UNITED KINGDOM*** (Application no. 7525/76), judgment of 22 October 1981.: The applicant, Mr. Jeffrey Dudgeon is a 35-year-old shopping clerk resident in Northern Ireland. Mr. Dudgeon is a homosexual, and his complaints are directed primarily against the existence in Northern Ireland of laws which have the effect of making certain homosexual acts between consenting adult males criminal offenses (para. 13). In this case, the ECtHR has concluded that Mr. Dudgeon has suffered and continues to suffer an unjustified interference with his right to respect for his private life and there is accordingly a violation of Art. 8 (Right to respect for private and family life) the ECHR (para. 63).

[20] In the Schalk and Kopf case, the ECtHR notes that "there is no European consensus regarding same-sex marriage." (European Court of Human Rights, *Schalk and Kopf v. Austria*, judgment of 24 June 2010, para. 58.): European Court of Human Rights, ***SCHALK AND KOPF v. AUSTRIA*** (Applications no. 30141/04), Chamber judgment of 24 June 2010. (The applicants are a same-sex couple living in Vienna, born in 1962 and 1960. On September 10, 2002, the applicants requested the Office for Matters of Personal Status to proceed with the formalities to enable them to contract marriage. By a decision of 20 December 2002, the Vienna Municipal Office refused the applicants' request. Referring to Article 44 of the Civil Code, it held that marriage could only be contracted between two persons of opposite sex. In a constitutional complaint, the applicants alleged that the legal impossibility for them to marry constituted a violation of their right to respect for private and family life and of the principle of non-discrimination. On December 12, 2003, the Constitutional Court dismissed the applicants' complaint as ill-founded, stating that "the fact that same-sex relationships fall within the concept of private life does not give rise to an obligation to change the law of marriage." Nevertheless, the ECtHR finds no violation of Article 12 (Right to marry) because Art. 12 does not impose an obligation to grant the applicants access to marriage. Furthermore, the ECtHR finds no violation of Article 14 in conjunction with Article 8, stating that states must enjoy a margin of appreciation in the timing of the introduction of legislative changes. This case is evaluated as one step forward decision because the case first held that the relationship of the same sex couples fell within the notion of "family life," just as the relationship of a different sex couple. And such interpretation to include same-sex couples as "family life" opens possibilities to recognize their status in the following decision. However, this decision is also a one step backward case because the ECtHR states that the Convention does not oblige a state to grant a same-sex couple access to marriage).

[21] Edel (2015), p. 92.

marriage.[22] To reconstruct methodological questions, this study will primarily work with the following specific cases of the ECtHR related to same-sex marriage: *Olliari v. Italy* (2015, about a positive obligation of a state to provide legal recognition for same-sex couples), *Schalk and Kopf v. Austria* (2010, about access for same-sex couples to marriage or another form of legal recognition), and *Hämäläinen v. Finland* (2014, concerning the possibility of refusing married persons the right to legal recognition of gender reassignment). Moreover, this work will also analyze the cases of *Vallianatos v. Greece* (2013, an important case on sexual orientation discrimination in civil partnerships), *Chapin and Charpentier v. France* (2013, about the same-sex marriage in France), *Pajic v. Croatia* (2016, about the requirements of a residence permit for family reunification with a same-sex partner), *Taddeucci v. Italy* (2016, about the refusal to grant a residence permit to a gay couple on family grounds), and *Aldeguer Tomás v. Spain* (2016, about the inability of the surviving partner of a same-sex relationship to receive a survivor's pension). To deal with the issue of European consensus, cases are chosen from different Member States which are the defendants in each case.

More cases are chosen for analysis referring to the factsheet of sexual orientation issues published by the ECtHR in April 2020. Among the European Convention articles related to sexual orientation issues, cases of Articles 8, 10, 11, 12, and 14 will be chosen. For the effectiveness of the analysis, at least one case of the relevant article's topic is analyzed. In the case of Article 8 the ECHR (right to respect for private and family life, the home, and correspondence), at least one case to cover each topic is chosen as follows: *E.B. v. France* (2008, adoption), *Orlandi and Others v. Italy* (2017, civil unions), *Perkins and R. v. the United Kingdom* (2003, discharge from the army), *Sousa Goucha v. Portugal* (2016, dismissal of the claim for defamation), *Beizaras and Levickas v. Lithuania* (2020, offensive comments or publication), *Salgueiro da Silva Mouta v. Portugal* (1999, parental authority, child custody, and access rights), *P.B. and J.S. v. Austria* (2010, social protection), and *Kozak v. Poland* (2010, succession to a tenancy).

In Article 10 the ECHR (freedom of expression), the following cases are chosen: *Vejdeland and Others v. Sweden* (2012, regarding the applicants' conviction in 2005 for distributing approximately 100 leaflets in an upper secondary school), *Mladina D.D. Ljubljana v. Slovenia* (2014, related to prosecuting journalists for their

[22] My focus in this work will be the criminalization of LGBTI (the right to sexual freedom: non-criminalization of same-sex relations) and sexual orientation and same-sex marriage mainly as a comparative aspect of the European Court of Human Rights and South Korea. The ECtHR cases are mostly analyzed as main examples of the sources because there are not enough cases related to sexual orientation in the Constitutional Court of Korea yet. Nevertheless, analyzing the ECtHR cases on this topic will have implications for future case law in the Constitutional Court of Korea to come towards the prohibition of discrimination based on sexual orientation. Under the jurisprudence of the ECtHR, there are many other issues in discrimination based on sexual orientation, such as in labor relations (the ECHR Article 11 of the Convention: the right to freedom of assembly and association), child adoption (the ECHR Article 8, right to adopt), which will be only briefly introduced. Since the two subjects are most relevant to the South Korean context, they will be mainly discussed.

publications on issues of public debate that may also offend a public figure, especially a politician), *Kaos Gl v. Turkey* (2016, concerning the seizure of all the copies of an issue of a magazine published in 2006 by *Kaos GL*—a cultural research and solidarity association for gay men and lesbians), *Bayev and Others v. Russia* (2017, concerning a complaint brought by three gay rights activist about legislation in Russia banning the promotion of homosexuality).

For the cases of Article 11 the ECHR (freedom of assembly and association), they are chosen as follows: *Baczkowski and Others v. Poland* (2007, regarding the unlawful refusal to grant permission for a march and meetings to protest against homophobia), *Genderdoc-M v. Moldova* (2012, concerning the banning of a demonstration organized by a non-governmental organization in Moldova to assist the LGBT community), *Lashmankin and Others v. Russia* (2017, regarding the severe restrictions on peaceful assemblies of a gay pride march and meeting), *Alekseyev and Others v. Russia* (2018, concerning the continued refusal by Russian authorities to approve organizers' requests to hold LGBT rallies), and *Zhdanov and Others v. Russia* (2019, concerning the authorities' refusal to register the organizations set up to promote and protect LGBT rights).

In addition, the Constitutional Court of Korea cases of 2002, 2011, and 2016[23] will be criticized to show how unconstitutional it is to punish same-sex relations between consenting adults under Article 92 of Korean Military Criminal Law. As a reference from other Asian countries, the Supreme Court of India's recent decision on the non-criminalization of same-sex relations will be analyzed. In the absence of same-sex marriage cases in the Constitutional Court of Korea, the district court decision[24] in Seoul is included in the references as the first case in Korea. The first same-sex marriage case in Asia is the Constitutional Court of China (Taiwan) in 2017, which will be analyzed as the reference case from Asia. As marriage is considered to have "deep-rooted social and cultural connotations"[25] of one society, the prohibition of same-sex marriage in Korea can be viewed as a matter of moral enforcement similar to adultery[26] which was prohibited in the past. By analyzing the Constitutional Court of Korea case on the prohibition of marriage between people

[23] There were three decisions by the Constitutional Court of Korea on the constitutionality of Korean Military Criminal Law Article 92 to punish same-sex relations between consenting adults: The Constitutional Court of Korea, 2001 Hun-Ba 70, decided on June 27, 2002, the CCK, 2008 Hun-Ga 21, decided on March 31, 2011, 2012 Hun-Ba 258, decided on July 28, 2016.

[24] This case is regarded as the first case to confirm the prohibition of same-sex marriage as a court ruling in Korea. (Seoul Seo-Bu District Court, 2014 Ho-pa 1842, decided on December 6, 2016).

[25] European Court of Human Rights, *Schalk and Kopf v. Austria*, Judgment of 24 June 2010, paragraph 62.

[26] The criminal law has punished adultery, and such punishment has been decided as unconstitutional in Korea in 2015. (The Constitutional Court of Korea, 2009 Hun-Ba 17, decided on February 26, 2015). Through non-criminalization of adultery, some applications can be adapted to the criminalization of same-sex relations and the prohibition of same-sex marriage in Korea.

with the same surnames and same places of origin,[27] important references can be acquired on the interpretation of marriage from the Constitutional Court of Korea.

1.4 Working Definitions

This work deals with making the prohibition of discrimination on the ground of sexual orientation workable in Korea through clear and foreseeable methods of adjudication applied by the ECtHR and other jurisdictions. I refer to the definitions that *F. Edel* uses in his writing. **Sexual orientation**[28] is defined as "each person's capacity for profound emotional, affectional and sexual attraction to, and intimate and sexual relations with, individuals of a different gender or the same gender or more than one gender."[29] I did not include gender identity as the reason because **discrimination on grounds of sexual orientation** in this work is understood as a broad concept involving "not just the equality right, but also the right to privacy and family life..., the basic right to the free development of one's personality."[30] I used LGBTI, which is the acronym to stand for "Lesbian, Gay, Bisexual, Transgender and intersexual"; however, the concept of "sexual minorities" has been used to include LGBTI more comprehensively than the use of "LGBT" or "LGBTI," and "LGBTIQ" to include queer. I decided to use the term of **sexual minorities** more extensively because my aim in using the term is to protect the rights of all those people who are discriminated against because of their sexual orientation. In addition, I want to point out that **legal recognition of same-sex relationships** is different from **legal recognition of same-sex marriage.**[31] Legal recognition of same-sex relationships refers not only to the institution of marriage, but also to some form of civil partnership or unions for same-sex couples. It is considered as if there was no European Consensus (to be defined in a later part of this work) in recognizing

[27] The ban on the marriage between the same surnames and same origins was decided as unconstitutional by the Constitutional Court of Korea in 1997. (The Constitutional Court of Korea, 1995 Hun-Ga 6, Grand Chamber Decision, decided on July 16, 1997). This case will be discussed in detail in Sect. 2.3 of Chap. 2.

[28] Sexual orientation and gender identity are often discussed together as the grounds of discrimination. (Recommendation 1915 (2010) Final version on "Discrimination on the basis of sexual orientation and gender identity" Article 2). However, in this work, I will focus only on sexual orientation for the following reason. Gender identity is defined as "a person's innate perception of him/herself as being a man or a woman, both or neither" (taken from Edel 2015, p. 8) while sexual orientation refers to heterosexuality and homosexuality. As my focus of case analysis is limited to same-sex marriage and non-criminalization of same-sex relations, I have titled my work as discrimination based on sexual orientation.

[29] Edel (2015), p. 7.

[30] Fredman (2011), p. 86.

[31] Schalk and Kopf case (the ECtHR, 2010) deals with legal recognition of same-sex marriage. And, the commentary "explicitly states that member states have no legal obligation in practice to unify their marriage laws in order to allow same-sex marriages." (cited from Ziyadov 2016, p. 395).

same-sex marriage. However, there is a European Consensus in recognizing same-sex relations.[32]

All other working definitions, particularly related to principles and theories, are explained in each chapter. Nevertheless, it is useful to put forward a preliminary idea here about the principles and important concepts discussed throughout this work. First, as the focus of this work is the prohibition of discrimination based on sexual orientation, it is important to understand what could be considered as acts of discrimination. I borrowed the concept from *the Yogyakarta Principles* (2007) because the principles provide meaningful terms and definitions related to the situation of people of diverse sexual orientation in a situation where there are no specific human rights treaties to address the discrimination based on sexual orientation.[33] The acts of discrimination include "violence, harassment, exclusion, stigmatization and prejudice" directed against persons because of their sexual orientation, and such acts "undermine the integrity and dignity of those subjected to these abuses" and may "weaken their sense of self-worth and belonging to their community, and lead many to conceal or suppress their identity and to live lives of fear and invisibility."[34] I find that such expressions show how problematic this situation is because sexual minorities suffer in the Korean society as a result of all the acts of discrimination that make them suppress their identity and live invisible lives.

Another important concept concerning the principle of non-discrimination is the notion of human dignity. I could not agree more with the following explanation of the acts of discrimination as those that "treat certain people as second class citizens, that demean them, that treat them as less capable for no good reasons, or that otherwise offend fundamental human dignity."[35] It is exactly how sexual minorities feel in everyday life all over the world because very often they have to conceal their sexual orientation or risk being refused admittance to certain educational institutions, companies, or communities because of their sexual orientation. Such treatment makes sexual minorities feel greatly inferior to others and harm their human dignity, even if "human dignity is inviolable. It must be respected and protected."[36]

The European Convention on Human Rights prohibits indirect discrimination as well as direct discrimination. **Indirect discrimination** is described by the ECtHR as "a difference in treatment (which) may take the form of disproportionately prejudicial effects of a general policy or measure which, though couched in neutral terms,

[32] European Court Human Rights, *Oliari and others v. Italy*, judgment of July 21, 2015, paragraph 53–54.

[33] For international instruments to address a specific ground of discrimination, there are International Convention on the Elimination of All Forms of Racial Discrimination (Race, 1966), Convention on the Elimination of All Forms of Discrimination against Women (Gender, 1979), Convention on the Rights of Persons with Disabilities (Disability, 2006).

[34] Yogyakarta Principles (2007), Preamble.

[35] Fredman (2011), p. 19.

[36] Article 1, Charter of Fundamental Rights of the European Union (2007), http://eur-lex.europa.eu, last accessed November 30, 2021.

discriminates against a group. Such a situation may amount to 'indirect discrimination', which does not necessarily require a discriminatory intent."[37] **Direct discrimination** is described by the ECtHR as being a case where "there must be a difference in the treatment of persons in analogous, or relevantly similar, situations, which is based on an identifiable characteristic."[38]

It is essential to understand the concept of **intersectionality** as combating discrimination based on sexual orientation because sexual minorities often suffer from discrimination in combination with other grounds such as age, disabilities, migration background, or gender.[39] Intersectionality is a concept introduced by *Kimberle Crenshaw* in 1989, referring to "the relationship and multidimensionality among various identities, social relations and subject formations and how such identities are connected to structures of oppression."[40] Intersectionality is a meaningful concept to discuss the discrimination based on sexual orientation because it puts sexual minorities in a more vulnerable position, as *Christiane Wilke* advocates for the consideration of intersectionality: "complex identities matter because they are targeted and mobilized in state violence."[41] More particularly, the concept of intersectionality is necessary to discuss the rights of sexual minorities considering their particular history of suffering.[42]

The **principle of proportionality** is suggested in this work as being the most important methodological tool to prohibit discrimination based on sexual orientation in the jurisprudence of the ECtHR and the Constitutional Court of Korea. Even if some argue that proportionality is not perfect and that it is necessary to discuss the future of proportionality to improve it,[43] and others claim that proportionality is not adequate to apply the cases of economic and social rights,[44] I examine the principle of proportionality as an effective methodological tool to prohibit discrimination based on sexual orientation throughout this work. I borrow the concept of the nature

[37] European Court of Human Rights, *Biao v. Denmark* (Application no. 38590/10), Grand Chamber judgment of 24 May 2016, para. 103.

[38] Ibid. para. 89.

[39] The Report of the Independent Expert on protection against violence and discrimination based on sexual orientation and gender identity takes some examples of intersectionality as women who are lesbian, bisexual, trans and gender diverse, young/older persons, persons living with disabilities, and asylum seekers, refugees, migrants and internally displaced persons. (United Nations, A/74/181, pp. 10–15).

[40] Crenshaw (1989), pp. 139–167.

[41] Wilke (2013), p. 137.

[42] In her recent article, *R. Xenidus* argues that it is most important that the term of intersectionality refers to a particular history, intellectual heritage and context of emergence (Xenidis 2018, p. 47). I find that such a definition is very relevant to the rights of sexual minorities considering their history of suffering from discrimination, and it is still ongoing all over the world.

[43] For more discussion on the future of proportionality, please see Barak (2012), pp. 528–547.

[44] One of the scholars to argue was Katharine G. Young. For further discussion on proportionality and Economic and Social rights, please see Young (2017). For contrasting arguments, please see Clérico (2018), pp. 25–48; Clérico (2017).

of the principle of proportionality from *Robert Alexy*[45] which consists of the three sub principles of suitability, necessity, and proportionality in the narrower sense. The principle of suitability assesses whether the means adopted to promote the principle actually promote this purpose or not. As there are fewer cases of unsuitability, the principle of necessity is becoming more important, which demands that measures that interfere less intensively will be chosen if the measures in question are equally suitable. The third subprinciple of the principle of proportionality in the narrower sense is called the "Law of Balancing" to state, "the greater the degree of non-satisfaction of, or detriment to, one principle, the greater must be the importance of satisfying the other."[46] This problem of balancing principles can be found in statements of the German Federal Constitutional Court such as "the more that statutory intervention affects the basic expressions of human freedom of action, the more carefully the reasons justifying it must be weighed against the citizen's basic right to freedom."[47] The basic rule of the "Law of Balancing" can be stated as "the permissible level of non-satisfaction of, or detriment to, one principle depends on the importance of satisfying the other."[48] And this idea of the "Law of Balancing" is applied as the meaning of the third subprinciple of the principle of proportionality in the narrower sense throughout this work.

Another important concept is the distinction between **positive state obligation** and negative state obligation. One of the main case analyses in this work is same-sex marriage and in the legal recognition of same-sex marriage the state's positive obligation is emphasized because the state must provide the institution of marriage to same-sex couples. I applied the definitions of positive state obligation by *L. Lavryson* to refer to "an obligation imposed under a human rights requiring the State to take action."[49] On the other hand, negative state obligation is related to abstaining from interference, and it further refers to state inaction. In discussing state obligations in human rights, the obligation to respect refers to the negative state obligations, while the obligation to protect and fulfill is considered as the positive state obligation.[50]

As the doctrine of **margin of appreciation** has occurred and developed in the jurisprudence of the European Convention on Human Rights, I borrow the definition of margin of appreciation from *Y. Arai-Takahashi*'s study on "The Margin of Appreciation Doctrine and the Principle of Proportionality in the Jurisprudence of the ECHR." The term of Margin of Appreciation used in this work refers to "the latitude a government enjoys in evaluating factual situations and in applying the provisions enumerated in international human rights treaties."[51] Understanding the

---

[45] Alexy (2017), pp. 14–16.

[46] Ibid. p. 16.

[47] Alexy (2010), p. 102.

[48] Ibid.

[49] Lavrysen (2016), p. 11.

[50] Ibid. p. 12.

[51] Arai-Takahashi (2002), pp. 2–5.

concept of margin of appreciation is particularly important when dealing with cases related to discrimination based on sexual orientation. The European Convention on Human Rights endorsed a minimum standard about shared traditions of democracy and fundamental rights but allows some discretion on the matters related to diverse cultural and legal traditions developed by each Member State.[52] Most of the issues in question in relation to discrimination based on sexual orientation such as same-sex marriages are considered diverse cultural and legal traditions embraced by each Member State.

1.5 Research Questions

Prohibition of discrimination on the ground of sexual orientation seems to be a challenging task, especially in the South Korean legal context. As *Abrusci* points out in her article,[53] the debate is particularly intense because it is closely related to cultural, social, legal, and religious concerns. It seems to be more serious in the South Korean case. While sexual minorities are almost invisible in Korean society as the most vulnerable group, the Constitutional Court of Korea still regards criminalization of same-sex relations under Korean Military Criminal Law as constitutional, and there is no official decision on same-sex marriages in the Constitutional Court of Korea. In this situation, the experiences from the courts of other parts of the world can give meaningful references especially with methodological tools in South Korea for upcoming decisions.

Positive inspiration for the prohibition of discrimination based on sexual orientation can be obtained from the ECtHR. *Lavrysen* mentioned in his book[54] that the renowned concurring opinion of Judge *Wildhaber* in the *Stjerna* case (the issue is about the authorities refusing a request for a surname change, and the ECtHR found no violation of Article 8 the ECHR)[55] has been influential in shaping his research questions. In the *Stjerna* case, the ECtHR examined the case under Article 8 ECHR (the right to respect private and family life) on the question of whether the essential

[52] Ibid. p. 3.

[53] Abrusci (2017), pp. 255–256.

[54] Lavrysen (2016), p. 23.

[55] European Court of Human Rights, ***STJERNA v. FINLAND*** (Applications no. 18131/91.), Chamber Judgment of 25 November 1994. (The applicant, Mr. *Stjerna* is a Finnish national living in Helsinki. On March 28, 1989, he applied to the County Administrative Board of Uusimaa for permission to change his surname *Stjerna* to "Tawaststjerna." He claimed that he and other Stjerna family members always felt it an injustice only to bear half of the original name, and it was difficult to pronounce as well. But, the Advisory Committee on Names opposed the change, saying that his ancestors had used the name because the ancestor had been born out of wedlock. The ECtHR holds that Article 8 is applicable, but there has been no violation of Article 8 nor Article 14 taken together with Article 8. The Court does not find that the sources of inconvenience the applicant complained of are sufficient to raise an issue of failure to respect private life, and the refusal by the Finnish authorities did not constitute a lack of respect for his private life in the meaning of Article 8.).

object of Article 8 is to protect the individual against arbitrary interference by public authorities, or if there are positive obligations inherent in an effective "respect" for private life.[56] In this work, such an interpretation is important because Article 8 of the Convention is also applied to the ECtHR case law on same-sex marriage.

Such contexts lead to the following research questions:

How does the ECtHR apply legal methodological tools particularly in the case law on discrimination based on sexual orientation? Is there any problem in applying such legal methodological tools as the principle of proportionality, the margin of appreciation, the concept of negative and positive obligations, the prohibition of discrimination, the argument of a European Consensus, and the standards[57] *to distinguish core rights from supplementary rights? How can the ECtHR enhance clarity in using a certain methodological tool especially in the case law on discrimination based on sexual orientation, to find more violations?*

At the same time, the criteria which the ECtHR uses to test the question of discrimination based on sexual orientation will be examined under the light of Article 12 (right to marry) and Article 14 (the prohibition of discrimination). This analysis will be done, using very well-known cases including *Schalk and Kopf vs. Austria* (2010, about non-obligation of Member States to legislate for legally recognized same-sex marriages) and *Oliari vs. Italy* (2015, about a positive obligation of Member States to provide legal recognition for same-sex couples). The lack of clarity as to the test and standards used by the ECtHR to examine the reasonableness of a justification is problematic,[58] especially in the Convention system. The ECtHR may provide interpretative guidance to the national authorities, and the national courts will implement them to prevent future violations only if the Convention standards are clear.[59] In this sense, what we can consider as alternatives is to reconstruct existing methodological tools to better clarify what the Court means when it uses a certain methodological tool. For example, when the Court differentiates between core and supplementary rights in a legal reasoning, it is important to know the standards used to distinguish one from the other. And we will have clearer ideas when the Court uses a specific methodology to find violations by analyzing the case law of a similar topic. Throughout the current study, these methodological tools will be analyzed by their main meaning and usages, such as the margin of appreciation, positive/negative obligation, and European consensus as related elements of argumentations used in the case law of the ECtHR on sexual orientation and same-sex marriage.

Other sub-questions that will be considered are the following:

Why is it important to analyze the jurisprudence of the ECtHR?

---

[56] European Court Human Rights, *Stjerna v. Finland*, judgment of 25 November 1994, paragraph 38.

[57] *J. Gerards* has criticized the distinction of the core of rights by ECtHR as "rather fuzzy" even if it is essentially important to the individual (taken from Gerards 2011, p. 80).

[58] Greer (2004), pp. 412–417.

[59] Wildhaber (2002), pp. 161–164.

How can we eventually improve the discrimination based on sexual orientation in South Korea?

Can South Korea overcome the current situations regarding discriminatory acts based on sexual orientation using experiences from other courts – legislation of general anti-discrimination law, principles to find out violations, the standards to distinguish the enforcement of morality, ethical entitlements, and moral ones?

The ECtHR has more important roles than other national courts, or as a court in the conventional system, for the following reasons: firstly, it checks national decisions and legislation for mistakes to ensure the observance of the engagements undertaken by the high contracting parties in the Convention. Secondly, it provides interpretative guidance to the national authorities for safeguarding fundamental rights.[60] For this reason, the Convention system requires close cooperation between the national authorities and the ECtHR. National authorities are only willing to mirror the Court's interpretative approach if it is clear, transparent, and persuasive. Therefore, the clarity in the use of methodological tools by the ECtHR is essential because it makes the legal argumentation foreseeable.[61] Although it is difficult to achieve full certainty in dealing with "hard" cases, the applications must be clear enough to lead, to be clear and transparent in judgments, and to be able to foresee the reference of future cases.

In addition, the methodological tools used by the U.S. Supreme Court and the Inter-American Court of Human Rights (IAtHR) will be analyzed regarding possible implications for the Constitutional Court of Korea, especially with the cases of discrimination based on sexual orientation. Comparing the *Oliari*[62] case of the ECtHR with the *Obergefell*[63] case of the U.S. Supreme Court about legal recognition of same-sex relations, *Zago* has claimed that "it is of notice that Strasbourg judges are sensible to new developments at the global level. Institutional dialogue can surely contribute to the consolidation of an international trend towards the recognition of same-sex relationships through marriage also in Europe."[64] From the perspective of such judicial dialogue, it is meaningful to analyze other courts' jurisprudence on the same issue as a matter of inspiration for the Korean Constitutional Court. The cases from India as well as Taiwan will be particularly relevant for developing new jurisprudence in South Korea.

The following sub-questions will be closely examined to answer the main research questions stated above:

[60] Gerards (2013), pp. 467–470.

[61] *S. Sottiaux* and *G. Van Der Schyff* used the terms of consistency, stability, predictability (taken from Sottiaux and Van Der Schyff 2008). However, I want to use the term "foreseeable" as the ECtHR used it in the case of *Sunday Times* as a law had to be formulated with sufficient precision to enable the citizen to regulate his conduct: that person must be able to *foresee*, up to a reasonable degree (European Court of Human Rights, *Sunday Times v. U.K.*, judgment of 26 April 1979, paragraph 49).

[62] European Court Human Rights, *Oliari and others v. Italy*, judgment of July 21, 2015.

[63] Obergefell v. Hodges, 576 U.S. 644 (2015).

[64] Zago (2015).

To make the prohibition of discrimination on the grounds of sexual orientation workable, how could the ECtHR and the Constitutional Court of Korea enhance clarity in applying methodological tools? To that end, how could the ECtHR and the Constitutional Court of Korea adapt their legal methodology in a more foreseeable way? Should the ECtHR and the Constitutional Court of Korea apply the structured proportionality, distinguish positive and negative state obligation, and establish the factors to determine the breadth of margin in the jurisprudence of discrimination based on sexual orientation? Which legal basis could the Constitutional Court of Korea apply to decide the criminalization of same-sex relations as being unconstitutional, and to legally recognize same-sex marriage through its jurisprudence? Will legal philosophical considerations of moral enforcement and legislation of anti-discrimination law work positively for the court to construct new jurisprudence with the goal of prohibiting discrimination based on sexual orientation?

1.6 Methodology of the Study

In the first court case of same-sex marriage in South Korea of May 25, 2016,[65] the court rejected the case as "inadmissible," stating that the state's legislative function has not made legislation to provide legal recognition of same-sex marriage in Korea. While rejecting it, the Korean court stated that the current Korean legal system presupposes marriage as only "between opposite sexes," not "between same sexes," although there are no articles to clearly define marriage as such in the Korean constitution. Furthermore, the court added that there is not yet any consensus about same-sex marriage among Korean citizens. There have been no further decisions on the constitutionality of the Korean Military Criminal Law Art. 92 (6) to criminalize same-sex relations after the last decision of July 28, 2016.[66] In this decision, the Constitutional Court of Korea decided the Art. 92 (6) does not violate the Korean Constitution.

My very first initiative starts with challenges to the existing jurisprudence related to discrimination based on sexual orientation: could the study about principles and tests as legal methodology and the analysis of case law of the ECtHR restructure legal reasoning in the decisions of other jurisdictions on the same matter and guide future decisions[67] of Korean courts, and vice versa? Such a question is in line with current discussions of comparative human rights law—the judicial dialogue between the national court and the regional human rights court. As the recent article

[65] Seoul Seo-Bu District Court, 2014 Ho-pa 1842, decided on December 6, 2016.

[66] The Constitutional Court of Korea, 2012 Hun-Ba 258, decided on July 28, 2016.

[67] The quote was inspiring—"how legal concepts are defined and fit together and the extent to which any general principles can be extracted by legal reasoning that can guide future decisions." (taken from Bell 2011, p. 155).

discusses, "a different type of communication between international and domestic courts has become a widespread phenomenon since the 1990s"[68] and my analysis of the ECtHR and the Constitutional Court of Korea case law can serve as another form of judicial dialogue between the two courts to positively guide future decisions.

Thus, the methodology in this work follows the academic discipline of "studying law as a normative system, limiting its 'empirical data' to legal texts and court decisions."[69] The analytical approach is used when analyzing court decisions in a legal study. In this work, court decisions of the ECtHR and the Constitutional Court of Korea are analyzed from a comparative perspective, which will examine the particularities of the Constitutional Court of Korea cases in depth. Such an analytical approach deals with the topic of an improved way to guarantee the rights in question by using the normative approach. Considering that the normative approach provides the legal philosophical foundation about the contents of law in the future, this work will discuss new legislation to guarantee better rights for sexual minorities. Finally, this work is concerned with an analytical approach by restructuring case law in different jurisdictions as well as with normative questions to prohibit discrimination based on sexual orientation in future decisions.

The first methodology is an *analytical* approach to study the case law on discrimination based on sexual orientation from a comparative perspective of different jurisdictions—mainly in the ECtHR and the Constitutional Court of Korea. Furthermore, restructuring the case law of the ECtHR according to legal methodological tools, including the principle of proportionality will show different applications of such tools in the Constitutional Court of Korea. The second methodology is a *normative* approach to study the role of states as well as the role of courts when dealing with discrimination based on sexual orientation using the distinctions of ethical and moral considerations. The two methodologies enable case law of different courts on the same topic to be analyzed to answer normative questions of transforming discriminatory acts. The enforcement of morality has been actively discussed in the context of Europe but mostly ignored in Korea. This discussion is particularly important since the enforcement of morality should be dealt with from a legal perspective as well as with philosophical considerations.

The *normative* approach makes it possible to deal with the relation between morality and the state's role to prohibit discrimination based on sexual orientation. Such a normative approach is necessary to attain the objective of this study, especially to emphasize a general anti-discrimination law in Korea by deconstructing similar laws in other jurisdictions such as Germany, England, and the U.S. This combined analytical and normative methodology goes beyond the simple claim that general anti-discrimination law is needed to prohibit discrimination based on sexual orientation. Instead, it allows us to profoundly deal with the content and the process of relevant laws in other jurisdictions. The need to enact general anti-discrimination legislation should be followed by the need to analyze counterarguments against it

[68] Maues et al. (2021), p. 1.

[69] Van Hoecke (2011), pp. 1–2.

beyond the mere legal debates, by analyzing case law from other jurisdictions according to generally accepted principles and theories. Therefore, such a task should clearly differ from a brief introduction of case law or processes which enact similar laws in other countries. This study will answer the main research questions particularly through the dismantling process of the relevant precedents to connect the two discourses—the ECtHR and the CCK—based on the analytical methodology of the precedents and the normative approach of considerations on morality and the role of the state.

1.7 Structure of the Study

This work comprises nine chapters:

The first chapter is the introduction in which this study's general aim, and the three specific analytical, critical, and normative aims are set out. In raising the issue, I have written some introductory thoughts on the limitations of the freedom of individuals and the role of the state, on moral coercion, and on the state's intervention to introduce some legal philosophical thoughts regarding the background to the discriminatory acts against sexual minorities. In the scope of the analysis, I introduce the important studies that have inspired my work and justify how my study will be different from existing ones. As the main normative sources, I elaborate on how I have chosen the ECtHR and the Constitutional Court of Korea's judgments and decisions. There are many topics related to discrimination based on sexual orientation, so it is impossible to deal with all of them. Therefore, I have narrowed them down to the two most important topics: criminalization of same-sex relations, and same-sex marriage, because the first topic is considered as sufficient protection given in the European context and the latter is not. In the section on working definitions, I define some of the important concepts and terms that will be used throughout this work. Lastly, I clarify research questions and the methodology of this study.

Chapter 2 discusses discrimination based on sexual orientation as a topic of the enforcement of morality and the role of states. To provide insights, Korean Constitutional Court cases on adultery and prohibition of marriage between people with same surnames and from the same places of origin will be analyzed.

The third chapter provides an overview of the legal recognition of same-sex relationships in South Korea as well as in Europe. The first point is whether sexual orientation is regarded as grounds not to discriminate. In Art. 14, the ECHR,[70] sexual

[70] Article 14 Prohibition of discrimination (the ECHR) states: "The enjoyment of the rights and freedoms set forth in this Convention shall be secured without discrimination on any ground such as sex, race, colour, language, religion, political or other opinion, national or social origin, association with a national minority, property, birth or other status.

orientation is not stated explicitly as grounds to prohibit discrimination. Art. 11 (1)[71] of the Korean Constitution stipulates the principle of non-discrimination; however, only sex, religion, or social status are explicitly stated as grounds. Nevertheless, sexual orientation should be regarded as grounds not to discriminate based on dynamic, teleological, and contextual interpretations. It is also important to be aware of South Korea and Europe's current situation to discern outstanding issues related to discrimination based on sexual orientation.

The fourth chapter provides a comparative perspective for applying the principle of non-discrimination in different jurisdictions. Firstly, the principle of non-discrimination in the European System of Human Rights is introduced. Then, the standards of the equality test in Korea are discussed focusing on the applicability of the prohibition of arbitrariness, and the principle of proportionality. Subsequently, the U.S. Supreme Court cases will be considered as sources of comparative analysis. Such a comparative analysis will enable us to look at the issues of equality from different angles[72] and the Constitutional Court of Korea regard the U.S. case as the source of reference. Following this, the principle of equality in German jurisdiction is introduced. It is especially important to understand this because the principle of equality has developed significantly through German public law and migrated to Asia including South Korea.[73] The fifth section is about anti-discrimination law. There is considerable resistance to the legislation of anti-discrimination law in Korea. To overcome some resistance, I have included the process and contents of equality law in the EU, Germany, and Britain, which are considered by the Ministry of Justice in Korea as important comparative laws for future legislation of Anti-Discrimination Law in Korea.

The fifth chapter is mainly dedicated to reconstructing the case law of the ECtHR according to the principle of proportionality. Firstly, I introduce how the principle of proportionality has been developed in the European context, followed by an analysis of the jurisprudence of Article 8 (Rights to respect for private and family life), Article 10 (Freedom of expression), Article 11 (Freedom of assembly and association) ECHR because those articles deal mainly with the case law on discrimination based on sexual orientation in the ECtHR. Finally, there is a discussion of the role of the judicature because it is often discussed together with the applicability of the principle of proportionality.[74]

In the sixth chapter, other relevant concepts in the case law of the ECtHR will be introduced. It is important to understand the positive state obligation, the margin of

---

[71] Article 11(1) of the Constitution of the Republic of Korea states: "All citizens shall be equal before the law, and there shall be no discrimination in political, economic, social or cultural life on account of sex, religion or social status."

[72] O'Regan and Khosla (2014), p. 309.

[73] Particularly, the principle of proportionality has developed in German administrative law, and in German constitutional law, and has migrated to all over the world including Asia. For more, please see: Barak (2012), pp. 199–200.

[74] Proponents of the proportionality are criticized as defending the expansive scope of judicial review (Webber 2018, pp. 94–95).

appreciation, and consensus argument because those are the methodological tools applied in the jurisprudence of discrimination based on sexual orientation in the ECtHR. This chapter particularly reviews the problem in the application in the case law and looks for some alternatives in future decisions.

Chapter 7 analyzes the cases where the standard of protection of sexual minorities in the European system is sufficient. In this chapter, the criminalization of same-sex relations under the Korean Military Criminal Law and the Constitutional Court of Korea's decisions will be criticized. In addition, a recent Supreme Court decision of India will be introduced. Chapter 8 presents a case analysis where the standard of protecting sexual minorities in the European system is insufficient because same-sex marriage case law of the ECtHR is considered a hard case. For a comparative analysis, a general discussion in South Korea will be first introduced. Subsequently, the development of case law in the United States of America and the Inter-American Court of Human Rights will be analyzed. Chapters 7 and 8 are dedicated to case analyses—non-criminalization of same-sex relations and same-sex marriage.

Chapter 9 presents general conclusions, and consists of a summary of findings, recent discussions, suggestions for further research, and personal reflections.

References

Abrusci E (2017) A tale of convergence? Discrimination based on sexual orientation in regional human rights bodies and the human rights committee. Nord J Hum Rights 35(3):240–257. https://doi.org/10.1080/18918131.2017.1355434. Accessed November 30, 2021.

Alexy R (2010) A theory of constitutional rights (trans: Rivers J). Oxford University Press, Oxford

Alexy R (2017) Proportionality and rationality. In: Jackson VC, Tushnet M (eds) Proportionality new frontiers, new challenges. Cambridge University Press, Cambridge, pp 11–12. https://doi.org/10.1017/9781316691724.002. Accessed November 30, 2021.

Arai-Takahashi Y (2002) The margin of appreciation doctrine and the principle of proportionality in the jurisprudence of the ECHR. Intersentia, Oxford

Barak A (2012) Proportionality: constitutional rights and their limitations (trans: Kalir D). Cambridge University Press, Cambridge

Bell J (2011) Legal research and the distinctiveness of comparative law. In: Van Hoecke M (ed) Methodologies of legal research. Hart, Oxford

Clérico L (2017) Proportionality and balancing. In: Mendes CH, Gargarella R (eds) Oxford handbook of constitutional law in Latin America. Oxford University Press, Oxford

Clérico L (2018) Proportionality in social rights adjudication: making it workable. In: Duarte D, Sampais JS (eds) Proportionality in law. Springer, Heidelberg, pp 25–48

Crenshaw K (1989) Demarginalizing the intersection of race and sex: a black feminist critique of antidiscrimination doctrine, feminist theory and antiracist politics. Univ Chic Leg Forum 1989: (1), Article 8, 139–167

Edel F (2015) Case law of the European Court of Human Rights relating to discrimination on grounds of sexual orientation or gender identity. Council of Europe

Fredman S (2011) Discrimination law, 2nd edn. Oxford University Press, Oxford

Gerards J (2011) Pluralism, deference and the margin of appreciation doctrine. Eur Law J 17:80–120. https://doi.org/10.1111/j.1468-0386.2010.00540.x

Gerards J (2013) How to improve the necessity test of the European Court of Human Rights. Int J Constit Law 11(2):466–490. https://doi.org/10.1093/icon/mot004

Greer S (2004) Balancing and the European Court of Human Rights: a contribution to the Habermas-Alexy debate. Camb Law J 63(2):412–434. https://doi.org/10.1017/S0008197304006634. Accessed November 30, 2021.

Habermas J (1996) Between facts and norms. Polity Press, Polity

Habermas J (2001) The postnational constellation. Polity Press, Polity

Kant I (1968) Metaphysik der Sitten, Einleitung in die Rechtslehre, § B, Kants Werke VI (Akademie Textausgabe)

Lavrysen L (2016) Human rights in a positive state. Intersentia, Antwerp

Maues AM et al (2021) Judicial dialogue between National courts and the Inter-American Court of Human Rights: a comparative study of Argentina, Brazil, Colombia and Mexico. Hum Rights Law Rev 00:1–24. https://doi.org/10.1093/hrlr/ngaa047

O'Regan K, Khosla M (2014) Equality in Asia. In: Dixon R, Ginsburg T (eds) Comparative constitutional law in Asia. Edward Elgar, Cheltenham

Ryu S-J (2013) US Supreme Court's recent decisions about homosexuality: analysis and meaning of US V. Windsor case. Public Law J 14(4):87–114. https://doi.org/10.31779/plj.14.4.201311.004

Sieckmann J (2012) The logic of autonomy: law, morality and autonomous reasoning. Hart Publishing, Oxford

Sottiaux S, Van Der Schyff G (2008) Methods of international human rights adjudication: towards a more structured decision-making process for the European Court of Human Rights. Hastings Int Comp Law Rev 31(1)

Van Hoecke M (2011) Legal doctrine: which methods for what kind of discipline? In: Van Hoecke M (ed) Methodologies of legal research. Hart Publishing, Oxford

Webber G (2018) Proportionality and absolute rights. In: Jackson VC, Tushnet M (eds) Proportionality new frontiers, new challenges. Cambridge

Wildhaber L (2002) A constitutional future for the European Court of Human Rights? Human rights law journal: in association with the International Institute of Human Rights. Hum Rights Law J 23(1-5-7):161–165

Wilke C (2013) Remembering complexity? Memorials for Nazi victims in Berlin. Int J Transit Justice 7(1):136–156. https://doi.org/10.1093/ijtj/ijs035

Xenidis R (2018) Multiple discrimination in EU anti-discrimination law: towards redressing complex inequality? In: Belavusau U, Henrard K (eds) EU anti-discrimination law beyond gender. Hart Publishing, Oxford

Young K-G (2017) Proportionality, reasonableness, and economic and social rights. In: Jackson VC, Tushnet M (eds) Proportionality new frontiers, new challenges. Cambridge University Press, Cambridge

Zago G (2015) Oliari and Others v. Italy: a stepping stone towards full legal recognition of same-sex relationships in Europe. https://strasbourgobservers.com/2015/09/16/oliari-and-others-v-italy-a-stepping-stone-towards-full-legal-recognition-of-same-sex-relationships-in-europe/. Accessed November 30, 2021.

Ziyadov N (2016) Same-sex marriage in US and European Court of Human Rights case law: a comparison. Int J Soc Sci Educ Res 2(2):387–401. https://doi.org/10.24289/ijsser.279052. Accessed November 30, 2021.

References

Chapter 2
Discussions on the Enforcement of Morality

2.1 Legal Philosophical Background

Most legal enforcement of morality reflects prevailing social values, obviously including the important question of which morals can be included in the legal concept and which cannot, as in the case of the Constitutional Court of Korea deciding[1] to abolish adultery from the criminal code, when it had been in force for more than 60 years. It is noticeable how the state's enforcement of morality has changed over time. However, deciding to what extent the state can enforce morality or can guarantee extended morals is still not a simple issue. Furthermore, this question is also the subject of both legal philosophical debates. Is it possible to use legal punishment or inaction to legally enforce certain immoral acts which do not have any visible victims?

Academic scholars in the past have thought deeply and thoroughly about this issue as the citations from *M. Ginsberg* show: "In liberal societies it is recognized that there are certain values or goods which cannot be promoted by compulsion or external standardization and which can flourish only in freedom, for example, religion, learning, research, science, philosophy and art. The state can, through

[1] The Constitutional Court of Korea, 2009 Hun Ba 17, decided on February 26, 2015 the unconstitutionality of the criminal punishment of adultery.

In this case, the Court pointed out changes in public awareness of social structure, marriage, and gender as well as of a growing emphasis on the right to sexual self-determination. Thus, the Court stated that it is difficult to indicate whether the public's perception is consistent with punishing adultery by the criminal code. Here it can be inferred how the Constitutional Court of Korea deals with moral coercion: Even if some acts are considered as immoral, if such acts are essentially a part of the private life of the individual and there is no specific harm to society or such harm is not so great, state punishment power must not intervene from the perspective of modern criminal law. Accordingly, adultery is decriminalized in many parts of the world. In addition, the protected interest by criminalizing adultery is the maintenance of marriages and families, which must be left to the parties' free will and affections. For this reason, adultery cannot be enforced through criminal punishment.

H. J. Lee, *Discrimination Based on Sexual Orientation*, Interdisciplinary Studies in Human Rights 8, https://doi.org/10.1007/978-3-030-95423-9_2

law, help by providing the external conditions these ends require, but it must avoid anything like direct control of the values themselves. The principle here is not that these matters are self- and no other-regarding. It is that freedom is a necessary condition to the pursuit of these values. Individuality, variety, spontaneity is essential to them."[2] The belief that some values can be legally enforced in a pluralistic society can be difficult to understand, especially for those who both believe in and follow liberal values. Nevertheless, according to *Ginsberg*'s statement, all state intervention is not always accepted only at the level of promoting individual liberties.

Even if a free society has different moral values, there is a need to specify some areas where the state must not intervene through law at all. However, the core problem is how to define the scope of the legal enforcement of morality, particularly when such moral values do no harm to other people. Examples include prostitution, adultery, gambling, euthanasia, suicide, pornography, and *same-sex relations*, which are the main topic of this work. The common characteristics of such topics lie in that (1) there are no direct victims from these acts, (2) the acts are usually performed voluntarily by the parties, (3) most acts are mutually agreed upon. Some may argue that victims exist in the case of adultery. However, it is characteristic of the victims of adultery that spouses are different from victims of other crimes. Unlike the victims of crimes such as murder, robbery, or rape, a spouse as a victim of adultery can get divorced and use civil litigation to claim for the damages that occurred.

Therefore, what has been the basis for punishing adultery under criminal law? Legislative grounds have been necessary to maintain marriages and families as the basis of a healthy society. Korean scholars of criminal law regard the protected interest either as sexual customs or morals[3] or the monogamous marriage system.[4] In fact, after the Constitutional Court of Korea decided that adultery is unconstitutional, not only Confucian scholars but also many other scholars who emphasized particular traditional Oriental values harshly criticized the Constitutional decision. One of the legal scholars, *Jisu Kim*, in his recent publication,[5] asked the following questions to rebuke the advocates for abolishing the criminalization of adultery:

– Can "I" gladly tolerate it when "my" spouse enjoys the right to sexual self-determination?
– Can "my" spouse peacefully coexist as willing to tolerate "my" freedom of infidelity?
– Will "my" children, as well as "my" parents, favor tolerating "my" freedom to infidelity?

[2]Ginsberg (1961), p. 68.

[3]Oh (2009), p. 791; Park (2011), p. 568.

[4]Lee (2010), p. 638.

[5]Kim (2016), p. 186.

- If the peace of "my" family has been threatened because of adultery of "my" parents as "I" was young, what would "my" feelings have been at that time or this moment?
- Can "you" claim to abolish adultery if "my" lovely daughter suffers from the infidelity of "my" son in law?

Although one can sympathize with these questions from *Kim*, the distinction between the realm of law and morality must not depend solely on the personal emotions of "mine." If most morals and values have immediate legitimacy, those who have different thoughts or values from the majority would always be easily exposed to legal discrimination. This is one reason why the fact that Confucian traditions have suppressed individual liberties cannot be ignored by using the excuse of morals as well as of the interests of the community.

The question is whether a simple conflict between values is the main topic of legal coercion of morals. Not necessarily, I would answer. Some of the following legislative examples are much more easily accessible around us and are not easily rejected: helmetless motorcycling, payment of wages even below the minimum wage, providing medicine without prescriptions, aggressive begging, or laziness.[6] In this regard, it is important to notice that agreements and contracts between adults do not always precede the state's legal intervention. This is the reason why there should be certain intervention over particular values. In other words, if the law enforces or punishes certain acts, it will probably justify punishing people who have different values from the majority through the use of coercion by the majority if the legislative objectives of such laws are not well clarified. To such questions, the *Wolfenden Committee* published the Report of the Committee on Homosexual Offences and Prostitution in 1957.[7] The committee responded with an opinion on prostitution and homosexuals, but the report still had some influence over the discussion of legal coercion of morals. The substance of the Committee's report lies in the fact that the Criminal Code functions to preserve public order and politeness, to protect citizens from aggressive or harmful acts, and to prevent acts designed to exploit or corrupt others. In other words, it is not possible to legally limit or punish anything that is not related to public manners or personal harm. In particular, the case of homosexuality or prostitution lies outside the realm of law because it applies to the individual freedom to choose, and act based on personal morals.

[6] Suber (1999), pp. 632–635.

[7] The Wolfenden Committee: Report of the Committee on Homosexual Offences and Prostitution. Presented to Parliament by the Secretary of State for the Home Department and the Secretary of State for Scotland, etc. [Chairman, Sir John Wolfenden.], Parliamentary Papers. Cmnd 247, 1957.

2.1.1 Moral Enforcement by Law

Some acts harm the individual while they do not harm other people: can the state's intervention in such cases be justified? Some of these acts have almost always been accepted in the East Asian Confucian culture, and their acceptance has been the subject of debate in Western European Society[8] regarding the possibility of legal sanctions. Supporters of legal morals, who favor the possible enforcement of morals by law, claim that immoral conduct can be punished even if there are no victims. According to such positions, homosexual activities that have been carried out by agreement between consenting adults can be legally punished because the acts are considered immoral. For instance, *P. Devlin*, a British judge and legal philosopher, has justified the punishment of prostitution or homosexuality in his book of "The Enforcement of Morals" since they could disrupt society by violating the common societal morals.[9]

On this matter of the relation between law and morals, Judges *Gyu-Gwang Cho* and *Moon-Hee Kim* of the Constitutional Court of Korea expressed their opinions in the adultery case:[10] The question of whether a particular human act is illegal and criminal and whether the state exercises the power to regulate or punish such an act, or leaves it to morals, depends on the interrelationship of humans and society so that the result depends on the time and space to be finally decided by the overall circumstances of society and the awareness of the individuals in that society. However, the state does not have the constitutional legitimacy to impose criminal sanctions on certain acts only to improve the citizens' morality level. According to the famous expression of "constitutional interpretation as a living instrument,"[11] the operation of the state's punishment power varies based on circumstances as well as on the awareness of the society's individuals. This constitutional case applied one of the famous modern constitutional interpretation tools of "living instrument"; however, the Constitutional Court of Korea concluded that the state must necessarily punish adultery. It took about 25 years until the criminalization of adultery was

---

[8]I do not agree with cultural anthropological dichotomy such as "East Asian Confucian Culture" against "Western European Society." The reason why I have referenced to "East Asian Confucian Culture" and "Western European Society" as its counterpart is to criticize the reasoning by the Constitutional Court of Korea. The CCK has used the cultural differences as an excuse not to accept universal human rights. I am not against the whole idea of enforcement of social morality. Rather, I want to emphasize that the enforcement of social morality can be justified based on the guarantee of individual autonomy and fundamental rights of individuals.

[9]Devlin (1959), pp. 129–151; Devlin (1965), pp. 1–25.

[10]The Constitutional Court of Korea, 89 Hun Ma 82, decided on September 10, 1990. Concurring Opinion from Judges *Gyu-Gwang Cho* and *Moon-Hee Kim.*

[11]"In 1994, Deane and Toohey JJ began to refer to the Constitution as a "living instrument" or "living force" that should not be constrained by the dead hands of the founders." (taken from Goldsworthy and Huscroft 2018, p. 201).

regarded as unconstitutional by the Constitutional Court of Korea,[12] claiming that the public consciousness has changed. Since then, it can no longer be justified that adultery must be regulated by the state's criminal code.

Such a great change of the Court between the previous two cases on the same issue indicates that it is not a simple matter to justify the enforcement of morals by law, even if there have been changes in the consciousness of society's members. In the past, when confidence in the neutrality of the state was strong, it was believed that state neutrality was directly related to the guarantee of individual freedom. It was believed to be desirable that the state would not intervene. In other words, the theme of legal coercion of morality led to the discussion of "legal guardianship" and "perfectionism" as one of the tides in such a large flow of discussions in social science.

The legal enforcement of morality by the state does not simply follow the prevailing social conditions but has some philosophical basis for further discussion. Naturally, from the standpoint of emphasizing the power of private contracts between individuals, it may not be easy to accomplish the happiness of individuals by state intervention. Yet, if individuals are considered to achieve happiness as a result of the state's interventions, another question arises related to individual autonomy because individuals will become happy when individual freedom is ensured and it is possible to improve individual autonomy. Seen from the perspective that moral enforcement is difficult to justify unless an individual harms other people, it is difficult to agree on the criminalization of same-sex relations in cases where different moral standards exist. Universal values refer to some moral standards shared by most people in the world; it is difficult to prescribe non-criminalization of same-sex relations as universal values. Particular values are embedded within each community's own traditions and morality. Nevertheless, there are universal values as well. For example, it is essential to universally accept the non-criminalization of same-sex relations to protect sexual minorities from discrimination based on sexual orientation. The question is how to justify this from a legal and philosophical perspective. Some East Asian Confucianists[13]

---

[12]The Constitutional Court of Korea, 2009 Hun Ba 17, decided on 26 February 2015. (Five judges express their opinion as unconstitutional as follows: In our society today, free exercise of the right to sexual self-determination is no less than the legal interest of maintaining traditional sexual morality or protecting the duty of marriage fidelity from the perspective of individual dignity and pursuit of happiness. With such a change in social structure, public awareness of marriage and gender, and a perception that places greater emphasis on the right to sexual self-determination, even if spouses may have had sexual relations with others (non-spouses), it is no longer clear if the state has right to regulate this by means of criminal punishment. It is unclear whether people will still agree with that since it is actually impossible to regard all the morally condemned actions as the subject of criminal punishment.)

[13]As examples of such East Asian Confucianists, there are *Lee Kuan Yew*, the former minister of Singapore, *Mahathir Mohamad*, the former Malaysian Prime Minister, and *Joseph Chan* who wrote "Legitimacy, Unanimity, and Perfectionism" published in Philosophy & Public Affairs 29, no. 1, Princeton University Press in 2000.

claim that certain values must be followed despite diverse opinions as to how to maintain the community as a whole.

In the adultery case, the Constitutional Court of Korea states that despite the great changes in the structure and public awareness of our society, the unique concept of fidelity in Korean society, especially that of a married couple, is still regarded as a case of enduring traditional ethics. Confucian culture has affected Korean society in that the importance of families has been emphasized. At the same time, Confucianism has brought a patriarchal culture. The social characteristics of criminalizing adultery can be attributed to the legal enforcement of morals that emphasize the importance of maintaining the family. Therefore, adultery is ultimately considered as undermining social order and seriously infringing the rights of other people. Furthermore, this legal awareness is still valid.[14] From this specific case, the Court identifies traditional ethics with morals and justifies the legal punishment of values in a moral scope. The Constitutional Court of Korea seems to use law as a means to strengthen the cultural identity of society's members. The areas represented as individual rights among legal regulations appear to be easily justified in criminal punishment. However, if the action in question infringes on fundamental rights, there are some cases which specify a particular individual whose rights are violated. If there are no specific individuals whose rights are infringed by a certain act, the legitimacy of the criminal punishment can be derived in terms of objective value order.[15] For example, some people argue that the legislation of same-sex marriage violates their ethical standards. Nevertheless, the legislation of same-sex marriage does not violate their human rights or constitutional rights.

In some cases, the legal enforcement of morals has been necessary. Adultery is one of the examples from Korean history, as mentioned above. From a liberalistic point of view, the focus is on infringing individual freedom and rights by criminalizing adultery. On the other hand, those who oppose such a standpoint emphasize the legal enforcement of moral values. In conclusion, supporters of legal moralism (claiming that moral values can be legally enforced) assert that one must use force if some actions in question are regarded as immoral, irrespective of whether they inflict harm on other people. Those supporters believe enforcing morality is one of the duties of the law. The aim of promoting good and preventing evil is good, and such an aim is legitimate enough to be easily understood as a legislative objective. In this respect, criminal law is seen as essentially something to liquidate evil.[16] Nevertheless, the standard to distinguish good from evil changes over time and it cannot only be decided by the state. Similarly, if states intervene in adultery by criminalizing it, it is difficult to justify this as the enforcement of morals since adultery is an act between consenting adults without harming others, and it is

[14]The Constitutional Court of Korea, 2000 Hun Ba 60, decided on October 25, 2001. Judicial Reports 13-2, pp. 480–486.

[15]Hörnle (2008), p. 317.

[16]Stephen (1872), pp. 96–98.

difficult to agree with the idea of enforcing morals using criminal law to achieve common social values.

2.1.2 Implications of Legal Paternalism

If the Harm Principle[17] justifies state intervention[18] against individual freedoms to prevent harm from others by Legal Paternalism, the scope of the state intervention can be extended in the name of benefiting individuals. Such a difference in scope can explain why different positions exist regarding the criminalization of same-sex relations. Some will argue that criminal punishment is unnecessary as long as homosexual acts do not harm others. Legal Paternalism seems to have gained considerable support, especially because it justifies intervening in the lives of others for the sake of another person's goodness, such as prohibiting drug abuse.[19] Nevertheless, questions still remain as to whether the state has the legitimacy to determine the goodness of an individual. There seems to be no significant difference between forbidding immorality or causing some discomfort to some without harming others and legally encouraging some moral behavior; however, there are differences. For example, the punishments for not wearing seat belts and the punishment for dwarf-tossing[20] are totally different, and the effect of both applications is quite distinct.

---

[17] *John Stuart Mill* first articulated the harm principle in the first chapter of On Liberty (1859): "The object of this Essay is to assert one very simple principle, as entitled to govern absolutely the dealings of society with the individual in the way of compulsion and control, whether the means used be physical force in the form of legal penalties, or the moral coercion of public opinion. That principle is that the sole end for which mankind is warranted, individually or collectively, in interfering with the liberty of action of any of their number, is self-protection. That the only purpose for which power can be rightfully exercised over any member of a civilized community, against his will, is to prevent harm to others. His own good, either physical or moral, is not a sufficient warrant. He cannot rightfully be compelled to do or forbear because it will be better for him to do so, because it will make him happier, because, in the opinion of others, to do so would be wise, or even right. . .The only part of the conduct of anyone, for which he is amenable to society, is that which concerns others. In the part which merely concerns himself, his independence is, of right, absolute. Over himself, over his own body and mind, the individual is sovereign." (Mill 1859, pp. 21–22).

[18] In this chapter, I distinguish state interventions from state positive duties (such as duties to protect, duty to fulfill or the minimum core obligation of state, as explained in Fredman 2008, pp. 70–87) or state positive obligations. I use the term "state intervention" in the sense of protecting the liberty or individual autonomy against state intervention such as criminalizing adultery or criminalizing same sex relations between consenting adults. This state intervention must be distinguished from the state's positive obligation, for example, to legalize same-sex marriage or provide of legal recognition of same-sex relations.

[19] Feinberg (1971), pp. 106–124; Dworkin (1972), pp. 64–84; Sunstein and Thaler (2003), pp. 1159–1202.

[20] Dwarf-tossing was regarded as one of the bar attractions, but it is outlawed in France and in the several US states and Canada. A United Nations Human Rights Committee ruled that the "sport" is contrary to human dignity. ("Dwarf Tossing – The Rules" https://www.hitc.com/en-gb/2010/07/25/dwarf_tossing_the_ru/. Accessed November 30, 2021.)

Legal Paternalism emphasizes the complementary role of morality and law. It is distinguished from the position that claims morals can be enforced by law because such a claim emphasizes the powerful role of law in the realization of morality. Another difficult case, along with the adultery case in the Constitutional Court of Korea, is illicit sexual acts under false marriage promises. Regarding this article, the Constitutional Court of Korea decided that it is unconstitutional because it violates the right of sexual self-determination as well as the freedom and privacy of personal life. The Constitutional Court stated in this case:

> It is included in the private, confidential sphere whether men choose women as their partners for loving acts without any harmful measures such as using their superior powers or violence. Therefore, by its nature, state intervention has to be restrained from interfering in such acts. There is no reason to punish sexual acts without any intention to marry because Korean criminal law does not punish any sexual acts before marriage. If women determine alone whether they will have sexual relations with men, yet later claim that their decision was the result of mistakes and that the relevant men should be punished, it is as if women would deny their own right to sexual self-determination. There have been many changes in citizens' legal consciousness regarding the need to criminally punish sexual acts before marriage. It is less necessary to use criminal law to protect women's mistaken premarital sexual acts; furthermore, the kinds of sexual acts any adults have, in principle, are based on the individuals' own freedom.[21]

The criminal code in question has been prescribed to punish men who have had sexual intercourse with women after promising to marry them. The purpose of such a prescription has been to protect women. As seen from the decision above, the distinction is necessary between the part directly regulated by law and morals. Furthermore, what should be in the sphere of morals must not be interfered with by laws, and the Court will not tolerate it. In other words, such a criminal provision where men will be punished when they do not marry a woman after having sexual relations with her after promising to marry her shows that women are seen as sexually incompetent. The legal interest to be protected by this provision is not to promise marriage to have sexual relations. It seems as if women's capacity to judge the reliability of such a promise to marry is very much underestimated. This shows that sometimes morals can be excessively applied with the following side-effects even if the legal interests apparently exist. The state actively guarantees an

---

As an example of a legislative ban, the Legislative Assembly of Ontario pronounced Bill 97, Dwarf Tossing Ban Act:

> 1. (1) No person shall organize a dwarf-tossing event or engage in dwarf tossing.
>
> 1. (2) A person who contravenes subsection (1) is guilty of an offence and on conviction is liable to a fine of not more than $5,000 or imprisonment for a term of not more than six months, or to both. (Legislative Assembly of Ontario, https://www.ola.org/en/legislative-business/bills/parliament-37/session-4/bill-97. Accessed November 30, 2021.)

[21] The Constitutional Court of Korea, 2008 Hun-Ba 58, decided on November 26, 2009. From this decision, Article 304 of the Korean Criminal Code has been deleted. In this article, it has been stipulated that any men who have sexual acts with women (who do not have any problem with sexual abuse) by suggesting that they will marry the women will be punished by imprisonment for not more than two years or by a fine not exceeding five million Korean won.

individual's right to sexual self-determination by means of legislation, but at other times active state legislation hinders the accomplishment of such a right.

In this decision,[22] the CCK states that even if each act is regarded as morally objectionable, it is essentially part of an individual's private life, and state intervention is not justified unless there is a social hazard and there is no obvious harm to the legal interests protected by law. As the CCK points out in the decision,[23] some provisions for punishment can sometimes harm community customs. In this case, criminal punishment could enforce unwanted marriages, which is not the original purpose of the legislation. In this regard, legal enforcement of moral matters or criminal punishment should not only consider the original legislative purpose but also their practical application. Otherwise, it can lead to completely different results. The original legislative intent was to maintain a monogamous marriage system as well as the preservation of the family. Nevertheless, the state should not intervene in enforcing unwanted marriage by criminalizing sexual relations even if the man does not intend to marry.

This is why understanding Legal Paternalism is important. As *Gerald Dworkin* argues: "By paternalism, I shall understand roughly the interference with a person's liberty of action justified by reasons referring exclusively to the welfare, good, happiness, needs, interests, of values of the person being coerced."[24] From the paternalistic point of view, the focus is on promoting individual welfare or happiness even if individual freedoms are interfered with during the process of the promotion. Paternalism deals with the legal enforcement in the scope of the welfare or happiness of individuals. The following paternalistic examples by *Dworkin* still seem to be a suitable topic of discussion.

1. Laws requiring motorcyclists to wear safety helmets when operating their machines.
2. Laws forbidding persons from swimming at a public beach when lifeguards are not on duty.
3. Laws making suicide a criminal offense.
4. Laws making it illegal for women and children to work at certain types of jobs.
5. Laws regulating certain kinds of sexual conduct, e.g., homosexuality among consenting adults in private.
6. Laws regulating the use of certain drugs may have harmful consequences to the user but do not lead to anti-social conduct.

[22] The Constitutional Court of Korea, 2008 Hun-Ba 58, decided on November 26, 2009.

[23] The Constitutional Court of Korea, 2008 Hun-Ba 58, decided on November 26, 2009. (In this decision, the Court states: Men who have sexual relations with the false promise to marry are subject to social criticism and sanctions based on ethics and individual moral standards in various fields such as home, society, and even workplace. Therefore, criminal law does not need to interfere with all such actions that are essentially part of individual's private lives. Another important point is that if men marry for fear of criminal punishment, even when unhappy marriage life is expected in the future, it is as if the criminal law compels such marriage that eventually breaks down. Therefore, enforcing this by law is unreasonable. It is the trend of modern criminal law that state power should not intervene in areas that are part of individuals' private lives unless the social hazard is very serious and there is obvious harm to the interests protected by law.)

[24] Dworkin (1972), p. 65.

7. Laws requiring a license to engage in certain professions with those not receiving a license subject to fine or jail sentences if they engage in the practice.
8. Laws compelling people to spend a specified fraction of their income on the purchase of retirement annuities. (Social Security)
9. Laws forbidding various forms of gambling (often justified because the poor are more likely to throw away their money on such activities than the rich who can afford to).
10. Laws regulating the maximum rates of interest for loans.[25]

As the above examples show, it is no longer obvious that individuals sufficiently recognize their own interests so that state intervention in some cases is not needed. The heart of legal paternalism is that the state restricts a person's freedom for the benefit of the person, contrary to the individual's will. The state uses criminal law to punish drug use at the expense of the individual's freedom for their own benefit. The issue of securing life or public welfare at the expense of individual freedom in many Asian countries, including South Korea,[26] is similarly based on this rationale for provisions that limit individual freedom. As we can see from the controversy over "Asian values," some political leaders and scholars in Asia still support the idea of illiberal democracy, which is different from liberal democracy in the West.[27] The logic of limiting individual freedom is still strongly supported in some Asian countries. From a liberalistic viewpoint, the term *Paternalism* itself can be negatively interpreted.[28] Nonetheless, it is difficult to regard Paternalism negatively from the perspective of the "Asian values" discourse. The distinction between weak paternalism and strong paternalism depends on the extent to which individual autonomy is respected: if individual autonomy is regarded as being more important, it refers to weak paternalism; if individual autonomy is regarded as less important, it refers to strong paternalism. According to *Feinberg*,[29] a state intervenes even in completely voluntary actions under the strong meaning of Paternalism, while a state intervenes only when an individual lacks the ability to make judgments which are in his/her best interest so that the actions are non-voluntary under the weak meaning of Paternalism.

The individual opinion is a significant factor to give the legitimacy. However, the problem does not end here. The question of the objectives for such interventions remains even after the legitimacy is accepted. Furthermore, if the interventions are even at odds with the person's intentions, the objectives of such interventions should be considered deeply. The discussion about the final objectives can return to the ultimate purpose of the happiness of other people or the community. In this sense,

[25] Ibid. pp. 65–66.

[26] Article 37, Paragraph 2 of the Constitution of the Republic of Korea stipulates as follows:

> The freedoms and rights of citizens may be restricted by Act only when necessary for national security, the maintenance of law and order or for public welfare. Even when such a restriction is imposed, no essential aspect of the freedom or right shall be violated.

[27] For the controversy over "Asian values" and the criticism on illiberal democracy, please see: Tatsuo (1997).

[28] Feinberg (1986), p. 4.

[29] Feinberg (1971), p. 124.

Paternalism can only be defined as interventions for the benefit of other people.[30] Nevertheless, the benefit to the individual is never an easy excuse for interfering in individual freedoms. Furthermore, it is not the state but individuals who should decide what is beneficial for individuals. Likewise, even if the state criminalizes same-sex relations between consenting adults for the benefit of others, the interference in the freedom of same-sex couples cannot be justified under the name of Paternalism.

2.2 Case Study in Korea: Adultery

The most representative case in the debate on legal coercion of moral matters in Korea is that of adultery. The crime of adultery[31] was abolished by the Korean Constitutional Court's decision in 2015. The legislative purpose of adultery is to control the maintenance of marriage by the state. The Korean Constitutional Court has relatively recently reversed four existing rulings.[32] In the current situation where there is no same-sex marriage case in the Korean Constitutional Court, it is significant to review the adultery case because it is also related to the institution of marriage. Furthermore, adultery has been regarded as one of the most important cases on morality enforced by law.

2.2.1 Previous Decisions:[33] Constitutional

In this section, the reasons why adultery is regarded as constitutional will be introduced. Details about the reasoning of the majority opinion and the dissenting opinion will show how the reasoning changed in the 2015 case, when adultery was declared unconstitutional.

According to the majority opinion of the 2001 case,[34] a person with a married spouse who has sexual relations with a third party who is not his/her married spouse offends against sexual morality or the institution of the monogamous marriage system. It also violates the duty of sexual integrity, which a person has towards

[30]VanDeVeer (1986), p. 24.

[31]Before eliminating the provision on January 6, 2016, Article 241, paragraph 1 of the Korean Criminal Code stipulated that "Adultery of the person with married spouse will be 2-year imprisonment. The counterpart of the adultery will have the same punishment as the person as above."

[32]The Constitutional Court of Korea, 2009 Hun-Ba 17, etc., decided on February 26, 2015.

[33]The Constitutional Court of Korea, 1989 Hun-Ma 82, Grand Chamber Decision, decided on 10 Sep. 1990; The Constitutional Court of Korea, 2000 Hun-Ba 60, Grand Chamber Decision, decided on October 25, 2001.

[34]The Constitutional Court of Korea, 2000 Hun-Ba 60, Grand Chamber Decision, decided on October 25, 2001. Judicial Report 13-2.

his/her married spouse. Therefore, to maintain sexual morality, the monogamous marriage system, the security of the family life, or to protect the marital sexual obligations, it is necessary to control the spouse's acts of adultery to prevent further social harm such as abandoning the spouse and the family, problems of children out of wedlock and divorce, etc. Furthermore, the majority opinion argued as follows: the question of whether a particular human act is considered illegal and whether the state can punish certain criminals or certain acts can only be controlled by an individual moral standard that depends on particular historical (and social) context as a function of the interrelationship between humans, and humans and society. Therefore, the problem of moral coercion or legal coercion will ultimately only be determined by social context as well as the social conscience of its members.[35]

The majority opinion defines protecting the sexual integrity of the married couple as one of the important roles of the state. In other words, the Court also regards the core of the debate in question as a matter of the historical situation and the social attitudes of the society's members. However, it should be pointed out how these attitudes are reached. In other words, even after determining that adultery as a crime is unconstitutional, many citizens will still consider the need to criminalize adultery again. This is because the social attitudes will not easily recognize the real change, and even if such a change is detected, opinions for and against it will still exist. Until such matters become issues for actual legislation, discrimination and unfair punishment will persist.

According to the Court's 2005 decision,[36] people's legal awareness of sex and gender have changed considerably as South Korean society has rapidly become more individualistic and open-minded. Especially considering adultery, criminal punishment of adultery has been abused as a means of fulfilling the demand for more alimony when couples get divorced. With the amendments of the Korean family law,[37] each counterparty has been granted the right to claim the division of property owned by both husband and wife, and custody of the children is also equally guaranteed without gender discrimination between men and women. For this reason, even from the perspective of women with a relatively poor social status compared to men, it has become more reasonable to respond to adultery with civil damage or family law litigation rather than criminal punishment. In this sense, the normative power of criminal punishment of adultery is weak compared to the situation in the past.[38]

The majority opinion has gone into detail to explain why adultery existed so long in the penal code. Unlike in the past, where several complementary means were

[35] Ibid. pp. 485–486.

[36] The Constitutional Court of Korea, 2000 Hun-Ba 60, Grand Chamber Decision, decided on October 25, 2001. Judicial Report 13-2, pp. 485–486.

[37] Korean Family Law was amended as of January 13, 1990 regarding the details of divorce. This is referred as Amendment to Civil Code No. 4199.

[38] The Constitutional Court of Korea, 1989 Hun-Ma 82, Grand Chamber Decision, decided on 10 Sep. 1990.

lacking, now that such supplementary means are in place, criminal punishment is no longer necessary. However, in the four previous decisions[39] before the decision of 2015, the majority opinion concluded as follows: despite major changes in the structure and public attitudes of our society, the notions of fidelity, especially those between married men and women, are deeply rooted in our traditions and ethics. Monogamy and the obligation of marital sexual integrity are still deeply rooted and established in our social, moral standards. Therefore, adultery or extra-marital affairs could ultimately impede social order in the current situation, by being harmful and infringing others' rights so that criminalizing adultery can still be seen as legally valid. The majority opinions before 2015 concluded that the criminal punishment of adultery was constitutional. On the other hand, the dissenting opinions have reasoned that adultery or affairs are not matters of criminal punishment but ethical as well as moral matters In other words, it would not be a crime that the state has to intervene and punish with its criminal code. Sexual intercourse is originally in the most private and confidential territory, and therefore an individual's duty of fidelity to their spouse can never be physically enforced. Neither should it be subject to state surveillance and criminal punishment.

Article 10[40] of the Korean constitution confirms the dignity and value of human beings as being the inviolable fundamental human rights of each individual. The basis of such fundamental human rights is the right to self-determination, which humans have not as a means but as the end in itself. In this sense, the core independence of the personality itself must be retained no matter what, even if some freedoms can be limited for the existence of a communal society. However, criminal punishment for adultery is like forcing affection and love on the spouse. Such enforcement violates human dignity because it deprives the person of his/her independence, that is, sexual self-determination.[41] This essential logic of dissenting opinion from the decision of the year 2001 led to the majority opinion of the decision of 2015.[42]

According to the decision of Adultery on October 25, 2001, the majority opinions state that criminal punishment of adultery is needed "to maintain good sexual ethics and a monogamous marriage system, to secure family life and to ensure the obligations of sexual integrity of both husband and wife. . .for the prevention of

---

[39] The Constitutional Court of Korea, 1989 Hun-Ma 82, Grand Chamber Decision, decided on 10 Sep. 1990; The Constitutional Court of Korea, 2000 Hun-Ba 60, Grand Chamber Decision, decided on October 25, 2001.

[40] Article 10 of the Constitution of the Republic of Korea reads as follows: All citizens shall be assured of human worth and dignity and have the right to pursue happiness. It shall be the State's duty to confirm and guarantee the fundamental and inviolable human rights of individuals.

[41] The Constitutional Court of Korea, 2000 Hun-Ba 60, Grand Chamber Decision, decided on October 25, 2001. Judicial Report of precedents 13-2, pp. 488–489.

[42] The Constitutional Court of Korea, 2009 Hun-Ba 17, 2011 Hun-Ga 31 consolidated, decided on February 26, 2015.

social harm."[43] The majority opinions regarded that adultery harms the order of society and violates the rights of others, and considered that the criminal punishment of adultery has the legitimate aim of protecting sound sexual customs or sexual ethics. To justify criminal punishment, the majority opinions stated: "For a particular human act, whether the state should intervene by criminal punishment and regulate it because the act is illegal and criminal, can only be determined by the situation of the times as well as the attitudes or consent among the members of the society."[44]

A rationale similar to the basis for such a ruling can be found in the argument of Lord *Devlin*.[45] He argues that the law must not punish specific acts that are still considered as being within the limits of tolerance. Even if the majority of people do not like such acts, such feelings are not sufficient for their punishment. Instead, there must be true feeling of condemnation to justify punishment, and the feelings of condemnation is the force behind morality. Lord *Devlin* regards all moral judgment as the emotion that reasonable people feel when others act in a way that is morally wrong. His argument is that the awareness or consent among the members of the society which the majority opinions refer to is not decided by the power of reasons but by the power of shared feeling.

The majority opinion seems to conclude that certain acts can be criminally punished since they produce feelings of condemnation. Such a conclusion is possible because the law of balancing[46] has not been applied. The majority opinion focuses only on the infringement of others' rights because adultery can be harmful to other family members. Nevertheless, it ignores the importance of the right to sexual self-determination. The argument for criminalizing adultery limits the scope of the right to sexual self-determination. The majority opinion argues that adultery is a crime established on the premise of the social system of marriage so that adultery has nothing to do with protecting the individual's right to sexual self-determination.

It is problematic that majority opinions consider the right to sexual self-determination to be interpreted in a very restrictive manner without legitimate grounds. Furthermore, they miss the opportunity to balance the right to infringe and the aim to protect through the criminal punishment of adultery. Even if public anger is considered serious, it cannot be legitimate not to apply the law of balancing. Especially when deciding whether the state should intervene by means of criminal punishment, it is more important to weigh the right to infringe because criminal punishment is considered the most serious intervention of the state. The majority opinion seems to believe that a society could disintegrate if the state does not enforce

[43]The Constitutional Court of Korea, 2000 Hun-Ba 60, Grand Chamber Decision, decided on October 25, 2001. Majority Opinion.

[44]The Constitutional Court of Korea, 2000 Hun-Ba 60, Grand Chamber Decision, decided on October 25, 2001. Majority Opinion.

[45]Devlin (1965), p. 17.

[46]According to the argument of Lord Devlin, balancing is appropriate only when public outrage is shown to be overstated. However, when the intolerance, indignation, and disgust are genuine, balancing no longer applies. After all, what is necessary is "nothing more than passionate public disapproval." (taken from Dworkin 1966, pp. 991–992).

the morals that are regarded as maintaining society's foundation. This can be criticized through the argument of *H.L.A. Hart*: "Apart from the one general statement that 'history shows that the loosening of moral bonds is often the first stage of disintegration,' no evidence is given in support of the argument and no indication is given of the kind of evidence that would support it, nor is any sensitivity betrayed to the need for evidence."[47]

2.2.2 The Decision of 2015:[48] Unconstitutional

In this section, different opinions[49] will be introduced in the decision from 2015 which made the criminal punishment of adultery unconstitutional. It is important to learn about this decision because it has many similarities with the issue of criminalizing homosexual relations as well as same-sex marriage in Korea: previously, many people in Korea supported the criminalization of adultery, which was considered an immoral behavior just as same-sex relations are considered immoral. However, it was finally decided that criminalizing adultery was unconstitutional, providing hope that future decisions will make criminalizing homosexual relations unconstitutional.

The majority opinions have adopted the principle of proportionality in their reasoning process. Maintaining marriage and family cannot be enforced through criminal punishment. Therefore, criminal punishment of adultery is not regarded as a suitable and effective means to obtain the objectives of protecting the monogamous marriage system and the family order. In addition, the majority opinions confirm that criminal punishment of adultery fails the *suitability* test of the proportionality. The criminalization of adultery is not suitable not only in the sense of achievement but also of promotion. To satisfy the test of suitability, the means should be "carefully

---

[47] Hart (1967), p. 3.

[48] In this section, I am analyzing the reasoning of the decision of the most recent case about adultery in 2015 (The Constitutional Court of Korea, 2009 Hun-Ba 17, etc., February 26, 2015). Following this decision, the criminal code of adultery was removed from the criminal code of Korea. It is meaningful to analyze the reasoning of this decision because it can show how the Constitutional Court of Korea dealt the moral coercion case, and in that sense, relevant considerations can be inferred as to the future case of same-sex marriage that has not been decided yet in the Constitutional Court of Korea.

[49] There are four different opinions (4 justices of unconstitutional, 1 justice of separate opinion—concurring opinion 1, 1 justice of separate opinion—concurring opinion 2, 2 justices of constitutional) in the decision. As majority opinions, there are five judges who regarded the criminalization of adultery as unconstitutional. Under the Korean Constitution, Article 113 (1), "When the Constitutional Court makes a decision of the constitutionality of a law, a decision of impeachment, a decision of dissolution of a political party or an affirmative decision regarding the constitutional complaint, the concurrence of six justices or more shall be required." Nevertheless, concurring opinion 1 and concurring opinion 2 are in the opinion of "unconstitutional" even if they have different reasoning from the majority opinion, the conclusion of this case has been "unconstitutional." Even if the reasons for unconstitutional are different, if the opinion of six or more justices is unconstitutional, the case will be declared as unconstitutional (referred from, Kim 2010, p. 1657).

designed to achieve the objective in question."[50] The criminalization of adultery does not achieve the objective of the protection of marriage and family order. Firstly, adultery in the Korean criminal code is a crime subject to the spouse's complaint, which is only possible after the legal marriage is dissolved, or divorce proceedings are filed. Therefore, criminal punishment of adultery cannot achieve the objective. A person punished for adultery is most unlikely to reunite with the spouse that had complained. Furthermore, the process of criminal punishment amplifies the couple's conflict and thus the order of a healthy family will not be protected. Secondly, the criminal punishment of adultery does not promote the objective in question either. Promoting the marriage system presupposes that a married spouse will avoid adultery because of the fear of being criminally punished. However, it is highly doubtful whether such pre-suppression measures are effective. In addition, no document that has empirically analyzed the actual state of law enforcement shows that criminal punishment has had a general preventive effect.[51]

To understand the meaning of the necessity test, there are useful metaphors such as "narrowly tailored," or "police cannot shoot a sparrow with a canon," or one "must not use a steam-hammer to crack a nut."[52] From such expressions, it is understood that the test of necessary addresses "whether there are less-restrictive ways"[53] for the state to achieve its aim other than the means in question. There are less restrictive measures to attain the objective of protecting the marital obligation of husband and wife without the criminal punishment of adultery in Korean law. First, an act of unchastity is considered as a cause for judicial divorce.[54] Second, a spouse who has committed adultery shall be obliged to compensate the spouse for property and mental anguish.[55] Furthermore, a certain disadvantage can be given to a spouse who commits adultery when the family court decides on matters concerning the right of child-rearing and restrictions and exclusions of visits for the children.[56] The criminal punishment does not fulfill the test of *necessity* because there are other less restrictive measures available in Korean law to promote the marital obligations

[50] Barak (2012), p. 306.

[51] The Constitutional Court of Korea, 2009 Hun-Ba 17, etc., decided on February 26, 2015, The Majority Opinions.

[52] Barak (2012), p. 333.

[53] Huang and Law (2015), p. 4.

[54] The Korean Civil Act Article 840 (Causes for Judicial Divorce) states as "Either husband or wife may apply to the Family Court for a divorce in each case of the following subparagraphs: 1. If the other spouse has committed an act of unchastity."

[55] The Korean Civil Act Article 843 (Provisions to be Applied Mutatis Mutandis) states that "Article 806 shall apply mutatis mutandis to the claims for damages from a judicial divorce." Article 806 (Dissolution of Matrimonial Engagement and Claims for Damages) states that "(1) When a matrimonial engagement has been dissolved between parties, one party may claim against the other party in negligence the damages therefrom. (2) In paragraph (1), the negligent party shall be liable for damages from mental anguish in addition to property damages."

[56] The Constitutional Court of Korea, 2009 Hun-Ba 17, etc., decided on February 26, 2015, The Majority Opinions.

of husband and wife. Furthermore, these alternative measures such as provision of alimony or payment of compensation according to family law are also regarded just as effective[57] as criminal punishment.

Moreover, the majority opinions hold that criminal punishment of adultery fails in the last step of proportionality, proportionality in the narrow sense, and balancing. On the one hand, the public interest in protecting the monogamous marriage system as well as the obligations of fidelity is hardly attained with the criminal punishment of adultery. On the other hand, the individual right to sexual self-determination and the freedom of private life is extremely restrained by making the realm of an individual's sexual life, which is very confidential, subject to criminal punishment. It fails in the balancing test of two legal interests. It is unconstitutional because it fails the test of suitability, necessity, and balancing of the principle of proportionality.

According to Justice *Kim*,[58] the core essence of adultery lies in committing an act which intentionally violates one's duty of fidelity towards his or her married spouse. A married individual's free sexual self-determination has essential limitations based on the exclusivity and sustainability of a sexual community, which was created by their own decision to marry. Justice *Kim* classifies and differentiates three types of adultery. According to him, the first type is sexual relations with another person out of simple sexual enjoyment even if they are married. The second type is to fall in love with another person who is more attractive than their own spouse. The third type is to meet a new loving partner and have sexual relations as marriage is virtually broken even if the existing marriage has not been legally dissolved or no divorce lawsuit has been filed. *Kim* argues that the first and second types are most likely to be major points of criticism and it must also be considered whether it is necessary to protect the existing marital relations, unlike the third type. For this reason, punitive

[57] The Constitutional Court of Korea did not assess other less restrictive measures such as the provision of alimony or payment of compensation by a spouse who commits adultery. Nevertheless, the CCK states that criminal punishment of adultery did not work as effective measure to promote marital obligation because there were no statistics to show the criminal punishment had been effective (referred from "Constitutional Court of Korea, 2009 Hun-Ba 17, etc., decided on February 26, 2015, The Majority Opinions). After the abolishment of criminal punishment of adultery, it was reported that the amount of alimony was much increased considering all the circumstances of couples involved. When the criminal punishment of adultery still existed, the Korean family court set the maximum amount of alimony as around 30,000 USD equivalence which is considered as being very low considering the economic status of the couples involved. It was because the family court considered that a spouse who commits adultery should be criminally punished. For this reason, the amount of alimony was much increased, which had the effect of promoting obligations (taken from the news article about the abolition of adultery in Korea. https://www.mk.co.kr/news/society/view/2017/12/854859/. Accessed November 30, 2021). Therefore, I argue that these alternative measures according to civil law or family law are equally effective as the criminal punishment.

[58] Justice *Yi-Soo Kim* expresses the first Concurring Opinion. The Constitutional Court of Korea uses the term of "separate opinion" instead of "concurring opinion." Nevertheless, I term Justice Kim's opinion as concurring opinion because it has the same conclusion as the majority opinion with different reasoning.

regulations regarding the first and second types are still required according to the general public's attitude. Therefore, criminal penalties for the first and second types of adultery are appropriate and effective since they have the legitimate aim of protecting social ethics at a minimum level that is recognized in the marriage system based on the obligation of sexual integrity between married couples. In this sense, such limitation is not regarded as excessive regarding the individual's right to sexual self-determination.

However, in the case of the third type, where the couple's marriage has already virtually broken down, there is no risk of violating the spouse's obligations to fidelity or hampering the marriage system through extramarital sexual relations. Therefore, punishment in such a case is not allowed since it would be an excessive use of the state's punishment power. Additionally, criminal punishment for the unmarried party is unreasonable given the nature of the adultery since it would be an excessive use of state penalties in view their right to sexual self-determination. Nevertheless, it is against the rule of clarity as well as foreseeability to punish all individuals affected uniformly without the chance to consider the individuality and specificity of the type of actor or types of specific actions. This uniform applicability of criminal penalties of adultery violates the Constitution as an excessive action of state criminal penalties that deviates from the necessary degree in fulfilling the purpose and the intended function through such penalties. Unlike the reasoning of the majority opinions, *Kim* highlights the unclear and ambiguous stipulations of the code to criminalize adultery, which diminishes *foreseeability* to find out which specific actions or who could be punished by such stipulations. Justice *Kang*[59] reasons that adultery of a married spouse is a serious threat to the monogamy that forms the basis of the marriage system, causing serious social problems such as the neglect of family members. For this reason, even if adultery is based on the individual's right to sexual self-determination as concerning the private sphere of an individual's confidential social life, the necessity of legal regulation is recognized because such acts could have a detrimental effect on marital relations.

The components of adultery[60] seem to be clear enough, but the negative prerequisite to prosecute in paragraph 2, such as "condones" or "pardons," is not so clear and thus people cannot *foresee* the scope and limitations to the extent with regard to the state exercise of state authority. Therefore, the article of adultery violates the principle of legality to state prerequisites of criminal codes very clearly for the foreseeability of the people. Justice *Kang* also applied the principle of proportionality in his reasoning. There must be many cases according to the types of adultery.

---

[59] Justice *Il-Won Kang* expresses the second Concurring Opinion.

[60] Article 241 (Adultery) was stipulated in the Korean Criminal Code (legislated on September 18, 1953, with the law number of 293) as follows:

> Paragraph 1. A married person who commits adultery shall be punished by imprisonment for not more than two years. The same shall apply to the other participant.
>
> Paragraph 2. The crime in the preceding paragraph shall be prosecuted only upon the complaint of the victimized spouse. If the victimized spouse condones or pardons the adultery, complaint can no longer be made.

Nevertheless, regardless of each detail or corresponding type of action, if all the cases are punished only with imprisonment, the stipulated provision violates the law of balancing because there is no reasonable balance between the actor's responsibilities and the related punishment. The provision violates the principle of proportionality because the responsibility is not proportionate to the punishment as it is against the principle of a substantive rule of law. Justice *Kang* did not properly apply all the steps of the principle of proportionality in his reasoning. However, he still applied the law of balancing and the core ideas of the principle of proportionality in the analysis to conclude the unconstitutionality of the criminal law article for punishing adultery.

According to the dissenting opinion,[61] adultery committed by a married person is an act which violates the duty of sexual fidelity after an individual has voluntarily chosen to marry, and the social system which marriage implies. Moreover, the other party to adultery, knowing that the person is already married, is inherently rejecting the community that protects marriage as a social and legal system. Adultery could become a serious threat to monogamy which is considered to be the heart of the marriage system and could cause social problems such as the neglect of spouses and families. The provisions criminalizing adultery are intended to ensure a marriage system based on monogamy and family life and to obey the obligations of marital fidelity. This is in line with the state's duty to maintain and protect marriage and family life based on an individual's human dignity and gender equality as stated in the Korean Constitution.[62]

Even if Justice *Lee* and *Ahn* do not clearly mention the analysis using the principle of proportionality, their reasoning can be restructured according to the steps of proportionality. They point out that the provisions stipulate only two years' imprisonment, which is not considered high or severe because the maximum length is limited to two years. Furthermore, some sentences can be suspended according to the details of the acts if they are considered to be a mild violation. These imply that the stipulation cannot be seen as an excessively hefty punishment compared to individual responsibilities. In that sense, they consider that adultery, when prosecuted, inevitably causes social problems arising from the destruction of the family regardless of the types of actions.[63] In this respect, even if the legislator did not stipulate a fine as a punishment, as different from other sexual customs, it cannot be considered as violating the law of balancing.

Furthermore, the public interest protected by criminalizing adultery is the constitutional value of protecting sexual morality and guaranteeing marriage and family

---

[61] Justice *Jung-Mi Lee* and *Chang-Ho Ahn* express the Dissenting Opinion to regard the criminal punishment of adultery as constitutional.

[62] In their dissenting opinions, Judge *LEE* and Judge *AHN* cited Article 36, paragraph 1 of the Constitution of the Republic of Korea, which stated as follows: Marriage and family life shall be entered into and sustained based on individual dignity and equality of the sexes, and the State shall do everything in its power to achieve that goal.

[63] If an individual wanted to accuse his or her spouse of adultery under the criminal law, they had to start divorce proceedings when making the accusations.

systems. On the other hand, restrictions on conduct under the clause of adultery apply to sexual acts in a specific relationship in which a counterpart has a legal spouse and both an actor and a counterpart know about it. Even if the counterpart of adultery is not married, obligations are imposed on them not to actively violate the legal and moral duty of another person with the knowledge of the violations. The article that stipulates criminalization of adultery does not violate the law of balancing because it does not limit the right to sexual self-determination excessively, considering material harm that could be brought by a violation. Therefore, it is still constitutional.

The first concurring opinion points out that comprehensive punishment, regardless of the type of adultery committed, is equivalent to the excessive use of the state's punishment power, which restricts an individual's right to sexual self-determination. In other words, if adultery is criminally punished when the marital relationship is maintained without any material problems, and a person is still liable for sexual fidelity towards his or her spouse, without this being regarded as an excessive restriction. The second concurring opinion confirms the necessity to regulate adultery legally. However, to punish all types of adultery only with imprisonment violates *the principle of proportionality*. It has also been pointed out that "condones" or "pardons" stipulated in Article 241, paragraph 2 (Adultery) in the Korean criminal code are not clear enough in their meaning. The intention of the second concurring opinion as well as the provision of adultery itself is not unconstitutional providing that it is amended to have punishment options according to the severity of violations, and those unclear terms of "condones" or "pardons" can be more clearly stated.[64]

Regarding the question of whether a particular human act is considered illegal or whether the state regulates such acts with punishment, or whether such an act is entrusted to the moral law, the answer depends on social and temporal conditions as a function of the interrelationship between humans, and between humans and societies. In the decision of the recent adultery case, the Constitutional Court of Korea concludes that the questions mentioned above can only be solved by considering the prevailing conditions in society and the attitudes of the members of society. The Constitutional Court of Korea seems to have difficulty interpreting the historical as well as the current situation, and the changes in people's attitudes.[65] This is exactly why considerations and debates over moral coercion are needed. Of course, while adultery is much more widespread than polygamous marriages, many scholars in Korea[66] still support the criminalization of adultery because it completely breaks

[64] Chung (2016), pp. 229–241.

[65] The Constitutional Court of Korea seemed to wait for the consensus of the Korean people to agree on the abolition of the criminal punishment of adultery as the CCK had previously decided that the criminal punishment as constitutional four times. The CCK also considered the consensus on the matter from a comparative law perspective. The decision of the year 2015 states that adultery was not a crime in other countries such as Denmark, Sweden, Japan, Germany, France, Spain, Switzerland, Argentina, and Austria. (The Constitutional Court of Korea, 2009 Hun-Ba 17, etc., decided on February 26, 2015, The Majority Opinions.)

[66] Kim (2016).

the relationship of trust between married couples, and is seriously opposed to traditional values.

2.3 Case Study in Korea: Prohibition on Marriage[67] Between Same Surnames and Same Places of Origin

The marriage system is recognized only by the state, so there are no substantive alternatives if the state prohibits or has no legal recognition of marriage. Currently, there is no legal recognition of same-sex relations in Korea. In the past, marriage between people with the same surnames and the same places of origin was prohibited in Korea. This ban put many people in a complicated situation until the Constitutional Court of Korea[68] decided that such a ban was unconstitutional. In the decision, there were three different opinions of five justices of majority opinions (unconstitutional), of two justices of concurring opinion, and of two justices of dissenting opinion. The current situation of no legal recognition of same-sex relations in Korea is very similar to the past case where many couples lived as "de facto" couples without any marriage registration because they shared the same surnames and same family origins. Because of the prohibition, the children born from these

[67] This case of prohibition on marriage is between same surnames and same places of origin. Same surnames (同姓) mean same family names, and same places of origin (同本) means the same birthplace of the founder or same ancestor. Same surnames and same places of origin do not mean that these persons are relatives.

[68] The Constitutional Court of Korea, 1995 Hun-Ga 6, Grand Chamber Decision, decided on July 16, 1997. (In 1997, the Constitutional Court of Korea ruled against the ban on same-surnames-same-origin marriage, as a result, which Article 809 of the Korean Civil Code came to stipulate a ban on blood-relative marriage.)

Article 809 of Civil Code (Prohibition of marriage between parties whose surname and ancestral home are common), which does not exist because of the abolishment after the Constitutional decision has stated as follows:

> Paragraph 1. A marriage may not be allowed between blood relatives, if both surname and its origin are common to the parties.
>
> After the decision of 1997 from the Constitutional Court of Korea, Article 809 of the Civil Code was reformed as follows, effective on March 31, 2005.
>
> Paragraph 1. Marriage may not be allowed between parties whose relationship of blood relative exists within the eighth degree (including the blood relatives for the real-adopted child kept before real-adoption).
>
> Paragraph 2. Marriage may not be allowed between parties if either of them is or was the spouse of blood relative within the sixth degree of relationship, or if either of them is or was the blood relatives within the sixth degree of relationship of the spouse, or if either of them is or was the spouse of blood relatives by affinity within the fourth degree of relationship of the spouse.
>
> Paragraph 3. Marriage may not be allowed between parties whose relationship of blood relative existed within the sixth degree of adoptive parent's lineage and within the fourth degree of adoptive parent's affinity.

relationships could not be legally registered under their parents, so that they had to be registered under relatives of the couples to be legally educated. As such, provision of the marriage system by the state are essential for the parties concerned.

Some may wonder what the same surnames and the same family origins in Korea mean: whether that means the two people are close relatives or not. The answer is absolutely no. The same surname and same family origin do not relate in any way with a close relative. For example, one of the most common surnames in South Korea is *Kim*. *Gimhae* in the *Gyeongsang* province[69] of Korea is the most common family origin among the surnames of Kim. Surprisingly, the population with the surname *Kim* with the family origin *Gimhae* is 4,456,700 according to the censorship in 2015. Considering the whole population of South Korea is some 51,360,000 in 2017,[70] it is easy to understand how absurd it is to prohibit marriages among people with the same surnames and the same family origin.

2.3.1 The Background of the Marriage Bans

How could such an absurd prohibition be possible in the first place? What was the background to such a prohibition in Korea? To find out, it is worth looking up the origins of the ban. As a background, the state followed the Confucian tradition[71]

[69] *Gyeongsang-do* province was one of the eight provinces of Korea during the *Joseon dynasty*. *Gyeonsang* was located in the southeast of Korea. The provincial capital was Daegu. The region is known as the birthplace of the Kingdom of Silla. The region also has a significant role in modern Korean history, since six previous South Korean presidents of *Park Chung-hee, Roh Tae-woo, Chun Doo-hwan, Kim Young-sam, Roh Moo-hyun*, and *Park Geun-hye*, as well as the current president of *Moon Jae-in*, were born in this Gyeongsang-do province.

[70] Statistic Korea, https://kosis.kr/visual/populationKorea/PopulationByNumber/PopulationByNumberMain.do?mb=Y&menuId=M_1_1. Accessed November 30, 2021.

[71] According to the opinion of five judges as unconstitutional in the decision as above (The Constitutional Court of Korea, 1995 Hun-Ga 6, Grand Chamber Decision, decided on July 16, 1997.), the ban on the same surname and the same origin originates from the Chinese tradition of the prohibition on marriage between the same surnames. It was legalized after *Joseon Dynasty* (*Joseon Dynasty* was a Korean dynastic kingdom that lasted for approximately five centuries. *Joseon* was founded by *Seong-Gye Yi* in July 1392 and was replaced by the Korean Empire in October 1897.) in Korea. At the time of establishing such a prohibition, national policies, national consciousness, ethics, economic structure, and family system were reflected in the marriage system. Such a ban served to maintain social order in a central patriarchal and social class in an agricultural society. According to the constitution's discord opinion by two judges in the same decision, the ban on the same surname and the same origin was regarded as the marriage tradition of the Korean people as inherited for hundreds of years. Furthermore, the institution of marriage is included in the legislative discretionary matters, as the legislature should decide as legislative policy considering various circumstances, including tradition, customs, and a sense of ethics. For this reason, these two judges claim that the Constitutional Court of Korea should not decide it to be unconstitutional even if the provisions to ban are unconstitutional. The discord opinion of the CCK intends to urge the legislature to decide a new marriage system after making full considerations on our country's marriage customs, ethical consciousness, notions of kinship and its change, whether the ban has lost

faithfully and forced the people to follow it as a moral value to protect the order of the community. The ban is a practice that was adopted by small groups of the noble class in the late *Joseon Dynasty*, following Confucian customs as an extended version of the prohibition of marriage between close relatives. The *Joseon Dynasty* strictly prohibited marriages between the same surnames after applying the provisions of *the Code of the Great Ming*[72] from China. At the beginning of the adoption, the prohibition was between the same surnames as in China. Such a prohibition changed to the ban on marriage between the same surnames and the same family origin in *Joseon* because many people had the same surnames, but different family origins. It was impossible to prohibit all the marriages between the same surnames in *Joseon* because the marriage had been recognized for a long time between the same surnames and different origins.

However, the fact that there was a lower class of people who did not have their surnames in the late *Joseon Dynasty* makes it difficult to say that the practice had been dominant in society, including the people of lower classes.[73] Unlike China, which abolished the ban on marriages between people with the same surnames in 1931, the Korean criminal code of the year 1905 stipulated the ban on marriages between same surnames and same family origin: anyone who marries someone who has the same surname, as well as the same origin, will be punished by being struck 100 times and by being forced to divorce.[74] Inferred from such an origin, the ban on the marriage between the same surnames and the same family origins is not a tradition that the Korean people have kept as a whole, but rather a product of confusion as it is stipulated as a law.

The question then arises as to what the reason for the justices of the Constitutional Court of Korea who defended the marriage ban in question was. According to the two justices who have dissenting opinions in the case,[75] the ban did not come from China, but was one of the Korean traditional cultures representing the beauty and

---

its social validity or rationality fully, possibilities of any new improvements on this system, and the need to follow-up new regulations after the prohibition of the ban. Article 809 of Civil Code (Prohibition of marriage between parties whose surname and ancestral home are common) lost its effectiveness because the legislature was not amended until 1998, which was given by the Constitutional Court of Korea when it decided "Constitution Discord" in July 1997. The article was amended only in 2005.

[72] The Code of the Great Ming (大明律) is a Chinese code that was distributed in 1397 and was a basis of the criminal law throughout the 500 years of the Ming Dynasty (明, the unified dynasty of China that existed from 1368 to 1644, it survived for 277 years with all 16 emperors.) and Qing Dynasty (清, the last unified dynasty in Chinese history, Qing was officially established on October 13, 1635, until 1924 when the imperial family was officially dismantled and the feudal dynasty that lasted more than 2000 years in Chinese history ended). This Code has influenced the laws of Korea and Japan (referred from "Encyclopedia of Korean Culture," https://encykorea.aks.ac.kr/Contents/Item/E0014348. Accessed November 30, 2021).

[73] So (2016).

[74] Kaku (2006), p. 292.

[75] The Constitutional Court of Korea, 1995 Hun-Ga 6, Grand Chamber Decision, decided on July 16, 1997, Dissenting Opinion.

ethnicity of our own nation. Furthermore, they pointed out that the social environment and attitudes in Korea, especially marriage practices, did not seem to have changed in essence in many ways despite the rapid economic growth since the 1970s. Their argument was that family law should reflect traditional practices in stipulating the marriage system. Nevertheless, since there is no evidence that the Korean marriage custom had changed, the two justices argued that there was no need to eliminate the prohibition on marriage between the same surnames and the same family origin. Therefore, the justices concluded that deciding that it was unconstitutional was not easy unless it was determined that the legislature's judgment was considered obviously unreasonable. Even if some of the areas were considered a legislative discretionary matter, the Court was able to decide it was unconstitutional if the legislative neglects its duty to amend or abolish; meanwhile, victims suffered tremendously because of legislative neglect.

Nevertheless, the two justices further insisted that Article 809, Paragraph 1 did not violate the principle of proportionality. As a first step, they claimed that the Article had a legitimate aim of maintaining social order by legislating and enforcing traditional marriage customs. Furthermore, it was regarded that such an aim corresponded to constitutional ideals. Regarding the claimed infringement of the right to pursue happiness, freedom of marriage, and freedom to choose whom to marry freely, these could also be limited by law under the necessary conditions. As long as a legitimate aim is recognized as just, the ban in question could not be considered as violating the essence of the right to marry, especially the right to choose whom to marry. Therefore, it did not violate the test of suitability, necessity, and proportionality in the narrow sense. However, such an argument by the two justices can be criticized because the ban violated the principle of proportionality, which will be analyzed in the following section.

2.3.2 *Criticism Based on the Principle of Proportionality*

In the case of the marriage ban between the same surnames and the same family origin, it is necessary to critically examine the basic structure of the relationship between, on the one hand, the state's obligation to protect fundamental rights and, on the other hand, the individuals whose rights have been infringed regarding their right to pursue happiness. In the relationship between objectives and means, the principle of proportionality generally requires the use of proportional means to achieve a certain objective. The principle of proportionality was developed in Germany and has traveled all around the world,[76] and the Constitutional Court of Korea derives this principle from Article 37(2) of the Korean Constitution.[77] In interpreting the relationship between the prohibition of violating an *essential aspect* stated in the

[76] Clérico (2018), p. 26.

[77] Article 37, Paragraph 2 of the Constitution of the Republic of Korea read as follows:

article and the principle of proportionality, it is important to understand the essential aspect of freedom or right.

To understand the essential aspect of freedom to marry, it is necessary to understand, firstly, what this essential aspect means, and secondly, how to interpret the content of freedom to marry. Firstly, the essential aspect in the Korean Constitution can be understood as a similar concept with an essential core. The essential core can be understood as a "core to a given right which cannot be limited under any circumstances."[78] To understand the content of the essential core, *Alexy* proposes the distinction between two theories: the absolute and the relative[79] notions of the essential core. According to the absolute theory, there is a core to each right that cannot be limited under any circumstances.[80] A relative theory of the essential core of rights applies if the essence is equivalent to whatever is left of the right after the balancing test has been carried out.[81] The Constitutional Court of Korea seems to generally reflect a relative theory of the essential core of the right to marry in this case because the Court applies the ordinary proportionality assessment. Secondly, it is essential to know the content of the right to marry in the Korean Constitution, which can largely be seen as one of the rights of the people to pursue happiness (Article 10[82]), or one of the freedoms of private life (Article 17[83]).

Under the idea of the essence of rights, if there is a certain "measure" to accomplish "legitimate aim," this specific "measure" cannot violate "the very essence" of the right. According to *Christoffersen*[84] to explain the idea of the essence of rights, "the very essence" of the right is represented by the circle in the very central part of the right. This center circle of the very essence of the right to marry can never be trespassed upon.[85] The essence of freedom to marriage can be interpreted as including the right to voluntarily choose a spouse, whereby restricting or forcing anyone in the choices is prohibited. The question then is whether the public order, or morals and traditions of Korea, which have traditionally been

---

> The freedoms and rights of citizens may be restricted by Act only when necessary for national security, the maintenance of law and order or for public welfare. Even when such restriction is imposed, no *essential aspect* of the freedom or right shall be violated.

78 Christoffersen (2010), p. 27.

79 Alexy (2010), pp. 76–77.

80 Ibid. p. 193.

81 Ibid. P. 193.

82 Article 10 of the Constitution of the Republic of Korea read as follows:

> All citizens shall be assured of human worth and dignity and have the right to pursue happiness. It shall be the duty of the State to confirm and guarantee the fundamental and inviolable human rights of individuals.

83 Article 17 of the Constitution of the Republic of Korea read as follows:

> The privacy of no citizen shall be infringed.

84 Christoffersen (2010), p. 27.

85 Ibid. pp. 26–27.

regarded as grounds to restrict marriage freedom, including the marriage ban on same-sex couples, are seen as legitimate grounds that can completely restrict marriage itself? To answer this question, it is essential to determine the differences between the marriage ban between the same surnames and the same origin and other marriage restrictions such as the prohibition of bigamy or prohibition of child marriage. In my view, it is different from other restrictions because the marriage ban between the same surnames and the same origin is only regarded as a limitation because of culture or tradition. There are no legitimate aims such as the protection of monogamy in the prohibition of bigamy, and the protection of children in the prohibition of child marriage.

The following pages will assess the marriage ban between persons with the same surnames and the same origin. The principle of proportionality is essential to determine whether the marriage ban violates the essence of the right to marry because no essential aspect of the freedom or right shall be violated under the Korean Constitution.

The suitability test assesses whether a complete ban on marriages between persons with the same surnames and the same origins is a suitable measure to achieve the aim of maintaining traditions and cultures. This assessment does not choose one suitable means to achieve the aim. Among the other available means, the prohibition on marriages is tested as a sufficient means to achieve the legitimate aims mentioned above.[86] What are specifically the legitimate aims of such a marriage ban? The general aim is to keep the marriage system in accordance with tradition. In other words, the marriage system cannot accept all new customs within the framework of law even if attitudes have changed over time. Another aim of the ban mentioned is eugenics, which is claimed to be the aim of the ban at present, but there were more arguments presented in its favor at the time of legislation. Therefore, to understand the role which eugenics played in justifying the ban, it is worth looking at the statement in the National Assembly's record of the enactment by *Byeong-Ro Kim*,[87] the first Chief Justice of the Supreme Court of Korea.

According to *Kim*'s statements, "Some of the important basics of people are that humans have a sense of awakening different from animals. Animals such as dogs and pigs recognize their mothers or younger brothers and sisters when they are breastfeeding. Nevertheless, animals no longer recognize their parents when they are grown up. This is human culture, which is different from these traits of animals. This is the starting point of the aim of a marriage ban between persons of the same surnames and the same origin. In many countries, marrying close relatives is prohibited, and then the scope becomes more and more widespread. Banning marriages between relatives in Korea has been passed down as our best culture

[86] For other specific examples of suitability analysis, see Clérico (2018), pp. 37–39.

[87] *Byung-Ro Kim* has served as the first Chief Justice of the Supreme Court of Korea from September 13, 1948 until December 16, 1957. During this period, KIM was judged to have made every effort to make the judiciary independent from all other pressures and obstructions from governments.

and tradition. For this reason, as moral and ethical cultures have improved, and physiology research has evolved in other countries, other countries will adopt such a good tradition from Korea sometime in the future. It can be in 100 years or 200 years from now. This is why many other countries in the West today seem to be better than us in terms of their scientific civilization. However, from the perspective of the basic culture of humanity, Korea is in a higher position than any other country."[88]

The claim regarding the purpose of preserving traditions sounds absurd, being based on the justification that humans are different from animals and that other Western countries will also learn this culture in the future. However, in the year 1957 in Korea, there were intense discussions regarding this issue. The aim of enacting such a marriage ban was justified for the preservation of tradition or ethnic pride at the time of its legislation and has been repeatedly claimed ever since; the discussion has focused on whether the marriage of entire groups of people with the same surnames and the same origin should have been prohibited or whether it is necessary to further subdivide the range of groups affected. For this reason, the initial enactment contained provisos such as "Marriage has been banned between persons with the same surnames as well as the same origins. However, it does not apply when the ancestry is not clearly distinguished."[89] The means for achieving the aim stated above can be an absolute ban or a conditional ban. Even if an absolute ban is not the most effective means to preserve the traditional marriage system, no further considerations could be given at this stage of the test as long as they are considered *suitable* to achieve such aims. Whether the means are the most effective measures or less intrusive measures will be considered in the next test of *necessity*.

At this stage, a marriage ban which was regarded as a suitable means to achieve the preservation of traditions will be assessed as to the less restrictive alternative means test[90] and the balancing[91] test to violate the fundamental right of freedom to marriage at a minimum level. In other words, if a large number of opinions support achieving one legitimate aim, but they greatly infringe and damage the realization of another legitimate aim, the means cannot pass the test of necessity. In this case, it is necessary to find alternative means other than a blanket ban of marriage between perons with the same surnames and same origins. In other words, to attain the

[88]The sources come from the 26th statement in the National Assembly's record of the enactment, the 30th edition, the National Assembly Secretariat, November 6, 1957, p. 9 (taken from Myung 2008).

[89]Myung (2008).

[90]There are different positions regarding the usefulness of the less restrictive means test among scholars. For this, please see Clérico (2018), pp. 39–41. I agree with Clérico because neither positions to claim it is useful nor positions to claim it is not useful are attractive. Rather, I would analyze this marriage ban case according to Clérico's position of "contextual approach that is sensible to the intensity of the interference of the right in question and the position of the vulnerability of the claimers."

[91]The test of necessity allows a comparison of suitable means, while the question of whether even the least restrictive means is acceptable is a balancing question (taken from Brems and Lavrysen 2015, p. 142). This is why I have titled this sub-section as less restrictive means test and balancing.

legitimate aim of preserving the tradition as well as some grounds of eugenics, less infringing measures than a total ban of marriage should be adapted.

As the prohibition on marriage between persons with the same surnames and the same origin is a comprehensive ban, it is necessary to take measures to limit and specify the scope of the marriage ban when considering contextual circumstances of the rights infringed by the ban. According to the necessity test, also referred to as "the less restrictive means" test, the legislator must choose which would least limit the right in question.[92] If there are multiple possible means available, two solutions are possible. Firstly, if a large number of possible means have the same degree of *suitability*, then the means with the least degree of interference with the rights or freedoms must be chosen. Secondly, if those many possible means have different degrees of *suitability*, then the means must be selected by comparing the degree of *suitability* and the degree of *necessity*.[93] If the marriage ban in question is applied to the sub-questions of the necessity test, (1) are there other suitable means available to promote the same end? (2) Are these means less restrictive of the right? (3) Are these means equally effective as the challenged means in promoting the same end?[94] A complete ban will not be the less restrictive measure to promote the aim of preserving traditions because there should be legislative measures other than the marriage system to promote the same end which are equally effective.[95] A comprehensive ban on marriage will excessively limit the freedom to marry.

Figure 2.1[96] illustrates the Pareto efficiency as well as optimality. If P_1 and P_2 are conflicting principles, P_1 is the protection of traditional morals, and P_2 is the freedom to marry in the case of the marriage ban between the same surnames and the same origin. Z_1, Z_5, Z_4 represent feasible solutions for balancing.[97] The curve connecting the points of Z_1, Z_5, and Z_4 is "the Pareto-optimality frontier," where a certain fulfilment of P_1 with the highest possible fulfilment of P_2 which is compatible with the fulfilment of P_1.[98] I_1 and I_2 represent indifference curves, and these solutions are hypothetical.[99] These curves represent the relationship between P_1 and P_2. As P_1/P_2

[92] Barak (2012), p. 317.

[93] Yi (2005), p. 25.

[94] Brems and Lavrysen (2015), p. 142.

[95] A complete ban on marriage did not work as an effective measure to promote the tradition in real life. There was not much difference before and after the abolition of a complete ban. Couples did not give up being together because of the marriage ban. Under the complete ban, the Korean government allowed couples to legally marry for the year of 1978, 1988, and 1996 with the special legislation of allowing marriage between same sex and same family origin. As the situation was not very different before and after the complete abolition and during the special permission, this suggests that less alternative measures such as the timely permission or complete permission are just as effective as the complete ban to promote the aim of preserving the tradition.

[96] Structure of a balancing problem (referred from Sieckmann 2018, p. 14).

[97] The important issue of balancing is how to justify a priority among normative arguments in conflict (taken from Sieckmann 2018, p. 14).

[98] Sieckmann (2018), p. 15.

[99] For more, please see Sieckmann (2018), pp. 14–16.

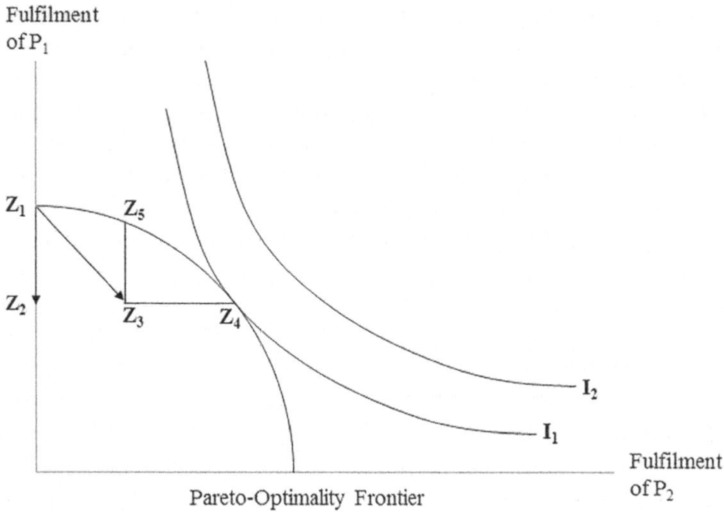

Fig. 2.1 The structure of a balancing problem (Requoted from Sieckmann 2018)

increases, P_2/P_1 decreases. If I_1 moves to I_2, the fulfilment of both P_1 and P_2 can increase. Nevertheless, I_2 exists outside of the Pareto-Optimality Frontier (Z_1-Z_5-Z_4), which is impossible to attain. In the case of a complete marriage ban between the same surnames and the same origin, the freedom of marriage is completely limited without any other alternatives to recognizing marriage (Z_1). In this case, traditional morals (P_1) are fulfilled to the maximum level, but freedom of marriage is not fulfilled. Therefore, Z_1 cannot be the optimal solution because optimal solutions represent those points which are also situated on the Pareto-optimality frontier as well as on the highest accessible indifference curve, where the indifference curve touches the Pareto-optimality curve but does not intersect with it.[100] Moreover, Z_4 is considered as an optimal solution[101] after balancing P_1 and P_2.

The Constitutional Court of Korea interpreted the state's obligation to prohibit discrimination in marriage and family matters in the case[102] which decided the unconstitutionality of Income Tax Law 61(1) to stipulate that the taxes will be imposed on all the income from assets of married spouses. According to the Court's interpretation, Article 36, paragraph 1[103] of the Korean Constitution guarantees the freedom to decide and form marriage and family life autonomously as a fundamental

[100] Sieckmann (2018), p. 16.

[101] An optimal solution occurs when there is no other outcome strictly preferred by at least one player that is at least as good for the others (taken from Ostrom 2018, p. 5). The complete marriage ban between the same surnames and same origin (Z1) is the outcome strictly preferred by the principle of preserving tradition. Therefore, it is not an optimal solution.

[102] The Constitutional Court of Korea, 2001 Hun-Ba 82, Grand Chamber Decision, decided on August 29, 2002.

[103] Article 36, Paragraph 1 of the Constitution of the Republic of Korea read as follows:

right and guarantees the institutions of marriage and family accordingly. In addition, Article 36, Paragraph 1, has the characteristics of constitutional principles or normative principles that affect all areas of public and private law relating to marriage and family. These characteristics include positive state obligations to support marriages and families, to protect them from infringement by third parties through various restrictive state measures. This is in line with a state's duty to prohibit discrimination related to marriages and families.

Furthermore, the Constitutional Court of Korea has acknowledged that marriage norms significantly impact society. Marriage is a state-controlled system whose effects could reach various parts of the society. The marriage system can be seen as a typical case where the state's power controls individual autonomy. Freedom to marry should be enjoyed to the extent that individuals could make their own decisions with full autonomy. However, there are various forms of restrictions in the marriage system by the state. The Korean case of a marriage ban between persons with same surnames and same origin is the case in which the government has excessively intervened beyond the basic control in the case of marriage at a too early age or marriage between close relatives. This case analysis reveals much about how Korean society solves the serious remaining task of same-sex marriage because the cases are similar. It took more than 40 years until the marriage ban between persons with the same surnames and the same origins was abolished by law. However, it was finally amended by law following the decision of the Constitutional Court of Korea. This is why we should never give up on the current situation of "no legal recognition of same-sex relations" in Korea. As was the case in Korea's history, it will happen in the future if we continue our efforts and do not give up.

2.4 Conclusion

The issue of enforcing or punishing moral matters by law is still a subject of intense debate. This is why state neutrality is emphasized in certain areas while strong state intervention is claimed in other contexts. However, there is no doubt that having a "general" position under some principles relating to state intervention will eventually bring about some degree of conflict. The overall insistence on strong state intervention would lead to conflict with the individual's right to self-determination. Discrimination due to sexual orientation is often based on public moral sentiment, particularly when it offends the sentiments of various groups, including religious ones. In South Korea, there are Christian churches that oppose the protection of the rights of sexual minorities and produce much fake news about same-sex relations which may consider sexual minorities as physically and psychologically sick people.

Marriage and family life shall be entered into and sustained on the basis of individual dignity and equality of the sexes, and the State shall do everything in its power to achieve that goal.

They also use "religious reasons" to legitimize their perceived offenses and hatred towards sexual minorities.

This chapter explained how it would be possible for the discussion on non-discrimination based on sexual orientation to be fully conducted in South Korean society. Considering the progress made in other areas, proper discourses on non-discrimination for sexual orientation have not started yet. This is because sexual orientation is largely considered as being an area lying between morals and law enforcement. To clarify this, it is important to review some important Korean Constitutional Court cases regarding the restriction on marriage. Currently there is no official decision regarding same-sex marriage in the Korean Constitutional Court, although some related decisions such as adultery punishment and the restriction on marriage between persons with the same surname and same place of origin have been reviewed. From the implications of those cases, it will be possible to build the foundation to continue discussions on discrimination based on sexual orientation, including same-sex marriage in Korean society.

The root of the question of whether to allow same-sex marriage or not is the extent to which the state can intervene in individuals' "good lives."[104] As the state manages and controls the institution of the marriage system, prohibition of same-sex marriage is seen as creating a very significant problem in terms of discrimination based on individual sexual orientation by the state. However, if following the majority opinion is an essential way to obtain a better life, these opinions will not consider the prohibition of same-sex marriage as discrimination. In such an opinion, a good life not only respects individual tastes, but ultimately a good life can be achieved in society as a whole when harmonizing communal life and individual life. The majority argues that a good life does not mean respecting all the preferences of all the members of society. In this sense, it is claimed that individual freedom must be recognized only within the realm where it does not harm society. Meanwhile, Korean courts can learn from previous experiences: the experience of non-criminalization of adultery will a provide a potential impetus to decriminalize same-sex relations, and the elimination of the prohibition on marriage between people with same surnames and same places of origin will represent a stimulus to legalize same-sex marriage in Korea.

[104] I borrowed the definition of good lives: "The good and good life are not equal concepts. In the Confucian culture of East Asia, the prominent role expected of the rulers is to realize the happiness of common people who are ruled by these rulers. In this context, happiness should be distinguished from the good, rather good life of common people in happiness itself. In this context, the good must be distinguished from happiness; rather, the concept of a good life is similar to the concept of happiness. While the good is different from a good life, happiness should not be distinguished from a happy life. Such happiness or happy life is only possible when the good and the justice are together because individual happiness is not a concept distinct from the good or the justice" (taken from Jun 2021, pp. 14–15).

References

Alexy R (2010) A theory of constitutional rights (trans: Rivers J). Oxford University Press, Oxford
Barak A (2012) Proportionality: constitutional rights and their limitations (trans: Kalir D). Cambridge University Press, Cambridge
Brems E, Lavrysen L (2015) 'Don't use a sledgehammer to crack a nut': less restrictive means in the case law of the European Court of Human Rights. Hum Rights Law Rev 15(1):139–168. https://doi.org/10.1093/hrlr/ngu040. Accessed November 30, 2021.
Chan J (2000) Legitimacy, unanimity, and perfectionism. Philos Public Aff 29(1). Princeton University Press, Princeton
Christoffersen J (2010) Straight human rights talk – why proportionality does (not) matter. Scand Stud Law 55:11–44
Chung JS (2016) A study on the decision of unconstitutionality for adultery. Law Research Institute Chonbuk National University, pp. 229–241
Clérico L (2018) Proportionality in social rights adjudication: making it workable. In: Duarte D, Sampais JS (eds) Proportionality in law. Springer, Heidelberg, pp 25–48
Devlin P (1959) The enforcement of morals. Proc Br Acad 45:129–151
Devlin P (1965) The enforcement of morals. Oxford University Press, Oxford
Dworkin R (1966) Lord Devlin and the enforcement of morals. Yale Law J 75(6):986–1005
Dworkin G (1972) Paternalism. The Monist 56(1):64–84. https://doi.org/10.5840/monist197256119. Accessed November 30, 2021.
Feinberg J (1971) Legal paternalism. Can J Philos 1:106–124
Feinberg J (1986) Harm to self, the moral limits of the criminal law, vol 3. Oxford University Press, New York
Fredman S (2008) Human rights transformed: positive rights and positive duties. Oxford University Press, Oxford
Ginsberg M (1961) The enforcement of morals (discussion note). Br J Sociol 12(1):65–68
Goldsworthy J, Huscroft G (2018) Originalism in Australia and Canada: why the divergence? In: Albert R, Cameron DR (eds) Canada in the world: comparative perspectives on the Canadian constitution. Cambridge University Press, Cambridge, pp 183–208
Hart HLA (1967) Social solidarity and the enforcement of morality. Univ Chic Law Rev 35(1), Article 2. https://chicagounbound.uchicago.edu/uclrev/vol35/iss1/2. Accessed November 30, 2021.
Hörnle T (2008) Strafrechtliche Verbotsnormen zum Schutz von kulturellen Identitäten. In: Dreier Ö, Hilgendorf (eds) Kulturelle Identität als Grund und Grenze des Rechts, ARSP Beiheft Nr: 113
Huang C-Y, Law DS (2015) Proportionality review of administrative action in Japan, Korea, Taiwan, and China. In: Bignami F, Zaring D (eds) Research handbook in comparative law and regulation. Edward Elgar, Cheltenham. https://ssrn.com/abstract=2496220. Accessed November 30, 2021.
Jun H-J (2021) Beyond Asiatic perfectionism – reflections on the legitimacy of moral enforcement and hopes for human nature through an in-depth study on 'Asian values' and Asiatic perfectionism. FAU University Press, Erlangen. https://doi.org/10.25593/978-3-96147-460-8
Kaku S (2006) Nationalism and family regarding the marriage ban between persons with same surnames and same family origins, a series of co-research Korea-Japan. Asiatic Research Institute, Korea University
Kim C-S (2010) New theory of Korean constitutional law. Pakyoungsa, Seoul
Kim J-S (2016) Unjustice of the decision of the unconstitutionality of adultery from the viewpoint of East Asian legal historical philosophy & an open proposal for a reform bill. Research Institute of North Eastern Asia, vol 9(3)
Lee J-S (2010) Korean criminal law. Pakyoungsa, Seoul
Mill JS (1859) On liberty, Oxford, England. Oxford University Press, Oxford

Myung S-K (2008) The Vicissitudes of Article 809 of the 1958 Korean Civil Code - along with a discourse on human rights matters of minorities from a legal policy perspective. An Am Law J

Oh Y-G (2009) Korean criminal law. Parkyoungsa, Seoul

Ostrom E (2018) Governing the commons. Cambridge University Press, Cambridge

Park S-G (2011) Korean criminal law. Parkyoungsa, Seoul

Sieckmann J (2018) Proportionality as a universal human rights principle. In: Duarte D, Sampaio JS (eds) Proportionality in law. Springer, Heidelberg, pp 3–24

So H-S (2016) The ban on same-surname-same-origin marriage as an 'invented tradition' and colonial politics. Dae Dong Res Cult 96(52)

Stephen J (1872) Liberty, equality, fraternity (Warner S (ed) Indianapolis: Liberty Fund, 1993)

Suber P (1999) Paternalism, the philosophy of law, an encyclopedia. Garland, New York

Sunstein C, Thaler R (2003) Libertarian paternalism is not an oxymoron. Univ Chic Law Rev 70: 1159–1202

Tatsuo I (1997) Liberal democracy and 'Asian values' (trans: Kim C-R), Law Review 38(1). Institute of Law Studies Pusan University Press

The Wolfenden Committee: Report of the Committee on Homosexual Offences and Prostitution. Presented to Parliament by the Secretary of State for the Home Department and the Secretary of State for Scotland, etc. [Chairman, Sir John Wolfenden.], Parliamentary Papers. Cmnd 247, 1957

VanDeVeer D (1986) Paternalistic intervention. Princeton University Press, Princeton

Yi Z-I (2005) The concept, structure, and specification of the principle of proportionality. Go Si Res 32(3)

Chapter 3
Legal Recognition of Same-Sex Relationships in Korea and Europe

3.1 Sexual Orientation as Grounds Not to Discriminate

Sexual orientation has been defined as referring to "each person's capacity for profound emotional, affectional and sexual attraction to, and intimate and equal relations with, individuals of a different gender or the same gender or more than one gender."[1] Sexual orientation has been interpreted as being one of the grounds of discrimination through an open-ended list of Article 14 of the 1950 Convention for the Protection of Human Rights and Fundamental Freedoms (ECHR). Furthermore, as *Frederic Edel* pointed out, the European Court of Human Rights (ECtHR) played "an essential pioneering role in this field at international and European level as it was instrumental in bringing about major legislative changes on certain issues related to sexual orientation, starting in 1981."[2] As such, the ECHR and ECtHR have played important roles in defining the rights related to sexual orientation at the European level. Under EU Law, the non-discrimination directives prohibit discrimination with the protected areas of gender,[3] sexual orientation, disability, age, religion or belief,[4] and racial or ethnic origin. Furthermore, Article 14 of the ECHR states that there shall be no discrimination "on any ground such as sex, race, color, language, religion, political or other opinions, national or social origin, association with a national minority, property, birth or other status." Even if the ECtHR does not exclusively state whether it interprets sexual orientation to be included as being

[1] Preamble to the Yogyakarta Principles of 26 March 2007 on the application of international human rights law in relation to sexual orientation and gender identity.

[2] Edel (2015), p. 9.

[3] Council Directive 2006/54/EC of the European Parliament and of the Council of 5 July 2006 on the implementation of the principle of equal opportunities and equal treatment of men and women in matters of employment and occupation, OJ L204, 26.7.2006, pp. 23–36.

[4] Council Directive 2000/78/EC of 27 November 2000 establishing a general framework for equal treatment in employment and occupation, OJ L 303, 2.12.2000, pp. 16–22.

H. J. Lee, *Discrimination Based on Sexual Orientation*, Interdisciplinary Studies in Human Rights 8, https://doi.org/10.1007/978-3-030-95423-9_3

part of "sex" or "other status," the ECtHR[5] clearly states that sexual orientation is a concept undoubtedly covered by Article 14 of the ECHR.

According to the survey results by the European Union Agency for Fundamental Rights (FRA),[6] the percentage of sexual orientation represented only 0.2% in the sense of experiences in four areas of daily life in the 5 years before the survey. These four areas are looking for work, at work, education, and housing. Looking only at this number, sexual orientation does not appear to be a very important reason for discrimination in the discussion in Europe. However, other statistics from the same report of the FRA show the respondents' comfort level[7] with other ethnic minorities or sexual minorities as neighbors. The statistics present the percentages of respondents who selected a value between 5 and 10 when asked how comfortable they would feel with people from different ethnic groups or sexual minorities as neighbors. Unlike the result of the previous statistics, the comfort level result indicates a high level of acceptance towards other ethnic groups, but surprisingly, negative views towards sexual minorities. In this case, it cannot be said that sexual orientation is a minor reason for discrimination in the discussion in Europe. On the contrary, sexual minorities might be exposed to serious discrimination if others do not accept them as neighbors.

Sexual orientation should be protected as a significant reason not to discriminate through the methods of interpretation. Interpreting the Convention articles as a "living tree"[8] is especially important in the anti-discrimination law because it is

---

[5]The ECtHR clearly states that the applicant's sexual orientation is a concept which is undoubtedly covered by Article 14 of the Convention. In addition, the ECtHR states that the list set out in that provision is illustrative and not exhaustive, as is shown by the words "any ground such as" (taken from European Court of Human Rights, *Salguiero Da Silva Mouta v. Portugal*, decided on 21 December 1999, paragraph 28).

[6]EU-MIDIS II, *Second European Union Minorities and Discrimination Survey Main results*, European Union Agency for Fundamental Rights, 2017, p. 23.: The percentage as grounds of discrimination experienced in four areas of daily life in 5 years before the survey—The percentage are as following: Ethnic origin 25%, Skin colour 12%, Religion 12%, Age 7%, Gender 2%, Disability 1%, Sexual orientation 0.2%, other 5%. Notes: Out of all respondents at risk of discrimination on different grounds in at least one of four domains of daily life asked about in the survey ("in 5 years before the survey": $n = 21{,}541$); weighted results. Domains of daily life considered for analysis: looking for work, at work, education (as parent or guardian) and housing.

[7]Figure 46 by FRA, EU-MIDIS II, *Second European Union Minorities and Discrimination Survey Main results*, European Union Agency for Fundamental Rights, 2017, p. 107.: shows respondents' comfort level with other ethnic minorities and gay, lesbian or bisexual persons as neighbors, by country and target group (%) Comfort level is much higher towards a person of another ethnic minority background (in case of target group of immigrants and descendants of immigrants from Turkey: 98% in Austria, 99% in Belgium, 93% in Germany, 96% in Denmark, 98% in Netherlands) than towards a gay, lesbian or bisexual person (44% in Austria, 79% in Belgium, 64% in Germany, 72% in Denmark, 67% in Netherlands).

[8]It is the Canadian metaphor of the constitution as a "living tree," and this means it is capable of growth yet rooted in a particular national text (Jackson 2010, p. 84) However, I want to emphasize more the capability of growth because there will be new grounds for discrimination as the society changes. And interpreting these as a "living tree" will be necessary to effectively protect victims who will suffer from grounds that are not explicitly stated in the law texts.

impossible to state all the grounds for discrimination. Some grounds could not have been included in the law at the time of legislation. Furthermore, if we take Germany as an example, there will be new grounds to discriminate as the society changes and proficiency in German, chronic disease, educational level, jobs or world views are included as grounds not to discriminate in the anti-discrimination law legislated in Berlin, Germany.[9] It is obvious how important it is to include new grounds not to discriminate resulting from methods of interpretation.

The first is evolutionary interpretation, which means it could evolve over time[10] as "living trees." It is also called a dynamic interpretation. Evolutionary interpretation considers "a continuous evolution in the norms and principles applied in international law or in the domestic law of the majority of Member States of the Council of Europe and shows, in a precise area, that there are common grounds for discrimination in modern societies."[11] Sexual orientation should be protected as grounds not to discriminate considering the reality where sexual minorities suffer from discrimination because of their sexual orientation and a more evolving conception of law over time.[12] According to the second approach of the teleological interpretation, sexual orientation should be protected as grounds of anti-discrimination. As *McCrudden* argues,[13] the court tries to interpret the provisions of the law in light of the "end" or "telos" of the law. Considering that the objective of the ECHR is to promote equality by securing the universal and effective recognition and observance of the rights as stated in the preface of the Convention, there is no legitimate reason not to include sexual orientation as grounds to prohibit discrimination, especially when human dignity and equality are considered as two dominant meta-principles[14] adopted in a teleological approach. Lastly, the contextual approach allows courts to take a case-by-case approach.[15] It is essential to take the contextual interpretation method because it can offer a perfect solution to a victim, especially in a vulnerable situation. There is no doubt that sexual minorities are put in an extremely vulnerable situation not only due to criminalization or prohibition of

[9]The law is called as "Landesantidiskriminierungsgesetz ('LADG')," which is the key anti-discrimination law of the Berlin Senate. The House of Representatives passed it in its session on 04.06.2020, and it came into force on 21. 06. 2020. It comprises three articles. Article 1 covers section 1 general provisions, section 2. Forms of discrimination, section 3 of legal protection, section 4. Diversity – Promoting a culture of valuing diversity, and section 4. Responsibility: Ombudsman. LADG emphasizes the responsibility of the public area in prohibiting discrimination: the scope of application in Article 4, explicitly states this law applies to public authorities, including courts, committees, prosecution, the constitutional court (for more, please see: Berliner Landes-Antidiskriminierungsgesetz (LADG), https://www.berlin.de/sen/lads/recht/ladg/. Accessed November 30, 2021).

[10]Jackson (2010), pp. 96–97.

[11]Besson (2019), p. 1232.

[12]Jackson (2010), p. 241.

[13]McCrudden (2017), p. 31.

[14]Ibid. p. 31.

[15]Shachar (2017), pp. 141–142.

marriage, which will be discussed in detail throughout this work, but also in their extended lifestyles such as when looking for a job, applying for a pension, or applying for a residence permit due to their sexual orientation. In that sense, considering their specific contexts, there is a need to provide them with equal protection.

Similarly, even if sexual orientation is not explicitly stated in the ECHR and the Korean Constitution, the rights of sexual minorities should be recognized with interpretative methods. Important implications can be found from the case of *Toonen v. Australia*,[16] which was submitted based on the individual complaint mechanism according to the optional protocol to the international covenant on civil and political rights in 1994. In this case, the applicant *Toonen* argued that the criminalization of same-sex relations in Tasmania, Australia violates Article 2(1)[17] (non-discrimination principle), Article 17 (right to privacy), and Article 26 (equality before the law) of the International Covenant on Civil and Political Rights. The state of Tasmania argues that criminalization is justified to attain the legitimate aim of preventing the extensive spread of HIV/AIDS. On the other hand, the Human Rights Committee found no reasonable relation between the legitimate aim and the means of criminalization. Moreover, criminalization makes same-sex relations more invisible, which could increase the risk of AIDS infection. Most importantly, the Committee interprets "sexual orientation" to be included in the extensive concept of "sex" that is stated explicitly in Article 2(1) of the Covenant. This decision by the Human Rights Committee is important because it shows that sexual orientation can be included in grounds for discrimination using interpretation.

Defining a minority as a protected sexual minority is also important when including sexual orientation as grounds not to discriminate. Firstly, the word minority does not mean the quantity. For example, even if women are equal to or even outnumber men, women can be considered a minority subject to discrimination. Therefore, the minority refers not to the concept of quantity but to the subjects of direct or indirect discrimination concerning the rights enjoyed by all humans. In this sense, even if all grounds to be the subject of discrimination are not explicitly stated, if some people belong to a certain group due to the factors that cannot be voluntarily selected such as individual biological, physical, congenial, or some other social factors and suffer from discrimination, such factors should be included as grounds for discrimination. Even if certain grounds are not recognized as the cause of discrimination at the time of enactment, any discrimination due to involuntary attribution should be included as prohibition.

On the other hand, the Korean Constitutional Court interpreted discrimination based on sex narrowly, and sexual orientation is not included as grounds not to

[16] *Toonen v. Australia* (1994), Communication No. 488/1992, U.N. Doc CCPR/C/50/488/1992.

[17] Article 2(1) ICCPR states that "Each State Party to the present Covenant undertakes to respect and to ensure to all individuals within its territory and subject to its jurisdiction the rights recognized in the present Covenant, without distinction of any kind, such as race, color, sex, language, religion, political or other opinion, national or social origin, property, birth or other status." In this article, sexual orientation is not explicitly stated as grounds not to discriminate.

discriminate.[18] In the same case, the Korean Court's different treatment of same-sex couples and different-sex couples is not a matter of discrimination based on grounds of sex, which is included in the protected scope of the Korean Constitution as such discrimination is not prohibited. However, different treatment based on sexual orientation is not included in the Constitution's scope to demand equal treatment. Therefore, the Court did not apply the strict security required to find violation discrimination based on sex. The Court found no violation and interpreted that discrimination based on sexual orientation was not included as gender-based discrimination that the Constitution protects. By excluding sexual orientation from the grounds not to discriminate, the Court ignores discrimination based on sexual orientation even if in reality serious discrimination occurs.

Such an interpretation by the Korean Constitutional Court has excluded sexual orientation from a subject of protection from discrimination even if a different treatment cannot be justified without a valid reason or reasonable excuse. In applying the principle of proportionality to find violations in the matter of discrimination, it focuses on the comparison between two objects in a comparable situation.[19] Therefore, the principle of proportionality examines whether there are differences between the objects who are treated differently, and whether such a difference is constitutionally legitimate. Even if judgment should be based on whether there is a difference in nature between the two groups, which could justify the different treatment in order to find discrimination,[20] the Constitutional Court of Korea only examines the relationship between the legitimate aim and the means—in this case, the legitimate aim of protecting sound culture in the military and the criminalization of same-sex relations as a means.[21] Not being included in the list of grounds in the provisions does not mean that there is no discrimination. The grounds to be explicitly stated in the provisions should be seen only as examples. Therefore, even if some grounds are not explicitly stated, these could still be regarded as grounds for discrimination. Sexual orientation should not be excluded from protection, and discrimination should be found by focusing on the different treatment between the two groups in a comparable situation, i.e., same-sex couples and different-sex couples.

[18] The Constitutional Court of Korea, decided on March 31, 2011, 2008 Hun-Ga 21, Case Law Book 23-1 (1), pp. 178, 189.

[19] Heun (2004), GG I, Article 3 Rn. 27.

[20] BVerfGE, 52, 277 (280).

[21] The Constitutional Court of Korea, decided on March 31, 2011, 2008 Hun-Ga 21, Case Law Book 23-1 (1), pp. 178, 189.

3.2 Background Information in South Korea

Compared to May 1980 when 1,000 to 2,000 innocent Korean citizens died fighting for democracy in the *Gwangju* uprising,[22] the level of general human rights protection has improved considerably in South Korea. However, there has been almost no or very little progress in some kinds of human rights violations, one of which is discrimination based on sexual orientation. Before going directly into the specific topic of discrimination based on sexual orientation in South Korea, it will be necessary to briefly discuss the development of constitutional law and the role of international human rights law and instruments in the Constitutional Court of Korea practice as background information. Understanding the role of the Constitutional Court of Korea and international human rights law is vital to solve the problem of discrimination based on sexual orientation. This understanding will show how Korean society can eventually overcome the problem of discrimination based on sexual orientation using the positive roles provided by international human rights law and the Constitutional Court of Korea.

The Constitutional Court of Korea plays a crucial role in South Korean society as seen from how the impeachment case surprised the world when the CCK announced its unanimous decision to impeach the president of the Republic of Korea, *Park Geun-Hye* on March 10, 2017.[23] International human rights law and instruments played a crucial role in interacting with constitutional rights in Korea in this decision, which greatly influenced Korean society itself. As *Jeremy Waldron*[24] pointed out, international human rights law is presented as a reference to be considered along with legislation or jurisprudence in other countries. The Constitutional Court of Korea also referred to the ECHR and cases of the ECtHR in its decision. For example, the CCK declared that the provisions prohibiting prisoners and probationers from voting were unconstitutional.[25] In this case, the CCK referred to the provision of the ECHR and the case of *Hirst v. the United Kingdom*[26] from the ECtHR. Furthermore, the CCK recently decided that if the Korean military service law does not stipulate alternative services for conscientious objectors, it is not constitutional, referencing the international human rights law.[27] Similarly, the Constitutional Court of Korea interacts with international human rights law, instruments, and human rights jurisprudence of the European Court of Human Rights. However, there are still no decisions in the Constitutional Court of Korea about discrimination based on sexual orientation.

---

[22] Plunk (1985), p. 5.

[23] The Constitutional Court of Korea, 2016 Hun-Na, decided on March 10, 2017.

[24] Waldron (2005), p. 129.

[25] The Constitutional Court of Korea, 2012 Hun-Ma 409·510, 2013 Hun-Ma 167 (Consolidated), decided on January 28, 2014.

[26] European Court of Human Rights, *Hirst v. the United Kingdom*, judgment of 6 October 2005.

[27] The Constitutional Court of Korea, 2011 Hun-Ba 379·383, decided on June 28, 2018. pp. 407–408.

The general situation in South Korea in terms of discrimination based on sexual orientation is much worse than in the EU in that the acceptance level is extremely low. The process of fighting for democracy has been ongoing in South Korea since the 1980s, leading to a continuous improvement in the level of general human rights protection. However, in some areas of human rights violations, there have been almost no or very little progress made so far. One such area is discrimination based on sexual orientation. Sexual minorities are considered one of the most vulnerable groups who suffer from severe discrimination in various sectors of society. In some areas the standard of protection is not sufficiently provided to sexual minorities, even in the European legal system, such as in the area of same-sex marriage or adoption. The level of protection is also surprisingly low in South Korea even in the cases where the protection is mostly given in the European context. One of those cases is the criminalization of same-sex relations between consenting adults, which will be criticized from the human rights perspective in the following chapters in this work.

The statistics show how badly Korean people have resisted acknowledging sexual minorities. One of the official public surveys conducted in the year 2013 shows that overall 78.5% of 1,500 adult respondents feel a degree of resistance towards same-sex couples.[28] Even worse, 73.8% of 1,000 adult respondents answered that they think a same-sex relationship is abnormal.[29] The debate on human rights abuses due to sexual orientation is particularly intense due to "the strong relevance of cultural, social and religious concerns."[30] Sexual orientation is a challenge as one of the most important grounds for discriminating against minorities in Korean society. The Christian groups, which form a major religion, are particularly opposed to any legal recognition of homosexual relations in Korea.

3.3 Legal Recognition of Same-Sex Relationships in Europe

This section will introduce the overview[31] of legal recognition of same-sex relationships in Europe. To effectively show the overview, the theoretical framework suggested by *Curry-Summer* will be employed. The theoretical framework

[28] Year 2013 public survey on homosexuality and same sex marriage by Donga Newspaper and Asan Policy Research Institution, 1,500 adults respondents, http://news.donga.com/3/all/20131031/58578866/1. Accessed November 30, 2021.

[29] Public survey on homosexuality by Media Research, 1,000 adults respondents, reported on May 30, 2013, http://www.christiantoday.co.kr/news/264192. Accessed November 30, 2021.

[30] Saiz (2004), p. 48.

[31] For an overview, I referred to the document of "Legal Recognition of Same-Sex Relationships in Europe" by *Samuel Fulli-Lemaire* from the Academy of European Law seminar on "Current Reflections on EU Anti-Discrimination Law Seminar" on 11–12 June 2018. Speakers' contributions are later published. (Fulli-Lemaire 2016. Forthcoming in the proceedings of the "Same-Sex Relationships and Beyond: Gender Matters in the EU" conference organized in Hamburg on

suggested by *Curry-Summer*[32] will be introduced to give an overview of the legal recognition of same-sex relationships in Europe because it is easy to categorize some groups of states according to each model. In the pluralistic model, "couples are offered two possibilities to formalize their relationship, irrespective of their gender, namely marriage or a form of non-marital registered relationship."[33] In the dualistic model, "couples are only provided with one institutionalized relationship form dependent on their sex: different-sex couples can marry, whilst same-sex couples are entitled to register their non-marital relationship."[34] Lastly, in the monistic model, "couples, irrespective of their gender, are presented with one institutionalized relationship form."[35]

The pluralistic model[36] shows the development of recognition of same-sex relations in Europe by dividing time periods into two. This model is particularly useful for understanding the difference between non-marital registered relationships and marriage as protecting institutions to recognize same-sex relations in Europe. In the first time period, both hetero-sexual couples and same-sex couples can enter into a non-marital registered relationship. In such a time period, marriage is only open to different-sex couples. However, this situation incurs discrimination against same-sex couples because marriage is still not open for them while different-sex couples can choose between marriage and non-marital registered relationships. Therefore, in time period 2, both hetero sex couples and same-sex couples choose the relationship forms of marriage and non-marital registered relationships.

Same-sex marriage has been introduced in France (2013), England and Wales (2013), Scotland (2014), Luxembourg (2015), and Ireland (2015).[37] Among Northern European countries, Denmark, Finland, and Sweden have enacted gender-neutral marriage and simultaneously abandoned their registered partnership. Such countries could be categorized as a monistic model, where a single, formalized institution is open to both same-sex and opposite-sex couples. Western European countries are showing steady progress in that same-sex couples can marry in all jurisdictions except Northern Ireland. In Northern Ireland, the Democratic Unionist Party has so far managed to block every attempt for a reform.[38] Therefore, Northern Ireland can be categorized as a dualistic system where different-sex couples can marry while same-sex couples can enter into non-marital registered relationships. Germany is

18–19 April 2016 by the Academy of European Law (ERA) and the Bucerius Law School, Available at SSRN: https://ssrn.com/abstract=2825874. Accessed November 30, 2021.)

[32] Curry-Sumner and Curry-Sumner (2009), pp. 242–244.

[33] Ibid. p. 242.

[34] Ibid. p. 243.

[35] Ibid. p. 243.

[36] "Pluralistic model tends to attain the end phase of this model by virtue of a two-stage process, thereby necessitating the division of the pluralistic model into two time-periods." Ibid. p. 243.

[37] Fulli-Lemaire (2016), p. 19.

[38] https://www.newsletter.co.uk/news/interview-dups-christian-values-will-not-change-says-foster-1278893. Accessed November 30, 2021.

categorized as a monistic system after abandoning registered partnerships and allowing same-sex marriages in 2017. Austria joined the pluralistic system after extending the registered partnership to opposite-sex couples.

Among Southern European countries, Italy fell into the dualistic model where different-sex couples can marry while same-sex couples can enter into non-marital registered relationships after the famous *Oliari*[39] case. The *Oliari* case is regarded as "a stepping stone towards full legal recognition of same-sex relationships in Europe,"[40] and the first judgment where "the ECtHR established the granting of legal recognition and protection to same-sex couples as a positive obligation"[41] for the state, based on Article 8 of the ECHR. In Greece, registered partnership is open to all couples following the case of *Vallianatos and others v. Greece*[42] in 2013. This case is considered as "another small step towards realizing full and equal protection for gay men and lesbians under the Convention."[43] The effect of the registered partnership falls somewhat short of the effects of marriage, particularly with regard to children.

[39] European Court of Human Rights, ***OLIARI AND OTHERS v. ITALY*** (Applications nos. 18766/11 and 36030/11), Chamber Judgment of 21 July 2015: The applicants are three same-sex couples of six Italian men who were born between 1959 and 1976 and live in Italy. The couples have been living together for several years in committed, stable relationships. Mr. Oliari and Mr. A requested the Trent Commune Civil status Office to register their marriage in July 2008. Following the rejection of their request, they challenged that decision before the Trent Tribunal. The Tribunal rejected their claim and referred to the Constitutional Court. In April 2010, the Constitutional Court declared their constitutional challenge inadmissible, concluding that the right to marriage did not extend to homosexual unions and was intended to refer to marriage in its traditional sense. The Court held that there had been a violation of Article 8 of the Convention (right to respect for private and family life) because Italy failed to comply with a positive obligation to ensure respect for the applicants' private and family life. After the case decision, the Italian Parliament passed the law 76/2016 in May 2016 to introduce same-sex civil unions in their domestic legal system for the first time.

[40] Lavrysen (2016).

[41] Ragone and Volpe (2016), p. 451.

[42] European Court of Human Rights, ***VALLIANATOS AND OTHERS v. GREECE*** (Applications nos. 29381/09 and 32684/09), Grand Chamber judgment of 7 November 2013: The applicants live together as a couple in same-sex relationships in Athens. The first and second, third, and fourth applicants had lived together for a long time as couples in Athens. The fifth and sixth applicants are in relationships but do not live together. The sixth applicant pays the fifth applicant's social security contributions. The seventh applicant is a not-for-profit association to support sexual minorities. On November 26, 2008, Law No. 3719/2008 "Reforms concerning the family, children and society" came into force. Under section 1 of the Law, "civil unions" can be entered into only by two adults of "different sex." Applicants complained that the fact the civil unions were designed only for couples of different-sex adults infringed their right to respect for their private and family life and amounted to unjustified discrimination between different-sex and same-sex couples. The court considers that the government had not offered convincing and weighty reasons capable of justifying same-sex couples' exclusion from the scope of Law No. 3719/2008. Accordingly, it found that there has been a violation of Article 14 of the ECHR taken in conjunction with Article 8.

[43] Johnson (2013).

No jurisdiction in Eastern Europe permits same-sex marriages. As of 2018, fifteen European countries authorized same-sex marriage: the Netherlands (2001), Belgium (2003), Spain (2005), Sweden (2009), Norway (2009), Portugal and Iceland (2010), Denmark (2012), France (2013), Great Britain (2014), Luxembourg and Ireland (2015), Finland (law adopted in 2014, effect in 2017), Germany and Malta (2017).[44] Even worse, some of the Eastern European countries have constitutional bans on same-sex marriage, and strikingly, most of these have been enacted fairly recently: Latvia (2006), Hungary (2011), Croatia (2013), and Slovakia (2014). Most of the Eastern European countries do not have same-sex marriage or same-sex registered partnership, and along with such bans, the people have a relatively low satisfaction level with the way democracy works.[45]

The *Oliari* case surely represents a cutting-edge judgment in the ECHR case law on the rights of sexual minorities, after having underlined the importance of granting legal recognition to de facto family life.[46] It also included same-sex unions as stable, committed relationships in the notions of family life.[47] In addition, the *Oliari* case clarified that when a state passes legislation to create a form of registered partnership, this format must be accessible to all couples regardless of their sexual orientation, which was set by the judgment of *Vallianatos*[48] case. Finally, it establishes the positive obligation of the state to ensure recognition of a legal framework for same-sex couples in the absence of marriage, in light of Article 8 of the ECHR.[49] Nevertheless, only 16 European countries out of 48 have legalized same-sex marriage.[50] Especially in the matter of same-sex marriage, EU countries are moving at different speeds and directions, and some degree of diversity exist among these countries.

---

[44] Schlagdenhauffen (2016). Permalink: https://ehne.fr/en/encyclopedia/themes/gender-and-europe/civil-law-a-tool-masculine-domination/same-sex-marriage-in-europe. Accessed November 30, 2021.

[45] Takács and Szalma (2011), p. 369, Figure 3. Accessed November 30, 2021.

[46] European Court of Human Rights, *X and others v. Austria*, judgment of 19 February 2013.

[47] European Court of Human Rights, *Schalk and Kopf v. Austria* (Applications no. 30141/04), Chamber judgment of 24 June 2010.: The applicants are a same-sex couple living in Vienna, born in 1962 and 1960. In the judgment, the Court notes "a rapid evolution of social attitudes towards same-sex couples" since 2001, resulting in many States having afforded them legal recognition. Therefore, the Court considers that the relationship of the applicants, "a cohabiting same-sex couple living in a stable partnership," fall within the notion of "family life." Cited from http://unionafirmativa.org.ve/unaf/wp-content/uploads/Case-schalk-kopf-vs-Austria-2010.pdf. Accessed November 30, 2021.

[48] European Court of Human Rights, *Vallianatos and Others v. Greece*, judgment of 7 November 2013.

[49] Zago (2015).

[50] International Lesbian, Gay, Bisexual, Trans and Intersex Association: Lucas Ramon Mendos, State-Sponsored Homophobia 2019 (Geneva; ILGA, March 2019), p. 277.

3.4 Convergence and Divergence

As introduced by some statistics in earlier sections, sexual minorities are vulnerable groups both in Europe as well as in South Korea. Some areas related to protecting sexual minorities are considerably underdeveloped. As *Johnson* states, "LGBT people have often encountered significant resistance from the ECHR organs when seeking the protection of the rights and freedoms guaranteed by the ECHR."[51] In addition, ECtHR's jurisprudence is currently relatively ambiguous, i.e., the ECtHR's jurisprudence on whether states are obliged to provide same-sex couples with access to an "alternative" to marriage or not is unclear, and the ECtHR still does not adopt a fully structured proportionality test including the test of necessity, and the Less Restrictive Measure test. Even the ambition of sexual minorities in European states to gain universal access to the rights and freedoms guaranteed by the Convention is still an "ongoing struggle."[52]

Nevertheless, there has been certain progress with the jurisprudence in the ECtHR in protecting sexual minorities unlike in South Korea. The ECtHR decided that criminalizing sexual acts between two consenting same-sex adult males in private amounted to a violation of Article 8 ECHR in *Dudgeon*[53] case in 1981. However, the Constitutional Court of Korea still decided the Korean Military Criminal Law criminalizing homosexual acts between two consenting males is constitutional in 2016,[54] which will be discussed in more detail in Chap. 7. Thus, Korea has not fulfilled decriminalizing same-sex relations yet.

The ECtHR already recognized "sexual orientation" as "a concept which is undoubtedly covered by Article 14 of the Convention" in *Salguiero*[55] case in 1999. In addition, the ECtHR also stated that "transsexualism was a notion covered by Article 14, which contained a non-exhaustive list of prohibited grounds for discrimination" in the case of *P.V. v. Spain*[56] in 2010. Furthermore, in 2015, "gender identity" was also included in the concept covered by Article 14 ECHR. The decision of *Identoba and Others v. Georgia* reiterates that "the prohibition of discrimination under Article 14 of the Convention duly covers questions related to sexual orientation and gender identity."[57] The ECtHR made a move forward to

---

[51] Johnson (2018), p. 27.

[52] Johnson (2018), p. 28.

[53] European Court of Human Rights, *Dudgeon v. United Kingdom*, judgment of 22 October 1981. Paragraph 63.

[54] The Constitutional Court of Korea, 2012 Hun-Ba 258, decided on July 28, 2016.

[55] European Court of Human Rights, *Salguiero Da Silva Mouta v. Portugal*, judgment of 21 December 1999, paragraph 28.

[56] Restriction of contact arrangements between a transsexual and her six-year-old son was in the child's best interests, European Court of Human Rights, *P.V. v. Spain*, judgment of 30 November 2010. Press Release issued by the Registrar of the Court, Decision of the Court.

[57] European Court of Human Rights, *Identoba and others v. Georgia*, judgment of 12 May 2015, paragraph 96.

protecting same-sex relationships with the right to respect family life under Article 8 ECHR in the case of *J.M. v. The United Kingdom* in 2010, stating that "the consensus among European States in favor of assimilating same-sex relationships to heterosexual relationships has undoubtedly strengthened"[58] and criticized the previous decision of *Mata Estevez*[59] in 2001.

However, Korea has not yet made the first step towards recognizing sexual orientation as grounds for not being discriminated against. Article 11 of the Korean Constitution stipulates that "all citizens shall be equal before the law, and there shall be no discrimination in political, economic, social or cultural life on account of sex, religion or social status." Sexual orientation is not explicitly included as grounds not to discriminate under the Korean Constitution. Nor are there any interpretations from the Courts that sexual orientation is protected under the scope of Article 11. Instead of moving forward, Korea is moving backward in terms of protecting the rights of sexual minorities. The only legal stipulation to include sexual orientation as grounds not to be discriminated against is the National Human Rights Commission of Korea Act.[60] But, a bill for amendment is currently being presented in the National Assembly in Korea, and, surprisingly, this amendment is about excluding sexual orientation from Article 2 of the National Human Rights Commission of Korea Act. By viewing the reasoning for excluding sexual orientation in the amendment bill, one can easily determine how absurd those reasons are: to include sexual orientation

---

[58] European Court of Human Rights, *J.M. v. The United Kingdom*, judgment of 28 September 2010, paragraph 50.

[59] European Court of Human Rights, ***Mata Estenvez v. Spain***, judgment of 10 May 2001. (The applicant lived with another man, Mr. G.C., for more than ten years. During that period, the applicant and Mr. G.C. ran a joint household, pooling their income and sharing their expenses. The applicant considered that their relationship's nature reflected their right to respect for their private and family life since, being homosexual, they could not sanction it by marrying because under Spanish law only heterosexual couples could marry. After Mr. G.C. died, the applicant claimed the social-security allowances for the surviving spouse. He had been refused to grant a survivor's pension because he was not considered as surviving spouse. In this case, the ECtHR reiterates that, according to the established case law of the Convention institutions, long-term homosexual relationships between two men do not fall within the scope of the right to respect for family life protected by Article 8 of the Convention.)

[60] Article 2, Paragraph 3 of the National Human Rights Commission of Korea Act states as follows:

> The term "discriminatory act violating the equal right" means any of the following acts, without reasonable grounds, on the grounds of sex, religion, disability, age, social status, region of origin (referring to a place of birth, place of registration, principal area of residence before coming of age, etc.), state of origin, ethnic origin, physical condition such as features, marital status such as single, separated, divorced, widowed, remarried, married de facto, or pregnancy or childbirth, types or forms of family, race, skin color, ideology or political opinion, record of crime whose effect of punishment has been extinguished, sexual orientation, academic career, medical history, etc.: Provided, That the temporary favorable treatment to a particular person (including a group of particular persons: hereafter the same shall apply in this Article) to solve the existing discrimination, the enactment and amendment of statutes and the formulation and enforcement of policy to this effect shall not be deemed a discriminatory act violating the equal right.

in the article harms school children with the risk of establishing a incorrect sexual identity as well as causing many health problems such as AIDS. In addition, the amendment bill argues that deleting sexual orientation can preserve the healthy tradition and sexual morals of Korean society.[61] Considering that the National Human Rights Commission of Korea is the frontier as well as a final backup organization to protect human rights, and the decision from the Commission only has an advisory effect unlike court decisions, this amendment bill shows how Korea is lagging behind in protecting sexual minorities.

Recently, a South Korean transgender soldier was dismissed only because of the soldiers' transsexuality, and this soldier *Byun Hui-Soo* continually applied to serve in the military after having sex change surgery in Thailand with the legal procedure with Korean military. *Byun* changed her legal sex from male to female with the decision of *Chongju* district Court[62] in February 2020. However, the Korean army dismissed her because a sex change is considered serious grounds for not continuing to serve in the military. *Byun* prepared an Administrative lawsuit claiming an administrative measure of dismissal; however, it does not seem to be easy due to society's negative feelings towards transgender people.[63] The Administrative lawsuit is expected to continue through the succession of the next of kin to *Byun,*[64] who killed herself on March 3, 2021.

Both in the EU and South Korea, sexual minorities are a vulnerable group and they are exposed to much discriminatory treatment in many sectors. Nonetheless, in the EU, there is slow but certain progress and development. For example, the Committee of Ministers in the Council of Europe has adopted a "recommendation designed to combat discrimination against lesbian, gay, bisexual and transgender people,"[65] and the ECtHR cited the recommendation in the cases relating to the rights of sexual minorities.[66] However, in South Korea, there are almost no

[61] Amendment on Article 2, Paragraph 3 of the National Human Rights Commission of Korea Act. Lawmaking information, https://opinion.lawmaking.go.kr/gcom/nsmLmSts/out/2023936/detailRP. Accessed November 30, 2021.

[62] This decision has been made as of February 20, 2020 to allow the legal gender of *Byun Hui-Soo* to change from male to female considering the medical operation, the life history, and the personal hope to continue to serve as a female soldier in the military.

[63] January 22, 2020, South Korea transgender soldier to sue over dismissal, BBC, https://www.bbc.com/news/world-asia-51204323. Accessed November 30, 2021.

[64] Daejeon District Court has accepted the application by the next kin of *Byun* regarding the succession of the lawsuit where the legitimacy of enforced dismissal will be decided. (Yonhap news article of April 9, 2021, https://www.yna.co.kr/view/AKR20210409138351063. Accessed November 30, 2021.)

[65] Recommendation designed to combat discrimination against lesbian, gay, bisexual and transgender people, Council of Europe, Recommendations, CM/Rec (2010) 5.

[66] European Court of Human Rights cited "Recommendation CM/Rec (2010)" in many cases of protecting sexual minorities:

freedom of expression and peaceful assembly: Alekseyev v. Russia (2010), Bayev and others v. Russia (2017)

The adoption of a child: Gas and Dubois v. France (2012), X. and others v. Austria (2013) protections for sexual minorities: criminalization of same-sex relations in the military criminal law, no same-sex marriage, and no anti-discrimination law. Moreover, except *Byun Hui-Soo* who was dismissed from Korean military, and *Kim Cho Gwangsoo* and *Kim Seung Hwan*[67] who are the first male same-sex couple who initiated legal action for the right to get married, all other sexual minorities are invisible. Their invisibility speaks volumes about how sexual minorities are in a severely vulnerable position.

3.5 Conclusion

Sexual minorities are one of the most vulnerable groups who have been discriminated against by various sectors of society. In that sense, sexual orientation is considered as important grounds not to discriminate. Unlike other grounds of discrimination such as gender, race, color, or religion, many areas in the scope of protection related to sexual orientation are underdeveloped. The promotion and protection of human rights and fundamental freedoms have been a core mission of the Council of Europe, however, some states in the Council of Europe, as well as some areas such as social benefits and services, are greatly underdeveloped in this regard. South Korea has made very little progress against the discrimination based on sexual orientation compared to other rights and freedoms and is showing a tendency to move backwards. In such situations, positive inspiration from other developed areas in Europe is necessary; even if Europe itself still has further progress to make, South Korea has something to learn from the experiences of Europe.

References

Barak A (2005) Response to the judge as comparatist: comparison in public law. Tul Law Rev 80: 195–202

Besson S (2019) Comparative law and human rights. In: Reimann M, Zimmermann R (eds) The Oxford handbook of comparative law. Oxford University Press, Oxford

---

The legal recognition of same sex relationships: Vallianatos and others v. Greece (2013), Oliari and Others v. Italy (2015)

Gender reassignment surgery: Y.Y. v. Turkey (2015)

Homophobic violence: Identoba and Others v. Georigia (2015), A.C. v. Romania (2016)

Family reunification: Pajic v. Croatia (2016)

Social security provisions: Aldeguer Tomas v. Spain (2016)

(taken from Johnson 2018, p. 13).

[67]The Hankyoreh, May 26, 2016, *Kim Cho Gwangsoo* and *Kim Seung Hwan* appeal against prohibition of same sex marriage http://www.hani.co.kr/arti/society/society_general/745609.html. Accessed November 30, 2021.

Curry-Sumner I, Curry-Sumner S (2009) Where will it all end? Common trends in American same-sex relationship recognition. Equal Oppor Int 28(3):233–248. https://doi.org/10.1108/02610150910947780

Edel F (2015) Case law of the European Court of Human Rights relating to discrimination on grounds of sexual orientation or gender identity. Council of Europe

Fulli-Lemaire S (2016) Legal recognition of same-sex relationships in central Europe: steady progress. In: Boele-Woelki K, Fuchs A (eds) Same-sex relationships and beyond: gender matters in the EU. Intersentia, Antwerp

Fulli-Lemaire S (2018) Legal recognition of same-sex relationships in Europe. Paper presented at the ERA seminar on the Current Reflections on EU Anti-Discrimination Law, the Academy of European Law, 11–12 June 2018

Heun W (2004) Gleichheit. In: Dreier H (ed) Grundgesetz Kommentar, 3. Auflage. Mohr Siebeck, Tübingen

International Lesbian, Gay, Bisexual, Trans and Intersex Association: Lucas Ramon Mendos, State-Sponsored Homophobia 2019 (Geneva; ILGA, March 2019)

Jackson V (2010) Constitutional engagement in a transnational era. Oxford University Press, Oxford

Johnson P (2013) Vallianatos judgment on sexual orientation discrimination in civil partnerships, article on Friday, 8 November 2013. http://echrblog.blogspot.com/2013/11/vallianatos-judgment-on-sexual.html. Accessed February 21, 2019

Johnson P (2018) The Council of Europe and the European Court of Human Rights. In: Ziegler AR (ed) International LGBTI law: sexual orientation and gender identity law from an international comparative perspective, forthcoming

Lavrysen L (2016) Aldeguer Tomas v. Spain: a missed opportunity for the Court to provide guidance concerning the legal recognition of same-sex relationships. https://strasbourgobservers.com/2016/07/07/. Accessed November 30, 2021

McCrudden C (2017) CEDAW in national courts: a case study in operationalizing comparative international law analysis in a human rights context. The Social Science Research Network Electronic Paper Collection: http://ssrn.com/abstract=2927707. Accessed November 30, 2021

Plunk DM (1985) South Korea's Kwangju Incident Revisited, Asian Studies Backgrounder No. 35 (September 16) 1985. https://www.heritage.org/report/south-koreas-kwangju-incident-revisited. Accessed November 30, 2021

Ragone S, Volpe V (2016) An emerging right to a "Gay" family life? The Case Oliari v. Italy in a comparative perspective. German Law J 17(03):451–485. https://doi.org/10.1017/S2071832200019830

Saiz I (2004) Bracketing sexuality: human rights and sexual orientation: a decade of development and denial at the UN. Health Hum Rights 7(2):48–80

Schlagdenhauffen R (2016) Same-sex marriage in Europe, Encyclopédie pour unehistoire nouvelle de l'Europe [online], 2016, published on 19/03/2018, consulted on 27/02/2019. http://ehne.fr/en/node/1225. Accessed November 30, 2021

Shachar A (2017) Constituting citizens: oaths, gender, religious attire. In: Albert R, Cameron DR (eds) CANADA in the world: comparative perspectives on the Canadian Constitution. Cambridge University Press, Cambridge

Takács J, Szalma I (2011) Homophobia and same-sex partnership legislation in Europe. Equal Divers Incl: Int J 30(5):356–378. https://doi.org/10.1108/02610151111150627

Waldron J (2005) Foreign law and the modern jus gentium. Harv Law Rev 119(1):129–147. https://www.jstor.org/stable/4093562. Accessed November 30, 2021

Zago G (2015) Oliari and Others v. Italy: a stepping stone towards full legal recognition of same-sex relationships in Europe. https://strasbourgobservers.com/2015/09/16/oliari-and-others-v-italy-a-stepping-stone-towards-full-legal-recognition-of-same-sex-relationships-in-europe/. Accessed November 30, 2021

Chapter 4
The Principle of Non-Discrimination and Anti-Discrimination Law

4.1 The Principle of Non-Discrimination in the European System of Human Rights

In this section, I will briefly discuss the principle of non-discrimination in the European system of human rights. I focus on the discussions of Article 14 of the ECHR and the cases of the European Court of Human Rights (ECtHR). First, I will introduce a general discussion related to the scope of Article 14, both direct and indirect discrimination, and an outstanding issue. Then, I will discuss the importance of the comparator in applying the principle of non-discrimination particularly in the case law of discrimination based on sexual orientation of the ECtHR.

4.1.1 General Discussion

Article 14 of the ECHR states that there shall be no discrimination "on any ground such as sex, race, color, language, religion, political or other opinion, national or social origin, association with a national minority, property, birth or other status." In the European Convention of Human Rights, there are two norms of equality codifications: Article 14[1] is a subordinate norm to prohibit discrimination in the

---

[1] Article 14, The European Convention of Human Rights (officially called as Convention for the Protection of Human Rights and Fundamental Freedoms (1950), as amended by protocols No. 11 and 14: Text amended by the provisions of Protocol No. 14 (CETS No. 194) as from the date of its entry into force on 1 June 2010) reads as follows:

> The enjoyment of the rights and freedoms set forth in this Convention shall be secured without discrimination on any ground such as sex, race, color, language, religion, political or other opinion, national or social origin, association with a national minority, property, birth or other status.

H. J. Lee, *Discrimination Based on Sexual Orientation*, Interdisciplinary Studies in Human Rights 8, https://doi.org/10.1007/978-3-030-95423-9_4

enjoyment of any right provided for by law which has an impact on the rights recognized by the Convention, and it is always applicable in conjunction with another Convention article setting forth a right or freedom. On the other hand, Article 1 of Protocol No. 12 ECHR[2] prohibits discrimination in the enjoyment of any rights provided for by any kind of law, whether or not it has an impact on the rights recognized by the Convention as an autonomous norm to generally prohibit discrimination. While Article 14 has been ratified by all the Council of Europe Member States,[3] Article 1 of Protocol No. 12[4] has only been ratified by some of them. Because Article 1 of Protocol No. 12 has a broader scope than Article 14, the applicability of Article 1 is very important. So far, the European Court of Human Rights tends not to find a violation of Article 14 when violations of other articles[5] are found. For this reason, it has not been decided whether the cases in question violate the prohibition of discrimination or not. However, if Article 1 of Protocol No. 12 is applied as an autonomous norm, it is expected that there will be more decisions which find violations prohibiting discrimination.

The scope of protected grounds is totally different between general guarantee provisions of equality and provisions of particular grounds. Similarly to Article 14 ECHR, Article 2(2) ICESCR[6] stipulates a general guarantee of

---

[2] Article 1, Twelfth Protocol (2000) the ECHR, General prohibition of discrimination:

1. The enjoyment of any rights set forth by law shall be secure without discrimination on any ground such as sex, race, colour, language, religion, political or other opinion, national or social origin, association with a national minority, property, birth or other status.
2. No one shall be discriminated against by any public authority on any ground such as those mentioned in paragraph 1.

[3] The total number of ratifications/accessions to the European Convention (Convention for the Protection of Human Rights and Fundamental Freedoms is 47. For an updated details, please see: https://www.coe.int/en/web/conventions/full-list?module=signatures-by-treaty&treatynum=005. Accessed November 30, 2021.

[4] Article 1 of Protocol No. 12 to the European Convention, as a general clause of prohibition of discrimination covers a broader scope than Article 14 of the European Convention. The total number of ratifications/accessions of Protocol 12 was 20. Please see for an up-to-date list: https://www.coe.int/en/web/conventions/full-list?module=treaty-detail&treatynum=177. Accessed November 30, 2021.

[5] For example, in the *Oliari* case (The European Court of Human Rights, *Oliari and others v. Italy,* decided on July 21, 2015), the ECtHR found violation of Article 8 (Right to respect for private and family life) because Italian Government has not provided a specific legal framework providing for the recognition and protection of their same-sex unions (paragraph 185–187). Nevertheless, the ECtHR does not assess whether this case is discrimination based on sexual orientation as stating "having regard to its finding under Article 8, the Court considers that it is not necessary to examine whether, in this case, there has been a violation of Article 14 in conjunction with Article 8 (paragraph 188)." I think this is because Article 14 is subordinate norm and the ECtHR can avoid further assessment of discrimination as finding violation of another article which is conjunction with Article 14. Nevertheless, the ECtHR will have difficulties in avoiding the further assessment when Article 1 of Protocol No. 12 is applied.

[6] Article 2, paragraph 2, International Covenant on Economic, Social and Cultural Rights (1966):

non-discrimination. The grounds of discrimination in this article are regarded only as examples, so that other grounds are not excluded because they are not included in the list. Because of this character as an open-ended list,[7] the UN Committee has clarified that "the examples of differential treatment presented in this section are merely illustrative and they are not intended to represent the full scope of possible discriminatory treatment under the relevant prohibited ground, nor a conclusive finding that such differential treatment will amount to discrimination in every situation."[8] On the other hand, there is an exhaustive[9] list in other international conventions. For example, Article 1 of CEDAW[10] as well as Article 1 of CRPD[11] protecting particular grounds has an exhaustive list, which has its own distinct limitations.

The scope of the principle of equality discussed in this work includes not only direct discrimination but also indirect discrimination based on sexual orientation. This is in line with "the purpose or effect of nullifying or impairing the recognition, enjoyment or exercise, on an equal footing"[12] that different treatment has in relation to the prohibition of direct or indirect[13] discrimination. Direct discrimination refers

---

State parties to the present Covenant undertake to guarantee that the rights enunciated in the present Covenant will be exercised without discrimination of any kind as to race, colour, sex, language, religion, political or other opinion, national or social origin, property, birth or other status.

[7] The open-ended list of grounds allows courts to include discrimination on grounds which are not included as grounds of prohibited discrimination. In addition, the courts are encouraged to do so by the international human rights instruments (taken from European Commission 2009, p. 57).

[8] UN Committee on Economic, Social and Cultural Rights (CESCR), General comment No. 20: Non-discrimination in economic, social and cultural rights (Article 2, para. 2, of the International Covenant on Economic, Social and Cultural Rights), Paragraph 15, 2 July 2009, E/C.12/GC/20, available at: https://www.refworld.org/docid/4a60961f2.html. Accessed November 30, 2021.

[9] The ECtHR uses the expression of "exhaustive" as the opposite term of "illustrative." The ECtHR states that "the list set out in that provision (referring to Article 14 the ECHR) is *illustrative* and not *exhaustive*" (taken from "European Court of Human Rights, *Salgueiro Da Silva Mouta v. Portugal*, judgment of 21 March 2000. Paragraph 28").

[10] Article 1 of Convention on the Elimination of All Forms of Discrimination against Women (1979): For the purposes of the present Convention, the term "discrimination against women" shall mean any distinction, exclusion or restriction made on the basis of sex which has the effect or purpose of impairing or nullifying the recognition, enjoyment or exercise by women, irrespective of their marital status, on a basis of equality of men and women, of human rights and fundamental freedoms in the political, economic, social, cultural, civil or any other field.

[11] Article 1 of Convention on the Rights of Persons with Disabilities (2006): The purpose of the present Convention is to promote, protect and ensure the full and equal enjoyment of all human rights and fundamental freedoms by all persons with disabilities, and to promote respect for their inherent dignity. Persons with disabilities include those who have long-term physical, mental, intellectual or sensory impairments which in interaction with various barriers may hinder their full and effective participation in society on an equal basis with others.

[12] International Convention on the Elimination of All Forms of Racial Discrimination (1966), Article 1, paragraph 1.

[13] "In particular, a first and important step towards the elimination of discrimination, *whether direct or indirect*, is for States to recognize the existence of diverse cultural identities of individuals and communities on their territories" (taken from Committee on Economic, Social and Cultural Rights,

to the situation "where one person is treated less favorably than another is, has been or would be treated in a comparable situation"[14] on any grounds including sexual orientation. One of the representative case laws to deal with direct discrimination in the ECtHR is *Konstantin Markin v. Russia*. In this case, the applicant, a male serviceman, was treated less favorably than another person, a servicewoman, in a similar situation for a reason related to a prohibited ground of gender because parental leave could only be granted to female military personnel.[15] On the other hand, the applicant who is the male serviceman could not have parental leave because of his gender. In another direct discrimination case, that of *Emel Boyraz v. Turkey*, the ECtHR found a violation of Article 14 of the Convention taken in conjunction with Article 8 because the applicant was refused appointment to the post of security officer because the post in question had been reserved for male candidates. And such a difference in the treatment of persons in comparable situations is discriminatory without objective and reasonable justification.[16]

On the other hand, indirect discrimination refers to the situation where there are seemingly neutral criteria for everyone, which, however, put a certain group of

General comment No. 21, paragraph. 23. https://www.refworld.org/docid/4ed35bae2.html. Accessed November 30, 2021).

[14]Council Directive 2000/78/EC of 27 November 2000 establishing a general framework for equal treatment in employment and occupation, Article 2(2)(a).

[15]European Court Human Rights, ***KONSTANTIN MARKIN v. RUSSIA*** (Applications no. 30078/06), Grand Chamber judgment of 22 March 2012 paragraph 46: The applicant was born in 1976 and lives in Velikiy Novgorod, Russia. He was serving as a radio intelligence operator after he signed a military service contract on 27 March 2004 which stated he "undertook to serve under the conditions provided for by law." Equivalent positions to his were held by service women and he was often replaced in his duties by female personnel (para. 9–11). After his third child was born in 2005, the court granted the petition for divorce which his wife has submitted (para. 12). After the wife left, the applicant asked the three years' parental leave, but the head of the military unit rejected this because three years' parental leave could be granted only to female military personnel (para. 15). He challenged the provisions of the Military Service Act as being incompatible with the equality clause in the Constitution, but the Constitutional Court concluded that the provisions were compatible with Constitution (para. 33–34). The ECtHR considers that the exclusion of servicemen from the entitlement to parental leave, while servicewomen are entitled to such leave, amounted to discrimination on grounds of sex. Therefore, the ECtHR concluded there has been a violation of Article 14 taken in conjunction with Article 8 (para. 151–152).

[16]European Court Human Rights, ***EMEL BOYRAZ v. TURKEY*** (Applications no. 61960/08), Judgment of 2 December 2014, paragraphs 48–56: The applicant was born in 1975 and was successful in the examination to become a public servant. The State Personnel Department appointed her to the post of security officer in the state-run Electricity Company. The human resources department of the Company informed the applicant that she would not be appointed because she is not a man who has competed military service. The Ankara Administrative Court annulled the decision of the Company and held that there had been no restriction on women working as security officers. But, the Supreme Administrative Court held that the requirement of military service demonstrated that the post was reserved for males and the requirement was lawful (para. 4–25). In this case, the ECtHR concluded that the difference in treatment amounted to discrimination on grounds of sex and that there was no proof that the difference in treatment pursued a legitimate aim. Therefore, there was a violation of Article 14 ECHR in conjunction with Article 8 (para. 56).

people in a disadvantaged position. A definition can be inferred from "where an apparently neutral provision, criterion or practice would put persons of one group at a particular disadvantage compared with other persons in a comparable situation."[17] The ECtHR accepted the concept of indirect discrimination in the case of D.H. and others v. The Czech Republic where, historically, Roma children have been sent to special schools considerably often than non-Roma children. The ECtHR accepted the statistics as evidence to find indirect discrimination from this case, and paid attention to the fact that "A Roma child in Ostrava was 27 times more likely to be placed in a special school than a non-Roma child."[18]

Yet, there is still an outstanding issue related to Article 14 ECHR.[19] It is semi-autonomous, meaning that a claim has to come within the ambit of another protected right. In the *Oliari* case as well, the Chamber decided to analyze a possible violation of article 8 alone, although most applicants claimed a violation of Article 8 in conjunction with article 14. By ignoring an evaluation of the case under Article 14, it missed the opportunity to verify in detail whether Italy satisfied the proportionality test under Article 14.[20] *Abrusci* also commented on this that "the ECtHR did not consider the alleged violation under Article 14, thus not assessing whether Italy was treating the applicants in a discriminatory way by denying them the possibility to enter into a marriage or civil partnership."[21] In the recent case of *Orlandi v. Italy*,[22] the ECtHR found a violation of Article 8 of the ECHR because Italy failed to strike a fair balance between competing interests in so far as they failed to ensure that the applicants had a specific legal framework available for the

[17] Taken from Council Directive 2006/54/EC of the European Parliament and of the Council of 5 July 2006 on the implementation of the principle of equal opportunities and equal treatment of men and women in matters of employment and occupation, Article 2(1)(b).

[18] European Court of Human Rights, *D.H. and others v. the Czech Republic*, judgment of 13 November 2007, paragraph 18.

[19] Article 14 The ECHR Prohibition of discrimination: The enjoyment of the rights and freedoms set forth in this Convention shall be secured without discrimination on any ground such as sex, race, colour, language, religion, political or other opinion, national or social origin, association with a national minority, property, birth or other status.

[20] Zago (2015).

[21] Abrusci (2017), p. 248. Last accessed on February 27, 2019.

[22] European Court Human Rights, ***ORLANDI AND OTHERS v. ITALY*** (Applications nos. 26431/12; 26742/12; 44057/12 and 60088/12), Judgment of 14 March 2018: The applicants of Ms. *Orlandi* and Ms. *Mortagna* are same-sex couple in a stable and committed relationship with each other. After they married on August 27, 2010 in Toronto during their stay in Canada for work purposes, they returned to Italy and transferred the relevant documents for the purposes of registration of their marriage in the Civil Status Office in Italy. However, the Commune of Ferrara informed the two applicants that it was not possible to register their marriage because Italian legal order did not allow marriage between same-sex couples (para. 11–17). In this case, the ECtHR found a violation of Article 8 ECHR because Italy failed to ensure that the applicants had available a specific legal framework providing for the recognition and protection of their same-sex unions (para. 210). Nevertheless, the ECtHR did not find a violation of Article 14 in conjunction with Article 8 or Article 12 ECHR, stating that it is not necessary to be examined because the Court had already found a violation of Article 8 the ECHR.

recognition and protection of their same-sex unions.[23] However, it still considered it unnecessary to examine whether there has been a violation of Article 14 of the ECHR,[24] leaving that as an outstanding question.

4.1.2 The Importance of the Comparator

To find a violation of Article 14 (Prohibition of discrimination), there must be a difference in the treatment of persons in relevantly similar situations.[25] It would be disproportionate if such differential treatment is not justified using the principle of proportionality. For the violation to be found using the proportionality analysis, it is important to have the right comparator to show a relevantly similar situation to the applicant's situation. *Laurens Lavrysen*[26] points out that it is problematic that the ECtHR chose the wrong comparator in the case of *Aldeguer Tomás.*[27] In the *Aldeguer* case, the applicant's situation is compared to the solution provided for by Law No. 30/1981(1981 Divorce Act) for different-sex cohabiting couples. While legally unable to marry before the law came into force, they were eligible for a survivor's pension by virtue of the retroactivity clause contained in its additional

[23] European Court of Human Rights, *Orlandi and others v. Italy*, judgment of 14 March 2018, paragraphs 210–211.

[24] Ibid. paragraph 212.

[25] European Court of Human Rights, *Aldeguer Tomás vs. Spain*, judgment of 14 June 2015, paragraph 79.

[26] Lavrysen (2016).

[27] European Court of Human Rights, ***ALDEGUER TOMÁS v. SPAIN*** (Application no. 35214/09), Judgment of 14 June 2016: The applicant, Mr. *Aldeguer*'s partner, with whom he had lived together in a same-sex relationship since 1990, died in 2002. In 2003 Mr. *Aldeguer* claimed social security allowances as a surviving spouse. The National Institute of Social Security refused to grant him a survivor's pension on the grounds that he had not been married to the deceased person. After legalizing same-sex marriage in Spain in July 2005, Mr. *Aldeguer* filed a complaint against the 2003 decision, which was dismissed because under the legislation in force he could not gain the status of a widower. The Supreme Court and the Constitutional Court in Spain decided against the applicant because the law had no retroactive effect in the applicant's circumstances. In this case, the ECtHR holds unanimously that there has been no violation of Article 14 read in conjunction with Article 8 of the Convention and Article 1 of Protocol No. 1 to the Convention. Particularly, the ECtHR concluded that the applicant's situation following the coming into force of the law legalizing same-sex marriage in Spain in 2005 had not been relevantly similar to that of a surviving partner of a heterosexual cohabiting couple, who had been unable to marry his or her partner before the law legalizing divorce came into force in 1981. Furthermore, the ECtHR stated there is wide margin of appreciation in the legal recognition of same-sex couples, and there is no established European consensus in the area of same-sex marriage (taken from Principal facts and Decision, press release issued by the registrar of the Court, ECHR 202 (2016) 14. 06. 2016).

provision no. 10(2).[28] The ECtHR considers that the legal impediment of the applicant is of a different nature from that of different-sex couples in the case of Law No. 30/1981. While the issue is about "an impediment to marrying" for same-sex couples in the applicant's situation, the issue of different sex couples in the case of Law No. 30/1981 is about "an impediment to remarrying."

As the judge *Keller* states in the separate opinion of *Aldeguer*,[29] the comparability of two groups makes the ECtHR's legal analysis more difficult. On the one hand, heterosexual partners lived in a de facto relationship with a new partner while being legally barred from divorce. On the other hand, same-sex partners live in a de facto relationship because they are not allowed to marry. The legislation was passed regarding the first group more than 25 years earlier than the second group. The argument of *Lavrysen* makes sense since it would have been much more relevant if a heterosexual partner who had been able to marry legally and to have enjoyed a survivor's pension were compared to the applicant before the 2005 same-sex marriage act. The point is that the applicant had been in a worse or less favorable situation than a heterosexual surviving partner when denied the benefit of a surviving partner's pension. By using the wrong choice of the comparator, the legal argument of the ECtHR finally failed to find a violation in this case.

Another case is *Taddeucci and McCall v. Italy*[30] where the right comparator plays an important role in finding a violation of Article 14 (prohibition of discrimination) taken together with Article 8 (right to respect for private and family life). When

---

[28] Law No. 30/1981 of 7 July 1981, amending the provisions of the Civil Code pertaining to marriage and the procedure to be followed for cases of annulment, judicial separation and divorce ("the Divorce Act") Additional provision no. 10 read as follows:

> On a provisional basis, until a definitive regulation is enacted in the relevant legislation, the following rules shall apply in matters concerning pensions and social security...
>
> 2. For those who have not been able to marry on account of the legislation in force until now but who have lived as a married couple, when the death of one of the partners has occurred before the entry into force of the present Law, the survivor will be entitled to the benefits provided for in the first paragraph of the present provision and to the corresponding pension in accordance with the following paragraph.
>
> 3. The right to a survivor's pension and other passive rights to benefits on account of a death shall be awarded to the person who has been the legal spouse in proportion to the time lived with the deceased spouse, irrespective of the causes that had determined the separation or divorce (taken from European Court of Human Rights, *Aldeguer Tomás vs. Spain*, judgment of 14 June 2015, paragraphs 32–33).

[29] European Court of Human Rights, *Aldeguer Tomás vs. Spain*, judgment of 14 June 2015, Separate Opinion of Judge Keller. Paragraph 6.

[30] European Court of Human Rights., ***TADDEUCCI AND McCALL v. ITALY*** *(Application no. 51362/09)*, judgment of 30 Sep. 2016: The applicants lived together as a same-sex couple since 1999. They lived in New Zealand as an unmarried couple until December 2003 and then they decided to settle in Italy. After moving to Italy, the second applicant, a New Zealand national applied for a residence permit on family grounds, which was rejected because same-sex partner could not be treated as a "family member." In this case, the ECtHR decided that Italy had violated Article 14 taken in conjunction with Article 8 because the state did not treat same-sex couples in the same way as heterosexual couples for the purpose of granting a residence permit for family reasons.

assessing whether there was a difference in the treatment of individuals in comparable situations, the Court of Cassation found no difference between the applicants and unmarried heterosexual couples. Each of the groups was excluded from being treated as a "family member" because it applies only to a "spouse," not to a cohabiting partner. Therefore, the Court of Cassation concluded that there was no discrimination based on sexual orientation because the exclusion of unmarried partners from the right to obtain a residence permit concerned all unmarried couples.

However, the European Court of Human Rights found that unmarried heterosexual couples could not be the right comparator. The reason for this is that the applicants could not get married or obtain any other form of legal recognition to enable them to be classified as "spouses" under national law, unlike unmarried heterosexual couples. What matters in finding discrimination of Article 14 is whether there is unequal treatment among groups in similar situations. Because of the content in Article 14, it is important to determine if there is unequal treatment of individuals whose situations are similar. The Court of Cassation failed to find a violation because it applied the wrong comparator, one who was in a different situation from the applicants. For this reason, to have the right comparator in a similar situation is particularly important to determine a violation of Article 14 ECHR.

4.2 Standards of Equality Test in Korea

The Korean Constitution determines the principle of equality as being that "all citizens shall be equal before the law" in Article 11. The Constitutional Court of Korea ("CCK") interprets this article not as promoting absolute equality but as promoting relative equality.[31] To promote relative equality means discriminatory treatment cannot be justified without reasonable grounds not only in the legislative acts but also in the applicability of law. To find violation of relative equality, the CCK needs the legal standard to determine whether there are reasonable grounds in specific treatments that differ. To identify such standards, the CCK applies the prohibition of arbitrariness as well as the principle of proportionality. On unreasonable unequal treatment, in a case dealing with different financial institutions from general creditors regarding overdue loans in 1989, the CCK states that "it means arbitrary discrimination, which is against justice." Furthermore, the CCK explicitly applies the principle of proportionality when stating "Any legislations that implies discriminatory treatment related to the fundamental rights of the people must have a

Furthermore, the ECtHR stated that there was a "significant trend" around the world towards recognizing the status of same-sex partners as "Family members." (paragraphs. 97–99).

[31] The Constitutional Court of Korea, 2005 Hun-Ba 34, decided on 26 Dec. 2008, Case Law Book 20(2) – II, pp. 594–607.

legitimate aim; furthermore, the means must have substantial relation to obtain such a legitimate aim, and the means have to be adequate".[32]

The CCK applies a standard of strict scrutiny in deciding on the violation of the principle of equality. For the strict scrutiny, the CCK applies the principle of proportionality in the cases where the margin of appreciation is considered narrow for legislators.[33] In this case, the CCK decided it is discrimination against women as well as disabled men who are not allowed to fulfill military service because only men who have finished their military service could receive considerable extra points for their exams to become public servants. In this case, the CCK applied the principle of proportionality because the legislators' margin is considered narrow in this matter, which deals with gender discrimination being protected particularly in the Constitution of Korea, and it could cause serious violation of the fundamental right to become a civil servant. Nevertheless, the application of proportionality does not presuppose a narrow margin of appreciation on the part of the legislators. The CCK states that the principle of proportionality applies when discrimination occurs especially in the scope where "the Constitutional particularly requests equality." In addition, the proportionality is applied when "there are serious limitations on exercising fundamental rights."[34] In cases such as those mentioned above, the margin of appreciation is granted narrowly to the legislators so that the principle of proportionality applies in many cases where a narrow margin is granted to legislators. Nevertheless, the CCK does not state the narrow margin of appreciation explicitly as a precondition for the application of proportionality. So far, the CCK has only explicitly clarified two preconditions—to be discussed in the following section—when applying the proportionality to determine the violation of the principle of equality.

Applying the principle of proportionality in finding discrimination is a criterion of stricter scrutiny than simply requiring any reasonable grounds for different treatment. Therefore, the following have to be tested when applying the proportionality test: the assessment of the correlation between different treatments, and the justifying grounds for such different treatments, an adequate balancing between the weight of legislative objective for different treatments, and the weight of different treatments.[35] In this case, the issue has been whether it is a discriminatory measure for men as well as for direct family members of national merit[36] to receive

---

[32]The Constitutional Court of Korea, 89 Hun-Ga 37·96 (Consolidated), decided on May 24, 1989.

[33]The Constitutional Court of Korea, 98 Hun-Ma 363 (Consolidated), decided on December 23, 1999.

[34]The Constitutional Court of Korea, 2007 Hun-Ma 870, decided on 30 July 2009, Case Law Book 21(2) – I, pp. 361–362.

[35]The Constitutional Court of Korea, 2000 Hun-Ma 25, decided on February 22, 2001.

[36]According to Act on the honorable treatment of and support for persons, etc. of distinguished service to the state, men of national merit is defined as "persons of distinguished service to the Republic of Korea who have made a sacrifice or contribution to the Republic of Korea" (Article 1). Direct family members of national merit include "a spouse, children, parents, grandparents who have no lineal adult descendant, minor siblings who have no lineal ascendant under 60 years of age and no adult senior sibling" (Article 5, Paragraph 1).

10% extra points as a benefit when they apply for the employment examinations conducted by the national institution. After applying the proportionality test, the CCK decided that such benefits neither violate the principle of equality, nor the rights to become civil servants of those who are not eligible for such benefits. In another case,[37] the CCK states that the proportionality test assesses whether strict proportional relation exists between the objective of discriminatory treatment and the means used.

Does the CCK accept the standards discussed in the Federal Court of Germany to decide whether discrimination has taken place? Many constitutional law scholars[38] in Korea argue that the CCK has adopted German standards to apply the prohibition of arbitrariness as well as the principle of proportionality, which I agree with. In the case of the benefit of extra points provided to discharged military members,[39] the CCK has stated, "In the case of equality, to apply stricter scrutiny or milder scrutiny depends on the breadth of the margin of appreciation given to legislators when forming legislations. In the area where the Constitution particularly stresses equality, the margin is considered narrow so that the stricter scrutiny of the proportionality test will be applied. In addition, when the Constitution provides certain grounds to prohibit discrimination, or presents particular sectors where discrimination is prohibited, the proportionality test will apply to the case of discrimination based on such grounds or in such particular sectors. Another factor to decide that the breadth of margin should be narrow is whether certain discriminatory treatment could cause significant harm in fulfilling the fundamental rights in questions." After all, considering such statements, the CCK seems to accept the prohibition of arbitrariness as well as the principle of proportionality from the Federal Court of Germany,[40] and it seems to apply those principles as criteria to find the violation of the principle of equality in the case of the benefit of extra points provided to discharged military members.

---

[37] The Constitutional Court of Korea, 2002 Hun-Ma 573, decided on 27 Mar. 2003: The issue of this case is whether Article 115, Paragraph 2 of local education autonomy law violates the principle of equality or not. The legal provisions of this case state that "In the local education committee election, if the number of experienced in education is less than one half of the number of elected among majority vote winners, regardless of the rate of vote, experienced in education will be appointed in the order of majority vote. The applicants who are not experienced have claimed such provisions violate the principle of equality and the applicant's right to be appointed as education committee member." The CCK decided the provisions are constitutional. However, five out of a total of nine judges are of the opinion that it is unconstitutional. The decision could not be made as unconstitutional because six judges are needed to decide that a measure is unconstitutional even if judges with the opinion that it is unconstitutional are more (five judges) than the judges whose opinion is that it is constitutional (four judges).

[38] One of the scholars is prof. *Dokyun Kim*. In his article of "*Die Struktur und Begründung der Abwägung im Recht*" (2007, Seoul National University), he has argued the principles and concepts of the Federal Constitutional Court of Germany influenced the case law of the Korean Constitutional Court.

[39] The Constitutional Court of Korea, 98 Hun-Ma 363, 98 Hun-Ba 33, 97 Hun-Ga 12 (Consolidated), decided on 23 Dec. 1999.

[40] For similar opinion, please see Hong (2012), p. 261.

In other words, according to the CCK, the stricter scrutiny of the principle of proportionality will be applied for the following cases: (1) the Constitution particularly emphasizes the obligation to achieve equality. The Constitution states some standards that cannot be used as grounds for differential treatment or for some particular sector to prohibit discrimination. Proportionality will be applied to discrimination based on such grounds or discrimination in those particular sectors,[41] (2) the margin of legislators is regarded narrow when discriminatory treatment could cause serious harm to the fulfillment of fundamental rights.[42]

4.2.1 The Prohibition of Arbitrariness

The Constitutional Court of Korea has adopted prohibition of arbitrariness in finding violations of the principle of equality. According to the CCK, "the principle of equality basically means the prohibition of arbitrary legislations in the case laws of the CCK. Thus, the CCK decides violation of the principle of equality when reasonable grounds cannot be found to justify different treatments in the decision of legislators. The legislator's obligation to fulfill equality under the Korean Constitution basically means prohibiting arbitrary legislation. After all, the norm controlled by the CCK does not assess whether the means are the most reasonable and valid, but rather assesses whether the political formation of legislators lies within the limitations set by the Constitution."[43] In this case, it has been questioned whether excluding those who are insured under a comprehensive traffic accident program from criminal prosecution violates the principle of equality against those who are not insured under such a program. The CCK has decided it does indeed violate the principle of equality because such a law treats the victims differently in traffic accidents that caused serious injury to the victim due to serious negligence of the drivers according to the insurance programs of the drivers responsible.

The CCK basically applies the prohibition of arbitrariness to assess whether legislators have been arbitrary with such discriminatory measures in deciding whether such discriminatory legal measures violate the principle of equality.[44] In

[41] The Constitutional Court of Korea, 2006 Hun-Ma 1192, decided on 26 Dec. 2009. Judicial Precedent 20-2 (II), pp. 787–805. (In the case regarding the standard to decide monthly payment of military servants, the CCK states when to apply *principle of proportionality*.)

[42] The Constitutional Court of Korea, 98 Hun-Ba 33, decided on 23 Dec. 1999. Judicial Precedent 11-2, pp. 732–749. (In this case, it has been questioned whether to bestow extra points within 5% range to veterans when they apply for the examination to become public officers. The CCK decided such 5% extra points are very critical to decide the result of the examination so that it violates the principle of proportionality so that the principle of equality is violated. Such a measure violates the right to be treated equally as well as the right to be appointed as public officer of the applicant who is not a discharged soldier.)

[43] The Constitutional Court of Korea, 90 Hun-Ma 110, decided on January 16, 1997. Judicial Precedent 9(1). pp. 90–115.

[44] The Constitutional Court of Korea, 2000 Hun-Ma 342, decided on 27 Sep. 2001. Judicial Precedent 13(2). pp. 434–437.

this case, there are different calculations of the retirement fund between the public officers with disqualifications and the public officers without such disqualifications. The CCK applied prohibition of arbitrariness to this case, and decided it does not violate the principle of equality because such differential treatments have reasonable grounds. CCK assesses two steps of the prohibition of arbitrariness in the case laws:[45] firstly, the existence of discriminatory treatments to regard matters that are fundamentally the same as different, and secondly, whether such different treatments can be regarded as arbitrary.

The Constitutional Court of Korea applied the prohibition of arbitrariness in the case law until 1999 when the CCK decided that providing extra points only to veterans is discriminatory against women and disabled people who are not eligible to serve in the military.[46] The principle of equality has been interpreted as meaning only the prohibition of arbitrary legislation and the principle of equality is violated when there is no reasonable ground to justify discriminatory legislation.[47] Nevertheless, as the Constitutional Court of Korea itself expresses,[48] it does not mean that the principle of proportionality had never been applied to find violation of the principle of equality before 1999. In the case of seeking to find whether civil procedure violates the principle of equality in 1996,[49] the CCK applied the principle of proportionality. The Court examined whether different treatments have a legitimate aim according to the Constitution (legitimate aim), whether the standards of different treatments have substantial relevance to the accomplishment of the stated aim (suitability), and whether discrimination is appropriate (necessity). The Constitutional Court of Korea applied the prohibition of arbitrariness as the main standard to decide the violation of the principle of equality before 1999. In addition, the principle of proportionality has been applied in some particular cases, which has affected the case law since 1999.

4.2.2 *The Principle of Proportionality*

Another important issue in applying the principle of proportionality in the case laws of the Constitutional Court of Korea is whether the principle will be applied in the

---

[45] The Constitutional Court of Korea, 2001 Hun-Ba 64, decided on January 30, 2003. Judicial Precedent 15(1). pp. 48–49.

[46] The Constitutional Court of Korea, 98 Hun-Ma 363, decided on 23 December 1999.

[47] The Constitutional Court of Korea, 90 Hun-Ma 110, decided on January 16, 1997.

[48] The Constitutional Court of Korea has stated that prohibition of arbitrariness was applied as a standard to decide the violation of the principle of equality up to year 1999. Nevertheless, the CCK stated that the principle of proportionality was also applied. In this case, the CCK did not apply the proportionality in the narrow sense or law of balancing in the case law (taken from The Constitutional Court of Korea, 2000 Hun-Ma 25, decided on February 22, 2001). After all, the CCK seems to have applied the principle of proportionality before 1999 even if it was not fully structured proportionality including the balancing test.

[49] The Constitutional Court of Korea, 93 Hun-Ba 57, decided on August 29, 1996.

same way both to rights of freedom and to rights to equality. The criteria to decide violation of the rights of freedom first confirm the scope of protection as well as the limitations, and assesses the interrelationship between the means to limit the rights of freedom and the legislative purpose as a matter of constitutional validity regarding the limitation. On the other hand, in the case of the rights to equality, the main issue is whether discriminatory treatment can be constitutionally justified after confirming such discriminatory treatment. Therefore, the principle of proportionality assesses whether the correlation between discrimination as a means and the aim of discriminatory legislation can be justified in dealing with the questions related to right to equality.[50]

The proportionality test examines "proportionality to limitations" in assessing the violation of the rights to freedom while it examines "the proportionality of discrimination" in assessing the violation of rights to equality. This is because rights to equality do not set a particular scope of protections so that there are justifiable discriminatory treatments and unjustifiable discriminatory treatments rather than limitations. The fundamental difference between the two lies in assessing "the proportionality of limitations" and "the proportionality of discriminations."[51] In other words, in assessing the violation of the rights to equality when applying the principle of proportionality, discriminatory treatments will only be justified when they pursue legitimate aims, are both suitable and necessary, and have considerable proportional relations to the values of such objective.

The proportionality test in the case laws of the CCK, as a means of stricter scrutiny, assesses whether the discriminatory treatments are strictly proportional relative to the objective of discriminatory treatments. To apply the principle of proportionality, which is stricter scrutiny than the test to see if there are reasonable grounds for discriminatory treatments, means that the legislators' margins will become narrower and that the positive obligation of the courts will be emphasized in guaranteeing the rights of equality. In terms of these difficulties, it is very important that the courts provide very clear standards when applying the principle of proportionality. The question then arises of whether the CCK provides such clear standards to apply Proportionality. The CCK applies the proportionality when finding violations of the principle of equality when the Constitution specially states that equal treatment has to be fulfilled, and when discriminatory treatment causes considerably weighty limitations to related fundamental rights.

However, such standards do not seem to be very clear, especially the second standard because "the case to bring about considerably weighty limitations" is a relatively subjective expression. Among the criticisms, professor *Boo-Ha Lee*[52] pointed out that it is difficult to classify the degree of infringement of basic rights based on the extent of seriousness to restrict basic rights. In addition, it is very ambiguous to suggest specific standards in making judgments about limitations to fundamental rights. "Considerably weighty limitations" should no longer be used or

[50] Son (2019), p. 4.

[51] Pieroth and Schlink (2000), p. 138.

[52] Lee (2011), p. 275.

would have to provide more specific sub-criteria to answer what this expression specifically means. Such arbitrary expression of "weighty limitations" can be seen as inappropriate standards.[53] As Professor *Lee* has pointed out, the standards must be clearly applied. Particularly, the question of the applicability of proportionality in the matters related to the principle of equality has to be very clear because decisions regarding violation can be different according to the standards applied. The CCK's current standards about the "weighty limitations" of fundamental rights are not clear enough because "weightiness" depends on a value judgment which can vary according to specific circumstances.

As mentioned above, the extent of seriousness in limiting related fundamental rights can also be confirmed after the process of examinations. In this sense, before entering the scrutiny it cannot be decided in advance whether stricter scrutiny of proportionality must be applied or less strict scrutiny of prohibition of arbitrariness should be applied.[54] This has to be decided according to the contexts and circumstances particular to each case. The CCK applies the proportionality as methods of adjudication to its case laws to find violation of the principle of non-discrimination; however, the standards with the applicability of proportionality are still both unclear and vague because the expressions of the standards provided are considered to be subjective. As an alternative, the Constitutional Court of Korea can consider what the Federal Constitutional Court of Germany has applied in the case of *Transsexuelle II*.[55] The principle of proportionality will apply especially when the discriminatory treatment is against a group of people on the grounds of sex, parentage, race, language, homeland, origin, faith or religious or political opinions as stated in Article 3 (3) of German basic law. Similarly, the grounds of sex, religion or social status listed in Article 11 (1) of the Korean Constitution should be interpreted only as illustrative[56] and other grounds cannot be disregarded only because they are not included in the list. In that way, discrimination against a particular group of people

[53]For more arguments, please see, Lee (2018a), p. 592.

[54]For similar criticism, please see, Yi (2001), pp. 14–15.

[55]BVerfGE 88, 87.

[56]There are two different positions when interpreting the stated grounds of discrimination in the Article 11(1) of the Korean Constitution. The first position is to interpret as illustrative. According to this position, the purpose of guaranteeing equality is that unreasonable discrimination cannot be accepted for any reason regardless of the stated grounds or not. Otherwise, it is difficult to protect the victims from the discrimination based on the grounds which could not be predicted at the time of the initial enactment of this constitutional article. Lastly, if the grounds in Article 11(1) are interpreted as a limited list, the scope of protecting equality become very narrow (Kwon 2010, p. 394). On the other hand, another position is to claim an interpretation of the grounds in Article 11(1) as a limited list to respect the intent of original legislators. This position claims that the Constitutional Court of Korea should apply the principle of proportionality only to the listed grounds to find the violation of principle of equality. To find out discrimination based on the grounds which are not listed, the CCK should apply the prohibition of arbitrariness (Kim 2000, p. 471). I agree with the first position to interpret only as illustrative because there are no legitimate reasons to differentiate the listed grounds of sex, religion or social status from other grounds such as sexual orientation.

can be prohibited. In addition, a particular minority group of people such as sexual minorities in South Korea can be protected from discriminatory treatment without legitimate grounds.

4.2.3 Case Study of the Constitutional Court of Korea[57]

In this section, one case of the Constitutional Court of Korea will be analyzed to demonstrate how the CCK applied the principle of proportionality in finding discrimination. It is important to study this specific case to see how the principle of proportionality is used to find violation of the principle of non-discrimination. The law[58] in question in this case provides benefits of extra points to veterans in the examination to become public servants. In this system, others who do not receive any extra points will be disadvantaged in the examination for employment. Whether such legal provisions violate the principle of equality or not will be decided by the Court's methods of adjudications. If the prohibition of arbitrariness is applied, the

---

[57] The Constitutional Court of Korea, 98 Hun-Ma 363, 98 Hun-Ba 33, 97 Hun-Ga 12 (Consolidated), decided on 23 Dec. 1999 (the case of benefit of extra points to veterans).

[58] The law in question is "Law concerning discharged army support" (legislated on 31 December 1997, Law No. 5482).

Article 8 (Additional points for recruitment examinations)

Paragraph 1. When the employment protection agencies conduct examinations for recruitment and discharged army officers apply for the examinations, the score for each subject in the written test will be added to the score of each subject within 5% of the full score for each subject as prescribed by presidential decree. If the employment protection agency does not conduct the written test, extra points will be added to the score of the practical test, document selection process, and interview test.

Paragraph 2. Omitted

Paragraph 3. Job categories subject to extra points in recruitment examinations conducted by the employment protection agency shall be determined by Presidential Decree.

Article 9 (Percentage of additional points for recruitment tests)

Paragraph 1. The rate of additional points against the full score for this recruitment test will be as follows:

1. Discharged military personnel who were discharged after completing a service period of 2 years or more: 5%
2. Discharged personnel who were discharged after completing service period of less than 2 years: 3%

Paragraph 2. Job categories subject to additional points for employment examinations in accordance with the provisions of Article 8, Paragraph 3 of the Act is as follows:

1. Of the civil servants prescribed in Article 2 of the National Public Service Act and Article 2 of the Local Public Services Act, all levels of civil servants of level 6 or lower and skilled civil servants.
2. As stipulated in Article 30, Paragraph 2 of the Act on Rewards and Supports of men with national merits, all levels of newly hired employees by employment protection agencies.

Court will assess only whether there are any reasonable grounds to justify such different treatments. In other words, if there are "factual differences between the two groups" or a "legitimate legislative purpose,"[59] it is likely to be regarded as no violation. On the other hand, if the principle of proportionality is applied, it assesses the strict proportional relations between discriminatory treatments and grounds to justify such different treatments: the characteristics as well as the importance of the differences between the two groups and the proportionality between the legitimate aim to be attained through such discriminatory measures, and the discriminatory acts will be assessed.

The CCK applies the proportionality differently from the structured proportionality test of Germany. As Professor *Soo-Woong Han*[60] points out, the CCK holds that "when the legislative purpose is legitimate, and discrimination is a suitable means to attain legitimate purpose, then such different treatments are considered reasonable." In other words, the CCK assesses only the legitimacy of the purposes for discrimination and the suitability of measures as discrimination, excluding both the third step of necessity and the fourth step of balancing. Even if the CCK states that it applies a stricter proportionality test, it is questionable how it is different from less strict prohibition of arbitrariness: a legitimate purpose is in most cases recognized, and suitability of discriminatory measures is likely to be easily passed when different treatments contribute to the fulfillment of legislative purpose on some level. If the CCK applies the principle of proportionality with only two steps, it is no different from the prohibition of arbitrariness. The case of the extra point system—which will be discussed in the following section—is regarded as having applied a more structured proportionality test to assess a legitimate aim, a suitability, a necessity and the proportionality in the narrow sense.

The main issue in this case is whether the extra point system can be justified according to Article 39[61] of the Korean Constitution. Paragraph 2 of Article 39 states prohibition of unfavorable treatment with the reason of the fulfillment of military obligation; however, the law in question bestows positive reward measures to those who have fulfilled military services by adding extra points to their employment examinations to become civil servants. The applicants in this case are female college students and university students with disabilities, who were preparing for civil servant examinations. They claimed the legislation in question violated their right to equality, right to work in public service, and the freedom to choose their jobs. The state argues that such benefits are based on the Constitution; however, Article 39, Paragraph 2 only prohibits unfavorable treatments to veterans. The Article

[59] The Constitutional Court of Korea, 88 Hun-Ga 7, decided on January 25, 1989.

[60] Han (2005), pp. 160–161.

[61] Article 39 of the Constitution of the Republic of Korea states as follows:

> Paragraph 1. All citizens shall have the duty of national defense under the conditions as prescribed by Act.
>
> Paragraph 2. No citizen shall be treated unfavorably on account of the fulfillment of his obligation of military service.

does not provide grounds to impose an obligation on the state to grant benefits or provide compensation measures to the people who fulfill their military service. To look at some statistics, 81.6% to 87% of the whole male population had been enlisted in military service for 5 years from 1994 to 1998.[62] This shows that more than 80% of Korean males will be veterans who would benefit from the law in question. Therefore, it discriminates against women and men who cannot carry out military services because of illness or disability.

In this case, the CCK assesses whether this case conforms to the standards of the proportionality in finding violations of the principle of non-discrimination and concludes this case fulfills both of the standards. The law in question treats men differently from women in the sector of employment although the Korean constitution[63] specifically requests protection of women related to employment. Nevertheless, the law in question discriminates against women who have to be specially protected in employment, which means their fundamental rights have been seriously violated so that stricter scrutiny of the proportionality test has to be applied.

On the steps of proportionality, the CCK first states that the objective is legitimate in that the law in question helps veterans to come back to society without any problems because they have lost all other opportunities to obtain employment or to prepare for employment during military service. Secondly, for suitability and necessity, the CCK decides that the law in question is not regarded as a reasonable support system because it deprives non-veterans of employment opportunities. Furthermore, it is not the choice of women and disabled people whether or not to do military service, but rather, they are not allowed to serve in the military. While very few women benefit, no disabled people benefit from this extra point system at all, yet most Korean men will benefit from it. Therefore, even if this extra point system is regarded as suitable to attain the legitimate aim of supporting people who have served in the military, the system will not be considered as a necessary measure because there should be less restrictive measures. The system in question bestows extra points of 5% or 3% which makes it impossible for other people without the extra points to pass the exam. In this situation, a system with a lower percentage of extra points or one that provides other types of benefits without hurting the rights of others could be considered a less restrictive measure. Nevertheless, it is not clear whether that would be regarded as an equally effective measure. Furthermore, it is not so easy to measure the effectiveness among all seemingly possible alternatives which are less restrictive.

Considering the characteristics of the aim which provides some support to people who have served in the military, a lower percentage of extra points can be argued as

---

[62] Taken from Statistics Korea Government Official Work Conference, https://www.index.go.kr/potal/main/EachDtlPageDetail.do?idx_cd=1718. Accessed November 30, 2021.

[63] The CCK referred to Article 32, Paragraph 4 of the Constitution of the Republic of Korea as grounds to apply the Principle of Proportionality in that the paragraph particularly asks for gender equality in the sector of employment. Article 32, Paragraph 4 stated as follows:

> Special protection shall be accorded to working women, and they shall not be subject to unjust discrimination in terms of employment, wages and working conditions.

being equally effective. Nevertheless, from the perspective of focusing only on the numbers of veterans who could become public servants because of the extra points, lower percentage of extra points cannot be argued as being equally effective. Nevertheless, it became obvious that it will fail from the next step of the proportionality in the narrow sense because neither women nor disabled persons could become civil servants on one hand, and only veterans could become civil servants on the other hand through the extra point system in question. Thirdly, the CCK assesses whether such discriminatory treatments are proportional to the weight of the legislative objectives. To assess the proportionality, the CCK emphasizes the two points: A large number of women are affected by this law. The effect of the given benefit is crucial to the result of the examination. Adding extra points of 5% or 3% to the total score by each subject is a decisive influencing factor in terms of passing or failing the examinations.

Considering such analysis of the proportionality, the CCK seems to interpret Article 32 (4) of the Constitution as a "special equality clause" compared to the general equality clause of Article 11, Paragraph 1.[64] What are the differences between special clauses and illustrative clauses? If Article 32(4) is interpreted as being an illustrative clause to provide an example of grounds for being treated as equal, it could not be regarded as fulfilling standards to apply the proportionality test. Since the CCK regards Article 32(4) as having constitutional meaning as stricter scrutiny has to be applied in the cases of gender discrimination, stricter proportionality could be applied. In that case, how different is such applicability from standards in finding gender discrimination by the Federal Constitutional Court of Germany? To deal with gender discrimination, the BVerfG has set a stricter scrutiny when stating "discriminatory stipulations. . .are justified only when it is 'absolutely necessary' to solve the problem that can only happen to men or women by nature."[65] Such

---

[64] Article 11 of the Constitution of the Republic of Korea is regarded as general equality clause and read as follows:

> Paragraph 1. All citizens shall be equal before the law, and there shall be no discrimination in political, economic, social or cultural life on account of sex, religion or social status.
> Paragraph 2. No privileged caste shall be recognized or ever established in any form.
> Paragraph 3. The awarding of decorations or distinctions of honor in any form shall be effective only for recipients, and no privileges shall ensue therefrom.

[65] 2 BvR 1870/07, paragraph 18, "Das Geschlecht ist nach Art. 3 Abs. 3 GG grundsätzlich kein zulässiger rechtlicher Anknüpfungspunkt für rechtlich unterschiedliche Behandlung. An das Geschlecht anknüpfende differenzierende Regelungen sind mit Art. 3 Abs. 3 Satz 1 GG nur vereinbar, soweit sie zur Lösung von Problemen, die ihrer Natur nach nur entweder bei Männern oder bei Frauen auftreten können, ***zwingend erforderlich*** sind, oder eine Abwägung mit kollidierendem Verfassungsrecht sie ausnahmsweise legitimiert." (translated in English: Under Article 3.3 of the Basic Law, gender is in principle not a permissible legal connecting factor for legally different treatment. Differentiating provisions based on sex are compatible with Article 3.3 sentence 1 of the Basic Law only insofar as they are ***absolutely necessary*** to solve problems that by their nature can only occur either in men or in women, or if weighing them against conflicting constitutional law legitimizes them by way of exception.) https://www.bundesverfassungsgericht.de/SharedDocs/Entscheidungen/DE/2008/11/rk20081107_2bvr187007.html. Accessed November 30, 2021.

standards imply that it is not enough to apply the prohibition of arbitrariness, and gender equality issues must be dealt with using stricter standards than just the prohibition of arbitrariness.

However, in this case, as *Zoonil Yi*[66] points out, the problem still remains as to how to solve actual existing inequality for veterans because the CCK does not propose any alternatives regarding the problem. However, some could argue that it is no longer the obligation of the Court to do so since it is not enough to find discrimination especially when the decision could lead to another possibility of discrimination. In fact, in Korean society, when this case was decided by the CCK, the conflicts between men and women became intense and men strongly argued that women also have to serve in the military. Furthermore, the CCK could have started a discourse with the aim of overcoming actual, existing inequality for veterans by suggesting some alternative measures. In that sense, it is another task for the CCK to reflect the changing reality and circumstances since it can no longer be justified for men to accept military service as national duty when receiving very low monthly incomes. In reflecting changing contexts, it is time to slowly discuss how to recalculate the disparity between legal equality and actual equality.

On the applicability of the principle of proportionality by the CCK in this case, there are several different opinions. The first opinion[67] is that the CCK applied the proportionality test of the *Trasnsexuelle II*[68] case of the Federal Constitutional Court of Germany. The second opinion[69] is that the CCK applied the standard of strict scrutiny of the US Supreme Court. The Constitutional Court of Korea applies the two standards of the prohibition of arbitrariness and the principle of proportionality in finding the violation of the principle of equality. These double standards are considered[70] similar to the double standards of the "rational basis test" and "strict scrutiny" in the US Supreme Court. On the one hand, the principle of proportionality in the case of Korea does not assess whether the discrimination of "suspect classification" or whether the matter violates the "fundamental rights"[71] of the applicants like the US Supreme Court. On the other hand, the Constitutional Court of Korea does not assess whether the discriminatory treatment in question is discrimination against a group of persons as the German Court does in the case of the *Trasnsexuelle II.*[72] For this reason, it is difficult to state that the CCK has adapted the standards of the equality test either from the US Supreme Court or from the Federal Constitutional Court of Germany. Nevertheless, the CCK has applied the principle of proportionality in this case, and has assessed the equality test according to legitimate aim, suitability, and proportionality in the narrow sense to find violation of the principle of equality.

---

[66] Yi (2001), p. 26.

[67] Jeong (2010), pp. 6–7.

[68] BVerfGE 88,87(96).

[69] Park (2001), p. 83.

[70] Lee (2007), pp. 48–49.

[71] Ibid. pp. 48–49.

[72] BVerfGE 88,87(96).

4.3 The Principle of Non-Discrimination in the US

In this section, the US Supreme court case of *Massachussetss v. Feeny*[73] will be briefly introduced because it deals with a similar issue as the case of the Constitutional Court of Korea introduced in Sect. 4.2.3 above. It is useful to look at the case dealing with similar topics from a comparative perspective in terms of judicial dialogues as well as judicial inspirations. Particularly, as discussed earlier, there are discussions as to whether the CCK has applied the standards of the equality test from the US Supreme Court. Additionally, this case is often referred to as providing counter-arguments by scholars[74] who claim that the extra point system in Korea does not violate the principle of equality. As the CCK applies methods of adjudications not only from Europe including Germany but also from case laws of the US Supreme Court, it would be helpful to analyze the similar case in the US

4.3.1 *Case Study of the US Supreme Court*[75]

Feeny has applied for a competitive civil servant position after 12 years in office as a state civil servant. Although she applied for the exams many times, ultimately, she failed because of the Massachusetts Act to give preference to veterans. According to this Act, all the veterans will be appointed for public office on a priority basis ahead of those who are non-veterans. Unlike the Korean case, this Act applies to those who have been in military service for at least 90 days and have participated for at least one day in warfare regardless of gender. However, the majority who benefit from this Act are men, and the numbers are overwhelming.

The US Supreme Court decided in this case that the Act in question does not discriminate against women in violation of the 14th Amendment regarding the Equality Protection Clause.[76] As reasons for the determination of constitutionality, it was stated that the Act has always been neutral in terms of sexual grammar for veterans. The US Supreme Court interprets the Massachusetts Act in question as one that does not categorize based on gender because the Act has consistently included women who served in the military as veterans. This Act does not categorize men and women, but veterans and non-veterans. Furthermore, the US Supreme Court stresses that this Act disfavors both men and women who are not veterans, and there are many men who are disadvantaged by this Act. However, as the European Court of Human Rights decided in the *D.H.* case,[77] indirect discrimination can be presumed

[73] Personal Administrator of *Massachussetts v. Feeny*, 442 U.S. 256(1979).

[74] For the argument by one of the scholars, please see, Jung (2012), pp. 79–80.

[75] *Personal Administrator of Massachussetts v. Feeny*, 442 U.S. 256(1979).

[76] Ibid. paragraphs 274–275.

[77] European Court of Human Rights, ***D.H. and Others v. The Czech Republic***, Grand Chamber Decision, judgment of 13 November 2007: This case originates in the Czech city of Ostrava, where

even if the law itself is stated as neutral because "large numbers of Roma children were still being placed in special schools" even if the law itself is written in neutral language. The same is true in this case as well since the US Supreme Court has mentioned "the number of men who benefit from this Act is overwhelming." The US Supreme Court should have carried out further assessments as to whether this can be regarded as indirect discrimination instead of coming to a conclusion that indicates the importance of the gender-neutral language of the Act.

4.3.2 Comparative Analysis of the Korean Case

For a similar topic, the two courts of the CCK and the US Supreme Court have decided differently: the CCK regarded it as unconstitutional because the act in question adds 3% to 5% extra points to veterans' scores, and thus it discriminates women from men. Such measures also violate the principle of proportionality. On the other hand, the US Supreme Court has decided such privilege given to veterans does not amount to gender discrimination. The focus of both courts has been different since the Supreme Court takes notice of the "discriminatory objective" of legislators while the CCK[78] pays attention to "discriminatory results" where the numbers of women who passed the examination are considerably low compared to the numbers of men.[79] Additional differences between the two cases are in the standards for applying a stricter scrutiny. The US Supreme Court applied milder scrutiny because a stricter scrutiny can only be applied when legislators intend to discriminate as a legislative objective. Nevertheless, the Constitutional Court of

---

between 1996 and 1999, *Denisa Holubova* and other 17 pupils of Roma origin were assigned to so-called special schools. These primary schools had been originally set up for children with learning difficulties and light mental retardation. Accordingly, graduates of such schools would receive inferior education based on a diluted curriculum. Due to the result of the entrance requirements of the ordinary primary schools and the resulting selection process, prior to 1989 most Roma children in Czech attended special schools. According to data supplied by the applicants, Roma children were 27 times more likely to be placed in a special school than non-Roma children. The Chamber found no violation because the Government had established that the system of special schools had not been introduced solely to cater for Roma children, and the rule governing children's placement in special schools did not refer to the pupils' ethnic origin. However, the Grand Chamber noted that as a *result* of their turbulent history and constant uprooting the Roma had become a specific type of disadvantaged and vulnerable minority, and found violation of principle of non-discrimination. (From Paragraphs 15, 18, 20, and 199.)

[78] Such standards of the CCK are similar to the standards to find indirect discrimination in the DH case of the European Court of Human Rights (European Court of Human Rights, *D.H. and Others v. The Czech Republic*, Grand Chamber Decision, decided on November 13, 2007.) because the CCK found gender discrimination in actually discriminatory results as "almost no women passed the examinations and furthermore, some female applicants failed the exam even if they receive full points from the written examinations because such extra points are given to the discharges soldiers." (The Constitutional Court of Korea, 98 Hun-Ma 363, decided on December 23, 1999.)

[79] For similar arguments, please see Lim (2007).

Korea applies the principle of proportionality as a stricter standard than the prohibition of arbitrariness on the following grounds. Firstly, even if the law does not directly discriminate against women and disabled people, the actual result that neither any women nor any disabled people passed the exam can serve as the ground to find discrimination. Secondly, Article 11(1) of the Korean Constitution[80] explicitly refers to sex as grounds not to discriminate. As such, it is very important both to find violations to apply the principle of proportionality as well as to apply the structured proportionality test with stricter scrutiny.

The *Feeny*[81] case cannot be used as a counter argument to claim that the Korean extra point system does not violate the principle of equality because the US Supreme Court has disregarded the two important matters in its decision. Firstly, the Supreme Court did not apply the strict scrutiny even if the case is related to discrimination based on "suspect classification" of gender and the "fundamental rights"[82] of the applicant's right to work. Secondly, the Supreme Court disregarded the concept of indirect discrimination because the Supreme Court states that a purpose to discriminate is needed to find the violation of the principle of equality rather than the results in a disproportionate impact.[83] However, as discussed in the case of *D.H.* of the ECtHR, if the results have a significantly disproportionate impact, it is recognized as indirect discrimination even if a purpose to discriminate on the basis of sex is not recognized.

4.4 The Principle of Equality in Germany

The Federal Constitutional Court of Germany ("BVerfG") has established standards to determine whether the equality principle is violated or not. Furthermore, it has established some principles such as the prohibition of arbitrariness and the principle of proportionality as determining the justifiability of limitations. It is meaningful to review these principles to promote equality because it affects jurisdictions all over the world, including the Constitutional Court of Korea.

[80] Constitution of the Republic of Korea, Article 11 (1) All citizens shall be equal before the law, and there shall be no discrimination in political, economic, social or cultural life on account of sex, religion or social status.

[81] *Personal Administrator of Massachussetts v. Feeny*, 442 U.S. 256(1979).

[82] Lee (2007), pp. 48–49.

[83] *Personal Administrator of Massachussetts v. Feeny*, 442 U.S. 256(1979).

4.4.1 The Prohibition of Arbitrariness ("Willkürverbot")

The BVerfG has applied the prohibition of arbitrariness as a standard to find violations according to the principle of equality. According to the interpretation by the BVerfG, the prohibition of arbitrariness means that "it violates the principle of equality when it is not possible to find in law as reasonable grounds based on the nature of the acts, especially objective grounds for discrimination."[84] In other words, it violates the prohibition of arbitrariness when some discriminatory measures are legislated to limit equal treatment, and there are no legitimate grounds to justify such discrimination. For example, if a legislator enacts a quota system for women, it could be discrimination against men so that reasonable grounds and explanations for such a quota system are necessary. If legislators set some fixed percentage to treat women favorably without any reasonable grounds to do so, this violates the prohibition of arbitrariness, thus; it violates the principle of equal treatment. In many cases, setting some rigid and fixed quotas to treat some specific group favorably is likely to be decided as unconstitutional.

What are the implications of the prohibition of arbitrariness in terms of the roles of legislators and the courts? By applying the prohibition of arbitrariness in the stage of legislations, the legislative authority could be given a relatively broader margin of appreciation in relation to equality compared to other fundamental rights. By applying the prohibition of arbitrariness, legislators could fulfill their duty of realizing equality regarding the contents of legislations that should correspond to the concept of justice or the legal consensus of the people.[85] It can thus be interpreted that equality in the substance of laws should be implemented in legislation. On judicial control competences, *Sieckmann*[86] argues that the constitutional weakening of the requirement to prohibit arbitrariness can be explained based on a limitation of judicial control competences because the prohibition of arbitrariness only requires factual reasons for differentiation instead of sufficient reasons for differentiation. And the requirement for a rational justification of the norm corresponds to the

[84] In the case of "2 BvR 2340/60" 1. a) states about prohibition of arbitrariness that "Der allgemeine Gleichheitssatz des Art. 3 Abs. 1 GG gebietet, wesentlich Gleiches gleich und wesentlich Ungleiches ungleich zu behandeln (vgl. BVerfGE 1, 14 <52>; 98, 365 <385>; stRspr). Aus ihm ergeben sich je nach Regelungsgegenstand und Differenzierungsmerkmalen unterschiedliche Grenzen für die Ausübung öffentlicher Gewalt, die vom bloßen Willkürverbot bis zu einer strengen Bindung an Verhältnismäßigkeitserfordernisse reichen" (https://www.bundesverfassungsgericht.de/SharedDocs/Entscheidungen/DE/2008/07/rk20080717_2bvr234006.html. Accessed November 30, 2021), which can be interpreted in English as: The general principle of equality in Article 3.1 of the German Basic Law requires that essentially equal things are treated equally and essentially unequal things are treated unequally (see BVerfGE 1, 14 <52>; 98, 365 <385>; stRspr). Depending on the object of regulation and differentiating features, this results in different limits for the exercise of official authority, which range from a mere prohibition of arbitrariness to a strict obligation to comply with proportionality requirements.

[85] Lee (2005), p. 117.

[86] Sieckmann (2018), p. 196.

requirement for a sufficient reason for differentiation, which can be applied by a balancing of conflicting interests.

Equality creates a limit since formal equality includes the prohibition of arbitrariness.[87] The concept of arbitrariness is understood in the German jurisdiction when a measure is actually and clearly unreasonable in relation to the situation it is intended to deal with.[88] Furthermore, the prohibition of arbitrariness is violated when the irrelevance of the differentiation is evident.[89] The prohibition of arbitrariness examines whether there are reasonable grounds in different treatments when deciding whether the measure violates the principle of equality or not. Such characteristics have allowed wide margins of appreciation to legislators and have limited judicial control competences to constitutional courts because constitutional courts can only control serious inequalities which are completely unreasonable. The Constitutional Court of Korea has accepted the prohibition of arbitrariness from the Federal Constitutional Court of Germany for finding violations of the principle of equality.

4.4.2 The Principle of Proportionality ("Verhältnismäßigkeit")

The objective of this section is to briefly introduce how the Federal Constitutional Court of Germany applies the Principle of Proportionality in deciding the principle of equality. A more important theme is how the Constitutional Court of Korea applied the principle of proportionality to its case laws, which will be discussed in more detail in the following section (Sect. 4.4). If the prohibition of arbitrariness is violated, the measures are regarded as not fulfilling the principle of equality. However, fulfilling the prohibition of arbitrariness does not directly mean conforming to the principle of equality. In this case, the principle of proportionality is required to test whether the means taken are in proportional relation to attain the objective.

In the case of *Transsexuelle II*, the Federal Constitutional Court of Germany applied the principle of proportionality when stating "the more the unequal treatment of persons or facts can have a detrimental effect on the exercise of freedoms protected by fundamental rights, the narrower the limits on the legislature's scope of action."[90] Such a statement can be interpreted as meaning that the principle of

---

[87] Sieckmann (2018), p. 244.

[88] BVerfGE 89, 1 - Besitzrecht des Mieters, Beschluß des Ersten Senats vom 26. Mai 1993 - 1 BvR 208/93 – "tatsächlich und eindeutig unangemessen sei" (paragraph 39).

[89] BVerfGE 88, 87 – Transsexuelle II, Beschluß des Ersten Senats vom 26. Jan 1993 - 1 BvR 38, 40 43/92 – "wenn die Unsachlichkeit der Differenzierung evident ist." (paragraph 36).

[90] BVerfGE 88, 87 – Transsexuelle II, Beschluß des Ersten Senats vom 26. Jan 1993 - 1 BvR 38, 40 43/92 – "wenn die Unsachlichkeit der Differenzierung evident ist" (paragraph 35): "Überdies sind dem Gestaltungsspielraum des Gesetzgebers um so engere Grenzen gesetzt, je stärker sich die Ungleichbehandlung von Personen oder Sachverhalten auf die Ausübung grundrechtlich geschützter Freiheiten nachteilig auswirken kann."

proportionality will apply as a stricter test than the prohibition of arbitrariness in the case where discriminatory treatment impacts the exercise of freedoms and fundamental rights. Furthermore, in this case, the Court pointed out the limitation of the prohibition of arbitrariness as a standard because "a violation of Article 3.1 of the Basic Law can only be established if the irrelevance of the differentiation is evident."[91] The Court implies the applicability of the proportionality as a stricter standard than the prohibition of arbitrariness especially in the case of "different treatment of groups of persons" or "a detrimental effect on exercising fundamental rights."[92] This is in line with *Sieckmann*'s argument of weighing conflicting concerns and sufficient reasons are needed for justification of differentiation.[93]

In this second transsexual decision ("*Transsexuelle II*"), the BVerfG suggested the criteria for applying strict proportionality tests. Additionally, the principle of proportionality will be applied in the case of discrimination against groups of persons. When groups of persons are discriminated against, and the grounds for discrimination are more similar to the grounds stated in Article 3, Paragraph 3 of German Basic Law and therefore such discrimination is regarded as unfair treatment against a minority, the intensity of scrutiny will increase and the demand for justification will be stricter. However, despite discrimination against groups of persons, if grounds to discriminate are not related to the characteristics of such groups of persons, the intensity of scrutiny will be between that of the prohibition of arbitrariness and strict standards. The principle of proportionality applies in cases of discrimination against groups of persons, as well as certain unfavorable treatments having negative impacts on compliance with other fundamental rights.

In terms of the cases being strengthened with the principle of proportionality, the BVerfG states such cases as: (1) the criteria of different treatment being more related with particular groups of individuals, and such different treatment is less dependent on situations or factual circumstances, (2) the more the criteria used for the unequal treatment resembles the prohibited criteria mentioned in Article 3, Paragraph 3 in German Basic Law as leading to discrimination against a minority, (3) the affected person having less influence on, (4) unequal treatment making the exercise of freedoms that are protected as fundamental rights more difficult.[94] On the applications of the principle of proportionality, the BVerfG states that "differentiations always require justification using factual reasons that are appropriate to the objective and the extent of the unequal treatment. A constitutional standard of review applies,

[91] Ibid. (paragraph 36): "Kommt als Maßstab nur das Willkürverbot in Betracht, so kann ein Verstoß gegen Art. 3 Abs. 1 GG nur festgestellt werden, wenn die Unsachlichkeit der Differenzierung evident ist."

[92] Ibid. (paragraph 36): "Dagegen prüft das Bundesverfassungsgericht bei Regelungen, die Personengruppen verschieden behandeln oder sich auf die Wahrnehmung von Grundrechten nachteilig auswirken, im einzelnen nach, ob für die vorgesehene Differenzierung Gründe von solcher Art und solchem Gewicht bestehen, daß sie die ungleichen Rechtsfolgen rechtfertigen können."

[93] Sieckmann (2018), p. 196.

[94] Rabe (2001), pp. 186–187.

when oriented to the principle of proportionality applicable here, the content and limits of which cannot be determined in abstract terms, but only according to the various factual and regulatory areas."[95]

In the case of *Nachtarbeitsverbot*, the Federal Constitutional Court of Germany applies the principle of proportionality in the matter of equality. In this case, the Court decided that "unequal treatment based on sex is only compatible ... as it is absolutely necessary to solve problems which, by their nature, can only occur either with men or with women."[96] This case confirms that the BVerfG applies the principle of proportionality when there is discriminatory treatment against a group of persons. In the case of *Risikostrukturausgleich*, the Federal Constitutional Court of Germany applied the principle of proportionality in finding the violation of the general principle of equality in Article 3 (1) of the Basic Law. Firstly, the Court assesses the legitimate aim as stating that "the objectives pursued by the legislator of the Health Structure Act with the introduction of risk structure compensation are legitimate."[97] Secondly, the test of suitability has been applied as "the resources used by the risk structure compensation are suitable for achieving the legislative goals."[98] Third, the Court applies the test of necessity to assess whether there are means which are equally suitable and can be considered to be milder.[99] Lastly, the Court applies the principle of proportionality in the narrow sense by stating that "in an overall weighing of the severity of the encroachment and the weight and urgency of the reasons justifying it, the limit of what is reasonable must be maintained."[100] As seen from the examples of case law, the Federal Constitutional Court of Germany applies the principle of proportionality in finding a violation of the principle of equality in specific cases of discriminatory treatment against a group of persons.

[95] 2 BvR 1961/10, paragraph 27, "Differenzierungen bedürfen jedoch stets der Rechtfertigung durch Sachgründe, die dem Ziel und dem Ausmaß der Ungleichbehandlung angemessen sind. Dabei gilt ein stufenloser am Grundsatz der Verhältnismäßigkeit orientierter verfassungsrechtlicher Prüfungsmaßstab, dessen Inhalt und Grenzen sich nicht abstrakt, sondern nur nach den jeweils betroffenen unterschiedlichen Sach- und Regelungsbereichen bestimmen lassen." https://www.bundesverfassungsgericht.de/SharedDocs/Entscheidungen/DE/2015/09/rk20150930_2bvr196110.html. Accessed November 30, 2021.

[96] BVerfGE 85, 191 - Nachtarbeitsverbot, paragraph 56: "Allerdings verstößt nicht jede Ungleichbehandlung, die an das Geschlecht anknüpft, gegen Art. 3 Abs. 3 GG. Differenzierende Regelungen können vielmehr zulässig sein, soweit sie zur Lösung von Problemen, die ihrer Natur nach nur entweder bei Männern oder bei Frauen auftreten können, zwingend erforderlich sind." https://www.servat.unibe.ch/dfr/bv085191.html. Accessed November 30, 2021.

[97] BVerfGE 113, 167 - Nachtarbeitsverbot, paragraph 167: "Die vom Gesetzgeber des Gesundheitsstrukturgesetzes mit der Einführung des Risikostrukturausgleichs verfolgten Ziele sind legitim." https://www.servat.unibe.ch/dfr/bv113167.html. Accessed November 30, 2021.

[98] Ibid. paragraph 173: "Die vom Risikostrukturausgleich eingesetzten Mittel sind zur Erreichung der gesetzgeberischen Ziele geeignet."

[99] Ibid. paragraph 242: "Die Zahlung von Bundeszuschüssen gemäß Art. 120 Abs. 1 Satz 4 GG an einzelne Krankenkassen mit schlechter Risikostruktur kommt als milderes Mittel nicht in Betracht."

[100] Ibid. paragraph 248: "Bei einer Gesamtabwägung zwischen der Schwere des Eingriffs und dem Gewicht und der Dringlichkeit der ihn rechtfertigenden Gründe muss die Grenze des Zumutbaren gewahrt bleiben."

4.5 Anti-Discrimination Law

Anti-Discrimination Law is the law where the principle of non-discrimination is conceptualized. In the section, some anti-discrimination laws and legislations will be reviewed so that they function as positive references for further legislation in Korea where there is no comprehensive anti-discrimination legislation. I will introduce EU Anti-Discrimination Law[101] first because it has been referred to as one of the main references in promoting legislation of the Anti-Discrimination Law in Korea. Subsequently, German Equality Law and British Equality Law will be discussed. I have specifically selected these two laws because firstly, these laws are national legislations, which could provide good references for future legislation of Korean anti-discrimination laws, and secondly, these two laws are included as important sources of comparative anti-discrimination legislation for the research by the Korean Ministry of Justice[102] for the future Korean anti-discrimination legislation.

4.5.1 EU Anti-Discrimination Law[103]

The year 2000 is considered the birth year of EU anti-discrimination law with the adoption of two major Equality Directives.[104] The grounds for race and ethnicity were introduced by the Race Equality Directive, and the grounds for religion, sexual orientation, age, and disability were introduced by the Framework Equality Directive.[105] Article 1 of the Race Equality Directive (Council Directive 2000/43/EC of 29 June 2000) clarifies the objective of the Directive as being "to lay down a framework for combating discrimination on the grounds of racial or ethnic origin,

---

[101] Even if the title and the topic of this work is not EU law but the case law of the ECtHR, I decided to introduce EU legislations because it may be motivation to find suggestions for South Korea to legislate Anti-Discrimination law and the principles of EU law determine the case law of the ECtHR. Above all, several academic articles introduce EU Directive as comparative references to promote legislating Anti-Discrimination Law in Korea (i.e., Kim 2014, pp. 177–179; Shin 2008a, pp. 210–222).

[102] Ministry of Justice of Korea (2008).

[103] "Anti-discrimination law" has been known as having originated from the US doctrine, EU anti-discrimination law is used in literature and law courses around the world with the same concept of "EU law of equal opportunities," "EU equality law," and "EU non-discrimination law" (taken from Belavusau and Henrard 2019, p. 615).

[104] Council Directive 2000/43, Implementing the Principle of Equal Treatment between Persons Irrespective of Racial or Ethnic Origin, 2000 ("Race Equality Directive") and Directive 2000/78, Establishing a General Framework for Equal Treatment in Employment and Occupation, 2000 ("Framework Equality Directive").

[105] Belavusau and Henrard (2019), p. 615.

with a view to putting into effect in the Member States the principle of equal treatment." Articles 2 and 3[106] clarify which situations are regarded as existing discrimination. What is unique about this Directive is that Member States can define the concept of harassment in accordance with the national laws and practice of the Member States in Article 2, Paragraph 3. The scope reaches both public and private sectors including public bodies, and the stipulation extensively relates to conditions for access to employment, access to all types and to all levels of vocational activities, conditions of dismissals, working conditions, social protection, education, and even access to housing (Article 3, Paragraph 1). Chapter 2 states "Remedies and Enforcement" including "defense of rights" (Article 7), "burden of proof" (Article 8), and "dialogue with non-governmental organizations" (Article 12). This Directive is regarded as a rather general guideline for Member States regarding racial and ethnic discrimination. Thus, it is necessary for each Member State to provide separate and concrete regulations according to their own specific situations. However, this Directive has a positive aspect in that it plays the role of a comprehensive rule. In addition, it serves as a standard for individual cases and Member States may be forced to abide by a fixed time limit. Notably, this Directive actually triggered Member States to enact comprehensive non-discrimination laws.

Another important piece of EU anti-discrimination legislation is the Framework Equality Directive (Council Directive 2000/78/EC of 27 November 2000) establishing a general framework for equal treatment in employment and occupation. This Directive prohibits discrimination based on religion or belief, disability, age or *sexual orientation*, and it covers a much wider scope of protection compared to the previous anti-racism directive. Article 1 clarifies the purpose of this Directive as "to lay down a general framework for combating discrimination on the grounds of religion or belief, disability, age or sexual orientation as regards employment and

[106] Council Directive 2000/43/EC of 29 June 2000

Article 2 Concept of discrimination 1. For the purposes of this Directive, the principle of equal treatment shall mean that there shall be no direct or indirect discrimination based on racial or ethnic origin.

Article 3. Scope 1. Within the limits of the powers conferred upon the Community, this Directive shall apply to all persons, as regards both the public and private sectors, including public bodies, in relation to: (a) conditions for access to employment, to self-employment and to occupation, including selection criteria and recruitment conditions, whatever the branch of activity and at all levels of the professional hierarchy, including promotion; (b) access to all types and to all levels of vocational guidance, vocational training, advanced vocational training and retraining, including practical work experience; (c) employment and working conditions, including dismissals and pay; (d) membership of and involvement in an organization of workers or employers, or any organization whose members carry on a particular profession, including the benefits provided for by such organizations; (e) social protection, including social security and healthcare; (f) social advantages; (g) education; (h) access to and supply of goods and services which are available to the public, including housing.

occupation, with a view to putting into effect in the Member States the principle of equal treatment." Article 2 stipulates the concept of discrimination, and clarifies that the "principle of equal treatment shall mean that there shall be no direct or indirect discrimination" based on any grounds according to Article 1. Furthermore, Article 2, Paragraph 5 as exceptional provisions stipulates that "this Directive shall be without prejudice to measures laid down by national law which, in a democratic society, are necessary for public security, for the maintenance of public order and the prevention of criminal offences, for the protection of health and for the protection of the rights and freedoms of others."

Directive 2002/73/EC of the European Parliament and of the Council of 23 September 2002 is the amended form from Council Directive 76/207/EEC on the implementation of the principle of equal treatment for men and women regarding access to employment, vocational training and promotion, and working conditions to implement gender equality. Article 2, Paragraph 2 defines direct discrimination, indirect discrimination, harassment, and sexual harassment.[107] In addition, Article 6[108] states that "Member States shall ensure that judicial and/or administrative

---

[107] Council Directive 2002/73/EC of the European Parliament and of the Council of 23 September 2002

2. For the purposes of this Directive, the following definitions shall apply:

- direct discrimination: where one person is treated less favorably on grounds of sex than another is, has been or would be treated in a comparable situation,
- indirect discrimination: where an apparently neutral provision, criterion or practice would put persons of one sex at a particular disadvantage compared with persons of the other sex, unless that provision, criterion or practice is objectively justified by a legitimate aim, and the means of achieving that aim are appropriate and necessary,
- harassment: where an unwanted conduct related to the sex of a person occurs with the purpose or effect of violating the dignity of a person, and of creating an intimidating, hostile, degrading, humiliating or offensive environment,
- sexual harassment: where any form of unwanted verbal, non-verbal or physical conduct of a sexual nature occurs, with the purpose or effect of violating the dignity of a person, in particular when creating an intimidating, hostile, degrading, humiliating or offensive environment.

[108] Article 6, Council Directive 2002/73/EC

Article 6 shall be replaced by the following: "Article 6

1. Member States shall ensure that judicial and/or administrative procedures, including where they deem it appropriate conciliation procedures, for the enforcement of obligations under this Directive are available to all persons who consider themselves wronged by failure to apply the principle of equal treatment to them, even after the relationship in which the discrimination is alleged to have occurred has ended.
2. Member States shall introduce into their national legal systems such measures as are necessary to ensure real and effective compensation or reparation as the Member States so determine for the loss and damage sustained by a person injured as a result of discrimination contrary to Article 3, in a way which is dissuasive and proportionate to the damage suffered; such compensation or reparation may not be restricted by the fixing

procedures, including where they deem it appropriate conciliation procedures" for "all persons who consider themselves wronged by failure to apply the principle of equal treatment to them" along with "real and effective compensation for reparation." Another Directive to promote gender equality is Council Directive 2004/113/EC of 13 December 2004, supplementing Directive 2002/73/EC as providing equal treatment in the non-employment related sectors as well. This Directive is to "lay down a framework for combating discrimination based on sex in access to and supply of goods and services, with a view to putting into effect in the Member States the principle of equal treatment between men and women." (Article 1)

Nevertheless, some shortcomings have been pointed out since the 2000 adoption of the EU Equality Directives.[109] Firstly, jurisprudence disproportionality exists among grounds of discrimination in the Court of Justice of the EU ("CJEU"). From 2000 until 2018, the CJEU decided a substantive number of cases on the grounds of age and disability, far fewer regarding sexual orientation, and scarcely any with regard to race and religion. Secondly, the material and personal scope of the two 2000 Equality Directives is unequal because the 2000 Directives are significantly different in their scope. The Framework Equality Directive is limited to the matter of employment, while the Race Equality Directive covers "social protection, including social security and health care, education, and access to goods and services available to the public, such as housing" (Article 3). In addition, Member States' resistance to implementing these directives is also considered a problem since a number of countries delayed the implementation of the directives.[110] Despite the stated problem, the EU anti-discrimination law is evaluated as offering one of the highest standards of protection from a comparative law perspective,[111] which is a positive aspect of the EU anti-discrimination law.

of a prior upper limit, except in cases where the employer can prove that the only damage suffered by an applicant as a result of discrimination within the meaning of this Directive is the refusal to take his/her job application into consideration.

3. Member States shall ensure that associations, organizations or other legal entities which have, in accordance with the criteria laid down by their national law, a legitimate interest in ensuring that the provisions of this Directive are complied with, may engage, either on behalf or in support of the complainants, with his or her approval, in any judicial and/or administrative procedure provided for the enforcement of obligations under this Directive.
4. Paragraphs 1 and 3 are without prejudice to national rules relating to time limits for bringing actions as regards the principle of equal treatment."

[109] Belavusau and Henrard (2019), pp. 625–635.

[110] Ibid. p. 615.

[111] Ibid. p. 635.

4.5.2 *German Equality Law*[112]

In Germany, as in other countries including Korea, individual anti-discrimination legislations existed according to particular grounds for discrimination until The General Equal Treatment Act (Allgemeines Gleichbehandlungsgesetz, "AGG") in 2006. Of course, Article 3, Paragraph 3 of German Basic Law also states the principle of non-discrimination that "no one shall be favored or disfavored because of sex, parentage, race, language, homeland and origin, faith, or religious or political opinions. No person shall be disfavored because of disability." In addition, Section 75, paragraph 1 of the Works Constitution Act ("Betriebsverfassungsgesetz" in German) stipulates equal treatment regardless of grounds such as "race, ethnic origin, descent or other origin, nationality, religion or belief, disability, age, political or trade union activities or convictions or on the grounds of *gender or sexual identity*." In the meantime, there have been a number of attempts to meet the need for a general anti-discrimination law, which was finally enacted in 2006. The original name of the act was changed to The General Equal Treatment Act from The Anti-discrimination Act ("Antidiskriminierungsgesetz") to alleviate the opposition to the strong tone of the name.[113] A general and comprehensive anti-discrimination law has gone through a rather difficult compromising process.

The legislative purpose of this Act is "to prevent or to stop discrimination on the grounds of race or ethnic origin, gender, religion or belief, disability, age, or sexual orientation." (Section 1, Purpose) Section 3[114] defines important concepts related to

---

[112] "The General Equal Treatment Act" Allgemeines Gleichbehandlungsgesetz, "AGG."

[113] Fuchs (2006), p. 377 onwards. (The AGG was adopted on 29 June 2006. The law came into force on August 18, 2006, after being signed off by the Federal President *Horst Köhler* in accordance with Article 82 (1) S.1 German Basic Law. This marked the end of a long process of implementing the anti-discrimination directives, which was accompanied by fierce controversy inside Germany.)

[114] General Equal Treatment Act, Section 3, Definitions

(1) Direct discrimination shall be taken to occur where one person is treated less favorably than another is, has been or would be treated in a comparable situation on any of the grounds referred to under Section 1. Direct discrimination on grounds of sex shall also be taken to occur in relation to Section 2(1) No. 1 to 4 in the event of the less favorable treatment of a woman on account of pregnancy or maternity.

(2) Indirect discrimination shall be taken to occur where an apparently neutral provision, criterion or practice would put persons at a particular disadvantage compared with other persons on any of the grounds referred to under Section 1, unless that provision, criterion or practice is objectively justified by a legitimate aim and the means of achieving that aim are appropriate and necessary.

(3) Harassment shall be deemed to be discrimination when an unwanted conduct in connection with any of the grounds referred to under Section 1 takes place with the purpose or effect of violating the dignity of the person concerned and of creating an intimidating, hostile, degrading, humiliating, or offensive environment.

(4) Sexual harassment shall be deemed to be discrimination in relation to Section 2(1) Nos. 1 to 4, when an unwanted conduct of a sexual nature, including unwanted sexual acts and requests to carry out sexual acts, physical contact of a sexual nature, comments of a sexual nature, as well as the unwanted showing or public exhibition of pornographic

discrimination: Direct discrimination (Section 3, Paragraph 1), Indirect discrimination (Section 3, Paragraph 2), Harassment (Section 3, Paragraph 3), and Sexual harassment (Section 3, Paragraph 4). In addition, "An instruction to discriminate against a person on any of the grounds referred to under Section 1 shall be deemed discrimination (Section 3, Paragraph 5). By specifically explaining the concept of discrimination in this way as stipulated in Section 3, ambiguous situations have been minimized. In other words, it strives to include a precise definition of the legal meaning of discrimination in a general and comprehensive anti-discrimination law, which is considered a very important part of the nature of such a law.

The principle of proportionality applies to justify differences in application in this Act. The law provided for exceptions to discrimination when there are occupational requirements that meet certain conditions: Section 8 (Permissible difference of Treatment on grounds of occupational requirements), Section 9 (Permissible difference of Treatment on grounds of religion or belief), and Section 10 (Permissible difference of treatment on grounds of age). These provisions state that differences in application is only permissible when the objective of different treatment is legitimate (legitimate aim), and such different treatment is suitable to attain such legitimate objective (suitability). For such different treatments to be justified, there must be "particular occupational activities" (Section 8, Paragraph 1[115]), which corresponds to a test of the necessity of the principle of proportionality.

The implications of the Act are as follows: Firstly, this law prohibits discrimination in all aspects that law regulates. It stipulates issues of equality that can be displayed in all aspects of the law, in terms of gender equality and grounds for not being discriminated against such as race, ethnic groups, religion, worldview, sexual orientation, age, etc. As such, it provides unified criteria for anti-discrimination. Secondly, compensation for damages allows not only material damages but also non-material damages. Such possibilities are very important in providing effective remedies. In many cases of discrimination, material damages are not enough to provide meaningful remedies for victims. Thirdly, the powers of the employee's

images, takes place with the purpose or effect of violating the dignity of the person concerned, in particular where it creates an intimidating, hostile, degrading, humiliating or offensive environment.

(5) An instruction to discriminate against a person on any of the grounds referred to under Section 1 shall be deemed as discrimination. Such an instruction shall in particular be taken to occur in relation to Section 2(1) Nos 1 to 4 where a person instructs an employee to conduct which discriminates or can discriminate against another employee on one of the grounds referred to under Section 1.

[115]General Equal Treatment Act, Section 8, Permissible Difference of Treatment On Grounds of Occupational Requirements

Paragraph 1. A difference of treatment on any of the grounds referred to under Section 1 shall not constitute discrimination where, by reason of the nature of the particular occupational activities or of the context in which they are carried out, such grounds constitute a genuine and determining occupational requirement, provided that the objective is legitimate and the requirement is proportionate.

council and the personnel committee were strengthened. Some provisions to prohibit discrimination arise under civil law contracts, which are very meaningful considering there are many cases of discrimination in the context of civil contracts.[116] Despite some criticisms[117] of the Act, public awareness of the working potential and the discrimination against older people was raised because an amendment to this Act in 2006 explicitly forbids discrimination on the basis of gender, origin, or age.[118] Furthermore, this German Act is evaluated positively especially in the discrimination based on race or ethnic origin because discrimination on the basis of nationality is generally regarded as possible indirect discrimination unlike the law of other Member States such as Estonia which does not provide protection against discrimination on the basis of citizenship.[119]

4.5.3 British Equality Law[120]

In the United Kingdom, all existing non-discrimination laws according to specific grounds for discrimination were abolished, and the content of such laws was included in the details of a newly enacted equality law in 2010. The new equality law serves as a general as well as comprehensive anti-discrimination legislation. One of the most important features of the Equality Act of 2010 regards age, disability, gender reassignment, marriage and civil partnership, pregnancy and maternity, race, religion or belief, sex, and *sexual orientation* as protected characteristics (Chapter 1, Section 4. The protected characteristics). *Sexual orientation* in particular is defined in Section 12[121] in detail. The main content of the Act includes types of

[116]Shin (2008b), p. 27.

[117]Prof. Dr. *Martin Diller* pointed out the central problem with AGG is age discrimination because a general belief to give older employees advantages before the law came into force is now considered as unequal treatment of young workers without objective and reasonable grounds (taken from Legal Tribune Online (2016), Zehn Jahre Antidiskriminierungsgesetz, https://www.lto.de/recht/hintergruende/h/zehn-jahre-agg-kritik/. Accessed November 30, 2021). Another criticism has been arisen in that the protection of the AGG does not apply to areas governed by public law even if discrimination is still prohibited in this context. And the Act provides protection in the field of education only to the extent that private contracts are involved (taken from Federal Anti-Discrimination Agency 2019, pp. 30–31).

[118]Caliendo and Hogennacker (2012), p. 17.

[119]European Commission (2009), pp. 74–75.

[120]The Equality Act 2010 (latest version available: https://www.legislation.gov.uk/ukpga/2010/15/contents. Accessed November 30, 2021.

[121]Equality Act 2010, http://www.legislation.gov.uk/ukpga/2010/15/section/12. Accessed November 30, 2021, Section 12. Sexual orientation.

(1) Sexual orientation means a person's sexual orientation towards—(a) persons of the same sex, (b) persons of the opposite sex, or (c) persons of either sex.
(2) In relation to the protected characteristic of sexual orientation—(a) a reference to a person who has a particular protected characteristic is a reference to a person who is of a

discrimination, prohibited conduct, non-discrimination measures in public services and functions, and positive actions.

Chapter 2 of the Act explicitly prohibits direct discrimination (Section 13) and indirect discrimination (Section 19). Direct discrimination is defined as "a person (A) discriminated against another (B) if, because of a protected characteristic, A treats B less favorably than A treats or would treat others." (Section 13, Paragraph 1) Generally, such direct discrimination is strictly prohibited. However, if the protected characteristic of direct discrimination is age, the principle of proportionality will apply when assessing whether such discrimination is considered proportionate means to attain legitimate aim.[122] On racial discrimination, "less favorable treatment includes segregating B from others." (Section 13, Paragraph 5) Especially, if the protected characteristic is gender, Section 13, Paragraph 6(a) specifically stipulates that it is discrimination if a woman receives less favorable treatment because she is breast-feeding. On the other hand, men cannot consider any special treatment to a woman regarding her pregnancy or childbirth as discrimination against them (Section 13, Paragraph 6(b)). In addition, the Act combines two relevant protected characteristics, and the victim can claim "combined discrimination: dual characteristics" in Section 14. This introduction of a combined discrimination clause is considered to be the concept of intersectionality[123] to protect victims from discrimination not on one single ground but on two grounds. Indirect discrimination is prohibited in the relevant protected characteristics of age, disability, gender reassignment, marriage and civil partnership, race, religion or belief, sex, and sexual orientation (Section 19, Paragraph 3).

Part 11 states the obligation of non-discrimination or equal treatment by public sectors in the advancement of equality. In Section 149, Paragraph 1, it is stated that "a public authority must, in the exercise of its functions, have *due regard* to the need to (a) eliminate discrimination, harassment, victimization and any other conduct that is prohibited by or under this Act; (b) advance equality of opportunity between persons who share a relevant protected characteristic and persons who do not share it; (c) foster *good relations* between persons who share a relevant protected characteristic and persons who do not share it." By stipulating the proper obligations of public institutions in the law very specifically, it can be said that the will to realize

---

particular sexual orientation; (b) a reference to persons who share a protected characteristic is a reference to persons who are of the same sexual orientation."

[122] Equality Act 2010, http://www.legislation.gov.uk/ukpga/2010/15/part/2. Accessed November 30, 2021, Section 13, Direct discrimination, Paragraph 2:

> If the protected characteristic is age, A does not discriminate against B if A can show A's treatment of B to be a proportionate means of achieving a legitimate aim.

[123] "Coined by *Kimberle Crenshaw* in 1989, the term intersectionality has become the key analytic framework through which feminist scholars in various fields talk about the structural identities of race, class, gender, and sexuality. Intersectionality emerged in the late 1980s as an analytic frame capable of attending to the particular positionality of black women and other women of color both in civil rights law and within civil rights movements" (taken from Cooper 2015).

the objective of this act is to eliminate discriminatory acts. In other words, it has been stipulated in as detailed as possible in order that superficial provisions would not detract from the original meaning of the enactment of law by unclear interpretation and application.

What are the significance and features of the 2010 Equality Act? This Act does not include the right of the National Commission on Human Rights to issue corrections, or the use of punitive damages, or the obligation to provide information related to discrimination in the sector of employment.[124] However, some very powerful measures are included in this Act such as references by a court to an employment tribunal (Part 9, Chapter 3, 122), the tribunal's powers to make wider recommendations, the role of the Equality and Human Rights Commission, and the ability of country courts to issue injunctions.[125] In addition, it is considered to be a positive means to deal with discrimination based on disability: failure to provide conveniences for persons with disabilities is considered to be a discriminatory act. However, some measures should be adopted to implement the principle of equality since the current Act does not define harassments or discriminatory advertising as forms of discrimination.

4.5.4 Legislation of Anti-Discrimination Law in Korea

South Korea does not yet have a general and comprehensive anti-discrimination law . There are discrimination-related laws, including the "Anti-discrimination against and Remedies for Persons with Disabilities Act,"[126] the "Equal Employment Opportunity and Work-Family Balance Assistance Act,"[127] the "Gender Equality Law,"[128] and the "Act on prohibition of age discrimination in employment and promoting elderly employment."[129] As such, there are laws to prohibit discrimination on

---

[124] Shim (2017), pp. 74–75.

[125] Authority of the House of Lords (2016), The Equality Act 2010: The Impact on Disabled People, Report of Session 2015-16, paragraph 423. https://publications.parliament.uk/pa/ld201516/ldselect/ldeqact/117/117.pdf. Accessed November 30, 2021.

[126] This Act was enacted on April 10, 2007 and has been in force since April 11, 2008. For details about this act, please *see* Woo et al. (2013).

[127] This Act was enacted in 1987 under the constitutional principle of gender equality, and is the first enactment to prohibit discrimination with employment opportunity. For details about this act, please see Park (2017).

[128] Initially it was enacted as "Framework Act on Women's Development" on December 30, 1995 and enforced on July 1, 1996 with the aim of promoting equality between men and women in all the areas of politics, economy, society and culture by stipulating fundamental rules with regard to the obligation, etc. of the State and local governments for realization of equality between men and women under the Constitution of the Republic of Korea (Article 1).

[129] Initially, the Act on promoting elderly employment was enacted on December 31, 1991 and has been in force since July 1, 1992. For some comparative aspect regarding the age discrimination act, please see Jung and Lee (2012), pp. 118–142.

particular grounds Accordingly, the National Human Rights Commission of Korea proposed a general and comprehensive anti-discrimination law to the prime minister in 2006 with a bill of recommendation, and the Ministry of Justice has since proposed an anti-discrimination law. Later, many legislators launched non-discrimination bills, all of which have since been abandoned according to Article 51[130] of the Korean Constitution.

I argue that Korea needs to enact a general and comprehensive anti-discrimination law to prohibit discrimination against social minorities in a more effective way. Currently, only individual anti-discrimination laws exist. Nevertheless, such individual anti-discrimination laws cannot protect the victims of multiple discrimination or intersectional discrimination because each individual anti-discrimination law covers only a single ground for discrimination. For example, how can individual anti-discrimination laws protect a victim who suffers discrimination on the grounds of gender, sexual orientation, age, and working status? Therefore, a comprehensive anti-discrimination law is needed, and different types of discrimination such as indirect discrimination, multiple discrimination, and intersectional discrimination should be defined as the scope of protection. Thus, despite the need for a general and comprehensive anti-discrimination law in Korea, further discussions to legislate a comprehensive anti-discrimination law have not yet been successful. In this sense, reviewing the non-discrimination laws of the EU, Germany, and the United Kingdom would have a positive impact to further discussions on non-discrimination law in Korea.

Some may ask why it is so important to have a general and comprehensive anti-discrimination law in Korea because there are already discrimination-related laws according to particular grounds for discrimination. It might be argued that such an exhaustive list of particular grounds can be extended by the notion of intersectionality[131] through combining grounds existing in the exhaustive list. However, the protection is still lacking compared to a comprehensive anti-discrimination law. This is true even if in the jurisdiction where a comprehensive anti-discrimination law such as the Court of Justice of the European Union is in force,

[130] Article 51 of the Korean Constitution states as follows: "Bills and other matters submitted to the National Assembly for deliberation shall not be abandoned on the ground that they were not acted upon during the session in which they were introduced, except in case where the term of the members of the National Assembly has expired." According to this Article, all of non-discrimination bills have been abandoned with the expiry of the members of the National Assembly, who have submitted those bills.

[131] The grounds of discrimination are regarded as being "extended in practice by the notion of *intersectionality* whereby the Committee addresses situations of double or multiple discrimination such as discrimination on grounds of gender or religion when discrimination on such a ground appears to exist in combination with a ground or grounds listed in article 1 of the Convention" (please see COMMITTEE ON THE ELIMINATION OF RACIAL DISCRIMINATION (2009): General Recommendation No. 32 – The meaning and scope of special measures in the International Convention on the Elimination of All Forms of Racial Discrimination, para 7, 24 September 2009, CERD/C/GC/32).

"no fully fledged jurisprudential clarification seems to be forthcoming"[132] despite recent engagement with intersectionality. As there are limitations to extend the grounds for discrimination through the concept of intersectionality in the jurisdiction which has a comprehensive anti-discrimination law, it will be more difficult to extend the scope of protection only through interpretation or engagement in the Korean jurisdiction where a comprehensive anti-discrimination law does not exist. A comprehensive law can provide a specific standard to define different types of discrimination, to determine the grounds for discrimination, and to find the violation and remedy it.[133] This is why the absence of a general anti-discrimination law in Korea is problematic. It is impossible to legislate for an individual anti-discrimination law on all the grounds for discrimination. Without a comprehensive anti-discrimination law, the applicability of new types of discrimination has to depend on the interpretation[134] of existing individual laws. As we can see from another example of a comprehensive anti-discrimination law, the German General Equal Treatment Act ("Allgemeine Gleichbehandlungsgesetz" in German), Section 1 of Part 1 General Provisions states the legislative purpose as: "the purpose of this Act is to prevent or to stop discrimination on the grounds of race or ethnic origin, gender, religion or belief, disability, age, or sexual orientation." It explicitly states that the prevention of discrimination and subsequent punishment or elimination of discrimination is the legislative objective of this Act.

Similarly, the presence of such general provisions plays a role in changing society's awareness of discrimination. I argue that awareness of discrimination can be improved by passing a comprehensive Anti-Discrimination Law. Korean society has previously experienced such awareness raising. For example, after the law on child abuse was passed, people began to recognize specific acts as child abuse.[135] This argument is in line with the impact of constitutional litigations as well as that of the courts. People's awareness regarding rights has been affected by the court's activities and jurisprudence.[136] For this reason, I argue that a comprehensive anti-discrimination law will be successful in changing the consciousness of Koreans, which in turn will prohibit discrimination.

Let us take as an example the Korean case where discrimination arises because there are no articles about same-sex marriage. The Constitution of Korea does not have any articles to directly permit or prohibit same-sex marriage. Therefore, whether or not same-sex marriages are allowed must be seen purely as a matter of legal interpretation. In such situations, the basic rights of same-sex couples who seek

[132]Xenidis (2018), p. 43.

[133]Kim (2014), p. 187.

[134]Interpretation can be various according to political, social situation. If protecting a certain minority group is provided for only by the interpretation of law without any specific standards given through a comprehensive anti-discrimination law, the vulnerable group will be put in an unstable situation in terms of protection.

[135]Lee and Kim (2019), pp. 633–635.

[136]Chen (2018), p. 25.

marriage are violated, and it is difficult to find a remedy for discrimination due to legal deficiencies is because there is no general and comprehensive anti-discrimination provision. In other words, if the case is interpreted to prohibit same-sex marriage, discrimination against same-sex couples is left solely to the interpretation of the legislator[137], and the judiciary does not have a positive role to resolve issues of discrimination.

In the absence of explicit articles, there are different interpretations of Article 36, Paragraph 1 of the Constitution to stipulate "marriage and family life shall be entered into and sustained on the basis of individual dignity and equality of the sexes, and the State shall do everything in its power to achieve that goal." Opinions are divided on the interpretation of the expression "equality of the sexes." People who are against same sex marriage interpret marriage as the integration of the two sexes, while people who are for same-sex marriage interpret such expression as enhancing the equality of both sexes. These debates have flowed in a direction which ultimately leaves the most important decisions not to the constitution, but to the sublegal provisions of civil law. However, if the constitutional provision is misinterpreted, same sex marriages are denied, and the rights of same sex couples are violated, so the result fails to find effective remedies to this serious violation of human rights. This cannot be simply regarded as a flaw arising from legislative deficiencies. Therefore, it is very important to introduce a comprehensive anti-discrimination law in Korea.

Additionally, I argue that to include sexual orientation as the ground for prohibition of discrimination in the comprehensive anti-discrimination law is particularly important in relation to protecting sexual minorities in Korean society. Instead, sexual orientation is recognized as a sickness to be cured instead of grounds for discrimination. It is one of the important legislative objectives of a comprehensive anti-discrimination law to protect sexual minorities who have never been protected in Korean society.[138]

4.5.5 Towards Korean Anti-Discrimination Legislations

So far, there have been about 6 legislative bills proposed by the government and different legislators in South Korea.[139] First, there was the proposal by the government in 2007 where indirect discrimination, harassment, and discriminatory advertisement were included in the concept of discrimination. This government proposal included 13 grounds for discrimination, but sexual orientation, gender identity and

[137] Even if it is not the only task of the legislator to interpret constitutional matters, the Korean court has stated that it is the task of the legislator to interpret whether same-sex marriage is allowed or not (taken from Seoul Seo-Bu District Court, 2014 Ho-pa 1842, decided on 6 December 2016).

[138] Kim (2014), pp. 193–194.

[139] Yi (2014), p. 252.

employment related discrimination were not included. As remedies for discriminatory acts, measures included positive actions taken by the courts as well as civil claims for damages. Criminal punishment of any discriminatory acts was also included as restrictions on discrimination. Anti-discrimination legislations proposed by ex-legislator *Hoe-Chan Roh* from the most progressive political party in Korea in the year 2008 define indirect discrimination, harassment and discriminatory advertisement as discrimination, and his bill included sexual orientation, gender identity, and types of employment 22 grounds for discrimination in total. As additional remedies of discriminatory acts, it is proposed that the National Committee of Human Rights can provide support for any related lawsuits. Restrictive measures of discrimination included punitive damage reimbursement, right to order correction by a human rights committee, and an enforcement levy.

All of these legislative bills have been scrapped[140] because the bills were not passed in the sessions, and the term of the members of the National Assembly had expired. The major opposition, not surprisingly has been against *sexual orientation*. The majority conservative power including Christian churches has strongly resisted the idea of the prohibition of discrimination based on sexual orientation. Legislators have considered that Korean society did not have any consensus on protecting sexual minorities or non-discrimination based on sexual orientation. However, discrimination based on sexual orientation is not a subject where social consensus is needed. Instead, it should be seen as a matter of universal human rights. Unfortunately, since 2013 when the last bill for an anti-discrimination law proposed by *Won-Sik Choi* came up, further discussions have stagnated. What is worse is that there are currently no grounds for expecting further progress.

In the absence of a general scope of anti-discrimination laws in Korea, it has become more difficult to protect minorities and vulnerable groups in relatively complex situations that cannot be protected by individual discrimination laws alone. This is especially the case as most discrimination cases that occur in today's society are based on multiple grounds and presented in a complex form such as a female, lesbian, part-time worker based on a short-term contract, or a disabled person is discriminated against in numerous sectors of education and services. Such complex discrimination cannot be easily and effectively corrected without a comprehensive anti-discrimination law.[141] Therefore, there is a need for a comprehensive anti-discrimination law as a general law for individual anti-discrimination laws in Korea.

[140] In the proposed bills in the past, there were some measures such as punitive damages and the right to correct of the Human Rights Committee. Although these measures were regarded as effective, the old bills were discarded and no further discussions on these measures have not been made.

[141] As mentioned previously, even if the concept of "intersectionality" is applied, the scope of protection is expected to be lacking compared to the legislation of a comprehensive anti-discrimination law. For example, even in the European human rights system where a comprehensive anti-discrimination law is inforce, it is argued that "no fully fledged jurisprudential clarification related to intersectionality seem to be forthcoming" (taken from Xenidis 2018, p. 43). Moreover, it will be more difficult to extend the scope of protection only through interpretation to apply the

Under the circumstances where comprehensive anti-discrimination legislation does not exist, there are eight individual discrimination prohibition laws[142] in Korea. Learning what these individual laws consider grounds to prohibit discrimination and in which sectors discrimination is prohibited provides implications on why a comprehensive anti-discrimination legislation is needed in Korea. The first is the "law to prohibit discrimination based on disability." The ground to prohibit discrimination of this law are disability, and the sectors to prohibit discrimination include employment, education, services, and public services. The second is the "law to prohibit discrimination based on age." Age is considered as grounds not to discriminate, and employment is the sector to prohibit discrimination. The third is the "Equal Employment Law." This law regards gender as grounds to prohibit discrimination and employment is the sector covered by this law. The fourth is the "law to prohibit discrimination of temporary workers." This law considers the forms of employment, particularly temporary and non-regular work as the grounds to prohibit discrimination compared to other forms of employment such as full-time and permanent jobs in the sector of employment. The fifth is the "bill to prohibit discrimination of information—disadvantaged group." Under this bill, the information—disadvantaged group is considered those having poor economic, regional, physical or social conditions. The protection scope is on the sector of information and communication services. The sixth is the "bill to promote gender equality." This bill focuses particularly on grounds such as gender, marital status, family status, pregnancy, childbirth, the physical condition of females such as appearance, height, and weight. It is designed to prohibit gender discrimination in the sectors of employment, education, services, social security, and public service. The seventh is the "bill to prohibit discrimination based on academic background." The aim of this bill is to not discriminate against people based on their educational background. Since there are rankings of universities in Korea, this law is to not discriminate on the grounds of which schools or universities people are from in the sectors of employment, granting national qualifications, educational institution, and vocational training. The last is the "Bill to prohibit discrimination based on region of origin." This bill considers particular tendencies of preferences according to the region of origin in Korea in the employment and education sectors.

Similarly, discrimination laws based on particular grounds in South Korea are mainly focused on the employment sector and tend to keep silent about protecting measures in the field of both services and education.[143] When putting comprehensive anti-discrimination law in place, all the grounds for discrimination and protected areas should be streamlined comprehensively for a more systematic legal system as

---

concept of intersectionality in the Korean jurisdiction where a comprehensive anti-discrimination law does not exist. Therefore, I argue that the application of the concept of intersectionality is not sufficient to provide a specific standard to apply to different types of discrimination. Furthermore, a comprehensive anti-discrimination should be legislated in Korea.

[142] Hong (2018), p. 7.

[143] For details about individual anti-discrimination laws in South Korea, please see Ahn (2017).

well as effective protection. The main reasons for the need for a general anti-discrimination law as a fundamental and integrated law on discrimination are:[144] firstly, for some grounds of discrimination, such as gender, disability, age, and race, there are individual anti-discrimination laws. However, it is practically impossible to enact an individual anti-discrimination law for all the various grounds. A General Law to prohibit discrimination can perform such functions that protect victims who are discriminated against based on the grounds that are not enacted as specific individual laws. Secondly, a comprehensive anti-discrimination law can provide legal standards to provide specific as well as unified guidelines about the definition, criteria and remedies for discrimination.

Furthermore, one of the most sensitive parts of the need for a general and comprehensive anti-discrimination law is the opportunity to intervene in equality violations by private actors. In previous discrimination cases, individuals suffered from discriminatory acts by state or public actors. However, in modern times, there are many cases of discrimination where violators are private actors. For example, when a private university recruits employees, will it allow a particular religion to be included as a necessary qualification? Furthermore, can such a qualification be included in the working contract? This was one of the discriminatory cases dealt with by the National Human Rights Commission of Korea (NHRCK).[145] Another case is that a commercial airline company includes physical conditions such as appearance and age when they hire female crew members.[146] Especially in this case, the age limit was set to the ages between 23 and 25 as the conditions for application. The NHRCK also decided that this is discrimination based on age, and such discrimination is not justified according to the principle of proportionality, since such measures do not have a legitimate aim. In the decision-making process, the NHRCK referred to the *Council Directive 2000/78/EC of 27 November 2000*, Article 2, Paragraph 2(a) as well as Article 4, Paragraph 1[147] from the EU equality

---

[144] Kim (2014), p. 187.

[145] The National Human Rights Commission of Korea, 09 Jin-Cha 1241 Recommendation of May 10, 2010. Recommendation of the National Human Rights Commission of Korea, the 4th edition, pp. 824–842.

[146] The National Human Rights Commission of Korea, 05 Jin-Cha 662, 06 Jin-Cha 468, 06 Jin-Cha 472, 06 Jin-Cha 502 (Combined) Recommendation of 13 November 2006. Recommendation of the National Human Rights Commission of Korea, the 2nd edition, pp. 403–409.

[147] Council Directive 2000/78/EC of 27 November 2000

> Article 2 (Concept of discrimination), Paragraph 2(a) states: direct discrimination shall be taken to occur where one person is treated less favorably than another is, has been or would be treated in a comparable situation, on any of the grounds referred to in Article 1;
>
> Article 4 (Occupational requirements), Paragraph 1 states: Notwithstanding Article 2(1) and (2), Member States may provide that a difference of treatment which is based on a characteristic related to any of the grounds referred to in Article 1 shall not constitute discrimination where, by reason of the nature of the particular occupational activities concerned or of the context in which they are carried out, such a characteristic constitutes a genuine and determining occupational requirement, provided that the objective is legitimate and the requirement is proportionate.

directive explained in Sect. 4.5.1 above. In addition, the NHRCK also referred to the Age Discrimination in Employment Act in America, the Employment Equality Act of Ireland, the Age Discrimination Act of Australia, and the Canadian Human Rights Act when finding any violations.

Other important cases of gender equality from the NHRCK are the practices in private companies where female employees have to retire when they get married.[148] This came to light during an investigation by the NHRCK, who recommended that the four private companies rectify the situation in terms of female employees' having to resign when getting married, secondary or lower positions for female employees, considering the military service experiences of male employees when promoting them, not promoting female employees above a certain position, and gender discrimination with holiday allowances. However, such recommendations from the NHRCK are only advisory and non-binding, illustrating that it is difficult in practice to correct violations unless violators are willing to improve the situation.

In the absence of a comprehensive anti-discrimination law in Korea, serious violations have been dealt with in civil law cases. One of the cases is that a private insurance company refused to enter into an insurance policy due to the disability of the applicant. Seoul's central district court[149] decided that refusals to issue insurance for persons with disabilities corresponds to unfair discrimination on the grounds of disability so that partial payments of the claim have to be made as liability for damages. In a similar case, the *Cheon An* district court[150] also decided that it is irrational to refuse insurance simply because of disability. The court decided that the private insurance company was responsible for the payment of alimony because the act is considered to be Tort in Korean civil law.

The Supreme Court of Korea also granted liability for damages against wrong-doing as an infringement of gender equality rights with discriminatory treatment between female members and male member of the YMCA (Young Men's Christian Association) as a private entity.[151] However, it is not very effective to seek remedies through civil litigations in South Korean courts. Applicants have no choice but to claim alimony because it is very complicated to calculate the concrete amount of damages. Often, in most discriminatory cases, it is difficult to compensate for damages suffered by the victim only with monetary indemnity. Furthermore, Korean civil courts tend to accept alimony in comparatively small amounts compared to damages caused by discriminatory acts. For this reason, it is not very effective to obtain damages caused by discrimination through civil proceedings. The issue of infringement of equality by private entities should no longer be neglected as a matter of private autonomy. Basic rights have a dual characteristic of subjective rights as

[148]The National Human Rights Commission of Korea, 16 Jik-Gwon 0000200 Recommendation of May 25, 2016.

[149]Seoul Central District Court, 2003 Ga-Dan 150880 Decision, decided on February 12, 2004.

[150]Dae-Jeon District Court, Cheon-Ahn branch court, 2005 Ga-Hap 5440 Decision, decided on July 20, 2006.

[151]Supreme Court of Korea, 2009 Da 19864 Decision, decided on 27. 01. 2011.

well as objective ordering of values, therefore the validity of fundamental rights between private persons is naturally recognized.[152] A comprehensive non-discrimination law should embody the effect of basic rights in a more concrete sense. Even if equality and private autonomy conflict in the scope of application, it does not mean that the basic rights of equality are not applied in the scope of private entities.

There are some concerns that have been raised in ensuring equality by enacting a comprehensive anti-discrimination law in Korea to prohibit discrimination in the scope of private entities:[153] (1) private autonomy can be violated; (2) freedom in the scope of privacy can be excessively limited; (3) if private companies are involved, the freedom and property rights of the companies can be infringed especially concerning employment contracts; (4) when sexual orientation is included as grounds not to be discriminated against, it can infringe on freedom of religion;[154] (5) the possibility of infringing on the autonomy of private organizations; (6) since there are already individual non-discrimination laws available, further disputes can be resolved through administrative measures, or through applications of general provisions of civil laws in the courts; (7) social consensus on comprehensive anti-discrimination law has not yet been reached. All of these concerns are regarded as reasons to oppose legislating for a general anti-discrimination law in South Korea.

Nevertheless, considering the complexities of a modern society, it is not easy to claim that infringement of equality cannot take place between private entities. Moreover, introducing a general law on non-discrimination may contribute to a change in the attitudes as well as the awareness of society's members.[155] Furthermore, legal transparency, legal stability, and *foreseeability* regarding discriminatory acts can be promoted with comprehensive anti-discrimination law, compared to applications of the general provisions of civil law.

4.6 Conclusion

In this chapter, I have discussed the principle of non-discrimination and the anti-discrimination law. The principle of non-discrimination is regarded as one of the important principles of international human rights law. I have introduced not only discussions in the ECtHR and the CCK, which are the main areas in this work but also discussions in EU,[156] Germany, US and Britain. Additionally, I have included

---

[152] Huh (2012), p. 249.

[153] Lee (2018b), p. 31, pp. 45–46.

[154] Especially for this concern, *Zoonil Yi* argued that prohibition of discrimination based on sexual orientation does not mean directly violations of religious freedom. These concerns should have come from Christian churches in Korea, who are strongly resist any measures related to same sex couples or homosexuality (taken from Yi 2014, p. 251).

[155] Park (2015), p. 1177.

[156] I have introduced EU legislations even if the title and the topic of this work is the jurisprudence of the European Court of Human Rights, not the European Court of Justice because EU Directives

these three particular jurisdictions because they are important as areas of research for future Korean anti-discrimination law. In addition, the use of comparative human rights law has advantages such as self-understanding the issue compared to other legal frameworks, learning lessons from other jurisdictions' experiences, and the clarification of the implications of certain institutional, textual, and interpretive options.[157] As shown from the cases above, a general and comprehensive anti-discrimination law will help to protect sexual minorities in Korea by prohibiting discrimination based on sexual orientation. In the current Korean situation, it is largely unexpected that there will be legislation for an individual anti-discrimination law based on sexual orientation. Neglecting discrimination could have a very negative effect on the formation of healthy public awareness. Of course, neglecting discrimination results in direct, considerable harm to the victims of discriminatory acts. Even if some conservative Christian churches are very reluctant to include sexual orientation as prohibiting grounds of discrimination, there is a strong need for comprehensive legislation on anti-discrimination laws. In addition, violations by private entities should be equally recognized in the same way as discrimination by the state or the public sector, so these should be also recognized as discrimination.

References

Abrusci E (2017) A tale of convergence? Discrimination based on sexual orientation in regional human rights bodies and the human rights committee. Nord J Hum Rights 35(3):240–257. https://doi.org/10.1080/18918131.2017.1355434. Accessed November 30, 2021.

Ahn J (2017) A study on the limits of individual anti-discrimination laws in South Korea. Chonnam Law Rev 37(3), Institute for legal studies Chonnam National University, 199–237. https://doi.org/10.38133/cnulawreview.2017.37.3.199

Authority of the House of Lords (2016) The Equality Act 2010: the impact on disabled people, Report of Session 2015-16, paragraph 423. https://publications.parliament.uk/pa/ld201516/ldselect/ldeqact/117/117.pdf. Accessed November 30, 2021.

Belavusau U, Henrard K (2019) A bird's eye view on EU anti-discrimination law: the impact of the 2000 Equality Directives. Cambridge University Press, Cambridge

Caliendo M, Hogennacker J (2012) The German labor market after the Great Recession: successful reforms and future challenges. J Eur Labor Stud 1(3):1–24

Chen AHY (2018) Western origins and Asian practice. In: Chen AHY, Harding A (eds) Constitutional Courts Asia: a comparative perspective. Cambridge University Press, Cambridge

Cooper B (2015) Intersectionality, the Oxford handbook of feminist theory. Oxford University Press, Oxford

Ellis E, Watson P (2014) EU anti-discrimination law. Oxford University Press, Oxford

European Commission (2009) Links between migration and discrimination – European Network of Legal Experts in the non-discrimination field Olivier de Schutter

Federal Anti-Discrimination Agency (2019) Guide to the General Equal Treatment Act. Antidiskriminiergunsstelle des Bundes

has been regarded as comparative references to promote legislating Anti-Discrimination Law in Korea.

[157] Fredman (2018), pp. 7–8.

Fredman S (2018) Comparative human rights law. Oxford University Press, Oxford
Fuchs M (2006) Zeitschrift für europäisches Sozial- und Arbeitsrecht (ZESAR), p. 377 onwards
Han S-W (2005) Die Prüfung des Gleichheitsverstoßes nach dem Verhältnismäßigkeitsgrundsatz. Hong Ik Law Rev 6
Hong K-H (2012) Eine Studie über die Prüfungsmaßstab und Prüfungsintensität des allgemeinen Gleichheitssatzes. Public Law 41(1). Korean Public Law Association
Hong S-S (2018) Why do we need comprehensive Anti-Discrimination Act as equal basic law in Korea? Ewha J Gend Law 10(3)
Huh Y (2012) Theory on Korean Constitution, 8th edn. Parkyoungsa, Seoul
Jeong M-S (2010) Verhältnismäßigkeit als Prüfungsmaßstab für Gleiheit. Institute of Law Studies Pusan National University, Law Review 51(1)
Jung Y-J (2012) Constitutional review on reintroduction of the veterans' extra point system. Public Law J 13(1), Korean Comparative Public Law Association
Jung S-D, Lee M-W (2012) Age discrimination in employment act in Korea, US, and Netherlands: its concepts and target groups. Health Soc Welf Rev 32(2):118–142. https://www.kihasa.re.kr/hswr/assets/pdf/640/journal-32-2-118.pdf. Accessed November 30, 2021.
Kim C-H (2000) The obligation of legislators to the principle of equality and the control over it, the Constitutional Court of Korea the 11th edition. Seoul
Kim D-K (2007) Die Struktur und Begründung der Abwägung im Recht. Seoul National University, Seoul
Kim M-S (2014) The minority protection and the Anti-Discrimination Act. Hongik Law Rev 15(3)
Kwon Y-S (2010) Constitutional law of Korea. Bubmoonsa, Seoul
Lavrysen L (2016) Aldeguer Tomás V. Spain: a missed opportunity for the court to provide guidance concerning the legal recognition of same-sex relationships, 7 July 2016, https://strasbourgobservers.com/2016/07/07/aldeguer-tomas-v-spain-a-missed-opportunity-for-the-court-to-provide-guidance-concerning-the-legal-recognition-of-same-sex-relationships/. Accessed November 30, 2021.
Lee U-H (2005) The equal right of both sexes. Public Law J 6(3). Korean Comparative Public Law Association
Lee N-H (2007) Standards of equality in the U.S. Constitution. Hongik University Press, Seoul
Lee B-H (2011) Die Prüfungsmaßstübe des Gleichheitssatzes im Verfassungsrecht. Leg Res 19(2)
Lee B-H (2018a) Constitutional research on the scrutiny standards for determining equality principles - an analysis of the decision of the Korean Constitutional Court. Res Law Policy 18(2)
Lee J-H (2018b) Private autonomy and anti-discrimination law. The Justice (165). Korean Legal Center
Lee K-E, Kim D-H (2019) A study on the change of perceptions of child abuse before and after special law. J Korean Contents Assoc 19(9). The Korea Contents Society
Lim J-B (2007) Case laws of U.S. Constitution: gender discrimination and the system to favour discharged veterans. Law Times, https://m.lawtimes.co.kr/Content/Opinion?serial=26095. Accessed November 30, 2021.
Ministry of Justice of Korea (2008) Anti-Discrimination Law in other countries, Seoul
Park K-S (2001) The interpretation of equality, Constitutional research on practice (憲法實務研究), Issue 2
Park S-U (2015) Eine Untersuchung über die zulässige unterschiedliche Behandlung im AGG für die Verabschiedung eines Gesetzes zum Benachteiligungsverbot. J Comp Priv Law 22(3). The Korean Association of Comparative Private Law
Park S-Y (2017) A study for effectiveness enhancement of women and family-related legislations: achievement and challenges of the equal employment opportunity act for the last 30 years. Korean Women's Development Institute, Seoul
Pieroth B, Schlink B (2000) Fundamental Rights of Germany, Grundrechte. Staatsrecht II, Chung T-H (translated), the Constitutional Court of Korea, Seoul
Rabe J (2001) Equality, affirmative action, and justice. Hamburg Univ., Diss., 2000/2001

Shim J-J (2017) The meaning of the Equality Act 2010 as a General Anti-Discrimination Law and its implications for Korea. Kangwon Law Rev 50
Shin O-J (2008a) Eine Studie über Anti-Diskriminierungsrichtlinien der EU. Public Law J 9(2). Korean Comparative Public Law Association
Shin O-J (2008b) The effect of EU anti-discrimination directives on promoting gender equality in employment in Germany. The 7th Korean Association of Gender and law
Sieckmann J (2018) Rechtsphilosophie. Mohr Siebeck, Tübingen
Son S-S (2019) Judgment of unconstitutional discrimination based on a proportionality review - with a focus on review over the decision by the Constitutional Court of Korea. World Constit Res 25(2)
Woo J-H, Kang J-G, Yoon S-J (2013) Evaluation of legislation on the anti-discrimination against and remedies for persons with disabilities act. Korea Legislation Research Institute on 16 September 2013
Xenidis R (2018) Multiple discrimination in EU anti-discrimination law: towards redressing complex inequality? In: Belavusau U, Henrard K (eds) EU anti-discrimination law beyond gender. Hart Publishing, Oxford
Yi Z-I (2001) Legal equality and actual equality. Ahn Am Legal Study, Seoul
Yi Z-I (2014) The need for legislation and legislative considerations of anti-discrimination law, parliamentary study 20(1)
Zago G (2015) Oliari and Others v. Italy: a stepping stone towards full legal recognition of same-sex relationships in Europe, https://strasbourgobservers.com/2015/09/16/oliari-and-others-v-italy-a-stepping-stone-towards-full-legal-recognition-of-same-sex-relationships-in-europe/. Accessed November 30, 2021.

Chapter 5
Principle of Proportionality in the Case Law of the ECtHR

5.1 Development of the Proportionality in a European Context

The principle of proportionality is widely used as a criterion of fairness and justice to assist in discerning the balance between the restrictions imposed and the severity of the prohibited act,[1] when two different rights conflict or rights conflict with a public aim. Proportionality analysis has come as a *constitutional* tool to enhance effectiveness in protecting individual rights. The proportionality is rooted in German Administrative and Constitutional Law and has since become the main test as a technique of rights adjudication[2] in many constitutional courts including those in countries, Israel, Canada, and South Africa. The German Federal Constitutional Court, which has developed the proportionality as a fundamental constitutional principle through case law, has already recognized that "the principle of proportionality possesses constitutional status."[3] The rights adjudication procedure based on the proportionality is regarded as one of the defining features in global constitutionalism in dealing with conflicts between two alleged constitutional "values" or "interests."[4] I argue that the German way of the structured proportionality is an important decision making tool, which should be applied by the ECtHR.

Under German law, the limitations of fundamental rights are only allowed when they pass the structured proportionality test.[5] The German proportionality test has

[1] According to *Sweet* and *Mathews*, proportionality Analysis is widely understood as an overarching principle of constitutional adjudication, the preferred procedure for managing disputes involving and alleged conflict between two rights claims, or between a rights provision and a legitimate state or public interest (taken from Sweet and Mathews 2008, pp. 1–2).

[2] Clérico (2021, forthcoming).

[3] Arai-Takahashi (2013), p. 447.

[4] Sweet and Mathews (2008).

[5] Koutnatzis (2011).

H. J. Lee, *Discrimination Based on Sexual Orientation*, Interdisciplinary Studies in Human Rights 8, https://doi.org/10.1007/978-3-030-95423-9_5

been structured in four steps: (1) *Legitimacy*: whether the aim of restriction is legitimate. (2) *Suitability*: whether the action taken by the government is appropriate to promote the state's objectives. (3) *Necessity*: whether there are other less restrictive alternative means for the government to achieve its objectives. (4) *Proportionality in a narrow sense*: whether the effects of the government's actions are disproportionate or excessive relative to the importance of the government's objectives.[6] The first stage is to assess legitimate aims. To justify the limitations on human rights, the aims of limitations are related to the protection of constitutional or human rights, or the realization of the public interest.[7] And the component of suitability is that the means or measures adopted by the law or state must be able to promote the proper purpose. The third stage of necessity test is also referred to as the less restrictive means test.[8] According to this test, the legislator has to choose the means which would least limit the human right in question among all those means that have legitimate aims and suitable relations between the aim and the means.[9] In addition, what is important is that less restrictive means must be equally effective as means in question. The last step of balancing[10] compares benefits gained by the public interest or other rights and the harm caused to the rights through the use of the means selected to gain the legitimate aim.[11] This strives at an optimal solution[12] of balancing such benefits and harm.

There are some criticisms about the proportionality principle, such as the lack of rationality, too wide a judicial discretion or insufficient protection of constitutional rights[13] or the existence of only diverse standards without unique content. Nevertheless, such criticisms are refuted by a number of constitutional scholars[14] as well. Furthermore, the principle of proportionality constitutes a core principle of EU law

[6]Barak (2012), pp. 243–370.

[7]Ibid., pp. 245–246, 253–257.

[8]Some argue that the test of necessity is different from less restrictive means test or the least-intrusive-means test. For example, *J. Gerards* argues that the two tests are different because necessity can be determined on its own while a less restrictive means test cannot be determined on its own (taken from Gerards 2013, p. 482). Nevertheless, I assume the two tests as equal in this work because the content of necessity test assesses what would least limit the protected human rights of all the available means (including hypothetical) (taken from Barak 2012, p. 317).

[9]Ibid., p. 317.

[10]The last test of proportionality is "proportionality in the narrow sense" or "balancing." Both terms are used as equivalent throughout this work.

[11]Barak (2012), p. 340.

[12]Sieckmann (2021, forthcoming), pp. 18–19.

[13]Barak (2012), pp. 481–491.

[14]One of the scholars is J. Sieckmann. Sieckmann argues that the principle of proportionality can be qualified as universal from the three aspects of the categorical structure of principles, the a priori-validity of some principles or norms, and the validity of norms for each legal system. I think this argument is particularly important to discuss the case law of discrimination based on sexual orientation in the context of Europe as well as South Korea because the principle of proportionality can work to prohibit discrimination in both jurisdictions as a norm of universal validity to each legal system (taken from Sieckmann 2018, pp. 4–10).

and is applied before EU courts in cases related to EU regulation or policy, and to national norms or national decisions[15] referring to EU law. In a reasoning process of the proportionality any grounds could be argued for or against the legitimacy, suitability, necessity of a means, or the balance between the means and the end. Furthermore, proportionality gives more strength to individual rights and freedoms, by placing the burden of proof on the intrusive state agency in proportionality analysis. Lastly, through the final stage of balancing, proportionality analysis protects rights and freedom even in cases where the limitation is regarded as necessary for the state's legitimate aim. It functions as the last bulwark for rights and freedom.[16] Therefore, I argue that the structured proportionality should be applied in the ECtHR.

The proportionality is considered as the strict level of review. *Gerards*[17] discusses four factors to determine the intensity of the EU Court's[18] review: The first factor is the seriousness and nature of the interference. The degree of interference with Community interests is important to the intensity of the courts' review, and the EU Courts apply the strictest level of review when a central community interest has been impaired. The second factor is the existence of consensus in the matter of protected interests. The EU Courts will apply a more deferential test when there is no consensus[19] regarding the contested issue within the EU. The European Court of Justice assesses the proportionality test when scientific consensus is lacking regarding the matter at hand. The third factor is the scope of the competences and powers of the relevant government institutions. The EU Courts apply a more deferential test in matters of legislation by the community institutions.[20] The fourth factors are fundamental rights. A strict level of review applies when the very essence[21] of a certain fundamental right has been affected. *Rivers* also introduces large, moderate, and

[15] Gerards (2011), p. 89.

[16] Schlink (2012), pp. 732–735.

[17] Gerards (2011), pp. 91–101.

[18] The term of European Courts is used when referring to both courts of "the European Court of Human Rights ('ECtHR')" and "the European Court of Justice ('ECJ')" in this work. Even if the main topic of this work is the ECHR and the jurisprudence of the ECtHR, I have included the discussion of the applicability of the proportionality in the European Court of Justice as well because the principles of the ECJ affects the case law of the ECtHR even if the two should be distinguished.

[19] Regarding this consensus argument, it will be discussed in the Chap. 6. Nevertheless, EU courts are criticized in applying the consensus argument because of the lack of clarity. It is pointed out that there is a lack of clarity as to what extent the consensus argument influences the intensity of review as well as how it inter-relates with other intensity-determining factors (taken from Gerards 2011, p. 96).

[20] *Gerards* further explains that the discretion may be limited to some extent (1) by the division of competence between the Community and the Member State, (2) by fundamental rights, and (3) by general principles such as the principle of subsidiarity (taken from Gerards 2011, p. 97).

[21] Regarding the "core right" doctrine where the level of review is intensified if the very essence of a certain fundamental right has been affected, further discussions will follow in Chap. 6 of this work.

small degrees of restraint.[22] There are controversies regarding which factors could determine different levels of intensity of review. In this context, *Lester* and *Pannick* claim the importance of the right at stake, the degree to which it is interfered with, and the existence of common ground[23] which has also been pointed out as the second factor of consensus argument by *Gerards* previously. In other words, the more important the right at stake is, the more intensely the right is interfered with and the less common ground is formed between Member States and the Convention determines whether the European Courts will analyze the case with standards of higher intensity of review. In this regard, as standards of higher intensity of review, I argue that the ECtHR should apply a fourfold test, which will be discussed in the following.

The doctrine of the proportionality uses a fourfold test of *legitimacy*, *suitability*, *necessity* and *fair balance* as the steps of the proportionality test. The proportionality in European jurisdiction is regarded as "first and foremost principle to identify the rational optimization of the common good."[24] Such extensive German experience in applying the principle of proportionality has influenced the jurisprudence of the European Court of Justice ("ECJ"), and the European Court of Human Rights.[25] However, the principle of proportionality in the ECtHR is different from the German Federal Constitutional Court. The ECtHR mainly reviews the legitimacy of the aim and then looks into whether the measure is "necessary in a democratic society or not."[26] The proportionality test in the reasoning process of ECtHR in general consists of a two-step structure. The first step focuses on "whether there exists an interference (infringement) with specific human rights as claimed by an applicant."[27] The following second step is to assess "whether such interference can be justified in the light of specific criteria of assessment."[28]

Unlike the German prolonged proportionality test, the reasoning process of the ECtHR proceeds by the following steps:

---

[22] *Julian Rivers* introduced three different degrees and introduced three different degrees of intensity of judicial review: (1) *a large degree of restraint*: the court will be very unwilling to question the view of the primary decision-taker that what is necessary to achieve a certain level of public interest is also balanced. (2) *moderate degree of restraint*: the court will want to check that the costs and gains are indeed roughly commensurable. (3) *small degree of restraint*: the court will need to be convinced that the decision, rule or policy in question is the best way of optimizing the relevant rights and interests (ibid., p. 203).

[23] Lester and Pannick (2004), p. 97.

[24] Alexy (2010), pp. 66–69.

[25] Arai-Takahashi (2013), p. 447.

[26] Article 8–11 of the European Convention stipulates limitations are justifiable if "necessary in a democratic society." The term was often criticized as a nontransparent use of terminology. In the case of *Sunday Times v. UK*, the Court elaborated the meaning as "whether the interference complained of corresponded to a pressing social need, whether it was proportionate to the legitimate aim pursued, whether reasons are relevant and sufficient" (European Court of Human Rights, *Sunday Times v. U.K.*, judgment of 26 April 1979, paragraph 62).

[27] Arai-Takahashi (2013), p. 450.

[28] Ibid., p. 450.

(1) Is there an *aim*? If so, is the aim legitimate? According to *Takahashi*,[29] in the ECtHR case law, the existence of "pressing social need" is necessary in assessing "proportionate balance between the interfering measure and the legitimate aim(s)." Nevertheless, "pressing social need" is not a fixed term. Therefore, "harmony with evolution of social forces and public opinions" is always needed to interpret whether there is such a pressing social need to legitimize the aim of the measure. The need to continually interpret the cases implies that the ECtHR's standard itself is unclear.
(2) Does interference exist? Have rights and freedoms in question been limited even if the state has to comply with its obligation? When asking this question, it is important to determine whether the interference is related either to the state's positive obligation or to its negative obligation.[30] To find out whether such interference is justified or not, the ECtHR examines the three different sub-tests in the cases of negative obligation. These three sub-tests are not the same as the steps of the proportionality because the sub-tests of the ECtHR are "in accordance with the law," "legitimate aim" and "necessary in a democratic society."[31] On the other hand, the ECtHR applies a single overall test of a fair balance in the cases of positive obligations.[32] According to this distinction of the ECtHR, it is necessary to decide whether the interference in question is a positive or a negative state obligation. Nevertheless, the ECtHR does not provide a clear distinction between the two obligations. For example, in the *Hämäläinen* case, the Grand Chamber considers allowing the applicant to have her new gender legally recognized while remaining married to involve a positive obligation on the state[33] while the chamber and the dissenting opinion considers it as a negative obligation.[34] The application of the test of the ECtHR depends on the distinction between positive and negative obligation, which differs in majority opinions and dissenting opinions or Chamber decisions and Grand Chamber decisions in the same issue. This reflects a problem of clarity.
(3) The doctrine of margin of appreciation will be assessed according to the breadth of the margin given to the states. To grasp the way in which the ECtHR delimits the scope of positive obligations at least to examine whether the state has complied with such obligations, it is necessary to discuss the application of the margin of appreciation doctrine in the cases concerning positive obligations.[35]

---

[29] Arai-Takahashi (2013), pp. 454–455.

[30] *Harris, O'Boyle, Bates,* and *Buckly* define a positive obligation as "one whereby a state must take action to secure human rights," while a negative obligation "is one by which a state is required to abstain from interference with, and thereby respect, human rights": Harris et al. (2009), p. 18.

[31] Ibid., pp. 344–359.

[32] Lavrysen (2016), p. 222. (For further discussion related to positive state obligation and negative state obligation, please see Sect. 6.1. Positive State Obligation of Chap. 6 in this work.)

[33] European Court of Human Rights, *Hämäläinen v. Finland,* judgment of 16 July 2014, paragraph 64.

[34] Ibid., paragraph 4.

[35] European Court of Human Rights, *Hämäläinen v. Finland,* judgment of July 16, 2014, p. 185.

Even if it is necessary to discuss this, the ECtHR does not provide clear standards to the breadth of the margin.

Nevertheless, the margin of appreciation is an important concept related to levels of scrutiny and it will be briefly discussed. According to *Arai-Takahashi*, the margin of appreciation is defined as the label used by the ECtHR "to indicate the measure of discretion allowed to the Member States in the manner in which they implement the Convention standards, taking into account their own particular national circumstances and conditions."[36] There are some factors[37] determining the width of the margin, and it is indicative of the level of scrutiny applied by the ECtHR: "a wide margin corresponds to light scrutiny, whereas a narrow margin corresponds to strict scrutiny."[38] The ECtHR has interpreted the phrase "necessary in a democratic society" in the limitation clauses as suggesting the existence of a "pressing social need." In addition, the ECtHR introduced the doctrine of a margin of appreciation in assessing the phrase "necessary in a democratic society" as well.[39] *Gerards* introduced "importance of the Affected Right" as one of the important factors to determine the scope of the margin of appreciation of the ECtHR.[40] While the ECtHR supposes that the narrower margin of appreciation is allowed for core rights, it leaves open the question of what exactly core rights[41] and supplementary rights are.

(4) The last step is adapting *the principle of proportionality*, but in most cases the ECtHR does not strictly follow the German three-pronged test of suitability, necessity, and the proportionality in a narrow sense. To restructure judgment of the ECtHR according to the principle of proportionality,[42] a less restrictive means test and the proportionality in the narrow sense[43] seem to be more

---

[36] Arai-Takahashi (2002), p. 2.

[37] *Yutaka Arai-Takahashi* analyzed a range of policy ground both favouring the margin of appreciation and determining stringent scrutiny: policy grounds underlying a margin of appreciation include moral considerations, national security and prevention of serious crime, issues closely associated with state sovereignty such as immigration controls, election systems, medical expertise, social and economic policy such as education policy, the right to property, European Consensus, positive obligations. Furthermore, Takahashi identifies variables that tend to narrow the parameters of national discretion: discrimination, non-derogable rights and other fundamental rights. (Ibid., pp. 206–230.)

[38] Lavrysen (2016), p. 189.

[39] Arai-Takahashi (2013), p. 454.

[40] Gerards (2011), pp. 112–113.

[41] The ECtHR does not explicitly provide the standards to distinguish core rights from other rights, but still uses the term of core rights as opposed to supplementary rights in the judgment. Regarding the core rights and obligations, *Martin Scheinin* argues that it is not justified to have any order of superiority or primacy between human rights although there are various reasons for the special characteristics of one or the other human rights. Martin further discusses each human rights contains an essential core and core obligations of states (taken from Scheinin 2013, pp. 527–540).

[42] Arai-Takahashi (2002), p. 15.

[43] The specific case law of the ECtHR to apply the test of necessity and the proportionality in the narrow sense will be discussed in Sect. 5.2.

relevant than legitimate aim and suitability. In some of case analysis, I have restructured case reasonings according to the necessity and the balancing test not because the legitimate aim and the suitability test are not important but because it seems more efficient to focus on the necessity and the balancing in some reasoning of the ECtHR. My thesis is that all four steps should nevertheless be analyzed in applying the principle of proportionality to enhance the clarity and consistency in its applicability as a legal methodological tool.

The principle of proportionality could apply not only to the issues of negative obligation, but also of positive obligation. The European Convention not only gives rise to so-called negative obligations requiring states to refrain from directly committing human rights violations, but also positive obligations to take steps to secure for individuals the effective enjoyment of their human rights.[44] In the case of negative obligations, whether state interference is "too excessive or not" will be assessed in the process of justification. On the other hand, whether the state "did enough or not" will be assessed in the case of positive obligations. The cases of discrimination based on sexual orientation involve both negative and positive obligations. For example, while the issue of non-criminalization of same-sex relations is whether there are interferences or not, the provision of legal recognition of same-sex relations is the problem of 'sufficiency' as to whether the state "did enough or not." Through restructuring the cases according to the proportionality in the following section will provide empirical analysis on that the proportionality can be applied to both cases of positive and negative obligations.

The distinction of positive and negative obligations are related to the breadth of the margin of appreciation and the core right arguments. In principle, the ECtHR applies a wide margin of appreciation in cases concerning positive obligations. One of the factors that mainly determines the width of the margin of appreciation is the importance of the affected right. *Gerards*[45] holds that "the margin will be narrow if the essence or 'core' of one of the Convention rights is affected." Likewise, the margin will be wider if the "supplementary" rights are affected, while it will be narrower in the cases of "core" rights affected. In the case of applying a narrower margin of appreciation, the ECtHR seems to apply stricter scrutiny than in the case of applying a wider margin of appreciation. This stricter scrutiny implies that the ECtHR applies a strict test of necessity to assess whether there are less intrusive measures.[46] On the other hand, the ECtHR frequently applies a rather procedural test where the margin is wide.[47] Nevertheless, the standard of the ECtHR to distinguish wide margin from narrow margin is as unclear as the distinction of positive and negative obligations. Therefore, I argue the structural proportionality can serve as an analytical tool for both wide margin and narrow margin, which will be done through

---

[44] Lavrysen (2016), p. 1.

[45] Gerards (2011), pp. 107–113.

[46] Ibid., p. 106.

[47] Ibid., p. 106.

the reconstruction[48] of the argumentation according to the steps of the proportionality in the following.

5.2 Proportionality Analysis in the Case Law of the ECtHR

This section will introduce how the ECtHR applies the principle of proportionality in the case law related to protecting the rights of sexual minorities. Even if the ECtHR states that limitations are justifiable if they are "necessary in a democratic society," and does not apply the proportionality test explicitly, my thesis is that the ECtHR's reasoning process can also be reanalyzed with the steps of proportionality and, furthermore, it would also be much clearer to apply the principle of proportionality explicitly with all the steps. In the following, the jurisprudence of Article 8 (Right to respect for private and family life), 10 (Freedom of expression), and 11 (Freedom of assembly and association) the ECHR will be reanalyzed according to the principle of proportionality. The reason why these articles especially are chosen is that they are the most relevant to the case law dealing with the issue of discrimination based on sexual orientation. Same-sex marriage will be discussed separately in Chap. 8.

5.2.1 *Jurisprudence of Article 8 (Right to Respect for Private and Family Life) ECHR*

Article 8 of the European Convention reads as follows:

1. Everyone has the right to respect for his private and family life, his home and his correspondence.
2. There shall be no interference by a public authority with the exercise of this right except such as is in accordance with the law and is necessary in a democratic society in the interests of national security, public safety or the economic well-being of the country, for the prevention of disorder or crime, for the protection of health or morals, or for the protection of the rights and freedoms of others.

Article 8 of the ECHR has always been very important in case law related to discrimination based on sexual orientation. The ECtHR held that "criminalizing homosexual acts between two consenting adult males in private amounted to a violation of Article 8"[49] in the *Dudgen* case. In the *J.M.* case, the ECtHR upheld

---

[48] I have reconstructed only the ECtHR cases. Nevertheless, that does not mean that the uses of the structure of proportionality can be only applied in the ECtHR cases. For example, the basic structure of the proportionality can be used to reconstruct overall assessment in the context of Latin American Courts. For that, please see, Clérico (2017).

[49] European Court of Human Rights, *Dudgeon v. United Kingdom*, judgment of 22 October 1981, paragraph 63.

the decision from the *Mata*[50] case as deciding that "a same-sex relationship fell within the ambit of Article 8."[51] There are many issues related to Article 8 such as state positive obligation,[52] margin of appreciation,[53] and the scope of Article 8 particularly such as private life, family life and the home,[54] however; my focus in this section is particularly restructuring court reasoning according to the steps of the proportionality in the case laws of the ECtHR related to Article 8 ECHR because my thesis is to urge the ECtHR to analyze all four stages of the proportionality test to enhance clarity as well as consistency of the applicability.

5.2.1.1 Legitimate Aim

The first element of the proportionality test requires that a law limiting a constitutional right has a proper purpose.[55] Article 8 ECHR states that there shall be no interference except as is in accordance with the law. The formal requirement of justifying limitations refers to the limitation which is in accordance with the law or the restrictions which are prescribed by law. Such legality[56] is not equal to legitimacy as the first stage of the principle of proportionality. The ECtHR requires legitimacy, in addition to legality as a justification for the limitation on the Convention rights. *Legitimate aim* is often regarded as a basic element, and the recent cases of the ECtHR has seemed to be more related with necessity or proportionality in the narrow sense. Such a tendency seems to give the impression that there are no problems with the applicability of the criterion of legitimate aim by the ECtHR. Nevertheless, as *Gerards* argues in her published works,[57] there are still problems

[50] European Court of Human Rights, *Mata Estenvez v. Spain*, judgment of 10 May 2001.

[51] European Court of Human Rights, *J.M. v. The United Kingdom*, judgment of 28 September 2010, paragraph 50.

[52] Lavrysen (2016), pp. 221–225: *Lavryson* discussed the different structure of the ECtHR's examination under Articles 8–11 in arguing the comparison of positive versus negative state obligations.

[53] Arai-Takahashi (2002), pp. 60–92: In Chap. 4, *Takahashi* discussed in detail the margin of appreciation doctrine in the jurisprudence of Article 8 ECHR, concluding that the breadth of the margin of appreciation varies and such a variability depends on such elements as the substance of the specific rights claimed under Article 8.

[54] Edel (2015), pp. 13–20: *Edel* analyzed case laws related to discrimination based on sexual orientation or gender identity according to the main freedoms relied on such as private life, family life, and the home.

[55] Barak (2012), p. 245.

[56] The principle of legality can be found in modern constitutions' limitation clauses, as well as in other international documents to state that any limitation must be "prescribed by law" or "in accordance with law." (Ibid., pp. 107–108.)

[57] Gerards (2019), pp. 220–228: In the Chap. 9 of legitimate aim, *Gerards* points out detailed discussion of situations when the ECtHR does not easily accept objectives as legitimate. Besides discrepancy between stated and real aims (9.3.), he also points out other difficult situations such as plurality of aims (9.4.) and interconnectedness of legitimate aim and proportionality (9.5.).

fulfilling the legitimate aim requirement in cases of the ECtHR. For example, the ECtHR will not often regard directly or indirectly expressive of discrimination or prejudice, gender stereotypes as legitimate objectives without providing clear reasons. Those problems need to be continuously discussed so that the ECtHR could improve the standard of *legitimate aim*.

In the *Oliari* case, the ECtHR found a violation of Article 8. To restructure the reasoning of the *Oliari* case, the issue in question is not considered to fulfill this first step. In this case, same-sex couples suffered from the absence of legal recognition of the same-sex partner. This absence did not pursue any legitimate aim. Furthermore, there was no legitimate aim of the state. The Italian government denied that such absence attempted to protect the traditional concept of family or the morals of society.[58] In the *Oliari* case, there was no legitimate aim for no provision of any legal recognition to same-sex couples.

In the *Orlandi*[59] case where the issue was the recognition of marriages obtained abroad, the ECtHR found a violation of Article 8 ECHR. The applicants *Orlandi* and *Mortagna* married in Toronto, Canada on August 27, 2010. After they got back to Italy, the two applicants submitted the relevant document to register their marriage, but the Commune of Ferrara rejected their applications stating that the Italian legal order did not allow marriage between same-sex couples. On the one hand, the applicants seriously suffered from "the consequences of being unable to benefit from a specific legal framework providing for the recognition and protection of their same-sex unions."[60] On the other hand, the Italian government failed to indicate any legitimate aim for the refusal to register the marriages except a general phrase concerning "internal public order."[61] Furthermore, the ECtHR states that "Article 8 does not enlist the notion of public order as one of the legitimate aims"[62] Restructuring the reasoning of the *Orlandi* case, it has been found to fail the test of a *legitimate aim*.

5.2.1.2 Suitability Test

Suitability addresses whether the action taken by the government is appropriate to promote the government's objectives. It means that "if the realization of the means does not contribute to the realization of the law's purpose, the use of such means would be disproportional."[63] In the *Oliari* case, the ECtHR decided that Italy had failed to fulfill its obligation to ensure that the applicants had "available a specific

[58] European Court of Human Rights., *Oliari and others v. Italy*, judgment of 21 July 2015, paragraph 176.

[59] European Court of Human Rights, *Orlandi and others v. Italy*, judgment of 14 December 2017.

[60] Ibid., paragraph 199.

[61] Ibid., paragraph 200.

[62] Ibid., Paragraph 200.

[63] Barak (2012), p. 303.

legal framework." To reconstruct the reasoning of the ECtHR in finding a violation of Article 8, such a specific legal framework is considered as a "means," providing for "the recognition and protection of their union" as an "aim." When the ECtHR assesses the legal protection measures which are currently available in Italy, it considers that they failed to provide for the core needs relevant to a couple in a stable committed relationship.[64] This consideration of the ECtHR can be restructured to conclude that the currently available measures are not appropriate to promote an aim of the recognition and protection of same-sex relations.

Restructuring the reasoning of the *Oliari* according to the *suitability*, the question is whether the legal protections currently available ("Means") are considered as appropriate to promote the recognition and protection of same-sex union ("Aim"). The first means are the "local registers for civil unions"[65] with the local authorities, which were available only in a small number of municipalities in Italy. This first means only had symbolic value as it did not confer any rights on same-sex couples which are needed for their legal protection. Therefore, the first means is not considered as an appropriate means to promote the aim. The second means were "cohabitation agreements,"[66] which had been available since December 2013 in Italy. These agreements could not provide some basic needs which were considered fundamental to the regulation of a relationship between a couple in a stable and committed relationship. For example, these agreements did not provide any mutual material support, maintenance of obligations, or inheritance rights. Furthermore, these agreements were open not only to couples in committed relationships but also to any people who cohabit, such as friends or flat-mates. Furthermore, living together was the precondition for these agreements. Nevertheless, the ECtHR had already accepted that the existence of a stable union should be independent of cohabitation in the case of *Vallianatos*.[67] Therefore, the second means is not considered as appropriate to fulfill the aforementioned aim either.

In the E.B. case,[68] the ECtHR has found a breach of Article 14 ECHR taken in conjunction with Article 8. In this case, the main issue is whether different treatment

---

[64] European Court of Human Rights, *Oliari and others v. Italy*, judgment of July 21, 2015, paragraph 169.

[65] Ibid., paragraph 168.

[66] Ibid., paragraph 169.

[67] European Court of Human Rights, *Vallianatos and Others v. Greece*, judgment of 7 November 2013, paragraph 73.

[68] European Court of Human Rights, ***E.B. v. FRANCE*** (Applications no. 43546/02), Grand Chamber judgment of 22 January 2008. (The applicant (E.B.) was a 45-year-old school teacher who had been in a stable relationship with another woman, R. since 1990. On February 26, 1998 E.B. applied to the Jura Social Services Department for authorization to adopt a child. In her application, E.B. noted her sexual orientation and her relationship with R. Despite French legislation expressly granting single persons a right to adopt, the adoption board recommended the application be refused on the ground that the child's best interests would not be served because of the lack of a paternal role model and R's lack of commitment to the adopted child. In this case, the ECtHR found that the refusal to grant authorization for the adoption violated Article 14 (prohibition of discrimination) in conjunction with Article 8 (the right to respect for private and family

of individuals adopting a child can be justifiable based on the applicant's sexual orientation. The applicant E.B. applied to adopt a child and she noted her sexual orientation and her relationship with R. Even if French legislation expressly granted single persons a right to adopt, the application of the applicant has been refused on the ground that the child's best interests would not be served first because of the lack of a paternal role model and R's lack of commitment to the adopted child.[69] The ECtHR considered the influence of the applicant's homosexuality was a "decisive factor leading to refuse her authorization to adopt."[70] Regarding Article 14 to find discrimination, the ECtHR considers two conditions—(1) whether the measure pursues a "legitimate aim," (2) there is "reasonable proportionality between the means employed and the aim to be realized."[71]

As to the first condition of "legitimate aim," the ECtHR admits means of prohibition of adoption to same-sex couple had pursued a legitimate aim. The legitimate aim has been to protect the health and rights of children who could be involved in an adoption procedure.[72] Whether the stated aim has legitimacy will not be separately assessed in this section because the ECtHR considers the state aims as legitimate and I do not have particular criticisms on that. *Suitability* test assesses a question of whether there is a rational connection between the means and the legitimate aim. In this case, the means applied is to prohibit the adoption of child to same-sex couple. Nevertheless, there are no national connection between this means and the aim of protecting the health and the right of a child in an adoption procedure for the following two reasons.

The first reason is related to the French law, which allowed the adoption of a child by a single person. The ECtHR points out that "French law allows single persons to adopt a child, thereby opening up the possibility of adoption by a single homosexual" and such comments are "not disputed."[73] Therefore, it is illogical that the current means is not to allow a same-sex couple to adopt a child even if the current law allowed a single person to adopt. The second reason is related to the reasons to reject adoption. French authorities stated that one of the reasons to reject adoption is

life) ECHR. The majority found that E.B. had been discriminated against, as a distinction was drawn based on consideration of her sexual orientation (taken from Human Rights Law Center, *Discrimination on the Basis of Sexuality a Violation of the Rights to Privacy and Equality* available at: https://www.hrlc.org.au/human-rights-case-summaries/eb-v-france-2008-echr-4354602-22-january-2008. Accessed November 30, 2021).

[69] Human Rights Law Center (2008).

[70] European Court of Human Rights, *E.B. v. France*, Grand Chamber judgment of 22 January 2008, paragraph 89.

[71] Ibid., paragraph 91.

[72] Ibid., paragraph 70: The ECtHR did not assess separately the legitimacy of aims in E.B. case alone. However, the Court cited the case of *Frette v. France* in E.B. case, and stated how the reasoning process in the E.B. case is different from the *Frette* case. During such reasoning, the Court seems to admit the similarity of the two first steps of Proportionality as legitimate aim and suitability because the Court has not pointed out those two besides citing from *Frette* case.

[73] Ibid., paragraph 94.

the lack of a paternal role model or referent.[74] It is highly questionable as to why a single person adoption does not have the lack of a paternal role model while same-sex couple adoption has the lack of a paternal role model. Furthermore, there is no evidence that children learn a paternal role only from a male parent. There are times that a mother plays a paternal role and a father plays a maternal role. Therefore, it is difficult to find rational connection between the complete ban on prohibition of adoption by a same-sex couple and the promotion of the health and the right of a child in an adoption process.

5.2.1.3 Necessity Test

Necessity assesses whether a measure or action appropriately suitable would intrude less upon the citizen's right, because the state has no good reason to use the more restrictive measures rather than the less intrusive means.[75] The ECtHR could improve its necessity test by the application of a least restrictive means test. Although the ECtHR has not explicitly endorsed the less restrictive means test, some of the ECtHR reasoning can be restructured as applying the less restrictive means test. In the *Oliari* case, "the Italian domestic court statement of formal recognition"[76] was available. Since the Italian law itself explicitly provides for the recognition of a same-sex partner only in very limited circumstances, even the most basic issues such as recognition of a relationship had to be determined judicially. Considering the complexities involved in this judicial determination of a relationship, the means of "the Italian domestic court statement of formal recognition" are considered as a significant hindrance to same-sex couples' efforts to obtain respect for their private and family life by their relationship being legally recognized. In this case, the option of "civil unions or registered partnership"[77] could be a less restrictive means than the means of "domestic court statement of formal recognition" because this option is less restrictive considering the complexities in the process obtaining court statement and equally effective in the legal recognition of same-sex couples. Reconstructing the reasoning, the means of "domestic court statement of formal recognition" did not satisfy the test of necessity because the government could provide less restrictive means than those currently available.

Another example of the *necessity* test can be found in the reasoning of the dissenting opinion in the case of *Schalk and Kopf*[78] because it was believed that there should be a better way than simply a registered partnership to recognize the

[74] European Court of Human Rights, *E.B. v. France*, Grand Chamber judgment of 22 January 2008, paragraph 25.

[75] Bernhard (2012), p. 724.

[76] European Court of Human Rights., *Oliari and others v. Italy*, judgment of 21 July 2015, paragraph 170.

[77] Ibid., paragraph 55.

[78] European Court of Human Rights, *Schalk and Kopf v. Austria*, judgment of 24 June 2010.

relationship of same-sex couples. This could be a legal framework offering same-sex couples, at least to a certain extent, "the same rights or benefits attached to marriage."[79] To reconstruct the reasoning by dissenting opinion, the case of *Schalk and Kopf* fails the necessity test because the currently available means of registered partnership was not the least restrictive means. A better mean should exist, which could provide the same rights or benefits as marriage to same-sex couples.

5.2.1.4 Proportionality in the Narrow Sense

Proportionality in a narrow sense addresses whether the effects of the government's actions are disproportionate or excessive relative to the importance of the government's objectives.[80] There are many cases related to Article 8 of the ECHR which have problems with the balancing test after restructuring reasoning even if the ECtHR does not explicitly state the applicability of the balancing test. To categorize, the first category refers to the cases of blanket exclusion or complete ban of persons in same-sex relations. It is argued that a complete ban relates to a less restrictive means test because alternative measures could be regularly suggested.[81] Nevertheless, I argue that a complete ban is a problem of *balancing* rather than a problem of *necessity*. To support the failure of a necessity test, alternative measures have to be suggested which need to be both less restrictive as well as equally effective as the means in question. Nevertheless, it is difficult to suggest such alternatives because a complete ban is usually considered as an effective means. The second category refers to the cases where the applicant's homosexuality has been considered as important in the making of certain decisions by the applicant. In those cases, the means in question does not exclude a certain group of persons such as homosexuals completely. Nevertheless, a person's sexual orientation is a factor which is considered as decisive in some important decisions or rejections. The third category refers to the issue of competing interests of individuals. For example, when an individual criticizes another person based on his/her sexual orientation, the issue is related to the freedom of expression of the individual against the right to reputation of another person.

The first category relates to complete ban or blanket exclusion of persons in same-sex relations. In the *Oliari* case, there were no possibilities of legal recognition of same-sex relations, which can be considered as blanket exclusion of same-sex couples from being legally recognized of their relationship. In this case, the violation of the Italian government is clear when the reasoning is restructured to find out the existence of "the fair balance between the competing interests of the individual and of the community as a whole."[82] On the one hand, "respect for applicants' private

[79] Ibid., Dissenting Opinion, paragraph 9.

[80] Barak (2012), p. 340.

[81] Brems and Lavrysen (2015), pp. 162–163.

[82] European Court of Human Rights, *Oliari and others v. Italy*, judgment of 21 July 2015, paragraph 160.

life" is negatively affected because there is no legal recognition of same-sex couples in Italy. On the other hand, the Italian government had not denied the need for legal protection of same-sex couples and failed to point to any community interests justifying the situation of no legal protection.[83] Furthermore, the absence of legal recognition is considered as a serious infringement of the right to respect for the private life of the applicants regarding the following circumstances.

Firstly, there is a trend among Council of Europe Member States towards legal recognition of same-sex couples. For example, 24 out of 47 Member States have legislated in favor of such recognition.[84] This trend shows there is a movement towards legal recognition of same-sex couples[85] in the EU and this movement has continued to develop rapidly in Europe since the ECtHR's judgment of the *Schalk and Kopf* case.[86] Secondly, the highest court of the Constitutional Court in Italy had also repeatedly emphasized the need for legislation to recognize same-sex relationships. This reflects the seriousness of the issue in question, the fact that the sentiments of a majority of the Italian population support legal recognition of same-sex couples, and the existence of an important social need for the recognition.[87] Lastly, despite the need, the Italian legislature had failed to provide for the recognition for a long time, which had caused a material problem for same-sex couples in Italy. In sum, the applicants' interests were seriously limited because of the absence of any legal recognition on the one hand. Nevertheless, the Italian government could not provide any sufficient reasoning to justify such a limitation. Furthermore, "the Italian Government has failed to explicitly highlight what, in their view, corresponded to the interests of the community as a whole."[88] Restructuring the reasoning, the Italian government failed the *balancing test* because limitations of the rights of the applicants are very serious while the community interest against the recognition is not considered important.

Another case in the first category is *Perkins and R. v. The United Kingdom,*[89] in which the ECtHR found a violation of Article 8 ECHR. The issue of the case was whether the applicants' discharge from the Royal Navy on the basis of their homosexuality can be justified. The methods of adjudication that the ECtHR applied are only whether such "direct interferences" can be justified as "necessary in a

[83] Ibid., paragraph 176.

[84] Ibid., paragraph 178.

[85] Ragone and Volpe (2016), p. 464.

[86] European Court of Human Rights, *Oliari and others v. Italy*, judgment of 21 July 2015, paragraph 178.

[87] Ibid., paragraph 178.

[88] Ibid., paragraph 176.

[89] European Court of Human Rights, *Perkins and R. v. the United Kingdom*, decided on 22 January 2003. (The applicants alleged that an investigation into their sexuality and their discharge from the Royal Navy on the basis of their sexual orientation as a result of the absolute policy against the presence of homosexuals in the armed forces violated their rights under Article 8 alone and in conjunction with Article 14 ECHR. The ECtHR held that there was violation of Article 8 ECHR and no violation of Article 8 in conjunction with Article 14 the ECHR.)

democratic society."[90] Nevertheless, the ECtHR tried to emphasize the problem with "the absolute policy of the Ministry of Defence against the presence of homosexuals in the armed forces."[91] Such a reasoning process of the ECtHR can be restructured according to the proportionality in a narrow sense. The expression of the "absolute policy" against the presence means the absolute ban of homosexuals in the armed forces. Nevertheless, it is highly questionable as to whether unconditional dismissal of homosexual soldiers from serving has a rational connection with the aim of promoting military culture.

The absolute ban of the Ministry of Defense in the case of *Perkins and R. v. The United Kingdom* violates the *balancing* test because the interference of the applicant through absolute expulsion is very serious. Yet, the state could not provide sufficient justification against the serious interference. Such reasoning as well as the decision of the ECtHR can be a good lesson to South Korean Courts for the upcoming case[92] where *Byun Hui-Soo*[93] was dismissed from South Korean army for violating army regulations following her sex change. The Korean Ministry of Defense dismissed her according to a similar absolute policy against the presence of transgender soldiers in the Korean military as the one in the *Perkins* case. Such army regulation of absolute dismissal violates the principle of proportionality in a narrow sense because the absolute ban without providing any alternative options such as the possibility to change the positions or department limits the right of an individual very seriously and it is difficult to find justification to balance the severe infringement of the right.

P.B. and J.S. v. Austria[94] is included in the first category because this case is related to blanket exclusion of persons in a same-sex relationship from insurance

[90] Ibid., paragraph 38.

[91] Ibid., paragraph 38.

[92] The case cannot continue anymore because Byun committed suicide in March 2021 after suffering from the decision of absolute expulsion from the Korean military. Nevertheless, the Korean courts should consider as to whether such expulsion can be against the law of balancing. The sad news about Byun was reported in BBC News Korea on March 3, 2021. (BBC, South Korea's first transgender soldier found dead. https://www.bbc.com/news/world-asia-56268409. Accessed November 30, 2021). As of April 9, 2021, the Korean courts decided that Byun's immediate family can continue to proceed with the legal case. (https://www.pressian.com/pages/articles/2021040916273008520#0DKU. Accessed November 30, 2021.) The decision from the district court has been pronounced on October 7, 2021. The Court decided Byun's dismissal is unlawful, and the decision of the district court became final as the chief of Korean army cancelled the appeal. (https://m.khan.co.kr/national/court-law/article/202110270854001. Accessed November 30, 2021.)

[93] January 22, 2020, South Korea transgender soldier to sue over dismissal, BBC, https://www.bbc.com/news/world-asia-51204323. Accessed November 30, 2021.

[94] European Court of Human Rights, *P.B. and J.S. v. Austria*, judgment of 22 October 2010: The applicants live together in a same-sex relationship. The second applicant is a civil servant, and he is insured with the Civil Servants Insurance Corporation (the "CSIC"). The first applicant asked the CSIC to include him in the second applicant's insurance cover, but the CSIC dismissed a request because the Act in question only referred to persons of the opposite sex living with the principally insured person (para. 6–8). On October 10, 2005, the Constitutional Court held that the two provisions in which the extension of insurance cover to unrelated persons living with the insured

coverage as dependents. In this case, the ECtHR found a violation of Article 14, read in conjunction with Article 8 in the first[95] and second period.[96] The ECtHR's reasoning of the first period as well as the second period[97] can be restructured according to the *balancing* test. The reasoning of the second period can be easily restructured according to the *balancing* test because the issue is no longer blanket exclusion of same-sex couples but still no sufficient justification was given by the Government for different treatments of heterosexual couples and same-sex couples. However, in the blanket exclusion in the first period is not easy to decide whether the issue is a problem of the necessity or the balancing. The first period was until the entry into force of Section 56(6a) of the Civil Servants Sickness and Accident Insurance Act (CSSAIA) on August 1, 2006: On July 1, 1997, the first applicant asked the Civil Servants Insurance Corporation (CSIS) to recognize him as a dependent of the second applicant and to extend the latter's health and accident insurance cover him. On September 2, 1997, the CSIC dismissed the request saying he did not qualify as a dependent because the first applicant was a same-sex partner.

---

were discriminatory because they were restricted to persons of the opposite sex. Accordingly, the amendment act entered into force on July 1, 2007 (para. 15–16). The ECtHR decided according to the three separate periods. (For the decisions of the ECtHR for the three separate periods, please see the footnote 502 below.)

[95] European Court of Human Rights, *P.B. and J.S. v. Austria*, decided on 22 October 2010, paragraphs 40–42.

[96] The ECtHR consider the three periods separately:

First period is until the entry into force of Section 56(6a) of the Civil Servants Sickness and Accident Insurance Act (CSSAIA) on August 1, 2006: On July 1, 1997, the first applicant asked the Civil Servants Insurance Corporation (CSIS) to recognize him as a dependent of the second applicant and to extend the latter's health and accident insurance cover him. On September 2, 1997, the CSIC dismissed the request saying he did not qualify as a dependent because the first applicant was of the same sex. The ECtHR found a violation of Article 14, read in conjunction with Article 8 in this period. (European Court of Human Rights, *P.B. and J.S. v. Austria*, judgment of 22 October 2010, paragraphs 40–42.)

Second period from the entry into force of Section 56(6a) of the CSSAIA on August 1, 2006 until the entry into force of the amended Section 56(6) and (6a) of the CSSAIA on June 30, 2007: The ECtHR considers that the discriminatory character of the CSSAIA did not change after the first amendment, because unmarried heterosexual couples qualified for preferential treatment, while unmarried same-sex couples are only qualified if they were raising children together. The ECtHR found a violation of Article 14, read in conjunction with Article 8, in respect of this period. (European Court of Human Rights, *P.B. and J.S. v. Austria*, judgment of 22 October 2010, paragraphs 43–44.)

Third period after the entry into force of the amended Section 56(6) and (6a) of the CSSAIA on July 1, 2007: The raising of children in the common household is formulated in a neutral way and applicants did not argue that under Austrian law homosexuals are excluded from caring for children. Therefore, the ECtHR found no violation of Article 14, read in conjunction with Article 8 in respect of this period. (European Court of Human Rights, *P.B. and J.S. v. Austria*, judgment of 22 October 2010, paragraphs 45–50.)

[97] The reasoning of the second period can be interpreted as focusing on the *balancing* test because the issue is no longer blanket exclusion of same-sex couples but still no sufficient justification has been given by the Government for different treatments of heterosexual couples and same-sex couples.

In the reasoning of the first period, the ECtHR stated that "the principle of proportionality does not merely require that the measure chosen is in principle suited for realizing the aim sought,"[98] when there is different treatment based on sexual orientation.

Furthermore, the ECtHR stated that "it must also be shown that it was necessary in order to achieve that aim to exclude certain categories of people."[99] Such statements can be interpreted that the test of *suitability* is not enough, and the *necessity criterion* must be met to justify such different treatment. Even if the ECtHR stated the standard of "necessary," the, blanket exclusion of a same-sex partner from qualifying as a dependent to be covered by the insurance of his/her partner is considered as a problem of the *balancing* rather than the *necessity* for the following two reasons. First, the seriousness of interference of the applicants by the blanket exclusion is very high and the state did not provide sufficient justification against this serious interference. Second, to regard this issue as a problem of the necessity, there must be an alternative which is less restrictive as well as equally effective as the blanket exclusion. Nevertheless, it is difficult to find less restrictive means to meet these two criterion.

The second category refers to the cases where the applicant's homosexuality has been considered as important in making certain decisions regarding the applicant. The case of *Salgueiro*[100] is an example in this category. In this case, child custody was taken from the father who lives with his same-sex partner after having divorced the mother of the child. The ECtHR found a violation of Article 8 taken in conjunction with Article 14.[101] The ECtHR stated that "the Court cannot find that a reasonable relationship of proportionality existed between the means employed and the aim pursued."[102] These statements of the ECtHR do not make clear which test of the proportionality was applied. Nevertheless, the reasoning can be restructured according to the *balancing* test. On the one hand, child custody was taken away from the father and the decision was made because of the father's sexual orientation. The degree of the interference of the father is very serious considering

[98] European Court of Human Rights, *P.B. and J.S. v. Austria*, judgment of 22 October 2010, paragraph 42.

[99] Ibid., paragraph 42.

[100] European Court of Human Rights, ***Salgueiro da Silva Mouta v. Portugal***, (Application no. 33290/96) the judgment of 21 March 2000: The applicant, Salgueiro da Silva Mouta is a Portugese national born in 1961. He was prevented by his ex-wife from visiting his daughter M., in breach of an agreement reached at the time of their divorce. The Lisbon Family Affairs Court granted him parental responsibility for the child in 1994. However, on appeal, the mother was given parental responsibility because the applicant was a homosexual and living with another man (para. 8–15). In this case, the ECtHR found a violation of Article 8 taken together with Article 14 because the applicant's homosexuality had been decisive in the final decision of Lisbon Court of Appeal (para. 35–36).

[101] European Court of Human Rights, *Salgueiro Da Silva Mouta v. Portugal*, judgment of 21 March 2000, paragraph 36.

[102] Ibid., paragraph 36.

that "the decision to award parental responsibility to the mother was based mainly on the father's sexual orientation,"[103] and "the applicant's homosexuality was a factor which was decisive in the final decision."[104] On the other hand, Portuguese authorities failed to balance against the serious interference of the applicant because they could not apply weighty reasoning to justify the serious interference.

The third category refers to the issue of competing interests of individuals. The ECtHR has found no violation of Article 8 ECHR in the case of *Sousa Goucha v. Portugal*[105] where the applicant's right to their reputation competes with the freedom of expression of television presenter F.C. to make a joke about the applicant's sexual orientation. The applicant is one of the most well-known television hosts in Portugal and he publicly declared his homosexuality in 2008. Nevertheless, the T.V. show presenter F.C. included him as "one of the best female Portuguese hosts."[106] The main issue in this case is "whether the State . . . achieved a fair balance between the applicant's right to protection of his reputation. . .and the other parties' right to freedom of expression."[107] The basis of the ECtHR's reasoning not to find any violation is the result of the test of *proportionality in a narrow sense.*[108] Nevertheless, the ECtHR's conclusion could be different because the ECtHR has regarded the degree of interference to the applicant moderate instead of high.

In this case, the television presenter *F.C.* made a joke about the applicant's sexual orientation by referring to the applicant as "one of the best female Portuguese hosts," leading the applicant to bring this case to the Criminal Investigation Court as a defamation case. The applicant claimed that the dismissal by the domestic courts of

[103] Ibid., paragraph 31.

[104] Ibid., paragraph 35.

[105] European Court of Human Rights, ***SOUSA GOUCHA v. PORTUGAL***, (Application no. 70434/12), judgment of 22 March 2016: The applicant is a well-known television presenter in Portugal, and he publicly declared his homosexuality in 2008 (para. 6–8). During the live talk-show, a quiz was asked to the guests – "Who is the best Portuguese female TV presenter?" And this question was identified as important in the quiz by the presenter F.C. The possible answers to the question included the name of three female presenters and the applicant's and the applicant's being the correct answer (para. 9–10). The applicant lodged a criminal complaint for defamation and insult against the TV company, the production company, the presenter F.C., the director of programs and contents. But, the Public Prosecutor before the Lisbon Criminal Department discontinued the proceeding because the defendants had not intended to offend the applicant (para. 11–17). In this case, the ECtHR found no violation of Article 8 because the television show's freedom of expression under Article 10 and the applicant's right to have his reputation respected are fairly balanced (para. 56). Furthermore, the ECtHR found no violation of Article 14 taken together with Article 8 because the passages in question were "debatable" and "could have been avoided," but did not have discriminatory intent (para. 66–67).

[106] European Court of Human Rights, *SOUSA GOUCHA v. PORTUGAL*, (Application no. 70434/12), judgment of 22 March 2016, paragraphs. 7–15.

[107] Ibid., paragraph 47.

[108] "The greater the degree of non-satisfaction of, or detriment to, one principle, the greater must be the importance of satisfying the other" (taken from Alexy 2010, p. 102).

his defamation proceedings against the television show violates his right under Article 8.[109] The ECtHR considers that interference with the applicant's right to his reputation is rather moderate in that the applicant is a "public figure"[110] and the disputes involve humor and satire.[111] Nevertheless, the dispute of confusion between gender and sexual orientation of the applicant constitutes a serious attack on his reputation[112] because the presenter regarded the male applicant as female presenter because of his homosexuality. The ECtHR considered the degree of interference in the non-satisfaction of the right to reputation of the applicant as moderate. Therefore, the ECtHR concluded that the dismissal by the domestic courts of his defamation proceedings does not violate the applicant's reputation and it is balanced between the television show's freedom of expression and the applicant's right to a reputation.[113] Nevertheless, the degree of interference should be high instead of moderate. It will be clear if the reasoning of *Kimel v. Argentina*[114] in the Inter-American Court of Human Rights is compared.

It is worth comparing the balancing procedure between the *Kimel* case in the Inter- American Court of Human Rights and the *Sousa Goucha* case in the European Court of Human Rights because both cases are related to the balancing of the freedom of expression and the right of a public person to sustain his reputation. In the case of *Kimel*, a journalist *Kimel* wrote a book about the San Patricio Massacre during the last military dictatorship and *Kimel* examined the judicial investigation into the massacre by pointing out the former federal judge. The judge brought a criminal action against *Kimel* for defamation, and *Kimel* was sentenced to one-year suspended imprisonment as well as the penalty of 20,000 pesos. The IACtHR found a violation of the right to freedom of thought and expression of *Kimel*. Both the applicant in *Sousa Goucha* case and the judge in the *Kimel* case are "public figures," however, a degree of interference in non-satisfaction of the freedom of expression of *Kimel* is considered as serious because *Kimel* was criminally punished. On the other hand, the importance of satisfying the right to honor of the judge is considered as moderate in that the judge is a public official and the issue in question is of public interest, which is not mere humor and satire as in *Sousa* case. Interference of the right of freedom of expression is serious compared to the right of the judge's honor; hence the interference cannot be justified in the proportionality test in a narrow sense.

The ECtHR considers the degree of the interference of *Sousa Goucha* moderate because he is a public figure and the content of the statement by F.C. was humor and satire. The IACtHR considered the right of the former judge to be honored as

[109] European Court of Human Rights, *Sousa Goucha v. Portugal*, judgment of 22 March 2016, paragraph 46.

[110] Ibid., paragraph 48.

[111] Ibid., paragraph 50.

[112] Ibid., paragraph 27.

[113] Ibid., paragraph 56.

[114] The Inter-American Court of Human Rights, Case of *Kimel v. Argentina*, judgment of 2 May 2008.

Table 5.1 shows how the ECtHR and the IACtHR decided the degree of interference in the *Sousa Goucha* case and the *Kimel* case. Since I agree with the opinion of the IACtHR, I have expressed my opinion as (I: serious) next to the opinion of the IACtHR. However, since I do not agree with the ECtHR, I have expressed my opinion differently next to the opinion of the ECtHR

	The right to be honored	Freedom of expression
The degree of the interference	Of *Sousa Goucha* ECtHR: Moderate (I: Serious)	Of T.V. Presenter F.C ECtHR: Moderate (I: Low)
	Of former judge IACtHR: Moderate (I: Moderate)	Of *Kimel* IACtHR: Serious (I: Serious)

moderate considering he was a public official and the content of the statement by *Kimel* was public interest. I agree with the IACtHR, but disagree with the ECtHR on that point for the following reasons. Firstly, the character of the public figure is completely different. The ECtHR considers the interference to *Sousa* to be moderate because he is a public figure. Nevertheless, he is a TV presenter, which is a different type of public figure than a politician or former judge because their image to the public is very important to a TV presenter. Therefore, a humiliating statement by F.C would have quite negatively affected the image of *Sousa* as a TV presenter. Second, the kind of content of the statements is completely different. The ECtHR considers the interference to *Sousa* to be moderate because the content of the statement was humor or satire. Nevertheless, the words in question are about *Sousa*'s gender and sexual orientation and the attack on personal honor or reputation related to such grounds should attain a certain gravity.[115] These words cannot be considered as humor because the intention of humor is make the listener happy instead of humiliating someone. For these reasons, the contexts of the ECtHR and the IACtHR are completely different so that the consideration of the ECtHR to the degree of interference to the right of a reputation of the applicant *Sousa* should have been considered serious instead of moderate. Then ECtHR could have found a violation of Article 8 the ECHR.

Another important case of the third category is *Beizaras and Levickas v. Lithuania*.[116] The first applicant was a secondary school student and he is an

[115] For more criticism on the judgment of *Sousa Goucha v. Portugal*, please see Tomlinson QC (2016).

[116] European Court of Human Rights, ***BEIZARAS AND LEVICKAS v. LITHUANIA***, (Application no. 41288/15) judgment of 14 May 2020: The applicants, *Beizaras* and *Levickas* are two Lithuanian nationals who are in a same-sex relationship. On 8 Dec. 2004, Mr. *Beizaras* publicly posted a photograph of them kissing on his Facebook page. The picture accrued some 800 comments, the majority of which were hateful (for example, "Kill…" "Fucking faggots – burn in hell, garbage," "it's not only the Jews that Hitler should have burned," "we should put your head under a car and into the noose, you fucking faggot.") (para. 6–10). The applicants attempted to have criminal proceedings opened, but by final ruling of February 18, 2015, the Klaipeda Regional Court dismissed the appeal. The regional court underlined the applicants' act to post the photograph can be interpreted as constituting "an attempt to deliberately tease or shock individuals with different views or to encourage the posting of negative comments." (para. 23.) In this case, the

openly gay man in a same-sex relationship with the second applicant, who publicly posted a photograph on Facebook page depicting a same-sex kiss. This post received more than 800 comments, and most of them had been aimed at inciting hatred and violence against LGBT people in general and numerous comments had directly threatened the applicants personally.[117] The applicants and LGL Association (National LGBT Rights Association) attempted to have criminal proceedings opened, but the prosecutor took the decision not to initiate a pre-trial investigation regarding the complaint.[118] The District Court dismissed the appeal as sharing the prosecutor's view that "mere use of obscenities" was not enough to incur criminal liability.[119]

The ECtHR finds a violation of Article 14, taken in conjunction with Article 8 ECHR in this case,[120] and the ECtHR's reasoning to find a violation can be restructured according to the *proportionality test in a narrow sense*. On the one hand, the degree of interference in non-satisfaction of the right of the applicant's honor is considered as very serious: the ECtHR states that offenses directed against a person's physical or mental integrity are so serious that only efficient criminal law mechanisms can ensure adequate protection.[121] The applicants had suffered: the secondary school headmaster of the first applicant had requested him "not to disseminate his ideas," the dean of the university theology faculty of the second applicant requested to change the course of the applicant's study.[122] Moreover, the comments affected the applicants' psychological well-being and dignity[123] very seriously.

On the other hand, the importance of satisfying the right of freedom of expression of the writers of hateful comments is light. Furthermore, such hateful comments cannot be protected under freedom of expression because they are very "offensive and vulgar."[124] Lithuanian authorities could not provide sufficient grounds to balance serious interferences of the applicants. In conclusion, the state failed to balance against the serious interferences to the applicants. In this case, the ECtHR started the assessment to refer to the particular importance of pluralism, tolerance and broadmindedness as the hallmarks of a "democratic society,"[125] which is very

ECtHR finds violation of Article 14 in conjunction with Article 8 ECHR and stated that "the very same discriminatory state of mind was at the core of the failure on the part of the relevant public authorities to discharge their positive obligation to investigate in an effective manner" (para. 129–130).

[117] European Court of Human Rights, *Beizaras and Levickas v. Lithuania*, judgment of 14 May 2020, paragraphs 7, 8, 9, and 10.

[118] Ibid., paragraph 18.

[119] Ibid., paragraph 20.

[120] Ibid., paragraph 130.

[121] Ibid., paragraph 111.

[122] Ibid., paragraph 24.

[123] Ibid., paragraph 117.

[124] Ibid., paragraph 117.

[125] European Court of Human Rights, *Beizaras and Levickas v. Lithuania*, judgment of 14 May 2020, paragraph 106.

impressive to show how the ECtHR takes the suffering of sexual minorities seriously. Lithuanian authorities' refusal to prosecute the authors of serious homophobic comments including undisguised calls for violence violate Article 14 in conjunction with Article 8 ECHR. Even if the ECtHR finds a violation in this case, the remaining task is how to make *discriminatory* national authorities such as Lithuania take a proactive role in providing truly effective domestic remedies to prohibit discrimination based on sexual orientation.[126]

5.2.2 Jurisprudence of Article 10 (Freedom of Expression) ECHR

Article 10 of the Convention reads as follows:

1. Everyone has the right to freedom of expression. This right shall include freedom to hold opinions and to receive and impart information and ideas without interference by public authority and regardless of frontiers. This article shall not prevent States from requiring the licensing of broadcasting, television or cinema enterprises.
2. The exercise of these freedoms, since it carries with it duties and responsibilities, may be subject to such formalities, conditions, restrictions or penalties as are *prescribed by law* and are *necessary in a democratic society*, in the interests of national security, territorial integrity or public safety, for the prevention of disorder or crime, for the protection of health or morals, for the protection of the reputation or rights of others, for preventing the disclosure of information received in confidence, or for maintaining the authority and impartiality of the judiciary.

Article 10 ECHR enshrines the principle of legality and the principle of proportionality in paragraph 2—prescribed by law, *legitimate aim* including national security and others, and "necessary in a democratic society" which can be interpreted as implying the test of *necessity* as well as that of the *proportionality in the narrow sense*.[127] I argue that applying the structured proportionality is a clearer standard than including these steps of the proportionality by implications. To back up my arguments, I am restructuring the cases according to the steps of the proportionality. In this section, the analysis focuses on the cases of Article 10. Nevertheless, I will not discuss in detail each step of the proportionality because it has been done in the previous section of Article 8. I have focused on some steps of the proportionality which have been regarded important in the cases. Of course, that does not mean that the steps I have not discussed do not have to be examined because my thesis is to apply all the steps of the proportionality. Article 10 is becoming more important in protecting rights of sexual minorities, mostly in the case law of the ECtHR because

[126]For more comments on the judgment of *Beizaras and Levickas v. Lithuania,* please see *A picture of a same-sex kiss on Facebook wreaks havoc: Beizaras and Levickas v. Lithuania* https://strasbourgobservers.com/2020/02/07/a-picture-of-a-same-sex-kiss-on-facebook-wreaks-havoc-beizaras-and-levickas-v-lithuania/. Accessed November 30, 2021.

[127]Lavrysen (2016), p. 222.

defamation and hate speech against sexual minorities are at issue. In this section, the four cases[128] of ECtHR will be analyzed mainly according to the steps of the proportionality.

5.2.2.1 Legitimate Aim and Suitability Test

The ECtHR found a violation of Article 10 ECHR, as well as of Article 14 taken in conjunction with Article 10 in the case of *Bayev and others v. Russia.*[129] The reasoning in the decision is interpreted focusing on the *legitimate aim* and the *suitability*. According to the factual information of the case, the first applicant was found guilty of a breach of Section 3.10 of the Ryazan Law on Administrative Offences so that he was ordered to pay a fine of 1500 Russian roubles for holding a static demonstration in front of a secondary school in Ryazan, holding two banners which stated that "homosexuality is normal."[130] The second and third applicants were found guilty of a breach of Section 2.13 §1 of the Arkhangelsk Law on Administrative Offences: the second applicant was ordered to pay a fine of RUB 1800, and the third applicant was fined RUB 2,000 for holding a static demonstration in front of the children's library and for holding a banner stating "Homosexuality is good," "Children have the right to know. Great people are also sometimes gay…"[131]

[128]In the case of article 10 ECHR (Freedom of expression), cases are chosen: Vejdeland and Others v. Sweden (2012, regarding the applicants' conviction in 2005 for distributing in an upper secondary school approximately 100 leaflets), Mladina D.D. Ljubljana v. Slovenia (2014, related to insults in an article concerning a parliamentary debate on the legal recognition of same-sex relationships), Kaos Gl v. Turkey (2016, concerning the seizure of all the copies of an issue of a magazine published by a cultural research and solidarity association for gays and lesbians), Bayev and Others v. Russia (2017, concerning a complaint brought by three gay rights activist about legislation in Russia banning the promotion of homosexuality).

[129]European Court of Human Rights, ***BAYEV AND OTHERS v. RUSSIA,*** (application nos. 67667/09, 44092/12 and 56717/12), Chamber judgment of 20 June 2017: The applicants *Bayev, Kiselev* and *Alekseyev* are Russian nations and gay activists. The laws banning "propaganda of homosexuality" were effective at regional level in 2003 and at federal level in 2013. According to the applicants, these laws constitute a virtually full prohibition on nearly any public mention of homosexuality. All the applicants were found guilty of administrative offenses and given fines because they had staged demonstrations between 2009 and 2012 as a protest against these laws. The applicants complained to the Constitutional Court, but the Constitutional Court stated that the ban was justified on the grounds of protection of morals because homosexuality could "create a distorted impression of the social equivalence of traditional and non-traditional marital relations" and lead children into non-traditional sexual relations (para. 6–25). In this case, the ECtHR found a violation of Article 10 the ECHR (freedom of speech). The ECtHR stated that the Russian authorities, by adopting such laws, had reinforced stigma and prejudice and encouraged homophobia, which was incompatible with the values of a democratic society such as equality, pluralism and tolerance (para. 83–84). In addition, the Russian Government violated Article 14 in conjunction with Article 10 because the differences were based solely on considerations of sexual orientation, which were unacceptable under the European Convention (para. 88–92).

[130]Ibid., paragraphs 10–11.

[131]Ibid., paragraphs 14–15.

The central issue in the *Bayev* case whether a legislative ban on the promotion of homosexuality or non-traditional sexual relations among minors[132] can be justified.

Firstly, the legislative ban does not have a *legitimate aim.* The applicants exercised their freedom of expression by displaying banners as activists for sexual minorities, who have been criminally punished according to a legislative ban. Since the legislative provision[133] has been applied to the criminal punishment to the exercise of freedom of expression of the applicants, it is important to examine the aim of this legislative provision. The state has argued that this legislative provision has the aim of "the protection of health and morals and the right of others,"[134] which has been legitimate. I argue that the aims claimed by government are not legitimate for the following reasons. First, the nature of proper purpose should consider creating "a foundation for living together."[135] Particularly, if different opinions can be criminally punished to protect morals, the nature of this aim does not serve to constitute a basis for living together. Second, the aims are not stated explicitly in a clear and specified way to be legitimate.

Furthermore, even if the state argues that the aims are legitimate, the legislative provisions in question are not considered as appropriate to fulfil the stated aims. The ECtHR has stated that the state is to "reinforce stigma and prejudice and encourage homophobia, which is incompatible with the notions of equality, pluralism and tolerance inherent in a democratic society"[136] by adopting these provisions. This reasoning of the ECtHR can be interpreted that the application of the legislative ban is not suitable to promote the stated aims of protecting, health, moral, and the rights of others. Rather, the ban is to negatively affect the society by reinforcing stigma and prejudice.

In addition, there are two more positive implications regarding this case. First, the vagueness and unforeseeability of the provisions have been considered a problem in this case. The ECtHR regards the legislative provisions[137] by which the applicants

---

[132] European Court of Human Rights, *Bayev and Others v. Russia,* judgment of 20 June 2017, paragraph 61.

[133] One of the relevant Russian Law at issue reads as follows:
Section 2.13 Public activities aimed at the promotion of homosexuality among minors

1. Public activities aimed at promoting homosexuality among minors – shall be punishable by an administrative fine for private citizens ranging from 1,500 to 2,000 roubles; for officials – from 2,000 to 5,000 roubles; for legal entities – from 10,000 to 20,000 roubles.
2. The activities referred to in point 1 of the present section, if repeated within one year, shall be punishable by the imposition of an administrative fine, ranging from 2,000 to 5,000 roubles for private individuals, from 5,000 to 10,000 roubles for officials, and from 20,000 to 25,000 roubles for legal entities. (European Court of Human Rights, *Bayev and Others v. Russia* decided on June 20, 2017, paragraph 27.)

[134] European Court of Human Rights, *Bayev and Others v. Russia,* judgment of 20 June 2017, paragraphs 45, 49.

[135] Barak (2012), p. 259.

[136] Ibid., paragraph 83.

[137] One of the relevant Russian Law at issue reads as follows:
Section 2.13 Public activities aimed at the promotion of homosexuality among minors

were criminally punished as inappropriately vague as well as unforeseeable in application; therefore, the law itself is open to abuse.[138] Even if these provisions are not about criminalizing homosexual relations, the problem that the law itself has is surprisingly similar to the Article 92 of the Korean Military Criminal Law (KMCL). Second, the ECtHR saw a violation of Article 14 taken in conjunction with Article 10 ECHR, and at the same time it found a violation of Article 10 ECHR. It clearly shows a different position from the *Oliari*[139] case as well as the *Orlandi*[140] case because the ECtHR in those cases decided that there was no need to examine the complaints under Article 14 in conjunction with Article 8 or Article 12 because the Court already found a violation of Article 8 ECHR. Instead of stopping further reasoning after finding a violating of Article 8, the ECtHR should explicitly decide whether the case in question violates Article 14. The decision of the ECtHR works not only as the subjective specific case decision but also functions as an objective standard of human rights protection for other Member States. The decisions of the ECtHR often function as inspiring sources to other courts in the world including the US Supreme Court as well as the Constitutional Court of Korea. Therefore, such a decision of discrimination could raise people's awareness to recognize sexual orientation as grounds to prohibit discrimination.

5.2.2.2 Necessity Test

The ECtHR found a violation of Article 10 the ECHR in the case of *Kaos GL v. Turkey*.[141] The reasoning process is considered as focusing on the test of *necessity*.

---

3. Public activities aimed at promoting homosexuality among minors – shall be punishable by an administrative fine for private citizens ranging from 1,500 to 2,000 roubles; for officials – from 2,000 to 5,000 roubles; for legal entities – from 10,000 to 20,000 roubles.
4. The activities referred to in point 1 of the present section, if repeated within one year, shall be punishable by the imposition of an administrative fine, ranging from 2,000 to 5,000 roubles for private individuals, from 5,000 to 10,000 roubles for officials, and from 20,000 to 25,000 roubles for legal entities. (European Court of Human Rights, *Bayev and Others v. Russia*, judgment of 20 June 2017, paragraph 27.)

[138] European Court of Human Rights, *Bayev and Others v. Russia*, judgment of 20 June 2017, paragraphs 63.

[139] European Court of Human Rights, *Oliari and others v. Italy*, judgment of 21 July 2015.

[140] European Court of Human Rights, *Orlandi and others v. Italy*, judgment of 14 December 2017.

[141] European Court of Human Rights, ***KAOS GL v. TURKEY***, (application no. 4982/07) Chamber judgment of 22 November 2016: Since the full case is only available in French and Turkish, I referred to the press release of this case issued by the registrar of the Court. ("Seizure of all copies of a magazine published by an association promoting LGBT rights in Turkey breached its right to freedom of expression" ECHR 378 (2016), 22.11.2016.) The applicant is a Turkish association known as "The Kaos cultural research and solidarity association for gays and lesbians" based in Ankara. Its aim is to promote the rights of LGBT community in Turkey. On July 21, 2006, the Ankara Chief Prosecutor seized three copies of issue 28 of the magazine *Kaos GL* before its distribution because the issue in question contained articles and interviews on pornography related to homosexuality. On the same day, the Criminal Court of First Instance ordered the seizure of the

This case concerns the seizure of all the copies of a magazine published by the applicant, which is a Turkish association known as "The Kaos cultural research and solidarity association for gays and lesbians." The aim of this applicant is to promote the rights of the LGBT community in Turkey. The Turkish authorities, when presenting their aim of protecting public morals, ordered the seizure and the confiscation of all the copies of issue 28 of the magazine for more than five years.

The ECtHR specifically pointed out that "the domestic authorities had not attempted to implement a less harsh preventive measure than seizure of all the copies of the issue in question,"[142] which can be interpreted as the failure of the test of a *less restrictive measure*. In this case, the ECtHR suggested the examples of such a less harsh preventive measure: "prohibiting sale of the magazine to persons under the age of 18 or requiring special packaging with a warning for minors." What is more important for the role of the ECtHR is to take a proactive role in finding violation of national authorities, rather than restricting itself to the formal negative role as a court. It was very progressive for the ECtHR in this case to apply the test of *necessity* and to show the examples of *less intrusive measures* to find a violation of Article 10 ECHR.

5.2.2.3 Proportionality in the Narrow Sense

Vejdeland and others v. Sweden[143] is the first case where the ECtHR applied the principles related to hate speech in the context of sexual orientation.[144] The ECtHR found no violation of Article 10 ECHR in this case. The reasoning of the ECtHR can be restructured according to *the proportionality in the narrow sense*. Looking at the facts of the case, the applicants distributed approximately a hundred leaflets[145] on the

---

375 copies of issue 28. Furthermore, the Ankara Chief Prosecutor charged the president and editor-in-chief of the *Kaos GL* magazine. In this case, the ECtHR found a violation of Article 10 ECHR because the seizure of all the copies of issue 28 of *Kaos GL* amounted to a disproportionate interference with the exercise of the applicant's right to freedom of expression.

[142] Press Release issued by the registrar of the Court (2016), *Seizure of all copies of a magazine published by an association promoting LGBT rights in Turkey breached its right to freedom of expression*, ECHR378 (2016), 22.11.2016.

[143] European Court of Human Rights, ***VEJDELAND AND OTHERS v. SWEDEN*** (Application no. 1813/07), judgment of 9 May 2012: The four applicants entered a secondary school and distributed approximately a hundred leaflets in and on pupils' lockers. The leaflets called homosexuality a "deviant sexual proclivity" that has a "morally destructive effect on the substance of society" (para. 7–8). The applicants were convicted by the Swedish Supreme Court for agitation against a national or ethnic group and they appealed to the ECtHR, complaining that their right to freedom of expression had been violated. In this case, the ECtHR finds no violation of Article 10 because the conviction and the penalties imposed were not disproportionate to the legitimate aim, relevant and sufficient (para. 59).

[144] Trimmer (2012).

[145] The leaflets included the following statements "Homosexual Propaganda

In the course of a few decades' society has swung from rejection of homosexuality and other sexual deviances to embracing this deviant sexual proclivity. Your anti-Swedish teachers know

pupils' lockers in an upper secondary school and they were charged with agitation against sexual minorities.[146] The issue in this case is whether such criminal punishment of applicants violates Article 10 the ECHR, freedom of expression of the applicants. The ECtHR finds in the *Vejdeland* case that the legal provisions[147] to punish the applicants regarding their statements that threatened or expressed contempt for a group of people with reference to their sexual orientation is justified according to two principles. Firstly, the interference with the freedom of expression through the applicants' conviction is in accordance with Chapter 16, Article 8 of the Swedish Penal Code meeting the requirements of *the principle of legality*.[148] Secondly, the interference has a *legitimate aim* of the principle of proportionality, which is "the protection of the reputation and rights of others."[149] Furthermore, the ECtHR is likely to consider the interference with freedom of expression of the applicants as light or moderate, while considering the importance of satisfying the right to honor of sexual minorities as very important. The ECtHR stresses that discrimination based on sexual orientation is as serious as discrimination based on "race, origin or color."[150] On the other hand, the statements made by the applicants are "serious and prejudicial allegations"[151] and "unnecessarily offensive."[152]

On the one hand, regarding the criminal punishment imposed on the applicants, the ECtHR considers that it is not serious interference compared to such unnecessary harmful statements made by the applicants. The applicants were not sentenced to imprisonment, and three of the applicants were given suspended sentences combined

very well that homosexuality has a morally destructive effect on the substance of society and will willingly try to put it forward as something normal and good.

- Tell them that HIV and AIDS appeared early with the homosexuals and that their promiscuous lifestyle was one of the main reasons for this modern-day plague gaining a foothold.
- Tell them that homosexual lobby organizations are also trying to play down paedophilia, and ask if this sexual deviation should be legalized." (European Court of Human Rights, *Vejdeland and others v. Sweden*, judgment of 9 February 2012, paragraph 8.)

[146]European Court of Human Rights, *Vejdeland and others v. Sweden*, judgment of 9 February 2012. paragraphs 8–9.

[147]The legal provisions in question is Chapter 16, Article 8 of the Penal Code: The Article provides that a person who, in a disseminated statement or communication, threatens or expresses contempt for a national, ethnic or other such group of persons with allusion to race, colour, national or ethnic origin, religious beliefs or sexual orientation, should be convicted of agitation against a national or ethnic group. The offence carries a penalty of up to two years' imprisonment. If the offence is considered minor the penalty is a fine, and if it is considered to be aggravated the penalty is imprisonment for no less than six months and no more than four years. (European Court of Human Rights, *Vejdeland and others v. Sweden*, judgment of 9 February 2012, paragraph 18.)

[148]European Court of Human Rights, *Vejdeland and others v. Sweden*, judgment of 9 February 2012, paragraphs 48–49.

[149]Ibid., paragraph 49.

[150]Ibid., paragraph 55.

[151]Ibid., paragraph 54.

[152]Ibid., paragraph 57.

with fines, and the fourth applicant was sentenced to probation. The ECtHR found that such penalties were not excessive considering their acts to distribute the leaflets containing serious and prejudicial allegations against sexual minorities. On the other hand, as interference of the right of freedom of expression is considered as moderate or light, and the importance of satisfying the right not to discriminate based on sexual orientation is very high, such interference is justified and there is no violation of Article 10 ECHR. In this case, the reasoning regarded the law of balancing to protect the rights of sexual minorities from harmful effects of expression of hate speech against sexual minorities.

The case of *Mladina D.D. Ljubljana v. Slovenia*[153] is another important case where the reasoning of finding a violation of Article 10 the ECHR can be understood as a question of balancing. To introduce the fact in the case, the applicant *Mladina* is a private company publishing the weekly magazine *Mladina.*[154] On June 27, 2005, the *Mladina* published a one-page article summarizing the parliamentary debate preceding the adoption of the Registration of Same-Sex Civil Partnerships Act ("the Act") and the responses of other parliamentarians to the speeches of the Slovenian National Party ("SNP") member. The article described the debate of the SNP, which strongly opposed the adoption and statements of one of the deputies, S.P., who was described by the author as a "typical attitude of a cerebral bankrupt." On August 26, 2005, the SNP member S.P. brought an action for defamation of his honor and reputation against the applicant. On May 16, 2006, the Ljubljana District Court ordered the applicant to pay S.P. the amount of 700,000 Slovenian Tolars (2,921.05 Euros) in damages as well as to publish this judgment itself in *Mladina*. On January 24, 2007, the Higher Court dismissed the applicant's appeal, and the Constitutional Court dismissed the applicant's complaint.[155]

This is another case of competing interests of freedom of expression with the right to honor as the *Kimel*[156] case of the Inter-American Court of Human Rights as well as *Sousa Goucha v. Portugal*, which were introduced in the previous section. In this

---

[153] European Court of Human Rights, ***MLADINA D.D. LJUBLJANA v. SLOVENIA*** (Application no. 20981/10), judgment of 17 April 2014: In 2005, the applicant of the private company *Mladina d.d. Ljubljana*, owner of the "Mladina" newspapers published an article regarding the adoption of the Registration of Same-Sex Civil Partnerships Act. The article described the debate of the Slovenian National Party, which strongly opposed the adoption and statements of one of the deputies, S.P., who was described by the author as a "typical attitude of a cerebral bankrupt." After publishing the article, S.P. pressed charges against the newspaper for defamation of his honor and reputation and the district court ordered the applicant to pay him damages 2,921.05 EUR in damages and to publish this judgment in newspapers (para. 5–20). The ECtHR found a violation of Article 10 ECHR in this case because the general interest in promoting freedom of expression in the issues of public interest is recognized. On the other hand, no pressing social need for the protection of S.P's reputation was found (para. 47–49).

[154] Ibid., paragraph 5.

[155] European Court of Human Rights, *MLADINA D.D. LJUBLJANA v. SLOVENIA* (Application no. 20981/10), judgment of 17 April 2014, paragraphs 6–20 (The Facts).

[156] The Inter-American Court of Human Rights, Case of *Kimel v. Argentina*, judgment of 2 May 2008.

case of *Mladina*, the ECtHR finds that the legal stipulations to punish the applicant company have a *legitimate aim* of protecting the reputation or rights of others.[157] Nevertheless, the main reasoning can be reconstructed as the test of *balancing*. On the one hand, the ECtHR considers the context of a political debate related to the public interest. In such a context, the ECtHR states that "a greater degree of tolerance"[158] is needed for a politician compared to a private individual. On the other hand, the ECtHR interprets that journalistic freedom can cover exaggeration or provocation or somewhat immoderate statements.[159] Therefore, the interference imposed on the applicants is not justified because it fails the *proportionality test in a narrow sense*.

The *balancing* scales of this case are very similarly applied as those in the *Kimel*[160] case of Inter-American Court of Human Rights. On the one hand, the degree of interference in non-satisfaction of the right of freedom of expression of the applicant *Mladian* and *Kimel* is considered as very serious. A criminal fine as well as introducing the judgment of such a criminal punishment must have a stigmatizing effect for magazine *Mladian* and criminal punishment for *Kimel*. On the other hand, the importance of satisfying the right to honor or reputation of S.P. and the former judge in the *Kimel* case are considered as moderate since the issues are of public interest, as both are public figures being politician and a public official, namely a former judge. The case *Mladina* particularly has implications in that it finds violation of Article 10 the ECHR for the legal actions against journalists by a politician, who made an insulting attack which degraded homosexuals. In the meantime, the ECtHR does not consider the criticism stated in *Mladina* as a personal attack on S.P. Rather, such criticism can be seen as the free debate of ideas, which a democratic society guarantees.[161] Convergence has been found in the case of the ECtHR and the IACtHR on the similar topic of competing interests of freedom of expression of journalist and of right to be respected of a public figure of politician and a former judge.

5.2.3 Jurisprudence of Article 11 (Freedom of Assembly and Association) ECHR

Article 11 of the Convention reads as follows:

---

[157] Ibid., paragraph 36.

[158] European Court of Human Rights, *MLADINA D.D. LJUBLJANA v. SLOVENIA* (Application no. 20981/10), Judgment of 17 April 2014, paragraphs 40.

[159] Ibid., paragraph 40.

[160] The Inter-American Court of Human Rights, Case of *Kimel v. Argentina*, judgment of 2 May 2008.

[161] European Court of Human Rights, *Mladina D.D.Ljubljana v. Slovenia*, judgment of 17 April 2014, paragraph 46.

1. Everyone has the right to freedom of peaceful assembly and to freedom of association with others, including the right to form and to join trade unions for the protection of his interests.
2. No restrictions shall be placed on the exercise of these rights other than such as are prescribed by law and are necessary in a democratic society in the interests of national security or public safety, for the prevention of disorder or crime, for the protection of health or morals or for the protection of the rights and freedoms of others. This article shall not prevent the imposition of lawful restrictions on the exercise of these rights by members of the armed forces, of the police or of the administration of the State.

It is becoming more important to exercise the right to openly proclaim one's sexual orientation by participating in demonstrations.[162] There are cases in which the ECtHR found violations of Article 11 as well as of Article 14 taken in conjunction with Article 11 related to demonstrations or assemblies to promote the rights of sexual minorities. In these cases as well, the *Principle of Proportionality* is particularly important as "a yardstick for assessing whether national authorities have overstepped the permissible bounds of discretion"[163] because national authorities and assembly organizers often conflict in the process of applications. In addition to the proportionality, "prescribed by law" is discussed in this section because it functions importantly particularly in the case law related to Article 11 as the mandate of legality as the limit in the limitations of the rights,[164] and the requirement of legality represents a formal aspect of the rule-of law principle.[165] Particularly, in the case law of Article 11, the *law of legality* often matters in the cases where states reject peaceful assembly without any legal grounds. As discussed earlier, the principle of legality is not part of the principle of proportionality. Nevertheless, legality is discussed because it is the important mandate as the limit of the limitations[166] on Freedom of assembly and association (Article 11 ECHR). Furthermore, the discussions on the steps of the proportionality will follow. This section will particularly discuss how legitimate aim, and the proportionality in the narrow sense functions in finding violation of Article 11 through analysis of the case law related to sexual orientation. Suitability and necessity are not included not because the test should not be examined[167] but because of the purpose of emphasizing the importance of legitimate aim and the balancing in the discussion of Article 11.

[162] Edel (2015), pp. 71–75: *Edel* analyzed case laws related to discrimination based on sexual orientation or gender identity related to Freedom to demonstrate in Section 6.

[163] Arai-Takahashi (2002), p. 145.

[164] Clérico (2021, forthcoming).

[165] Barak (2012), p. 108.

[166] Clérico (2021, forthcoming).

[167] I agree with *J. Sieckmann* in that "the principle of proportionality is of crucial importance" among the standards of constitutional law, which applies for the justification of an interference with the rights. Furthermore, the principle of proportionality requires that (1) the interference pursues a legitimate objective and the three sub-criteria of (2) the demand of adequacy (as "suitability" expressed in this work), (3) the demand of necessity, (4) the demand of proportionality in a strict sense (as "the proportionality in the narrow sense" expressed in this work) (taken from Sieckmann 2018, p. 11).

5.2.3.1 The Principle of Legality

The Principle of Legality requires that the interference should have legal grounds, because "a constitutional right cannot be limited unless such a limitation is authorized by law."[168] As stipulated in Article 11, Paragraph 2, ECHR, restrictions have to be prescribed by law. Even if the legality principle is regarded as a basic requirement of the rule of law, there are shockingly still cases that do not fulfill this requirement when limiting the rights of sexual minorities. One of those cases is the case of *Baczkowski and others v. Poland.*[169] In this case, the applicants are a group of individuals and the Foundation for Equality, and they wanted to hold an assembly in Warsaw to alert public opinion to the issue of discrimination against minorities including sexual minorities.

The complaint of the applicants is directed against the refusal without grounds as well as the non-timely legal protection. On June 3, 2005, the Traffic Officer on behalf of the Mayor of Warsaw refused permission because the organizers did not submit a "traffic organization plan."[170] On June 9, 2005, the Mayor issued decisions banning the assemblies organized by the applicants who work for the benefit of persons of homosexual orientation. On the same day the authorities allowed three other planned assemblies concerning discrimination against women.[171] On June 10, 2005 the applicants appealed to the *Mazowsze Governor* against the Mayor's refusals of June 9, 2005, and the Governor noted that the requirement lacked legal basis[172] in the provisions of the Assemblies Act.[173] On June 28, 2005 the applicant

---

[168] Barak (2012), p. 107.

[169] European Court of Human Rights, ***BĄCZKOWSKI AND OTHERS v. POLAND*** (App. No. 1543/06) judgment of 24 September 2007: The applicants of a group of individuals and an association sought permission from the Warsaw municipal authorities to stage a march (from June 10 to 12, 2005) through the city and hold a series of meetings to alert public opinion to the issue of discrimination against various minority groups including homosexuals and women. The authorities refused permission for the march (June 3, 2005) and 6 of the 8 planned stationary assemblies (June 9, 2005) on the ground of road traffic regulations (according to Road Traffic Act) and the risk of violent clashes with other demonstrators. The Mayor of Warsaw said in an interview that he would refuse the applicants' request in all circumstances because "propaganda about homosexuality is not tantamount to exercising one's freedom of assembly." Because the applicants knew the real reason of the refusal, they went ahead with the planned march (June 11, 2005) despite the refusal. On June 17, 2005, the governor and on August 22, 2005, the Local Government Appellate Board quashed the decisions of June 9 and 3, respectively. The ECtHR found a violation of Article 11, Article 13 in conjunction with Article 11, Article 14 in conjunction with Article 11 ECHR.

[170] Ibid., paragraphs 7–11.

[171] Ibid., paragraphs 13–15.

[172] European Court of Human Rights, *Baczkowski and others v. Poland,* judgment of 24 September 2007, paragraphs 21–24.

[173] Under Section 2 of the Assemblies Act, freedom of assembly can be restricted only by statue and where it is necessary for the protection of national security or public safety, for the protection of health or morals or for the protection of the rights and freedoms of others.

Under Section 8 the municipality shall refuse permission for the demonstration if its purpose is in breach of the Act itself or of provisions of the Criminal Code, or if the demonstration might entail a

Table 5.2 shows what happened according to timeline in the case of Baczkowski and others v. Poland because understanding the timeline is important to see why the state violated the applicants' rights

Timeline	What happened
May 12, 2005	The Applicants applied to the City Council Road Traffic Office for permission to organize the march for June 10-12, 2005 according to an instruction of the Warsaw Mayor's Office on May 11, 2005.
June 3, 2005	The Traffic Officer refused permission for the march
June 9, 2005	The Mayor issued decisions banning the assemblies to be organized by the Organizers including the applicants. On the other hand, three planned assemblies related to gender discrimination have been allowed
June 10, 2005	The applicants appealed to the Governor against the Mayor's refusals of June 9, 2005
June 17, 2005	The Governor quashed the contested June 9 Refusals of authorization to hold the assemblies
June 28, 2005	The applicant appealed to the Local Government Appeals Board against the decision of June 3, 2005

appealed to the Local Government Appeals Board against the decision of June 3, 2005, arguing that the requirement to submit "a traffic organization plan" lacked legal basis and the applicants had never been requested to submit such a document before. The Board then quashed the contested decision as being unlawful.[174]

As Table 5.2 shows, although the municipal authorities' decisions were subsequently quashed on appeal, the applicants argued that the remedy came too late (June 17, 2005) since the dates planned for the demonstrations (from June 10 to June 12, 2005) had already passed. The ECtHR found a violation of Article 11 ECHR in this case because the interference with the applicant's right to freedom of peaceful assembly was not prescribed by law.[175] Even if the assemblies were eventually held on the planned dates, the applicants took a risk in holding them given the official ban in force at that time. Furthermore, legal remedies by the national authorities could not change the situation of the applicants because the decisions were only given after the date of the assemblies.[176]

The reasoning of the ECtHR in this case can be restructured according to the principle of legality because it did not have legal ground prescribed by law.[177] In addition, the ECtHR found a violation of Article 13 (Right to an Effective Remedy) in conjunction with Article 11 because timing could be very important to the political

danger to life or limb, or a major danger to property (taken from European Court of Human Rights, *Baczkowski and others v. Poland,* judgment of 24 September 2007, paragraphs 32, 35).

[174] European Court of Human Rights, *Baczkowski and others v. Poland,* judgment of 24 September 2007, paragraphs 19–20.

[175] European Court of Human Rights, *Baczkowski and others v. Poland,* judgment of 24 September 2007, paragraphs 69.

[176] Ibid., paragraphs. 67–68.

[177] Ibid., paragraphs 70.

and social impact of a public assembly and the impact of the meeting can be seriously diminished.[178] In addition, the ECtHR found a violation of Article 14 in conjunction with Article 11 ECHR because of the strong personal opinions publicly expressed by the Mayor against "propaganda about homosexuality."[179] Such decisions could work as an objective standard for other Member States not to interfere with the grounds that are not prescribed by law, not to unlawfully refuse assemblies,[180] and not to discriminate against sexual minorities.

5.2.3.2 Legitimate Aim

Existence of a legitimate Aim is the first requirement in the four steps of structured proportionality test, and it is explicitly required in the second paragraph of Article 11 ECHR. *Gerards*'s interpretation is that it is not only required that the aims pursued are legitimate, but also interferences have to be "in the general interest or in the interests of national security or public safety, or they must be necessary for the protection of public order, health or morals, for the protection of the rights of others for preventing the disclosure of information received in confidence" as exhaustive lists of the aims.[181] *Legitimate Aims* are needed for the state interference of the rejection of applicants' requests to hold an assembly.

In the case of *Alekseyev and Others v. Russia*,[182] which concerned the continued refusal by Russian authorities to approve organizers' requests to hold LGBT rallies, the ECtHR found a violation of Article 11, Article 13 (Right to an effective remedy) in conjunction with Article 11, and Article 14 (Prohibition of discrimination) in conjunction with Article 11 ECHR. The ECtHR's assessment does not go into detail in terms of the applicability of the adjudication methods, merely stating that "the ban on holding LGBT public assemblies imposed by the domestic authorities did not correspond to a pressing social need and was thus not necessary in a democratic society."[183] Nevertheless, considering the ECtHR's statement that "the decision to

---

[178] Ibid., paragraphs 82–24.

[179] Ibid., paragraphs 100–101.

[180] For further insights related to the reasoning of the ECtHR on the case of *Baczkowski and others v. Poland,* please see Van den Bogaert (2019).

[181] Gerards (2019), pp. 220–221.

[182] European Court of Human Rights, ***ALEKSEYEV AND OTHERS v. RUSSIA*** (Applications nos. 14988/09 and 50 others), Judgment of 6 May 2019: The case brought together 51 applications by seven Russian nationals, who submitted notices to local authorities informing them of their intention to hold public rallies on the issue of LGBT rights. The local authorities rejected the proposed date and location of the rally. The domestic courts uphold these decisions and the result of the appeal came after the proposed date of the rally (Paragraphs 1–7.) In this case, the ECtHR found a violation of Articles 11, 13 in conjunction with Article 11, and 14 in conjunction with Article 11 ECHR because the ban on holding LGBT public assemblies imposed by the domestic authorities was not necessary in a democratic society.

[183] Ibid., paragraph 21.

reject the applicants' requests to hold public LGBT events could not be justified by concerns over public disorder,"[184] it seems that the ECtHR considers that the state's rejection does not have legitimate aims. In Article 11, Paragraph 2 explicitly states that "for the prevention of disorder" is stated as an example of a legitimate aim, but Russian authorities failed to provide proof that their decision to reject LGBT events was a legitimate aim to prevent disorder. In addition, "opposition to the events from a majority of society"[185] is not accepted as a legitimate aim to reject the applications to hold public rallies.

In another case against Russian authorities of *Zhdanov and Others v. Russia,*[186] the ECtHR also finds a violation of Article 6 (access to court), Article 11 (freedom of association), and Article 14 (prohibition of discrimination) in conjunction with Article 11. Particularly the reasoning to find a violation of Article 11 can be reconstructed according to the test of a legitimate aim. Russian authorities claim that the refusal to register an association defending LGBT rights aims to protect Russia's sovereignty, safety and territorial integrity which are linked to the legitimate aims of the protection of national security and public safety.[187] However, the ECtHR considers such aims to be interpreted restrictively so that they cannot be considered as legitimate for the refusal. Furthermore, the ECtHR points out that there is no relation between the promotion of homosexuality and the demographic situation, and the also state failed to explain "how a hypothetical decrease in the population could affect national security and public safety."[188] In this case, the state's refusal to register organizations to promote and protect the rights of LGBT people in Russia does not have any legitimate aims because there are no reasonable relations between the aims of organizations and Russia's sovereignty caused by a hypothetical decrease in the population. This argument put forward by the Russian authorities is surprisingly similar to the Korean church's arguments against sexual minorities. Korean churches are against providing any protective measures to sexual minorities because such measures could promote homosexuality, cause a decrease in

[184]Systemic measures required to address issues of free assembly and discrimination as evidenced in ban on LGBT rallies, European Court of Human Rights, *Alekseyev and Others v. Russia,* judgment of 27 November 2018. Press Release issued by the Registrar of the Court, Decision of the Court. p. 1.

[185]Ibid., p. 2.

[186]European Court of Human Rights, ***ZHDANOV AND OTHERS v. RUSSIA*** (Applications nos. 12200/08 and 2 others), judgment of 16 October 2019: The applicants are three Russian organizations to defend LGBT rights, and four Russian nationals who are the founder or presidents of these organizations. The applicant organizations applied for registration, but the local authorities and the domestic courts refused their requests because the aim was to promote LGBT rights (para. 6–30). In this case, the ECtHR found a violation of f Article 6 § 1 (access to court), Article 11, Article 14 in conjunction with Article 11 because the ECtHR found the decisive grounds for refusal cannot be reasonably justified (para. 102, 165, 182–183).

[187]Ibid., paragraph 156.

[188]Ibid., paragraph 156.

population,[189] and threaten national security. Nevertheless, such aims cannot be recognized as legitimate as seen from the reasoning of the ECtHR in *Zhdanov* case.

5.2.3.3 Proportionality in the Narrow Sense

In the Case of *Genderdoc-M v. Moldova*,[190] the State admitted that there had been a violation.[191] Regarding Article 14 in conjunction with Article 11, the majority opinion found a violation while the dissenting opinion claims no violation. The reasoning of both opinions can be restructured according to the *proportionality test in a narrow sense*, yet nevertheless, leading to two different conclusions. In this case, the applicant as a non-governmental organization applied to authorities for authorization to hold a peaceful demonstration to encourage the adoption of laws to protect sexual minorities from discrimination. However, the authorities refused permission on the ground that there was already a law on the protection of minorities[192] (even if they are not sexual minorities specifically). The applicants argued that the government's rejection is discriminatory because the grounds for the ban was the fact that the assembly was promoting the interests of sexual minorities.

Regarding the violation of Article 14, the assessment of the majority opinion can be reconstructed according to the *proportionality in a narrow sense*. On the one hand, the degree of interference with the non-satisfaction of the right of assembly is regarded as serious because the state forbids demonstrations which they consider to be promoting homosexuality without offering clear reasons. On the other hand, the degree of freedom of religion of the government seems to be very light because rejecting assembly to promote the rights of sexual minorities is not connected with religious freedom or the religious intolerance of the Orthodox Christian church in Russia, to which a majority of people belong.

The dissenting opinion of judges *Gyulumyan* and *Ziemele* agrees with the seriousness of interference to the right of assembly of applicants. What was different

---

[189] The decrease of population is often discussed as grounds not to recognize same sex relations in Korea (taken from "Christian today" of 29 January 2018, https://www.christiantoday.co.kr/news/308909. Accessed November 30, 2021).

[190] European Court of Human Rights, ***GENDERDOC-M v. MOLDOVA*** (Application no. 9106/06), judgment of 12 September 2012: The applicant is a non-governmental organization (NGO) based in Moldova whose object is to provide information and to assist the LGBT community. The applicant applied to the Municipal Council for authorization to hold a peaceful demonstration in front of the Parliament to encourage the adoption of laws to protect sexual minorities from discrimination. But, the application was rejected by the Council. The Supreme Court of Justice found that the applicant association had failed to give undertakings as regards the obligations required by the law in respect of assemblies. Furthermore, the court considered that there was a risk that the demonstration would cause a breach of public order (para. 6–17). In this case, the ECtHR found a violation of Articles 11, 13 in conjunction with Article 11, and 14 in conjunction with Article 11.

[191] European Court of Human Rights, *Genderdoc-M v. Moldova,* judgment of 12 September 2012, paragraph 26.

[192] Ibid., paragraphs 6–9.

from the majority opinion concerns the government's justifications. The dissenting opinion considers that the government submitted reasonable arguments in rejecting the assembly applications. The dissenting opinion argues that the majority opinion should have assessed "as compared to other possible assemblies that were or were not allowed for the same reasons of public order"[193] as discriminatory treatment, which is missing. However, if interference of the right to assembly is serious, authorities have to present very weighty reasons for justifying interference as the state bears the burden of proof. Therefore, if the state fails to present "such analysis," the conclusion should find violation of Article 14 as the majority opinions do according to the *law of balancing*.

In the recent case of *Lashmankin and others v. Russia*,[194] the ECtHR finds violations of Articles 11 (Freedom of assembly), 13 (right to an effective remedy) in conjunction with 11, 5 (right to liberty), and 6 (right to a fair trial) of the ECHR. The applicants submitted a formal notice to the appropriate local authority of their intention to hold peaceful events such as a picket, a march, a gay pride march, and a meeting, which were repeatedly refused by the authorities. On the one hand, interferences by such a general ban on the right to assembly of applicants are regarded as serious; much worse, Russian authorities "disperse(d) some of the applicants' public events" and "arrest(ed) three of them,"[195] which makes interference even more serious. On the other hand, potential public disorder that might be caused by such peaceful events must be light. In addition, it does not fulfil the test of *the proportionality test in a narrow sense*.

---

[193] European Court of Human Rights, *Genderdoc-M v. Moldova,* judgment of 12 September 2012. Dissenting opinion, Paragraph 4.

[194] European Court of Human Rights, ***LASHMANKIN AND OTHERS v. RUSSIA*** (Applications nos. 57818/09 and 14 others) judgment of 29 May, 2017: The applicants are 23 Russian nationals who submitted a formal notice to the appropriate local authority to notify their intention to hold several assemblies. However, the authorities refused to approve its location, time or manner of conduct. In most of the cases, the applicants complain that these refusals meant that they could not hold their event at all. In numerous cases, the applicants challenged the rejection by making an appeal in court. However, the claims were rejected because the courts found the refusals were lawful and properly reasoned ("I. The Circumstances of the case"). In this case, the ECtHR found a violation of Article 11(1), Article 13 (Effective Remedy) in conjunction with Article 11. In addition, The ECtHR also unanimously found violations of Article 5 (Right to liberty and security § 1 and 6 (Right to a fair trial) § 1 in respect of certain applicants ("Legal Summary").

[195] Local authorities repeatedly undermined public protests against alleged corruption, ineffective governance, and the repression of civil liberties, Chamber judgment of *Lashmankin and others v. Russia,* judgment of 7 February 2017. Press Release issued by the Registrar of the Court, Decision of the Court. p. 4.

5.3 The Role of Courts and the Proportionality[196]

Human Rights protection is often concerned with minorities, as we discussed with regard to the right to marry for same-sex couples in the previous chapters. The ECtHR suggests that any distinctions based on membership of any "particularly vulnerable group in society that has suffered considerable discrimination in the past"[197] should be justified with very weighty reasons. Such vulnerable groups naturally include people from sexual minorities. Likewise, the protection of vulnerability, such as disability, age, and sexual orientation, has always been a major concern in Human Rights Protection. Another important issue regarding "the dilemma of human rights adjudication"[198] is whether the judiciary justifiability[199] on human rights could work to implement the right if the state fails in its role to guarantee and implement the right.

Jeremy Waldron advocates the democratic ideal by claiming that at least all important decisions should be made by the people, rather than by "unelected and unaccountable judges."[200] *Waldron* opposes the idea of allowing the judiciary to make contested value judgments. On the other hand, *Taggart*[201] argues that the special role of the courts is an ultimate enforcement mechanism for justification of all public power by providing adequate reasons for the decisions. In this sense, we can understand that the role of courts does not replace the role of decision makers, but requests decision makers to fulfill their obligations.

In the case of *DeShaney*[202] in the United States Supreme Court, *Joshua DeShaney*'s mother filed a lawsuit on his behalf against Winnebago County,

---

[196]Considering that Chap. 5 focuses on the principle of proportionality in the case law of the ECtHR, this section can be seen irrelevant with the topic of Chap. 5 because the case examples in this section are not from the ECtHR. Nevertheless, I wanted to include this section in Chap. 5 because discussions about the role of courts are discussed in the context of the principle of proportionality. The discussion in this section is only briefly introduced. Considering the importance of the topic of the role of courts and judicial review, it should be dealt more in depth as a topic of further research of mine.

[197]Moeckli (2014), pp. 168–169.

[198]Fredman (2013), p. 292.

[199]One of the main focuses of this work is about the right to marry as discrimination based on sexual orientation, and right to marry does not have any problem with **justifiability** because it is justifiable. The problem with the right to marry is rather the intensity of the judicial review. The reason is mainly that applying the fully structured proportionality is related to the role of judicature, especially with the test of necessity in searching for the less restrictive measure and the test of the proportionality in the narrow sense.

[200]Waldron (1999), p. 251.

[201]Taggart (1997), p. 305.

[202]***CASE OF Joshua DeShaney, by his guardian ad litem, and Melody DeSahney, Petitioners v. Winnebago County Department of Social Services, et al.,*** decided on February 22, 1989, by the Supreme Court of the United States: Joshua DeShaney lived with his father Randy DeSahney, who moved to Winnebago County in Wisconsin after a divorce court in Wyoming gave custody of Joshua to Randy in 1980. A police report of child abuses and a hospital visit in January, 1983,

claiming that by failing to intervene and protect him from violence about which they knew or should have known about, the agency violated Joshua's right to liberty without the due process guaranteed to him by the Fourteenth Amendment to the United States Constitution. The court opinion, by Chief Justice *William Rehnquist*, held that the process clause protects against state action only, and as it was *Randy DeShaney* who abused *Joshua*, a state actor of Winnebago County was not responsible. A state's failure to protect an individual against private violence generally does not constitute a violation of the Due Process Clause, because the Clause imposes no duty on the state to provide members of the general public with adequate protective services. The Due Process Clause in the case of *DeShaney* is phrased as a limitation on the state's power to act, not as a guarantee of certain minimal levels of safety and security. While it forbids the state itself to deprive individuals of life, liberty, and property without due process of law, its language cannot fairly be read to impose an affirmative obligation on the state to ensure that those interests do not come to harm through other means. The Supreme Court of the United States held that a state government agency's failure to prevent child abuse by a custodial parent does not violate the child's right to liberty for the purposes of the Fourteenth Amendment to the United States Constitution.

However, I do not agree with the holding of the *DeShaney* case because the role of the court is to monitor and to urge fulfillment of their responsibilities.[203] About ten years ago, almost all the medical doctors in Korea were very unkind to the patients. They never explained things in detail to the patients and only communicated with the nurse using some specialized words which the patients could not understand. After the court gave the doctors "the duty to explain" through judgment, their behavior changed dramatically. As such, the court judgment works as a catalyst to provide society with some issues to discuss. In that sense, the experiment by Indian courts is impressive in that the court extended the meaning of standing to sue, which was regarded as a weakness in an adversary judiciary system. The case of the Indian Supreme Court is regarded as a successful case of the positive role of the judicature. In dealing with the case of *Sheela Barse v. Union of India*,[204] the Indian Supreme Court directly appointed a fact finding committee and investigated the case. This case concerned thousands of adults and children who were put in prison without

---

prompted the country Department of Social Services(DSS) to obtain a court order to keep the boy in the hospital's custody. But, three days later, the juvenile court dismissed the case and returned the boy to the custody of his father. A DSS social worker recorded suspicion of child abuse, but no action was taken. Visits in January and March 1984, when the worker was told Joshua was too ill to see her, also resulted in no action. Eventually, Joshua suffered very severe brain damage after Randy beat him severely.

[203] Taggart (1997), p. 305.

[204] I introduced the United States Supreme Court case and the Indian case here although they are not cases of sexual orientation or same-sex marriage because I think these cases could be a good example of the role of the judicature. These cases show how far the Court could involve itself in the processes such as fact-finding and execution. Also especially the Indian Supreme Court cases are evaluated as successful incidents of an active role of judicature (related: Fredman 2008, pp. 124–133).

a limit to the detention period, on the grounds of regarding them as having a "non-criminal mental disorder." By the judgment,[205] the Indian Supreme Court imposed positive obligations on the state to improve facilities in mental hospitals and cure sick people in the hospital, as well as negative obligations not to imprison people with mental disorders.

Jeremy Waldron is regarded as one of the scholars who is against an active role of the judicature.[206] *Waldron* argues that it is a serious challenge for democratic as well as representative competences of the people, if judges have the authority to decide the content of human rights. His argument is that "a judge's decision should be firmly preserved in the isolated area which the action of the legislature cannot reach because some suggestion devised by legislators who will be elected next year or ten years later can be erroneous or can contain a real intention different from it revealed."[207] In addition, he claims that we have to trust "common people," who are politically responsible.[208] However, the judgment of the court appeared as a form of social conversation linking judicial activism, social movements and the human rights movement. Through this, social conversation regarding law, rights and justice no longer remains solely in the area of specialists' discourse. Judicial judgments initiate democratic communication between the people and the state, without being restricted to being simply the judgment about some limited individual's interests. Furthermore, judicial conversations could be seen as playing a positive role in overcoming the limits of democracy. Hence, the positive role of the judicature does not violate the principle of democracy.[209]

Judicial review is a theme which is closely related to the principle of proportionality,[210] which requires a deeper discussion than what has been introduced in this

---

[205] *Sheila Barse v. Union of India* [1995] 5 Supreme Court Cases 654 (Indian Supreme Court): "The case was initiated in 1990 by the social activist Sheela Barse, who forwarded to the Court a copy of an article in which she exposed the plight of the thousands of children and adults in Calcutta who were committed to jail under the category of 'non-criminal lunatics' and left there indefinitely in miserable conditions with no recourse to either medical treatment or judicial proceedings. Having received an inadequate response to its direction to the State to provide the relevant facts, the Court appointed a Commission to ascertain the facts itself. Consisting of a professor of psychiatry and an academic lawyer, the Commission was required to visit a representative sample of prisons or institutions and gauge relevant facts, including the total number of mentally ill inmates, the procedure for admission, the care and facilities provided, the existence of mental health facilities in the relevant district, the pattern of qualified staff, and procedures for after-care and rehabilitation." (Fredman 2008, p. 129.)

[206] Fredman (2008).

[207] Waldron (1999), p. 222.

[208] Ibid., p. 251.

[209] Related: Fredman (2008), pp. 128–134.

[210] The principle of proportionality is widely misunderstood as being the same as a strict judicial review, while a reasonableness review was equivalent to a more deferential approach, but *Matthias Klatt* argues against such a misunderstanding. According to his position, both the proportionality and reasonableness review are merely different sets of questions to ask, which do not predetermine the scrutiny and the degree of scrutiny must be established separately (taken from Klatt 2015, p. 357). *Katharine Young* offers a contrasting opinion to that of *Klatt* by suggesting that the

work. Furthermore, the intensity of review is also associated with the role of the courts because the approach to the discussion of the role of the judicature is similar to the approaches to decide the degree of intensities of judicial review. Variable intensities of review are understood in relation to the proportionality test as the courts will assess different degrees of intensity in reviewing the cases, depending on the subject matter in question. Variable intensity of review claims that there are different levels of intensity, for example, a relatively low, moderate, and high intensity. The level of intensity is decided by various factors, for example, the more serious a limitation of rights is, the more evidence the court will require. At the same time, the court will require more arguments if it could justify alternative measures.[211] In different intensities of review, a light intensity of control only applies for clear and evident legislative mistakes. The German Federal Constitutional Court applied a moderate intensity of control in its second abortion decision. By this intermediate intensity of review, the Court analyses whether the protection was "appropriate and effective," and whether it was from "a thorough and careful investigation of the facts and on justifiable assessments."[212] Lastly, the German Federal Constitutional Court applied a serious intensity of control in its first abortion case in 1975, where the Court "purported political necessities or a predominant view in society."[213]

Matthias Klatt suggests that courts should adopt a flexible approach instead of various intensities of judicial review such as either a weak or a strong review. A flexible approach allows for the whole range of intensities of review, fully dependent on the circumstances of each concrete case. This case-sensitive approach is sensitive to the particular legal system and to the circumstances of each case. However, this approach can be criticized because too much flexibility "may be unstable in practice."[214] *Klatt* responds by arguing that the flexible approach could enhance stability by the constitutional system, which considers the relation between competences on a more abstract level. The flexible approach to intensity of judicial review is meaningful in that it gives the courts a chance to have a whole range of intensities of review, considering the specific and unique circumstances each case has. In that way, the court will have more chances to find violations in concrete cases than the abstract determination in its judicial review. So far, the discussion of democracy and the courts has been introduced relatively briefly, but this topic could be much deeper than this as a topic of further research.

---

reasonableness standard, which follows a methodology of contextualized rights-evaluation, rather than the separate rights-identification and justification-of-limits associated with the proportionality, delivers greater rights protection (taken from Young 2017, p. 35). I agree with *Klatt* in that the decision of deference should depend on each case and context, and it delivers greater rights protection when considering all the circumstances of the case with proportionality as context-based criteria.

[211] Rivers (2006), pp. 205–203.

[212] Klatt (2015), p. 362.

[213] Ibid., p. 363.

[214] Klatt (2015), p. 373.

5.4 Conclusion

In this chapter, case law of the ECtHR related to sexual orientation issues has been analyzed according to the principle of legality as well as the principle of proportionality. The particular aim of this analysis is to show that the ECtHR could enhance clarity through consistently applying the structured proportionality in the cases of discrimination based on sexual orientation. At the same time, the case analysis shows that the ECtHR's standard of "necessary in a democratic society" itself does not make clear enough what exactly the ECtHR examines in finding a violation. However, when reanalyzing the reasoning of the ECtHR according to the specific steps of the proportionality, it is easily found that the specific step of the proportionality plays an important role in finding a violation. Furthermore, the conclusions of other cases in which the ECtHR did not find a violation could have been different if a structured proportionality test had been applied.

To enhance the clarity of the application of its methodological tools in its case law, it would be particularly helpful for the ECtHR to apply the more structured proportionality test of legitimate aim, suitability, necessity, and proportionality in a narrow sense. However, the test of necessity and the balancing are argued to require the ECtHR to make a complex empirical assessment, which leads to the discussion of the role of judiciary. Some scholars[215] are against the idea of an active role of the court because it could raise the problem of the separation of powers in the institution of democracy. Of course, it is true that the right of enactment and enforcement of law is given to both the legislative branch and to the administration. Nevertheless, we could not purely depend on the legislation even in the case of the lack of legislation where the legislator consistently ignores vulnerable human rights victims. An active role of the judiciary is needed to preserve the democratic system as well as to protect the human rights of vulnerable groups in particular. Nevertheless, the applicability of the principle of proportionality cannot be limited to emphasize formal democracy because the case analysis in this chapter shows how important it is to apply the structured test of the proportionality.

References

Alexy R (2010) A theory of constitutional rights (trans: Rivers J). Oxford University Press, Oxford

Arai-Takahashi Y (2002) The margin of appreciation doctrine and the principle of proportionality in the jurisprudence of the ECHR. Intersentia, Oxford

Arai-Takahashi Y (2013) Proportionality. In: Shelton D (ed) The Oxford handbook of international human rights law. Oxford University Press, Oxford

[215]For example, one of such scholars is *J. Waldron*. *Waldro*n argues that court is not allowed to decide the positive role of the state to fulfill human rights. He argues that the positive role of the court is considered as serious challenge to the democratic principle (taken from Waldron 1999, pp. 213, 222, 251).

Barak A (2012) Proportionality: constitutional rights and their limitations (trans: Kalir D). Cambridge University Press, Cambridge

Bernhard S (2012) Proportionality. In: Rosenfeld M, Sajó A (eds) The Oxford handbook of comparative constitutional law. Oxford University Press, Oxford

Brems E, Lavrysen L (2015) 'Don't use a sledgehammer to crack a nut': less restrictive means in the case law of the European Court of Human Rights. Hum Rights Law Rev 15(1):139–168. https://doi.org/10.1093/hrlr/ngu040. Accessed November 30, 2021

Clérico L (2017) Proportionality and balancing. In: Mendes CH, Gargarella R (eds) Oxford handbook of constitutional law in Latin America. Oxford University Press, Oxford

Clérico L (2021, forthcoming) Proportionality. In: Mendes CH, Gargarella R (eds) Oxford handbook of constitutional law in Latin America. Oxford University Press, Oxford

Edel F (2015) Case law of the European Court of Human Rights relating to discrimination on grounds of sexual orientation or gender identity. Council of Europe

Fredman S (2008) Human rights transformed. Oxford University Press, Oxford

Fredman S (2013) From dialogue to deliberation: human rights adjudication and prisoners' rights to vote. Public Law:292–311. https://doi.org/10.5040/9781474201704.ch-022

Gerards J (2011) Pluralism, deference and the margin of appreciation doctrine. Eur Law J 17:80–120. https://doi.org/10.1111/j.1468-0386.2010.00540.x. Accessed November 30, 2021

Gerards J (2013) How to improve the necessity test of the European Court of Human Rights. Int J Const Law 11(2):466–490. https://doi.org/10.1093/icon/mot004. Accessed November 30, 2021

Gerards J (2019) General principles of the European Convention on Human Rights. Cambridge University Press, Cambridge

Harris D et al (2009) Law of the European Convention on Human Rights, 2nd edn. Oxford University Press, Oxford

Human Rights Law Center (2008) Discrimination on the basis of sexuality a violation of the rights to privacy and equality, facts. https://www.hrlc.org.au/human-rights-case-summaries/eb-v-france-2008-echr-4354602-22-january-2008. Accessed November 30, 2021

Klatt M (2015) Positive rights: who decides? Judicial review in balance. Oxford University Press, Oxford

Koutnatzis S-IG (2011) Verfassungsvergleichende Überlegungen zur Reyeption des Grundsatzes der Verhältnismäßigkeit in Übersee, Verfassung und Recht in Übersee, Heft 1

Lavrysen L (2016) Human rights in a positive state. Intersentia, Antwerp

Lester A, Pannick D (2004) Human rights: law and practice, 2nd edn. LexisNexis, London

Moeckli D (2014) Equality and non-discrimination. In: Moeckli D, Shah S, Sivakumaran S (eds) International human rights law, 2nd edn. Oxford University Press, Oxford

Ragone S, Volpe V (2016) An emerging right to a "Gay" family life? The Case Oliari v. Italy in a comparative perspective. German Law J 17(03):451–485. https://doi.org/10.1017/S2071832200019830

Rivers J (2006) Proportionality and variable intensity of review. Camb Law J 65(1):174–207. http://www.jstor.org/stable/4509179. Accessed November 30, 2021

Scheinin M (2013) Core rights and obligations. In: Shelton D (ed) Oxford handbook of international human rights law. Oxford University Press, Oxford

Schlink B (2012) Proportionality. In: Rosenfeld M, Sajó A (eds) The Oxford handbook of comparative constitutional law. Oxford University Press, Oxford

Sieckmann J (2018) Proportionality as a universal human rights principle. In: Duarte D, Sampaio JS (eds) Proportionality in law. Springer, Heidelberg

Sieckmann J (2021, forthcoming) To balance or not to balance - the quest for the essence of rights. In: Sieckmann J (ed) Proportionality, balancing, and rights

Sweet AS, Mathews J (2008) Proportionality, balancing and global constitutionalism. Columbia J Transnatl Law 47:68–149

Taggart M (1997) The province of administrative law. Hart, Oxford

Tomlinson QC H (2016) Case Law, Strasbourg: Sousa Goucha v. Portugal, Failure to prosecute homophobic "joke" not a breach of Article 8. https://inforrm.org/2016/04/03/case-law-strasbourg-sousa-goucha-v-portugal-failure-to-prosecute-homophobic-joke-not-a-breach-of-article-8-hugh-tomlinson-qc/. Accessed November 30, 2021

Trimmer A (2012) Anti-Gay Hate Speech: Vejdeland and Others v. Sweden. https://strasbourgobservers.com/2012/02/14/anti-gay-hate-speech-vejdeland-and-others-v-sweden/. Accessed November 30, 2021

Van den Bogaert S (2019) ECHR rules on illegal ban of Warsaw Equality Parade: the case of Baczkowski and others v. Poland. German Law J 8(9):889–902. https://doi.org/10.1017/S2071832200006039

Waldron J (1999) Law and disagreement. Oxford University Press, Oxford

Young KG (2017) Proportionality, reasonableness, and economic and social rights. Boston College Law School, Boston

Chapter 6
Other Relevant Concepts in the Case Law of the ECtHR

6.1 Positive Obligation of the State

In this section, I will first discuss the general scope of positive obligation of the state, and then, how the general scope is applied in the specific case law. The cases are related to Article 8 as well as Article 11 of the ECHR because these articles are importantly dealt with in the cases of discrimination based on sexual orientation in the ECtHR.

6.1.1 General Discussions

Positive rights require the state to take action to actually do something while negative rights are considered as refraining from unjustified interference.[1] Despite such a definition, it is not easy to clearly distinguish negative rights from positive rights.[2] Some argue that it is somewhat useless to limit the positive dimension of rights to certain types or categories of rights, because all rights can impose negative as well as positive obligations on the authorities.[3] Such explanations apply to non-discrimination based on sexual orientation. To provide legal recognition of same-sex relations, the right not to discriminate involves positive obligations on the states. *R. Alexy*[4] divides negative rights into three groups. Firstly, certain "acts" of the right holder cannot be prevented by the state such as expressing an opinion or assembling on a street. Secondly, certain "characteristics" or "situations" of the right

[1] Klatt (2015), pp. 354–355.

[2] *M. Tushnet* noted as well about "the well-known difficulties associated with drawing the line between negative and positive rights. Tushnet (2018), p. 224.

[3] Fredman (2008), pp. 65–69.

[4] Alexy (2010), pp. 122–126.

H. J. Lee, *Discrimination Based on Sexual Orientation*, Interdisciplinary Studies in Human Rights 8, https://doi.org/10.1007/978-3-030-95423-9_6

holder should not be adversely affected. For example, *Alexy*[5] regards life, health, liberty, dignity, etc. not as objects which humans have but as "characteristics" which define their concrete existence. Thirdly, certain "legal positions" of the right holder should not be removed by the state because the existence of a certain legal position means that a corresponding norm applies. For example, the right of the citizen means that the state should not remove a legal position of the citizen. In addition, the state should not repeal certain norms applied to the right holder of the citizen.[6]

On the other hand, positive rights are often discussed with regard to social rights such as the right to education, health, housing or water. However, positive dimensions are not only confined to socio-economic or social rights. *Lavryson* defined three broad analytical categories of positive state obligations after analyzing the ECtHR case law.[7] The first category is substantive vs. procedural positive obligations. In the *Hatton*[8] case, the ECtHR explains the two aspects of positive state obligations in relation to Article 8 ECHR (Right to respect for private and family life):[9] Firstly, the Court may assess the substantive merits of the government's decision, to ensure that it is compatible with Article 8 (Substantive aspect). Secondly, it may scrutinize the decision-making process to ensure that due weight has been accorded to the interests of the individual (the procedural aspect). Substantive positive obligations aim to promote a particular human good or end, while procedural obligations do not directly aim to contribute to a particular state of affairs but are primarily concerned with considerations of fairness.

---

[5]Alexy (2010), p. 124.

[6]Ibid., p. 126.

[7]Laurens (2016), p. 23. pp. 45–130.

[8]European Court of Human Rights, ***HATTON AND OTHERS v. THE UNITED KINGDOM*** (Application no. 36022/97), the Grand Chamber judgment of 8 July 2003: The applicant Ruth Hatton and the other seven applicants all live, or have lived, near Heathrow Airport and complained about the noise levels caused by night flights at the airport between 4 a.m. and 7 a.m. They all suffered from sleep disturbances and sleep prevention, and most of them had to move to get away from the noise. From the year 1993 on, they allege to have experienced significantly higher levels of noise at night than before following the introduction that year of a new night noise regulatory regime for the airport. This new regime 1993 has led to a considerable increase in the number of flights at night. According to the consultation paper issued in 1995, the result of the 1993 Scheme was that more noise was actually allowed than in 1988. Despite these findings, the night restrictions remained unaltered (the facts taken from Tsioumani (2002)). In this case, the ECtHR found no violation of Article 8 (Right to respect for private and family life) ECHR because the ECtHR does not find that the U.K. failed to strike a fair balance between the right of the individuals to respect for their private life and the conflicting interests of others by those regulations. Furthermore, the ECtHR found no fundamental procedural flaws in the 1993 regulations on limitations for night flights (para. 129–130). Nevertheless, the ECtHR found a violation of Article 13 (Right to an effective remedy) ECHR because the scope of review by the domestic courts was not sufficient to comply with Article 13. The ECtHR pointed out that the scope of review did not consider whether the claimed increase in night flights under the 1993 Scheme represented a justifiable limitation on the right to respect for the private and family lives of the applicants (para. 141–142).

[9]European Court Human Rights, *Hatton and Others v. the United Kingdom*, judgment of 8 July 2003, paragraph 99.

The second category is horizontal or vertical positive state obligations. Horizontal positive obligations govern relations between private persons.[10] Horizontal effects of human rights refer to how one private person interferes with another private person.[11] Even if human rights have been affected through these horizontal relations, it is not sufficient to find that the state failed to comply with its positive obligation. Instead, this third party intervention by another private person should be linked to a failure of the state's compliance with positive obligations.[12] On the other hand, vertical positive obligations directly govern the relations between the individual and the state.[13] For an example of such vertical positive obligations, the ECtHR held that Article 8 requires that a transsexual must be able to obtain legal recognition of his or her gender re-assignment in the case of *Christine Goodwin*[14] because the state has the monopoly on the legal recognition of a person's sex.[15]

A third way to categorize positive obligations is to distinguish between positive obligations requiring the state to put in place a legal and administrative framework and positive obligations requiring ad hoc measures to be taken. *Lavryson* explains this distinction with *Xenos*' two elements of "core content" and the obligation to take ad hoc measures.[16] For example, regarding positive obligations of a legal and administrative framework, the ECtHR held in the *Osman*[17] case that the state is

---

[10] Laurens (2016), p. 78.

[11] Nowak (2003), p. 51.

[12] Ibid., p. 79.

[13] Ibid., p. 79.

[14] European Court of Human Rights, ***CHRISTINE GOODWIN v. THE UNITED KINGDOM*** (Application no. 28957/95), The Grand Chamber judgment of 11 July 2002: The applicant, Christine Goodwin is a post-operative male to female transsexual. The applicant claimed that she had problems and faced sexual harassment at work during and following her gender re-assignment. Furthermore, she experienced difficulties concerning her national insurance contributions because she has to continue to pay contributions until the age of 65 as she is still a man legally. (She would have ceased to be liable at the age of 60 if she had been recognized as a woman.) In addition, she alleged that her employer has been able to discover that she previously worked under another name and gender, which resulted embarrassment and humiliation (taken from "Council of Europe/ European Court of Human Rights, *Information Note on the Court's case-law No. 44*"). In this case, the ECtHR found a violation of Article 8 (right to respect for private and family life), Article 12 (right to marry) ECHR. Nevertheless, the ECtHR found no violation of Article 13 (right to an effective remedy) and it found no separate issue had arisen under Article 14 (prohibition of discrimination).

[15] Laurens (2016), p. 104.

[16] Ibid., p. 113.

[17] European Court of Human Rights, ***OSMAN v. THE UNITED KINGDOM*** (Application no. 23452/94), the Grand Chamber judgment of 28 October 1998: The applicant's husband was killed by her son's former teacher and her son was seriously wounded. The teacher had already threatened the applicant and his family before the accident happened. The applicant complained of the failure of authorities to protect the right to life of her husband from the threat posed by the teacher (Paragraph 10). In this case, the ECtHR states that Article 2 (Right to life) ECtHR implied a positive obligation on the state authorities to take preventive measures to protect an individual whose life is at risk from the criminal acts of another individual (horizonal effect of human rights

under a "primary duty to secure the right to life by putting in place effective criminal-law provisions."[18] In the case of *Georgel and Georgeta Stoicescu*,[19] the ECtHR stated that the state had failed to take ad hoc preventive measures to implement the existing legal framework.[20] *Lavrysen*'s three broad analytical categories of positive obligations are helpful to understand the concept of positive obligations, and show the diversity of contexts and ways in which the ECtHR required the contracting state to actively protect human rights.

Yet, to provide a comprehensive overview, the categorical framework of positive state obligations can be improved. Firstly, the factual/ normative distinction is explained by *R. Alexy*,[21] who divides rights to positive acts into two groups of a right to positive "factual" act and rights to positive "normative" state acts. Specific examples of a positive "factual" act are the right of an owner of a private school to a state subsidy or the right to an existential minimum.[22] Examples of the rights to positive "normative" state acts are the rights of a fetus, or the right of a beneficiary of the constitutional right to academic freedom.[23] The right not to be discriminated against based on sexual orientation could refer to normative performance as well as factual performance. For example, the right to be legally recognized as a same-sex couples can be considered as the right to an existential minimum[24] (a right to a

infringement). However, the ECtHR concluded that the facts in the case did not show that the police "knew or ought to have known" ("Osman Test" in Laurens (2016), p. 114.) that the lives of the Osman family were at real and immediate risk from the teacher. Therefore, the ECtHR found no violation of Article 2 of the United Kingdom (para. 121–122).

[18] European Court of Human Rights, *Osman v. the United Kingdom*, judgment of 28 October 1998, paragraph 115.

[19] European Court of Human Rights, ***GEORGEL AND GEORGETA STOICESCU v. ROMANIA*** (Application no. 9718/03), judgment of 26 July 2011: In October 2000, the applicant was attacked by a pack of stray dogs in front of her home in Bucharest in Romania. As a result of the attack, she suffered very serious injuries and became disabled. Even if the applicant tried on several occasions to bring civil action for damages, her case was repeatedly dismissed without examination because she had failed to identify the correct local authority responsible for the control of stray dogs. At the time of the incident, the population of stray dogs in Bucharest alone numbered some 200,000, which had been a public health issue for many years (para. 6–19). In this case, the ECtHR concluded that the state breached its positive obligations to safeguard and protect the right to respect for private life by failing to prevent dog attack. In conclusion, the ECtHR found a violation of Article 8 because the Romanian authorities had failed to take sufficient measures to address the issue of stray dogs which, in combination with their failure to provide adequate redress to the applicant (para. 60–63). In addition, the ECtHR found a violation of Article 6 (Right to a fair trial) § 1 because the applicant did not have an effective right of access to a court (para. 76).

[20] European Court of Human Rights, *Georgel and Georgeta Stoicescu v. Romania*, judgment of 26 July 2011, paragraph 61.

[21] Alexy (2010), pp. 126–127.

[22] Ibid., p. 126.

[23] Ibid., p. 127.

[24] Regarding the question of to what extent recognition of same-sex partnership can be part of subsistence level, I would argue that same-sex couples basically should enjoy the same level or the same extent in the legal recognition of their partnership. Nevertheless, even if it can be considered

positive "factual" act). At the same time, the right to same-sex marriage is analogous to granting a power to participate in a society's marriage system and the right to benefit from the constitutional right to marry (a right to positive "normative" state acts). Secondly, a general positive state obligation could be the enactment of a comprehensive anti-discrimination law as discussed in Chap. 4. Furthermore, by including sexual minorities in the scope of protection under the law, a general norm will be pronounced if discrimination based on sexual orientation is prohibited. Examples for individual positive state obligations can be a positive obligation to protect sexual minorities from homophobic speech[25] or positive obligation to put in place a legal framework for the legal recognition of same-sex relationships.

To explain the concept of positive state obligations, firstly, the differences between positive obligations and negative obligations will be explained. Secondly, it is important to discuss positive state obligations in a reconstruction of the court case analysis. The negative obligations of the contracting states require them to refrain from directly committing human rights violations. As the European Court of Human Rights often mentions in its judgments, negative obligations compel the state to abstain from arbitrary interference because the object of the Convention rights is "essentially" protecting individuals against arbitrary interference by the public authorities.[26] On the other hand, positive obligations require the contracting states to take steps to secure for the individuals the effective enjoyment of their human rights. Positive obligations are considered to be something "additional" to negative obligations that "may" flow from a particular convention right[27] whereas in the case of negative obligations, whether state interference is excessive or not is assessed. On the other hand, in the case of positive obligations, there will be an assessment as to whether the state did enough or not.

Why is the concept of positive state obligation important as a methodological tool in the case law of the ECtHR? Firstly, whether it is a positive or a negative obligation is related to the breadth of the margin of appreciation. The choice between positive and negative obligation is critical because the ECtHR grants states a wider margin of appreciation concerning their positive obligations than their negative ones.[28] Secondly, the ECtHR tends to apply stricter standards in negative obligations cases than in positive obligations where a single overall determination of whether a balance is fair is assessed.[29] The stricter standards of the ECtHR are not the same as the structured analysis of the proportionality of suitability, necessity, and proportionality

---

difficult to provide exactly same legal measures, there should be the same measures to legally recognize their partnership such as civil recognition or civil partnership for the time being. Nevertheless, the end goal is to provide the same extent of recognition of partnership should be provided both for same-sex couples and different sex couples.

[25] Tryfonidou (2020), pp. 101–103.

[26] Ibid., pp. 214–215.

[27] Ibid., p. 215.

[28] European Court of Human Rights, *Hämäläinen v. Finland*, judgment of 16 July 2014, dissenting opinion paragraph 4.

[29] Laurens (2016), p. 222.

in a narrow sense. The standards of the ECtHR in negative obligations cases consist of (1) legality as "in accordance with the law" or "prescribed by law" (2) legitimacy as "legitimate aim" (3) "necessary in a democratic society,"[30] which is different from necessity test because the ECtHR does not clarify less restrictive and equally effective measures as the one in question. A narrow margin of appreciation and the strict scrutiny analysis results in a higher probability of finding a violation than a wider margin and an overall test. Therefore, the decision between positive and negative obligations plays a very important rule in the case law of the ECtHR.

6.1.2 Application in the Case Law

In cases related to sexual orientation, the main freedom relied on by the applicants is Article 8 ECHR, which protects the right to respect for private and family life and the home.[31] Regarding the scope of Article 8, ECtHR has expressed both negative obligations as well as positive obligations on the part of the state: "Art. 8 signifies firstly that the State cannot interfere with the exercise of that right. Nevertheless, it does not merely compel the State to abstain from such interference. There may be positive obligations inherent in an effective 'respect' for family life."[32] Likewise, positive obligations on the part of the state exist in other articles related to sexual orientation although the ECtHR does not explain further what the legal basis for the recognition of positive state obligations is, and how and to what degree such positive obligations can be defined and imposed on the states.[33]

The ECtHR ensures such an emphasis on positive state obligations to protect sexual minorities from homophobic speech[34] regarding Article 8 ECHR in the recent case of *Beizaras and Levickas v. Lithuania*. The Court finds a violation of Article 14 in conjunction with Article 8 ECHR regarding Lithuanian authorities' refusal to prosecute authors of serious homophobic comments towards the applicants' Facebook posts. In this case, the Court held that Lithuania failed to fulfil its positive obligation to sexual minorities to effectively investigate, prosecute and punish homophobic hate speech,[35] pointing out the particular importance of such an obligation for vulnerable groups of minorities. Moreover, the ECtHR states that positive state obligations are "inherent in the right to effective respect for private life

[30] Ibid., p. 222.

[31] Edel (2015), p. 13.

[32] European Court of Human Rights, *Marckx v. Belgium*, judgment of 13 June 1979, paragraph 31.

[33] Gerards (2019), p. 109.

[34] Tryfonidou (2020), p. 101.

[35] European Court of Human Rights, *Beizaras and Levickas v. Lithuasnia*, judgment of 14 January 2020, paragraph 108.

[36] Ibid., paragraph 110.

under Article 8."[36] The ECtHR particularly emphasizes the substantive positive obligations of the state as "the adoption of measures even in the sphere of the relations of individuals between themselves"[37] in protecting compliance with Article 8. In this case, the ECtHR emphasizes the positive state obligations, especially for the purpose of minorities' rights in relation to Article 8 ECHR as referring to the hallmarks of a democratic society as pluralism, tolerance and broadmindedness.[38]

In another case of *Orlandi v. Italy* where the ECtHR found a violation of Article 8 ECHR in the state's refusal to register the applicants' marriage, the ECtHR considers the legal vacuum in Italy as a problem. In its reasoning, the ECtHR affirms that the state has positive obligations "inherent in effective respect for family life" in fulfilling the essential object of Article 8 as protecting the individual against arbitrary action by the state authorities.[39] In the meantime, the ECtHR expressly states that it is not necessary to distinguish positive and negative obligations in relation to the protection under Article 8 ECHR. Nevertheless, in this case, the ECtHR imposed a positive obligation on states derived from Article 8 ECHR to provide some means of recognition to same-sex marriages contracted in other jurisdictions when people attempt to register them in their territory.[40]

Positive state obligations are also applied in cases regarding Article 11 of the ECHR. In the case of *Baczkowski and others v. Poland*, the ECtHR found a violation of Article 11 of the ECHR when the authorities refused the applications to hold a campaign for homosexual rights. While freedom of assembly and association has been traditionally believed to require the government to abstain from interference,[41] the ECtHR explains that the state has positive obligations "to secure the effective enjoyment of these freedoms" as well as negative obligations of "not to interfere."[42] *Johnson*[43] has also explained that Article 11 of the ECHR can be breached as a result of a violation of negative obligations as well as positive obligations. The *Baczkowski* case indicates that the ECtHR recognizes the positive state obligations to provide effective protection to freedom of assembly to sexual minorities.

---

[36] Ibid., paragraph 110.

[37] European Court of Human Rights, *Beizaras and Levickas v. Lithuasnia*, judgment of 14 January 2020, paragraph 110.

[38] Ibid., paragraph 106.

[39] European Court Human Rights, *Orlandi and others v. Italy*, judgment of 14 December 2017, paragraphs 196–197.

[40] Tryfonidou (2020), p. 102.

[41] Gerards (2019), p. 123.

[42] European Court of Human Rights, *Baczkowski and others v. Poland*, judgment of 24 September 2007, paragraph 64.

[43] Johnson (2014), p. 184.

6.2 The Margin of Appreciation Doctrine

The margin of appreciation doctrine applied in the case law of ECtHR functions "to allow the States some leeway in deciding the regulation of the enjoyment of fundamental rights."[44] The doctrine plays a particularly important role in finding discrimination based on sexual orientation in the case law of the ECtHR because the scope of protection is related to the state's positive obligations as discussed in 6.1. above and states are granted some leeway to provide some systems such as marriage or social security systems. In such sense, it is important to consider the factors to determine the breadth of the margin, and how this doctrine is applied in the case law related to sexual orientation.

6.2.1 General Discussions

According to *Arai-Takahashi*, the margin of appreciation doctrine is defined as "the label used by the Court to indicate the measure of discretion allowed to the Member States in the manner in which they implement the Convention's standards, taking into account their own particular national circumstances and conditions."[45] For a more extensive theoretical discussion, substantive, structural, epistemic, and normative concepts of the margin of appreciation will be briefly introduced. The *substantive* concept of the margin of appreciation has been introduced by *Letsas.*[46] The main idea behind understanding the substantive concept is merely "a general point on the limitability or non-absoluteness of Convention rights."[47] The *substantive* concept of the margin of appreciation introduced by *Letsas* focuses on the fact that the use of the doctrine does not bring one single answer but a "range of permissible options," which leads to striking a "balance between individual rights and the public interest."[48] This is also in line with *Arai-Takahashi's* argument "the principle of proportionality should be deployed as a device to ascertain whether national authorities have overstepped their margin of appreciation."[49] In other words, the use of the margin of appreciation considers a "range of permissible options" and helps us to strike a balance through the principle of proportionality. Nevertheless, the doctrine itself adds nothing to the legal methodological tools of the ECtHR[50] because of the lack of normative force[51] of the margin of appreciation doctrine.

[44] Gerards (2019), p. 168.

[45] Laurens (2016), p. 185.

[46] Letas (2007), pp. 80–81.

[47] Ibid., p. 86.

[48] Ibid., p. 86.

[49] Arai-Takahashi (2002), pp. 14–15.

[50] Laurens (2016), p. 188.

[51] Letas (2007), p. 86.

The *structural* concept of the margin of appreciation can be explained using the subsidiarity argument. *Gerards* explained that the subsidiarity argument inspired the ECtHR to develop the margin of appreciation, which is based on the premise that the ECtHR should only intervene if it is clear that the states have not succeeded in securing the rights protected by the Convention.[52] *Letas* also considered the structural concept of the doctrine as being the reason for its existence in terms of subsidiarity."[53] This structural concept of the doctrine can be explained by "the better placed argument."[54] A margin of appreciation should be bestowed on the states by the ECtHR because they are in principle better placed than an international court to evaluate local needs and conditions.[55] In other words, the ECtHR can intervene only in the cases justified by the subsidiarity argument.

The *epistemic* concept of margin of appreciation can be borrowed from *Alexy*'s explanations about epistemic discretion.[56] *Alexy* distinguishes structural discretion from two other different forms of discretion, which are epistemic discretion in respect of the normative problem of balancing, and an epistemic discretion in respect of the empirical problem of effectivity. Epistemic discretion in respect of the normative problem of balancing can be linked to the prevalence of a margin of appreciation in cases where a fair balance needs to be struck between a Convention right and other rights or the public interest.[57] For example, the ECtHR considers that "very weighty reasons" are needed to balance unequal treatment based on sexual orientation, which leaves a narrow margin of appreciation.[58] Epistemic discretion in respect of the empirical problem of effectivity is concerned with the effect of current measures in the future, which is known as the problem of prognosis.[59] Problems of the margin of appreciation are pointed out as being the ECtHR's "tendency not to consistently establish the actual scope of the margin left in the concrete case" as well as "not making a clear connection between the margin of appreciation and standards of review."[60] Nonetheless, since the ECtHR still relies on the doctrine and the factors determining its scope, the margin of appreciation doctrine will continue to be relevant under the Convention system by supplementing and development by means of case law.[61]

---

[52] Gerards (2011), p. 104.

[53] Letas (2007), p. 81.

[54] Gerards (2019), p. 177.

[55] European Court of Human Rights, *Dudgeon v. United Kingdom*, decided on 22 October 1981, para. 52: "it is for the national authorities to make the initial assessment of the pressing social need in each case; accordingly, a margin of appreciation is left to them. However, their decision remains subject to review by the Court. . .However, not only the nature of the aim of the restriction but also the nature of the activities involved will affect the scope of the margin of appreciation."

[56] Alexy (2010), p. 310.

[57] Laurens (2016), p. 186.

[58] Gerards (2019), p. 171.

[59] Alexy (2010), p. 310.

[60] Gerards (2019), p. 197.

[61] Ibid., p. 197.

As *Letsas* pointed out,[62] "the idea of the margin of appreciation in itself clearly lacks any normative force that can help us strike a balance between individual rights and the public interests." Despite a limited normative basis for the margin of appreciation, looking for a normative concept of the margin of appreciation will help to understand the meaning of the doctrine. *Arai-Takahashi* argues that deference to democratic and pluralistic values provides a coherent normative core in the applicability of the margin of appreciation doctrine.[63] Balancing individual rights and majority interest in decision-making on human rights in a pluralist democracy[64] seems to be inevitable. Nevertheless, the margin of appreciation doctrine should not function to create "space"[65] between international human rights treaties and the interpretations because there are certain areas where no "space" is allowed. For example, sexual minorities are vulnerable people who have historically been discriminated against. The ECtHR should not apply the margin of appreciation doctrine in the cases where the rights of a certain vulnerable group must not be restricted.

In implementing the positive obligation under the Convention, the states enjoy a certain margin of appreciation. When determining the breadth of the margin, several factors must be considered. It is up to the Court to judge whether a fair balance between the competing interests of the individual and the community is concretely respected.[66] In the context of "private life," the Court has considered that where a particularly important facet of an individual's existence or identity is at stake, the margin allowed to the state will be restricted. On the other hand, there will usually be a wide margin available if the state is required to strike a balance between competing private and public interests of the Convention rights.[67] One of the important factors affecting the breadth of the margin of appreciation is the importance of the affected right, more specifically whether the rights are regarded as supplementary rights or core rights. According to *Gerards,*[68] "the margin will be narrow if the essence or 'core' of one of the Convention rights is affected." The ECtHR has considered that the margin must be narrow where "a particularly intimate aspect of an individual's private life" is concerned, such as a person's sexuality or identity.[69]

---

[62] Letas (2007), p. 86.

[63] Arai-Takahashi (2002), p. 243.

[64] Ibid., p. 243.

[65] *V. C. Jackson* argues engagement approach, which allows "space" between international human rights treaties and the interpretations of those same treaties by their expert committees in discussing CEDAW and national constitutions. Furthermore, the Committee's comments should not be regarded as steps toward an inevitable universalization of their content, but as simply points in a dialogue that could turn out quite differently. Nevertheless, I argue that there are certain vulnerable groups who need protection imminently and no "space" is allowed to protect their human rights. (For further discussions, please see Jackson (2016), pp. 437–464.)

[66] Ragone and Volpe (2016), p. 463.

[67] European Court of Human Rights, *Oliari and others v. Italy*, judgment of 21 July 2015, paragraph 162.

[68] Gerards (2011), 80, p. 112.

[69] Ibid., p. 113.

Arai-Takahashi suggests that a wide margin of appreciation necessarily applies because the scope of positive obligations is decided by "policy choice of Member States in allocation of their limited public resources" as well as by other factors that are difficult to evaluate "such as the severity of effect that a failure of a government to act causes on the rights as well as personal circumstances of individuals."[70] Furthermore, a wide margin of appreciation corresponds to a lax standard of proportionality, whereas a narrow margin corresponds to an intense proportionality appraisal.[71] When the margin is narrow, the Court will apply a full and thorough analysis with intensified, careful scrutiny requiring convincing and compelling reasons or very weighty reasons.[72] When all other conditions are regarded as being equal, there is a higher probability that the ECtHR will find a violation of the European Convention (ECHR) when the margin is narrower. On the other hand, the wider the margin is, the more likely it is that the ECtHR will not find a violation of the state.

6.2.2 Application in the Case Law

The European Court of Human Rights states that the relevant factors to determine the breadth of margin in the case of *Orlandi and others v. Italy*[73] are the existence or non-existence of common ground between the laws of the Contracting States. Accordingly, the ECtHR states that the margin will be wide when there is no consensus among Member States and the issue of whether to register marriages contracted abroad as marriage lacks consensus, thus affording a wide margin. To narrow such a wide margin so as to find violation of Article 8 ECHR in this case, the ECtHR emphasizes that this case "concerns facets of an individual's existence and identity."[74] In this case, the ECtHR seems to adjust the breadth of the margin where several factors are involved; yet, the ECtHR still does not suggest clear guidance as to which factors prevail over other factors so it is important to find out how the state applies the margin of appreciation doctrine in specific case law. In the case of *Orlandi*, the ECtHR considers the margin as narrow because the recognition of marriages obtained abroad is a core issue to an individual's identity although consensus is lacking.

In the case of *Sousa Goucha v. Portugal*, where the applicant's right to his reputation competes with the freedom of expression of television presenter F.C. to make a joke of the applicant's sexual orientation, the ECtHR cited the Court of Justice of

[70] Arai-Takahashi (2002), p. 218.

[71] Arai-Takahashi (2002), p. 204.

[72] Laurens (2016), p. 192.

[73] European Court of Human Rights, *Orlandi and others v. Italy*, judgment of 14 December 2017, paragraphs 203–206.

[74] Ibid., paragraph 206.

the European Union. The ECtHR explains that "a particularly wide margin of appreciation should be given to parody in the context of freedom of expression."[75] In this case, the ECtHR states that wide margin of appreciation is given in "the specific context of carnival festivities in Portugal in which citizens take the opportunity to use satire and caricature to criticize politicians,"[76] and the reasoning process is easy to find no violation of Article 8 ECHR in this case. Nevertheless, the ECtHR does not provide clear guidelines as to whether a wide margin is always applied in the case of satire or parody. Furthermore, what other specific factors can make the margin narrower in the context of freedom of expression is not clearly stated by the ECtHR.

In another important case of *Beizaras and Levickas v. Lithuania,*[77] the ECtHR finds a violation of Article 14 in conjunction with Article 8 ECHR regarding Lithuania's refusal to prosecute authors of serious homophobic comments about the applicants. In this case, the ECtHR recognizes the positive state obligations to adopt measures in the sphere of the individual relations in relation to Article 8. *Gerards* and *Senden* argue that the ECtHR has a tendency to allow a considerable margin of appreciation in almost every case concerning positive obligations, regardless of the importance of the individual right at stake.[78] Despite positive state obligations, the ECtHR considers that the state's margin of appreciation is narrow in this case because different treatment is based on the sexual orientation of the applicants. In this case, the ECtHR concludes that the breadth of margin is narrow even if it relates to positive state obligations to adopt measures. The ECtHR may have considered the ground of sexual orientation as the more important factor to decide the breadth of the margin.

In the case of *Salgueiro da Silva Mouta v. Portugal*, the ECtHR finds a violation of Article 8 taken in conjunction with Article 14 regarding the removal of child custody from the father who is in same-sex relations with his partner. In this case, the ECtHR states that the state enjoys a wide margin of appreciation concerning parental responsibility because national authorities know better how to work in the child's interests.[79] However, the ECtHR points out that national court decision "clearly showed that the decision to award parental responsibility to the mother was based mainly on the father's sexual orientation."[80] As in the *Beizaras* case, the ECtHR considers sexual orientation as being the more decisive factor to make the margin of appreciation narrow even if the state enjoys a wide margin in matters of parental responsibility for the child's interests.

---

[75] European Court of Human Rights, *Sousa Goucha v. Portugal*, judgment of 22 March 2016, paragraph 50.

[76] Ibid., paragraph 51.

[77] European Court of Human Rights, *Beizaras and Levickas v. Lithuasnia*, judgment of 14 January 2020.

[78] Gerards and Senden (2009), p. 651.

[79] European Court of Human Rights, *Salgueiro Da Silva Mouta v. Portugal*, judgment of 21 March 2000, paragraph 25.

[80] Ibid., paragraph 31.

In the *P.B. and J.S. v. Austria* case, the ECtHR concludes that blanket exclusion of same-sex partners from qualifying as a dependent who can benefit from the partner's insurance violates Article 14 in conjunction with Article 8 ECHR. On the breadth of margin of appreciation, the ECtHR first states that there is no consensus among Member States and therefore bestows a wide margin of appreciation, and there is still no consensus to recognize stable de facto partnerships between homosexuals legally and judicially despite a growing social acceptance of such partnerships.[81] However, another strongly relevant factor is different treatment based on sexual orientation, which affords a narrow margin of appreciation to the states.[82] In this case as well, the Court considers different treatment based on sexual orientation as the decisive factor to make the breadth of margin narrow although states generally enjoy a wide margin in the issues of no consensus. Such considerations are also seen in the case of *Kozak v. Poland* where the succession of a tenancy right of same-sex partner is at issue, as the Court states that "where a difference of treatment is based on sex or sexual orientation the margin of appreciation afforded to the State is narrow."[83] The ECtHR considers different treatment based on sexual orientation as being a more decisive factor when several other factors affect the breadth of the margin.

Nevertheless, the language used in explaining the breadth of the margin of appreciation is not likely to be very clear: in the case of *Genderdoc-M v. Moldova* concerning the refused permission for a demonstration organized by a Moldovian non-governmental organization to assist the LGBT community, the ECtHR states that "the contracting states enjoy *a certain* margin of appreciation"[84] in assessing the justification of different treatment in law in similar situations. It is not easy to foresee whether the expression of "a certain" margin means a wide margin or narrow margin because there are no further clarifications related to the breadth of margin. The ECtHR concludes that the margin is narrow because the different treatment is based on sexual orientation.[85] The ECtHR seems to apply the context approach as the scope of the margin varies according to the circumstances of the case;[86] whilst also considering different treatment based on sexual orientation as a decisive factor to make the margin narrow.

This is also shown in the case of *Bayev and others v. Russia* when the ECtHR concludes that Russia violates Article 10, and Article 14 taken in conjunction with Article 10. If the matter is related to sensitive moral or ethical issues and there is no consensus among Member States, the ECtHR accepts a wider margin of

[81] European Court of Human Rights, *P.B. and J.S. v. Austria*, judgment of 22 October 2010, paragraph 28.

[82] Ibid., paragraph 42.

[83] European Court of Human Rights, *Kozak v. Poland*, judgment of 2 March 2010, paragraph 92.

[84] European Court of Human Rights, *Genderdoc-M v. Moldova*, judgment of 12 September 2012, paragraph 50.

[85] Ibid., paragraph 51.

[86] Ibid., paragraph 50.

appreciation.[87] In this case, the ECtHR notices that there is a consensus about the recognition of a right to identify themselves as sexual minority. However, the Court does not explicitly state how such a clear consensus affects the breadth of margin of appreciation. Nevertheless, the ECtHR reaffirms that different treatment based on sexual orientation makes the state's margin narrow.[88]

In the cases concerning discrimination based on sexual orientation, the ECtHR confirms that different treatment due to sexual orientation is a very important factor to make the breadth of margin narrow. Particularly when a restriction on fundamental rights applies to a vulnerable group in society, the state's margin of appreciation is narrower and it must have very weighty reasons for the restrictions.[89] Sexual minorities are included in such a vulnerable social group in Europe as well as in Korea because they have been historically subject to discrimination and they have not enjoyed what heterosexuals enjoy in many areas including marriage, employment or social benefits.

6.3 The Core Right Argument

In the case law related to discrimination based on sexual orientation, the European Court of Human Rights uses some expressions such as core rights and supplementary rights, and core content of the rights.[90] One of the important factors to affect the breadth of the margin of appreciation is the importance of the affected right, more specifically whether the rights are regarded as supplementary rights or core rights. Even if the ECtHR has not provided clear and general criteria to determine which elements specifically consist of the core of those rights,[91] understanding the core right argument is important regarding the prohibition of discrimination based on sexual orientation for two reasons. Firstly, the ECtHR considers the margin of appreciation narrow when the essence or "core" of one of the Convention rights is affected.[92] The ECtHR has considered that the margin must be narrow where "a particularly intimate aspect of an individual's private life" is concerned, such as dealing with a case with respect to a person's sexuality or identity.[93] Secondly, when

---

[87] European Court of Human Rights, *Bayev and Others v. Russia,* judgment of 20 June 2017, paragraph 66.

[88] Ibid., paragraph 89.

[89] McGoldrick (2016), p. 329.

[90] I distinguish core rights from core content of the rights. For example, I argue that the right to marry is core right instead of supplementary right. When the right to marry is affected, the ECtHR should examine "the facts and arguments advanced in favour of certain restrictions and limitations more closely" (taken from Gerards (2011), p. 116). Core content of the right to marry includes the contents such as whom to marry or whether to marry or not.

[91] Gerards (2019), p. 188.

[92] Ibid.

[93] Ibid., p. 113.

the constitutional right of personal liberty is affected in its essential core, the restriction is considered as intense, which can only be justified by sufficiently weighty reasons.[94] If the rights of sexual minorities are considered as core rights, there is greater probability of finding violations by the ECtHR because only a narrow margin will be granted to the state's measures and sufficiently weighty reasons are needed to justify the different treatments.

Gerards[95] argues that there are four main values of *democracy*, *pluralism*, *human dignity* and *autonomy* underlying the European Convention. The closer a certain aspect of a right is related to these four values, the more it is considered to be a core right.[96] Discrimination based on sexual orientation is deeply related to *human dignity* because sexual minorities are concerned about failure to accord them equal dignity and respect.[97] Sexual minorities are exposed to homophobic bullying at schools as well as at workplace, which endangers the right to be respected as well as right to human dignity.[98] As autonomy emphasizes human characteristics of subjective self-determinating, discrimination based on sexual orientation is also highly related to the concept of autonomy. For example, freedom to marry is an autonomous decision of an individual because whether to marry or not, whom to marry, enter an intimate partnership with, and to legally recognize the relations is one of the most important decisions of an individual's private life. Yet if the state does not take any measures to recognize same-sex relations such as in Korea, the right to autonomy will be seriously limited because an individual cannot exercise his/her autonomous decision due to the inaction of the state. *Pluralism* is regarded an important characteristic of a *democratic* society along with tolerance and broadmindedness.[99] Accordingly, any interference with the right to respect for private life must be "proportionate to the legitimate aim pursued."[100] For example, many laws that criminalized homosexuality were struck down because they were not related to the legitimate aim of maintaining public morals at all, especially since such laws stigmatized homosexuality in the private sphere.[101] The right not to be discriminated against based on sexual orientation can thus be regarded as core right because it is related to the four main values of *democracy*, *pluralism*, *human dignity* and *autonomy*.

---

[94] Alexy (2010), p. 194.

[95] Gerards (2019), pp. 59–67.

[96] Ibid., p. 188.

[97] Fredman (2011), p. 92.

[98] *S. Fredman* referred to the recent statistics in her argument: One survey of over 1000 students in British schools in 2007 showed that almost two-thirds of LGB young people have experienced direct bullying; 70 percent of LGB respondents believed that they are more likely to be insulted and harassed than heterosexual persons; close to 50 percent said that they were a greater risk of physical assault. In conclusion, sexual minorities are identified as one of the most stressed groups of individuals in society (taken from Fredman (2011), pp. 92–93).

[99] Johnson (2016), p. 23.

[100] Ibid., p. 23.

[101] Megret (2014), p. 112.

Martin Scheinin[102] discusses three different approaches of identifying core rights and obligations within the framework of human rights law. The first approach defines some human rights as being superior to other human rights. This approach is in line with the judgment in the case of *Oliari*, which stated "the instant case is not concerned with certain specific supplementary (as opposed to core) rights."[103] The second approach supposes that each human right encompasses an essential core which is not a subject to be limited. In the General Comment by the Human Rights Committee, the Committee also took this approach by prohibiting limitations to the right to access to court (Article 14 of ICCPR: Right to Equality before Courts and Tribunals and to a Fair Trial) because it would "undermine the very essence of the right."[104] While the two approaches focus on the right-bearer of human rights, the third approach is to identify core obligations of the state as a duty bearer. The state will have core obligations in certain areas of the rights with respect to the holders of those rights. In the *Oliari* case, the ECtHR "finds that the Italian Government have failed to fulfill their positive obligation to ensure that the applicants have available a specific legal framework."[105] This could be interpreted as stating that the state has violated its "core" positive obligation, because same-sex marriage is the essential core of an applicant's private life and the state fails to fulfill its obligation to provide legal recognition measures to same-sex couples.

Same-sex marriage, like the freedom to get married, is undoubtedly protected as a civil and political right of the Convention and the Constitution of each Member State. Therefore, the state should not interfere with the individual in principle, because the state has to guarantee the right as a core right. The ECtHR uses the dichotomy of both core and supplementary rights in the *Oliari* case in its reasoning because the ECtHR recognizes same-sex marriage as a core right or essential core of private life. Thus, the essential core theory could be the answer for the ECtHR when it regards legal recognition of same-sex couples as a "core" right. As the guarantee of an essential core will not exceed the limitability contained in the principle of proportionality, respecting, protecting, and fulfilling the right to marry or create an intimate partnership between couples will be the essential core of individuals' private life.

Except in the *Oliari* case, there are no statements from the ECtHR concerning direct expressions of core and supplementary rights in other case law related to discrimination based on sexual orientation. Nevertheless, in some cases, the ECtHR seems to apply the essential core theory. In the case of *Baczkowski and others v. Poland,* the Court finds a violation of Article 11 of the ECHR regarding the

[102] Scheinin (2013), pp. 527–540.

[103] European Court of Human Rights, *Oliari and others v. Italy*, judgment of July 21, 2015, paragraph 177.

[104] Human Rights Committee, *General Comment No. 32: Right to Equality before Courts and Tribunals and to a Fair Trial (Article 14)*, 23 August 2007, UN Doc CCPR/C/GC/32, para 18.

[105] European Court of Human Rights, *Oliari and others v. Italy*, judgment of 21 July 2015, paragraph 185.

state authorities' rejection of an application to hold an assembly to promote the discrimination issues against minorities including sexual minorities in Warsaw. The ECtHR assesses whether interference impairs the core part of the right. One such example is the case of *Zhdanov and Others v. Russia*. In this case, the ECtHR finds violation of Article 6, Paragraph 1 ECHR because state authorities refuse to register organizations to promote LGBT rights and the applicants' appeal had not been examined. In the reasoning, the ECtHR states that failure to examine the applicants' appeal on the merits impairs "the very essence of their right to effective access to a court,"[106] and this violates Article 6 paragraph 1.

6.4 The Consensus Argument

As *Takahashi* introduced in his book,[107] the Consensus Argument looks closely at the law and practice of other Member States to indicate any European consensus on a controversial issue. However, the ECtHR often does not clearly provide a standard to decide when it considers having European Consensus or not. Particularly with the cases dealing with sexual orientation, the existence of a European consensus may serve to reinforce the ECtHR in pursuit of uniform European standards on certain matters, sometimes along with a living instrument[108] argument. A convention as a living instrument means that a convention should be interpreted under present day conditions to consider developments and changes in society. This includes the fact that there is not just one way or one choice when it comes to family or private life.[109] Similarly, interpretation of the Convention as a "living instrument" entails "common ground interpretation" or "consensus interpretation,"[110] therefore, the ECtHR should refer to evolving consensus to reflect a clear trend in Member States.

Especially in the case law related to discrimination based on sexual orientation, the ECtHR tends to find violation when there is sufficient consensus among the Member States on the matter. For example, in finding a violation of Article 14 (Prohibition of discrimination) in conjunction with Article 8 (Right to respect for private

[106] European Court of Human Rights, *Zhdanov and Others v. Russia*, judgment of 16 July 2019.

[107] Arai-Takahashi (2002), p. 215.

[108] In relation to the living instrument argument, there exists the concept of a living constitution. *David Strauss* defined a living constitution as "one that evolves, changes over time, and adapts to new circumstances, without being formally amended" in his book of *The Living Constitution* (2010). In contrast to *David*'s elaboration, *Dieter Grimm* criticized it as not being quite accurate, in that the change he speaks of is not brought about by the constitution itself; rather the change is a result of interpretation (taken from Grimm (2012), pp. 99–100).

[109] European Court of Human Rights, *Vallianatos and Others v. Greece*, judgment of 7 November 2013, paragraph 84.

[110] Gerards (2019), p. 53.

and family life) in the case of *Vallianatos*,[111] the ECtHR states that there is as yet no European consensus among the legal systems of the Council of Europe Member States, although a trend is clearly emerging with regard to the introduction of forms of legal recognition of same-sex relationships. Nevertheless, it is not clear what the ECtHR exactly means by "a clear trend" and under which condition it could be interpreted as "having European consensus." In the same case, the ECtHR mentions that "Lithuania and Greece are the only ones to reserve it (the recognition) exclusively for different-sex couples." However, the full elaboration is still lacking regarding the use of the consensus argument in assessing the stage of balancing[112] as a step of its proportionality analysis.

Another example is the *Dudgeon* case. In this case, the ECtHR relied on the existence of European consensus to find a violation of Article 8 ECHR stating that the great majority of the Member States of the Council of Europe no longer consider homosexual practices to be subject to the criminal law.[113] On the one hand, on the issue of same-sex marriage, the ECtHR states that there is not enough European consensus.[114] However, such a tendency could bring about the problem of not effectively protecting minority rights, since, as the ECtHR itself points out, "democracy does not simply mean that the views of the majority must always prevail."[115] Furthermore, as *Clérico* points out there are two problems of the use of the European consensus argument.[116] The first problem is the insufficiency, and the second is the incoherency problem. The insufficiency problem arises when the argumentation stops at this stage to later conclude that a proportionality or equality test will be conducted with low scrutiny. The incoherency problem arises when incoherent use is made of the European consensus argument in cases concerning similar cases.

The problem of incoherency can be found in the ECtHR cases related to sexual orientation. The ECtHR states that there is a European consensus about "Member States recognition of the right of individuals to openly identify themselves as gay, lesbian or any other sexual minority, and to promote their rights and freedoms."[117]

[111]European Court of Human Rights, *Vallianatos and Others v. Greece*, judgment of 7 November 2013, paragraph 91.

[112]The Court did not clearly about the effect of the consensus argument in the *Vallianatos* case. But the ECtHR seemed to include the European trend in the balancing stage to compare the law excluding same-sex couples v. including. The ECtHR did not explicitly apply the Consensus argument related with a narrow margin of appreciation, but it certainly considered the Consensus argument in the last step of a proportionality analysis when balancing competing interests. (European Court of Human Rights, *Vallianatos and Others v. Greece*, judgment of 7 November 2013, paragraph 91.)

[113]European Court of Human Rights, *Dudgeon v. United Kingdom*, judgment of 22 October 1981, paragraph 60.

[114]Johnson (2016), p. 171.

[115]European Court of Human Rights, *Beizaras and Levickas v. Lithuania*, judgment of 14 January 2020, paragraph 106.

[116]Clérico (2014).

[117]European Court of Human Rights, *Beizaras and Levickas v. Lithuania*, judgment of 14 January 2020, paragraph 119.

Furthermore in the same case, the ECtHR also acknowledges a "growing general tendency to view relationships between same-sex couples as falling within the concept of family life."[118] In addition, the ECtHR admits the existence of European consensus in matters "such as the abolition of criminal liability for homosexual relations between adults, on homosexuals' access to service in the armed forces, to the granting of parental rights, to equality in tax matters and the right to succeed to the deceased partners' tenancy,"[119] However, the ECtHR still does not consider a European consensus on questions of adoption by or marriage between homosexual people.

In some cases, such as *P.B. and J.S. v. Austria*, the ECtHR does not state very clearly whether the specific case is about a lack of European consensus or the existence of one. On the legal and judicial recognition of stable de facto partnerships between homosexuals, the ECtHR admits a "growing tendency"[120] that implies the existence of consensus. However, the ECtHR states in the same case that there is "little common ground between the Contracting States,"[121] which implies no consensus and a wide margin of appreciation accordingly. Finally, the ECtHR again mentions "a rapid evolution of social attitudes towards same sex couples"[122] in a considerable number of Member States, which seems to imply a tendency towards consensus. Similarly, there seem to be uncertainty regarding the level of abstraction the ECtHR uses to establish a consensus.[123] For European consensus to function well as one of the most objective criteria in determining the scope of the margin of appreciation as *Dzehtsiarou* argues,[124] the ECtHR should develop consistencies when applying the consensus argument through its judgment and should not use the consensus argument as an excuse not to recognize the rights of minorities.

6.5 Conclusion

In this chapter, relevant concepts other than the principle of proportionality have been introduced with the examples of case law of the ECtHR related to discrimination based on sexual orientation. The case law of non-criminalization of same-sex relations as well as same-sex marriage cases are only briefly discussed in this chapter

[118] Ibid., paragraph 122.

[119] Press Release issued by the Registrar of the Court (2010), *Repeated unjustified Ban on Gay-Rights Marches in Moscow*, European Court of Human Rights, *Alekseyev v. Russia*, Chamber judgment of 21 October 2010, Press Release issued by the Registrar of the Court, p. 3.

[120] European Court of Human Rights, *P.B. and J.S. v. Austria*, judgment of 22 October 2010, paragraph 28.

[121] Ibid., paragraph 28.

[122] Ibid., paragraph 29.

[123] Gerards (2019), p. 105.

[124] Dzehtsiarou (2015), p. 142.

because they will be discussed separately in the following Chaps. 7 and 8. The ECtHR applies many concepts in its reasoning of the cases related to sexual orientation, which are positive and negative state obligation, the margin of appreciation doctrine, the core right argument, and the consensus argument.

The doctrine of margin of appreciation suggests an ambit of discretion, "latitude of deference" or "room for maneuver" given to national authorities in assessing appropriate standards of the ECHR rights.[125] The ECtHR tends to assess positive state obligation, the core rights argument and the existence of established European consensus when it decides whether the National Authorities have overstepped the margin of appreciation. Furthermore, those concepts are not separate but relevant to each other. For example, the ECtHR makes the margin of appreciation narrower when the issue in question is related to positive state obligation, considered as core right, or when there is sufficient common ground among the Member States. Nevertheless, the conditions of the applicability of these concepts are neither consistent nor clear. The consensus argument is particularly problematic in the area of the protection of minority rights[126] such of sexual minorities because a lack of consensus is often used as an excuse not to recognize a right as, for example, the right to same-sex marriage.[127] As an alternative to this problem, the ECtHR can refer to the Inter-American Court of Human Rights ("IACtHR") because the IACtHR has explicitly rejected the consensus argument as stating that "the alleged lack of consensus in some countries regarding full respect for the rights of sexual minorities cannot be considered a valid argument to deny or restrict their human rights or to perpetuate and reproduce the historical and structural discrimination that these minorities have suffered."[128] Moreover, the ECtHR should develop consistencies when applying these concepts in the cases related to discrimination based on sexual orientation, which will ultimately serve to recognize the rights of sexual minorities.

References

Alexy R (2010) Rivers J (translated), A theory of constitutional rights. Oxford University Press, Oxford

Arai-Takahashi Y (2002) The margin of appreciation doctrine and the principle of proportionality in the jurisprudence of the ECHR. Intersentia, Oxford

Clérico L (2014) Notas y preguntas sobre los usos del derecho comparado por la Corte Interamericana de Derechos Humanos, IN: Discusiones, https://www.researchgate.net/

[125] Parras (2015), pp. 8–9.

[126] Dzehtsiarou (2015), pp. 127–128.

[127] Johnson (2016), p. 171.

[128] Inter-American Court of Human Rights, *Atala Riffo and Daughters v. Chile*, judgment of 24 February 2012, para. 92.

publication/299413196_Notas_y_preguntas_sobre_los_usos_del_derecho_comparado_por_la_Corte_IDH. Accessed 30 Nov 2021
Dzehtsiarou K (2015) European consensus and the legitimacy of the European court of human rights. Cambridge University Press, Cambridge
Edel F (2015) Case Law of the European Court of Human Rights relating to discrimination on grounds of sexual orientation or gender identity, Council of Europe
Fredman S (2008) Human rights transformed: positive rights and positive duties. Oxford University Press, Oxford
Fredman S (2011) Discrimination law, 2nd edn. Oxford University Press, Oxford
Gerards J (2011) Pluralism, deference and the margin of appreciation Doctrine. Eur Law J 17:80–120. https://doi.org/10.1111/j.1468-0386.2010.00540.x. Accessed 30 Nov 2021
Gerards J (2019) General principles of the European convention on human rights. Cambridge University Press, Cambridge
Gerards J, Senden H (2009) The structure of fundamental rights and the European Court of Human Rights. Int J Const Law 7(4):619–653, https://doi.org/10.1093/icon/mop028. Accessed 30 Nov 2021
Grimm D (2012) Types of constitutions. In: Rosenfeld M, Sajó A (eds) The Oxford handbook of comparative constitutional law. Oxford University Press, Oxford
Jackson VC (2016) Feminisms, pluralisms, and transnationalism: on CEDAW and national constitutions. Cambridge University Press, Cambridge
Johnson P (2014) Homosexuality and the European court of human rights. Routledge, London
Johnson P (2016) Going to Strasbourg: an Oral history of sexual orientation discrimination and the European convention on human rights. Oxford University Press, Oxford
Klatt M (2015) Positive rights: who decides? Judicial review in balance. Oxford University Press, Oxford
Laurens L (2016) Human rights in a positive state. Intersentia, Antwerp
Letas G (2007) A theory of interpretation of the European convention on human rights. Oxford University Press, Oxford
McGoldrick D (2016) Affording states a margin of appreciation. In: Buckley CM, Donald A, Leach P (eds) Towards convergence in international human rights law: approaches of regional and international systems. Nottingham Studies on Human Rights, 5. Brill/Nijhoff, Leiden
Megret F (2014) Nature of obligations. In: Moeckli D, Shah S, Sivakumaran S (eds) International human rights law. Oxford University Press, Oxford
Nowak M (2003) Introduction to the international human rights regime. Martinus Nijhoff Publishers, Leiden
Parras FJM (2015) Democracy, diversity and the margin of appreciation: a theoretical analysis from the perspective of the international and constitutional functions of the European Court of Human Rights. 1–18, https://doi.org/10.17103/reei.29.10
Ragone S, Volpe V (2016) An emerging right to a "gay" family life? The case Oliari v. Italy in a comparative perspective. German Law J 17(3):451–485. https://doi.org/10.1017/S2071832200019830
Rivers J (2006) Proportionality and variable intensity of review. Cambridge Law J 65(1):174–207. http://www.jstor.org/stable/4509179. Accessed 30 Nov 2021
Scheinin M (2013) Core rights and obligations. In: Shelton D (ed) Oxford handbook of international human rights law. Oxford University Press, Oxford
Tryfonidou A (2020), Positive state obligations under European law: a tool for achieving substantive equality for sexual minorities in Europe. Erasmus Law Rev 13(3):98–112, SSRN: https://ssrn.com/abstract=3737539. Accessed 30 Nov 2021
Tsioumani E (2002) Case Notes of Hatton and others v. United Kingdom (Application No 36022/97), Reciel 11(2) 2002. ISSN 0962 8797, Blackwell Publishers Ltd, Oxford
Tushnet M (2018) Rights inflation in Canada and the United States. In: Albert R, Cameron DR (eds) CANADA in the world: comparative perspectives on the Canadian constitution. Cambridge University Press, Cambridge

Chapter 7
Case Analysis: Non-Criminalization of Same-Sex Relations

7.1 Towards Non-Criminalization of Same-Sex Relations in Korea

Non-criminalization of homosexual relations is mostly protected in the European system. Nevertheless, the South Korean military law still punishes homosexual relations between consenting adults. Considering some progress made in South Korea, it is barely credible that Korea has not fulfilled the initial requirements of protecting sexual minorities. Therefore, this section discusses how Korea should make progress towards non-criminalization of same-sex relations between consenting adults.

7.1.1 Criminalization of Same-Sex Relations in Korea

An important issue related to the protection of sexual minorities in Korea is criminalization of homosexual relations under the Korean Military Criminal Law (KMCL). Article 92,[1] paragraph 6 of KMCL stipulates that a person who engages in "anal sex or other indecent acts" shall be subject to no more than two years of

[1]Korean Military Criminal Law Revision Act 2016.5.29. [Law No. 14183, enforced on May 11, 2016.]

Article 92 (Rape). A person who rapes a person prescribed in Article 1, Paragraphs 1 to 3 under assault or intimidation shall be subject to five years or more imprisonment.

Article 1 (Applicable Party). (1) This Law shall apply to a Korean soldier who has committed a crime prescribed in this law. (2) In Paragraph 1, "Soldier" means an officer, a warrant officer, a noncommissioned officer, and enlisted men, except for those in conversion service. (3) This Law shall apply to a person who falls under any of the following subparagraphs: (a) Civilian worker in the military (b) Students and candidates enlisted in the army pursuant to Article 57 of the Military Service Law (c) Reserve and supplementary forces who were called into service.

H. J. Lee, *Discrimination Based on Sexual Orientation*, Interdisciplinary Studies in Human Rights 8, https://doi.org/10.1007/978-3-030-95423-9_7

imprisonment. What is the problem with Article 92, paragraph 6[2] from the perspective of discrimination based on sexual orientation? Unlike other paragraphs,[3] the provision contains penalties for sexual contacts and acts without violence, assault or intimidation. Such elements are generally required in sexual violence crimes under the criminal law. In this regard, this provision could be interpreted as if homosexuality was punished unconditionally. Therefore, it could punish sexual contact or acts which were committed by two adults who are fully consenting.[4] A further problematic point is that it could provide the legal grounds to punish a victim as well. The CCK has already decided three times that this provision is constitutional, including the most recent decision on July 28, 2016. In this decision, the CCK decided that Article 92 does not violate the Korean constitution. However, it is actually unconstitutional since it punishes and restricts an individual's right to self-determination regarding sexual activities by means of the state's power to punish offenders.

7.1.2 Cases of the Constitutional Court of Korea ("CCK")

The CCK has already decided in three cases regarding the constitutionality of the Korean Military Criminal Law Article 92(6) on July 28, 2016 (2016 Case),[5] March 31, 2011 (2011 Case),[6] and June 27, 2002 (2002 Case).[7] In the 2002 case, the CCK decided that "other indecent acts" stipulated in Article 92 do not violate the principle of legality (void for vagueness) because soldiers with sound common sense and a feeling for law can easily grasp the meaning as to what extent an act corresponds to "other indecent acts." In addition, the CCK stated that the aim of the legislation is not

[2]KMCL Article 92(6) (Indecent Act). A person who engages in anal sex or other indecent acts to a person prescribed in Article 1, Paragraph 1 to 3 shall be subject to not more than 2 years' imprisonment.

[3]KMCL Article 92(2) (Similar Rape). A person who puts his/her genitals into the inner bodily parts (except genital) such as the mouth or anus of a person or puts bodily parts like fingers or tools into genitals, anus of a person prescribed in Article 1, Paragraphs 1 to 3 under an assault or intimidation shall be subject to 1 year or more imprisonment.

Article 92(3) (Forced Sexual Harassment). A person who sexually harass a person prescribed in Article 1, Paragraph 1 to 3 under an assault or intimidation shall be subject to 1 year or more imprisonment.

Article 92(4) (Semi Rape, Semi Forced Sexual Harassment). A person who rapes or sexually harasses a person prescribed in Article 1, Paragraphs 1 to 3 using the state of physical or mental impairment or inability to resist shall be subject to Article 92, 92(2), and 92(3).

Article 92(5) (Attempted Sexual Assault). A person who attempted a sexual assault prescribed in the Article 92, 92(2) to 92(4) shall be punished.

[4]Lee (2013), p. 33.

[5]The Constitutional Court of Korea, 2012 Hun-Ba 258, decided on July 28, 2016.

[6]The Constitutional Court of Korea, 2008 Hun-Ga 21, decided on March 31, 2011.

[7]The Constitutional Court of Korea, 2001 Hun-Ba 70, decided on June 27, 2002.

to protect individual sexual freedom, but to protect sound public life inside the army, which is social protection of military community. Therefore, it does not violate the principle of proportionality, especially the proportionality in the narrow sense. In the following 2011 case, the CCK similarly decided that the provision does not violate the principle of legality, the principle of proportionality, or the principle of equality. Hence, the article does not violate the Korean constitution.

Looking into the facts of the cases, in the 2002 case, the applicant, during his military service, was prosecuted on the grounds of sexually harassing the victim by putting his hands into the underwear of the victim and touching the victim's genitals. During the trial in the general military court, the applicant filed for adjudication on the grounds of constitutionality, but this was rejected. Then the applicant directly filed a constitutional appeal against the CCK based on Article 68(2)[8] of the constitutional court's law. In the 2011 case, the applicant, a platoon sergeant, was prosecuted on the grounds of sexually harassing the victim by touching the victim's belly, hips, and genitals. Later, the victim cancelled the accusation against the applicant, but the applicant was prosecuted because his act fell under "other indecent acts" of Article 92(6). This is because the accused could still be punished without the victim's accusation under the Article 92(6). The general military court, by its own decision, submitted an appeal to the CCK. When it is a premise of a lawsuit whether the law violates the Constitution or not, the court in charge of the case shall submit an appeal to the CCK for the judgment of the constitutionality by the court's own decision or by the application of the complainant.

Whilst the Constitutional Court did not see a violation of the Constitution, the dissenting opinions claimed the unconstitutionality of Article 92 KMCL. In the 2002 case,[9] the dissenting opinion stated that it violates the principle of legality, especially the vagueness doctrine[10] because the stipulations are vague. Under Korean criminal law, "indecent acts" involved with violence or intimidation are punishable.

---

[8]The complainant could appeal to the court for adjudication on constitutionality. In a case where such an appeal has been rejected, the complainant could file a constitutional appeal against the CCK directly, under the Article 68(2) of the Constitutional Court Act.

The Constitutional Court Act, Article 68 (Grounds for Request): (1) Any person whose fundamental rights guaranteed by the Constitution is infringed due to exercise or non-exercise of the public authority, excluding judgment of the court, may request adjudication on constitutional complaint to the Constitutional Court: Provided that any procedure for remedy is available by other laws, he/she may make a request after having taken all such procedures. (2) If a request made for adjudication on constitutionality of a law under Article 41 (1) is dismissed, the party who has made the request may request adjudication on constitutional complaint to the Constitutional Court. In this case, the party shall not request adjudication again on the constitutionality of a law, for the same reason in the litigation procedure of the case concerned. [This article was wholly amended by Act No. 10546 on April 5, 2011.]

[9]The Constitutional Court of Korea, 2001 Hun-Ba 70, decided on June 27, 2002.

[10]In this case, the Constitutional Court of Korea stated the vagueness doctrine, which seemed to have been adopted from the case law of the US Supreme Court. For example, in the cases of Franklin v. State, the Florida Supreme Court ruled that the state's felony ban on sodomy was unconstitutionally vague because an "average person of common intelligence" could not reasonably know, without speculating, whether "abominable and detestable crime against nature" included oral

However, Article 92 (6) stipulates that "indecent acts" are those without violence or intimidation. Therefore, the statement is vague as to whether the article intends to punish only the "indecent acts" without any violence or intimidation involved, or whether any "indecent acts" can be punished regardless of violence or intimidation. Likewise, in the 2011 case,[11] the dissenting opinion acknowledged that the provisions use only abstract, vague, and comprehensive terms such as "other indecent acts," thus, it is unclear whether it requires coercion, as well as what the degree of conduct, the subject of conduct, the counterparty, or the place of the acts should be. For these reasons, the dissenting opinion in the 2011 case[12] concluded that it is difficult for an average person of common intelligence to understand what is criminally punishable from the stipulations of the article. Furthermore, it could cause the law execution agencies to interpret the law arbitrarily. Therefore, it violates the principle of legality, especially the vagueness doctrine because what is punishable is stated too vaguely in the article.

The dissenting opinions of both the 2002[13] and 2011[14] cases analyze the violation of the principle of legality. Furthermore, they pointed out that Article 92 does not stipulate anything about the subject of the act or the counterparty. For example, it is not clear whether it means only between males or with females. Therefore, Article 92 is totally vague and thus violates the principle of legality. Yet the dissenting opinions of the two cases show differences in analyzing the violation of the principle of proportionality. In the 2002 case, the dissenting opinions stated that Article 92 violates the principle of proportionality for the following reasons: there is no possibility that there is a danger of directly causing any harm to the preservation of the combat power through same-sex relationship without any publicity or force. This can be interpreted to mean that it is not suitable to achieve the legislative aim of the provision through punishment, and not necessary because it exceeds the degree needed to achieve the aim. In this sense, the dissenting opinion concluded that Article 92 could not pass the *suitability* test and the *necessity* test in the proportionality. On the contrary, in the 2011 case, there was no mention at all of the violation of the principle of proportionality.

When comparing the two cases of 2002 and 2011, how could the 2011 case be evaluated? Is it a step forward or rather a step backward? It is rather a step backward for two reasons. Firstly, in the 2011 case, there was no mention of the analysis regarding the violation of the principle of proportionality although it was a much more recent case than the 2002 case. Secondly, in the 2002 case, the CCK made the decision only relating to the "indecent acts" in the Article 92(6) and concluded that it does not violate the Constitution. However, in the 2011 case, the CCK made the

sex or only anal sex (taken from Supreme Court of Florida, *Franklin v. State*, Nos. 40758, 40757, the decision of December 17, 1971).

[11] The Constitutional Court of Korea, 2008 Hun-Ga 21, decided on March 31, 2011.

[12] Ibid.

[13] The Constitutional Court of Korea, 2001 Hun-Ba 70, decided on June 27, 2002.

[14] The Constitutional Court of Korea, 2008 Hun-Ga 21, decided on March 31, 2011.

decision not only based on the "indecent acts," but also "anal sex."[15] The court also then concluded that it still does not violate the Constitution. In short, as the 2011 case concluded the constitutionality on both acts more extensively than the 2002 case, it goes backwards rather than forwards from the human rights perspective.

The most recent 2016 case[16] is similar to the second case of 2011. Nothing has particularly moved forward in terms of a human rights perspective. In the 2016 case, the CCK decided that "other indecent acts" stipulated in Article 92(6) do not violate the principle of legality particularly because the vagueness doctrine is not violated. The CCK stated that it can be interpreted as meaning acts conferring sexual satisfaction between homosexual soldiers which could objectively cause feelings of hatred among the general public. In addition, the provision does not violate the principle of proportionality because it is possible to suspend the court decision or the execution of punishment even after the court decision. The CCK stated in the decision that it was not violating the freedom of privacy, corporal liberty, or the right to sexual self-determination.

Looking into some of the relevant factual information of the 2016 case,[17] the applicant, during his military service, was prosecuted on the grounds of sexually harassing the victim by putting his hands into the underwear of the victim. The applicant was sentenced to six months in prison, and one-year probation by the general military court of Korea. During the appeal trial, the applicant filed the military court for adjudication on constitutionality of the Article 92, but the application was rejected. Then, the applicant directly filed a constitutional appeal to the CCK. The majority opinions of the case elaborated that Article 92 does not violate the principle of legality: Soldiers with sound common sense and legal sense could fully understand what acts the subject subscribed in the article could be. Therefore, there is no concern that the law enforcement agencies arbitrarily took a broad interpretation on this article. In conclusion, it is neither vague nor violates the principle of legality. On the other hand, the dissenting opinions stated that it violates the principle of legality. The reasons for that are: firstly, Article 92 does not clearly state whether coercion is needed or not in order to be punished. Secondly, the required degree of conduct is not stated specifically enough. Lastly, Article 92 does not state certainly about the subject, object, and place of the action to be punished.

7.1.3 Criticizing the Constitutional Court Decisions

In this section, the Korean Constitutional Court decisions that are introduced in the previous sections will be criticized according to the principle of legality, the principle of proportionality and the principle of non-discrimination.

[15] Park (2011), p. 77.

[16] The Constitutional Court of Korea, 2012 Hun-Ba 258, decided on July 28, 2016.

[17] The Constitutional Court of Korea, 2012 Hun-Ba 258, decided on July 28, 2016.

7.1.3.1 Violation of the Principle of Legality

A criticism on the Constitutional Court of Korea cases concerns the violation of the principle of legality. Article 92(6) KMCL stipulates only "anal sex or other indecent act," but it does not state anything as to whether the acts in question should include compulsion or not. Therefore, it is very difficult to judge whether certain acts are regarded as a forced offense liable to be criminal punishment. Article 92(6) is ambiguous as to the subject and the object of the punishable actions. The article is particularly unclear as to whether it is applicable only to a soldier or a civilian as object, or whether both males are punishable, and whether females or heterosexual acts are also included or not. It is also unclear whether the article punishes the acts between soldiers and civilians, or is confined to a military hierarchical relationship, or whether mutually consenting relationships between peers could be also punished.

It is unclear whether "other indecent acts" in Article 92(6) can be criminally punished even if there is an explicit or implicit agreement between the actors. As *Chan-Gul Park*[18] pointed out, compulsion should be decided according to the specific circumstances of the concrete cases. Furthermore, it is questionable whether the scope of criminal punishment can be extended even up to the acts with agreement or consent. As the Article 92 does not specify[19] the place and the time, therefore, the punishment could be extended irrespectively of whether the act is done at home or after work, or even on vacation. If the terms of a criminal statue are not sufficiently explicit those who are subject to it cannot know what conduct on their part will render them liable to its penalties,[20] In that case, more room is given to the state authorities to arbitrarily interpret the terms of article which are insufficiently explicit. Since it provides for the possibility of excess punishment due to this arbitrary interpretation by state authorities, unclear stipulations in the Article 92 definitely violates the principle of legality.

---

[18] Park (2011), p. 77.

[19] Such an unspecified stipulation is particularly problematic if it is a criminal statue. The Constitutional Court of Korea also stated explicitly that "the law must be stipulated in clear terms to protect public trust and ensure legal stability. Especially, clarity is needed when the law stipulates criminal punishment" (taken from The Constitutional Court of Korea, 90 Hun-Ba 27, April 28, 1992).

[20] The Constitutional Court of Korea stated the vagueness doctrine in its decisions related to the constitutionality of Article 92 KCML, which seemed to have been adopted from the US Supreme Court. The Constitutional Court of Korea interprets that the law violates the principle of legality when it violates the doctrine of the void for vagueness. The void for vagueness doctrine was made by Justice Sutherland in the US Supreme Court case of *Connally v. General Construction Co.*, 269 U.S. 385, 391 (1926): "The terms of a penal state ... must be sufficiently explicit to inform those who are subject to it what conduct on their part will render them liable to its penalties. . .and a statute which either forbids or requires the doing of an act in terms so vague that men of common intelligence must necessarily guess at its meaning and differ as to its application violates the first essential of due process of law" (taken from The Supreme Court of the United States, *Connally, Commissioner, et al. v. General Construction Company*, 269 U.S. 385 (1926)', full case available at Connally v. General Constr. Co., 269 U.S. 385, 46 S. Ct. 126, 70 L. Ed. 322, 1926 U.S. LEXIS 929 – CourtListener.com. Accessed November 30, 2021).

7.1.3.2 Violation of the Principle of Proportionality

The Constitutional Court of Korea assesses whether criminal punishment stipulated in the criminal code meets the sub-criteria of the principle of proportionality, which refers to legitimacy of aims, suitability of means, less restrictive measures, and proportionality in the narrow sense.[21] Firstly, the legislative aim of the Article 92 KMCL is not legitimate because it is ambiguous. The CCK points out that "other indecent acts" violate healthy military life and military discipline. However, it is very difficult to prove a correlation between sexual morals and good, healthy military life. A further point raised by *Myung-Su Kim*[22] is also importantly related to the ambiguous expressions in the article. The CCK describes the purpose and interests of protection as "the sexual health of the military," but it is too ambiguous to determine the exact meaning of the expression. Article 92 is problematic in that the legislative aim and interests of protection are too ambiguous to foresee Acts prohibited by the provision. This ambiguous legislative aim cannot be solved using interpretation according to the constitution because there is no specific constitutional provision with a relevant stipulation in relation to interpretation methodology. Instead, the Constitutional Court of Korea has recognized that this ambiguity is particularly problematic in criminal law stipulations.[23]

Secondly, suitability assesses whether a measure is an effective, appropriate or rational means of pursuing the desired end.[24] In other words, the suitability test assesses whether there are reasonable connections between the means and the proper aim.[25] Nevertheless, it is particularly difficult to find a rational connection between the means of criminal punishment of same-sex relations in the military under Article 92 and the intended purpose of a "healthy military life and military discipline" because the purpose is already very ambiguous. Moreover, even if the state authorities claim that there is a rational connection between criminalization of same-sex relations and the attainment of healthy military life and discipline, criminal punishment cannot be considered as less restrictive measures, which is the third step of necessity. In a modern society where individual consciousness and corresponding social systems are relatively open, criminal punishment without considering taking

[21] The Constitutional Court of Korea, 2016 Hun-Ba 408, decided on May 25, 2017: In this case, the Constitutional Court of Korea applied the four sub-tests of proportionality – legitimate aim, suitability, necessity, and the proportionality in the narrow sense to decide whether criminal punishment under the cosmetics law which bans the sale of sample cosmetics is constitutional or not.

[22] Kim (2011), p. 67.

[23] The Constitutional Court of Korea, 90 Hun-Ba 27, decided on April 28, 1992.

[24] Kirk (1997), p. 6.

[25] Barak (2012), p. 306.

other milder measures such as disciplinary actions is not proportionate at all.[26] Since criminal sanctions are the most powerful and infringing measures, the use of criminal sanctions should be restricted if it can be controlled by other less restrictive means. In that sense, Article 92 KCML fails the necessity test.

Finally, proportionality in the narrow sense can be assessed through the lens of rules of weight.[27] The restriction on the freedom of homosexual soldiers' privacy through criminalization of consensual same-sex sexual acts is considered to be very intense. On the other hand, the public interest of good and sound military life and discipline[28] seems to be attained without criminalizing same-sex relations. There could be many other methods to enhance sound military life not by criminal punishment but by alternatives such as education, training, other administrative measures. If the same goal can be served to the same extent without restricting the right, the restriction is considered as disproportionate,[29] particularly as homosexual soldiers do not serve in the military voluntarily, but by compulsory conscription in South Korea. Nevertheless, if they engage in any kind of same-sex sexual acts, then they are subject to punishment including imprisonment. The restrictions on freedom of privacy of these homosexual soldiers cannot be justified because the limitations are considered as very intense.

7.1.3.3 Violation of the Principle of Non-Discrimination

The last criticism concerns violation of the principle of non-discrimination. According to this principle, the state should not arbitrarily differentiate between individuals.[30] Firstly, the state differentiates solders from civilians because there is no criminal punishment for homosexual relationship between consenting civilians. Only homosexual acts committed by soldiers are punished. The CCK tries to justify such different treatment because the public interest in maintaining a sound military life and discipline as a military community is much more important than the individual's right to sexual self-determination. Nevertheless, the CCK justification does not make sense by itself, because it cannot explain the reason why heterosexual acts by consenting soldiers are not punished. Furthermore, serving in the military is not the voluntary choice of an individual but a compulsory duty in Korea. In this situation, it is difficult to justify the different treatment between soldiers and civilians.

Secondly, the state differentiates homosexual soldiers from heterosexual soldiers because only homosexual acts are criminally punished. Even if the law does not explicitly state that only homosexual acts are punished, Article 92 (6) stipulates that "anal sex" is punished. Furthermore, Article 92 has been only applied to homosexual

---

[26] Lee (2013), p. 44.

[27] Schauer (2014), p. 179.

[28] Kim (2011), p. 85.

[29] Ibid., p. 179.

[30] Fredman (2011), p. 8.

acts.[31] If it is a matter of sound military life and discipline, heterosexual relationships should also be punished according to the CCK's logic.[32] However, heterosexual acts between consenting soldiers are not criminally punished. Only homosexual acts are punished. There are no justifications as to why only homosexual acts endanger sound military life while heterosexual acts have nothing to do with sound military life. Formal equality before the law[33] is violated because the law does not punish heterosexual acts but only the same-sex sexual acts of soldiers. Hence, the law treats the two groups in similar situation differently without justification.

7.1.4 Comparative Analysis with the ECtHR Cases

This section will briefly introduce what South Korea can learn from European experiences towards non-criminalization of homosexual relations. There are many other related case laws in the ECtHR, but the comparative analysis will focus on two cases: the first case is *Dudgeon v. United Kingdom*[34] because this is the case where the principle has been established in relation to the ban on criminalizing homosexual relations between consenting adults. Another case is *Bayev and others v. Russia*[35] of the year 2017. Even if the main issue of this case is not about criminalizing homosexual relations, there are lessons for Korean courts in terms of the methodology applied.

There are several similar contexts between the *Dudgeon* case and the Korean situation. Firstly, homosexual acts committed in private between two consenting males aged 21 or over were no longer criminal offenses in England and Wales, but these were punishable in Northern Ireland. Likewise, Korean military law criminalizes homosexual acts between two consenting adults, but civilians who are not subject to military law are not punished by such acts. Secondly, as the opponents of abolishment of Korean military law articles argue, the law in question no longer gives rise to many cases of prosecutions in either the *Dudgeon* case or the Korean case. Even if there are a few prosecutions, the existence of the law to punish homosexual acts is still a problem because possibilities for prosecutions remain based on arbitrary decisions of state authorities. Moreover, the existence of the law makes homosexuals and the society consider homosexual acts to be criminal. Thirdly, the aims of such interferences are claimed in both cases as being similar

[31] Between January 1, 2004 and December 31, 2007, 176 cases have been criminally punished and all of them were on homosexual acts. Moreover, four cases of homosexual acts between consenting adults have been punished (Lee 2008, p. 73). In the Court's proceedings, interrogations on the convicted have focused on the questions related to homosexual acts which is regarded as "abnormal acts." (Ibid., p. 97.)

[32] Noh (2009), pp. 284–285.

[33] Fredman (2011), p. 86.

[34] European Court of Human Rights, *Dudgeon v. United Kingdom*, judgment of 22 October 1981.

[35] European Court of Human Rights, *Bayev and Others v. Russia*, judgment of 20 June 2017.

to "the protection of morals" or "the protection of the rights and freedoms of others."[36] Fourthly, majorities' opinions are very much against homosexual acts in both cases.

Regarding the legal impact of differences in law between Northern Ireland from England and Wales, the ECtHR stated the effort of the UK government to "bring Northern Ireland law on the matter broadly into line with that of England and Wales"[37] in the case. Regarding the second point, the ECtHR clearly states that "even if there was no prosecution or threat of prosecution, the mere existence of the legislation had constant direct repercussions on the applicant's private life,"[38] which could be a counter argument against the opponents of non-criminalization in Korea. The opponents claim that the existence of law does not restrict the right of homosexual soldiers much because there are not many cases of prosecution. Yet as the ECtHR points out, the very existence of such law to punish same-sex sexual acts between consulting adults itself interferes with the right of sexual minorities. It is also not desirable to depend on the authorities' power to prosecute or not as the law remains problematic.

The third point referring to the law's aim can be criticized. The ECtHR seems to admit the legitimacy of the aims claimed by the state authorities, as stating "the general aim pursued by the legislation remains the protection of morals in the sense of moral standards obtaining in Northern Ireland."[39] However, applying the reasoning in the more recent case of *Bayev and others*, such aims as "protection of morals," "protection of health," or "the protection of rights of other" are not considered as legitimate aims any more due to "the vagueness of the terminology" as well as "the potentially unlimited scope of their applications."[40] Such reasoning can also be exactly applied to the article of the Korean Military Law as the authorities state these vague and abstract aims regarding criminalization.

A fourth point relates to the consensus argument. Although the ECtHR made a pronouncement in terms of the consensus among Member States and the Korean Constitutional Court argues about the sentiment in the general public, the background behind both considers the opinion of the majority. However, as the ECtHR emphasizes, the hallmarks of a democratic society are particularly pluralism, tolerance and broadmindedness;[41] furthermore, ignoring the minority opinion because it is different from the majority cannot be acceptable in a democratic society.

In conclusion, Article 92 of the KMCL should be abolished. It cannot be justified that the state exercises its power to punish individuals according to sexual identity,

---

[36] European Court of Human Rights, Dudgeon v. United Kingdom, judgment of 22 October 1981, paragraph 45.

[37] Edel (2015), p. 46.

[38] Ibid., p. 46.

[39] European Court of Human Rights, *Dudgeon v. United Kingdom*, judgment of 22 October 1981, paragraph 46.

[40] European Court of Human Rights, *Bayev and Others v. Russia*, judgment of 20 June 2017, paragraph 83.

[41] European Court of Human Rights, *Beizaras and Levickas v. Lithuasnia*, judgment of 14 January 2020, paragraph 106.

preferences or sexual orientation of individuals. Article 92 (5) under the KMCL exists to punish male soldiers with homosexual tendencies. Moreover, it is highly unclear what the law intends to protect through the provision. The CCK's justification as "sound military life and discipline" is too ambiguous for the stipulation of criminal punishment. There is no clear evidence that homosexual relationships have significant, fundamental negative impacts on military cultures. The state cannot execute the power to punish the sexual relationships between fully consenting adults. Therefore, the CCK must decide that Article 92(5) KMCL violates the Constitution and accordingly the article must be abolished. It will be a small positive step towards realization of non-discrimination based on sexual orientation in Korea.

7.2 Non-Criminalization of Same-Sex Relations in India

What is the situation regarding legal recognition of same-sex relations in Asia? The actual situation in Asia is even worse than in Europe. Including South Korea, where there has been almost no or very little progress, in many countries in Asia sexual minorities are considered to be one of the most vulnerable groups suffering from various forms of discrimination. Anti-discrimination laws based on sexual orientation do not exist in most Asian countries and the right to change one's legal gender is also not recognized in many Asian countries. For example, as the statistics in year 2019 shows at the beginning of this chapter, 21 countries in Asia still criminalize consensual same-sex sexual acts between adults while no country in Europe still does this.[42] The section will introduce the recent case from India about criminalization of homosexual relations,[43] as decided in September 2018 (*Navtej Singh Johar* case). In this case, India's supreme Court unanimously ruled that Section 377 of the Indian Penal Code (1860) (IPC) was unconstitutional insofar as it penalized any consensual sexual activity between two adults regardless of whether they are homosexuals, heterosexuals, or lesbians.

7.2.1 Criminalization of Same-Sex Relations in India[44]

India is a country bordering Pakistan, China, Nepal, Bhutan, and Bangladesh, and it is the seventh largest country by area. The country also has the second largest

[42] Mendos (2019), p. 197.

[43] Navtej Singh Johar and Others v. Union of India through Secretary Ministry of Law and Justice, Writ Petition No. 76 of 2016, Indian Supreme Court decided on September 6, 2018.

[44] I referred to the report of Jindal Global Law School on Recent Legal Reforms on Gender Recognition: A Global Review, written by J. Dipika, R. Kimberly, and S. Surabhi, published in May 2019. pp. 26–37.

population in the world, with more than 1.3 billion people. From a cultural perspective, India has no official religion, but more than 80 percent of Indians are Hindu while about 13 percent are Muslim. Other religions in India include Buddhism, Sikhism, and Jainism, which all began in India. Hindi is the official language of the Indian government, and English is spoken as a subsidiary language.

The Constitution of India was adopted by a Constituent Assembly on November 26, 1949 as the supreme law in India, and it became effective on January 26, 1950.[45] The Supreme Court of India is the highest constitutional court, and the law declared by the Supreme Court is binding on all other courts in India. As a widely respected judicial institution, the Supreme Court has a high reputation for its independence and impartiality and for encouraging the development of litigation in the public interest to help poor and marginalized people.[46] As one of the most powerful judiciaries in the world, the Indian Supreme Court laid down procedural as well as substantive rights and has made a major contribution to human rights jurisprudence in many areas.[47]

Historically, most of the Indian sub-continent was under British rule from 1858 to 1947, and British settlements and possessions were administered by the East India Company until the Indian Rebellion of 1857. The IPC was introduced in 1860 as the first codification of criminal law in the British Empire, and the model was replicated in many other British colonies, but never in the United Kingdom itself.[48] According to the report by Human Rights Watch,[49] the law was imposed on India by the government of British India as part of a package of laws against public vice. Afterwards, the same language or substance was replicated in other British colonies including Bangladesh, Myanmar, Singapore, Malaysia, Brunei, Sri Lanka, Papua New Guinea and some 17 African countries. As seen from the wording of Section 377[50] of the IPC, the problem with it is that the code was interpreted as criminalizing same-sex activities because they were "unnatural" even if it made no reference to homosexuality or same-sex intercourse. It is similar to Article 92 of the KMCL in that it could punish any sexual acts between consenting adults.

More specifically, Section 377 of the IPC has the following problems. Firstly, it was initially introduced as an attempt to civilize the Indian population through the imposition of standards of morality from the Victorian era. There, sexual activities were considered to be mainly for procreation, which is no longer valid. Secondly, it is a clear human rights violation to criminalize same-sex relations between

[45] McGoldrick (2019), p. 3.

[46] Chandra (2018), pp. 710–711.

[47] Lokaneeta (2017), p. 354.

[48] Han and O'Mahoney (2014), pp. 2–6.

[49] Human Rights Watch (2008), *This Alien Legacy: The Origins of "Sodomy" Laws in British Colonialism*, 17 December 2008, available at: www.hrw.org. Accessed November 30, 2021.

[50] Section 377 of the IPC states: Unnatural Offences: Whoever voluntarily has carnal intercourse against the order of nature with any man, woman or animal shall be punished with imprisonment for life, or with imprisonment of either description for a term which may extend to ten years, and shall also be liable to a fine.

consenting adults from the anti-discrimination and equality perspective.[51] Therefore, it is highly problematic to prosecute consensual as well as non-consensual sexual acts under the Section 377.[52] According to the data provided by International Commission of Jurists,[53] fewer than 150 persons have been prosecuted under Section 377 in India since 1860. In the modern era, prosecutions have become increasingly rare. However, that does not mean that Section 377 is no longer problematic because it is used as the basis for continuous violence against sexual minorities by the authorities. This is supported by the statistics given in the news article[54] from *the Times of India*: police in different states and union territories arrested 1491 people under Section 377 in 2015, and 207 minors and 16 women were included. Such numbers show how sexual minorities suffered from the law. Regardless of the rare prosecutions, the existence of the law itself causes severe discrimination for them.

7.2.2 The Supreme Court Decisions of India

Prior to the landmark *Navtej Singh Johar* case in 2018, there were several cases examining the constitutionality of Section 377 of the IPC. In 2009, the Delhi High Court held in the *Naz Foundation* case[55] that Section 377 violated Article 21 (right to life and personal liberty), Article 14 (right to equality), and Article 15 (non-discrimination) of the Indian Constitution. In the decision, the court declared that Section 377 IPC, insofar as it criminalizes consensual sexual acts of adults in private, violates Articles 21, 14, and 15. It held that Section 377 does not apply to consensual sexual relationships between adults regardless of their sex. The decision seemed to have a positive impact on same-sex relationships in India until the Supreme Court overturned this decision in the *Suresh Kumar Koushal* case[56] in December 2013.

Those who attempted to stop positive progress in the rights of sexual minorities were not the government, but astrologer *Suresh Kumar Koushal*, religious individuals, and faith-based groups, including Hindus, Muslims, and Christians.[57] Such

---

[51] General Comment No. 22 (2016) on the right to sexual and reproductive health (Article 12 of the International Covenant on Economic, Social and Cultural Rights), E/C. 12/GC/22, 4 March 2016.

[52] Narrian (2010), p. 87.

[53] International Commission of Jurists (2017), *Unnatural Offences" Obstacles to Justice in India Based on Sexual Orientation and Gender Identity*, available at: www.icj.org. Accessed November 30, 2021.

[54] Thomas (2019).

[55] The Naz Foundation v. Government of NCT of Delhi (2009) 160DLT277, Writ Petition (Civil No. 7455/2001).

[56] Suresh Kumar Koushal v. Naz Foundation and Others (2014) 1 SCC 1, Civil Appeal No. 10972 of 2013.

[57] Ibid., paragraphs 24–28.

groups did not seem to share their common religious beliefs considering the elements of their various religions, but they were likely to unite against homosexuality. It is not surprising that the most radical resistance against all the legal instruments supporting same-sex relationships in Korea comes from Christian churches. Considering that Catholic churches have been against legalizing same-sex relationship historically, no religious group seemed to have been actually in favor of the rights of sexual minorities. The Indian Supreme Court decided that the abuse of Section 377 by police officers and others in power to target and harass innocent queer people did not affect the constitutionality of the law, because misuse does not mean that such legislation is unconstitutional.[58] In addition, the Supreme Court pointed out that the Delhi High Court relied too much on international precedent to decriminalize homosexuality even though such precedent could not directly apply to the Indian context.[59] Therefore, the Supreme Court decided that Section 377 is constitutional and refused to decriminalize homosexual relations.

However, the decision attracted much criticism not only from a substantive perspective but also a procedural point of view. As *Vikram Raghavan* pointed out in his criticism,[60] the Indian Supreme Court's decision to allow an appeal from *Koushal* was already problematic, because the party had not participated in the previous High Court proceedings in which the appellants did not satisfy the requirement to bring the case before the Supreme Court. In addition, *Raghavan* further explained that the appeal by *Koushal* was filed under Article 136[61] of the Indian Constitution, which is not a regular appellate provision but only confers residual jurisdiction. For this reason, the Supreme Court could accept an appeal only if its interference is warranted. Nevertheless, the party's explanation never met such a procedural requirement. For this reason, the Supreme Court decision of *Koushal* was problematic in its procedure from the beginning when the proceedings of appeal started.

From the substantive perspective, similar to the cases of the Constitutional Court of Korea, Section 377 of IPC is highly problematic in terms of human rights. Primarily, "unnatural offences" or "against the order of nature" is itself vague in expression to be regarded as a legal term to justify criminal punishment. This vagueness of the stipulations could make over-punishment highly possible because it does not specify many constituents to define what is punished including the place and the time of the act which can be punished. Secondly, it is not proportionate in that criminal punishment must be allowed as supplementary or as the last means.

[58] Kumar Koushal v. Naz Foundation and Others (2014) 1 SCC 1, Civil Appeal No. 10972 of 2013, paragraphs 76–78.

[59] Ibid., paragraph 78.

[60] Raghavan (2013).

[61] Article 136, The Constitution of India 1949 reads as follows: Special leave to appeal by the Supreme Court (1) Notwithstanding anything in this Chapter, the Supreme Court may, in its discretion, grant special leave to appeal from any judgment, decree, determination, sentence or order in any cause or matter passed or made by any court or tribunal in the territory of India. (2) Nothing in clause (1) shall apply to any judgment, determination, sentence or order passed or made by any court or tribunal constituted by or under any law relating to the Armed Forces.

"Imprisonment up to ten years" is not considered as necessary since other alternative measures could substitute. Lastly, it violates the final step of the proportionality test in that there is no balancing because the limitation of private interests is much more serious than the vague public interest of sound morals. It seriously violates the individual rights of self-determination of individuals' sexual acts because Section 377 punishes "whoever voluntarily has carnal intercourse." Despite much criticism, Section 377 remained valid through the *Koushal* case until the Supreme Court decision of the *Navtej Singh Johar* case in 2018.

The recent Indian Supreme Court decision of the *Navteh Singh Johar*[62] case in September 2018 is regarded as a landmark judgment, as it challenges Section 377. In this decision, the Court stated that Section 377 is unconstitutional as long as it criminalizes consensual sexual conduct between same sex adults, and it found its prohibition against "unnatural acts" (read to include same-sex sexual acts) unconstitutional.[63] According to *Dominic McGoldrick*,[64] there are four conceptual tools which the Indian Supreme Court adopted in this case: firstly, the Court regarded the Constitution as a tool for "transformative constitutionalism,"[65] where the role of the Constitution is understood as transforming a society in a better way. This better way considers that the society develops in a more inclusive way where the voice of minority groups is respected. Secondly, the so-called principle of "constitutional morality"[66] was applied in the decision. This "Constitutional morality" in this context means the core values set forth in the preface to the Constitution, which includes even greater values which could lead to a more diverse and comprehensive society. Thirdly, the Court focused on the decency of every individual because all other rights could lose their own meanings without the right to dignity. Lastly, the Indian Supreme Court enhanced the privacy rights, following the decision of *Puttaswamy*.[67]

[62] Navtej Singh Johar and Others v. Union of India through Secretary Ministry of Law and Justice Writ Petition No. 76 of 2016. The representative petitioners were a dancer (Navtej Singh Johar), a journalist (his partner), a chef, a hotelier and a businesswoman.

[63] Dipika et al. (2019), pp. 27–28.

[64] McGoldrick (2019), p. 6.

[65] Ibid., p. 6.

[66] Ibid., p. 6.

[67] Supreme Court of India, Justice K.S. Puttaswamy (Retd.) and Anr. Vs Union of India and Ors. Writ Petition (Civil) No. 494 of 2012, decided on August 24, 2017, 29(2017)10SCC1: The case was brought by 91-year-old retired High Court Judge Puttaswamy against the Union of India to determine whether the right to privacy was guaranteed as an independent fundamental right following conflicting decisions. In the latest case, the government's Aadhaar scheme (a form of uniform biometrics-based identity card) which the government proposed making mandatory for access to government services was challenged because the scheme violated the right to privacy. However, the Attorney General argued that the Indian Constitution does not grant specific protection for the right to privacy. Finally, the nine-judge bench of the Supreme Court unanimously recognized that the Constitution guaranteed the right to privacy as an intrinsic part of the right to life and personal liberty under Article 21 of the Indian Constitution (cited from Global Freedom of Expression in Columbia University, https://globalfreedomofexpression.columbia.edu/cases/puttaswamy-v-india/ last accessed on September 13, 2019).

There are four concurring opinions in the judgment, and the international perspective is extensively referred to countries such as the United States, Canada, South Africa, the United Kingdom, and other courts/jurisdictions including the Philippines, and the Human Rights Committee. *Justice Chandrachud* referenced other international jurisprudences, claiming that international jurisprudences have gone even further to protect rights for homosexuals instead of stopping at decriminalizing same-sex relations.[68] One of the jurisprudences referred to in this context is the famous case of *Oliari v. Italy* (2015)[69] from the European Court of Human Rights where the ECtHR affirmed that same-sex couples are in need of legal recognition and they can equally enter into "stable and committed relationships" as different sex couples.[70] The following refers to the US Supreme Court case *United States v. Windsor* (2013)[71] in order to show that it is unconstitutional to interpret "marriage" and "spouse" to apply only to opposite sex couples.[72] And the historical US Supreme Court case of *Obergefell v. Hodges* (2015)[73] is referenced to prove the court's view where "the right to personal choice regarding marriage is inherent in the concept of individual autonomy."[74] A comparative perspective on the same topic will provide the opportunity for mutual learning by means of the process of judicial dialogues.[75] The Indian case tried to justify its reasoning to decriminalize homosexual relations and the comparative perspective has been adopted in the process of its reasoning.

7.3 Discussions in the United States

It is difficult to claim that all other areas in human rights are underdeveloped in South Korea compared to the United States of America. However, since Korea is certainly underdeveloped in the protection of sexual minorities, there are lessons to be learnt from America. Particularly, the Korean Constitutional Court refers to cases from America as inspiring sources. In this respect, it will be helpful to look at some of the American experiences in the discussion of non-criminalization of homosexual

[68] Navtej Singh Johar and Others v. Union of India through Secretary Ministry of Law and Justice Writ Petition No. 76 of 2016, paragraph 115 (*per* Justice Chandrachud).

[69] European Court of Human Rights, *Oliari and others v. Italy*, judgment of 21 July 2015.

[70] Ibid., paragraphs 119–120 (*per* Justice Chandrachud).

[71] United States v. Windsor, 570 U.S. 744 (2013).

[72] Ibid., paragraph 121 (*per* Justice Chandrachud).

[73] Obergefell v. Hodges, 576 U.S. 644 (2015).

[74] Ibid., paragraph 121 (*per* Justice Chandrachud).

[75] Judicial dialogues between national courts and international courts improve the implementation of international human rights especially in order to fulfil the common missions (taken from Maues et al. 2021, p. 2). I argue that prohibition of discrimination based on sexual orientation is regarded as the common mission to be accomplished. Criminalization of consensual same-sex relations should be particularly abolished.

relations and how such a discussion increasingly influences the prohibition of discrimination based on sexual orientation in this section.

7.3.1 Getting Rid of the Sodomy Law

The *Bowers v. Hardwick* (1986)[76] case examined whether private homosexual acts between consenting adults can be protected as a fundamental right. *Mr. Hardwick* had been arrested on the grounds of violating the sodomy law of Georgia, and the prosecutors questioned the scope of the "right to privacy." They claimed that the scope of the "right to privacy" is limited to the marriage, family, childbirth, abortion, childcare, and education. For this reason, if the sodomy law was abolished, it could lead to all the laws prohibiting polygamy, homosexuality, same-sex marriage, or adultery being challenged. Regarding these claims, the applicant Hardwick focused on how far the government intervenes into an individual's life: that is, whether the state of Georgia has the power to instruct adult citizens how to handle their closest and intimate relationships in their bedrooms. On June 30, 1986, Georgia's sodomy law, which punishes homosexual conduct, was regarded as being constitutional by five to four votes.

The majority opinion of the *Bowers v. Hardwick*[77] case focused on the fact that same-sex relations have always been subject to punishment in the history of Western civilization. According to this opinion, whether same-sex relations are carried out in the context of private family life does not alter the conclusion. As the dissenting opinion, Justice *Blackmun*[78] viewed this case as "the right to be let alone" in relation to "the right to privacy." As to this opinion, many precedents had already acknowledged that the Federal Constitution has implemented a commitment to preserve the private freedom of individuals broadly as the government cannot be involved in this sphere. The most important point from this dissenting opinion is that no matter how a certain minority discomfort the majority, mere intolerance or hatred expressed by the majority cannot deprive the individuals of their right to physical freedom. This cannot be constitutionally justified in any cases. In this regard, it is important to understand the concept of privacy which determines the moral fact of an individual belonging only to him or herself instead of to another person or society as a whole. According to this concept, for example, the reason why the "decision" to marry is protected is because marriage is believed to promote a way of life, harmony in life, and sincerity towards the spouse rather than great causes, political beliefs, or economic or social plans. Similarly, protecting decisions about having children is not due to demographic considerations or biblical commands, but because being a parent could dramatically change how an individual defines him or herself.

[76] Bowers v. Hardwick, 478 U.S. 186(1986).

[77] Bowers v. Hardwick, 478 U.S. 186(1986).

[78] Ibid., Justice Blackmun, dissenting.

The majority opinion of the *Bowers* case can be criticized from two points. Firstly, the majority opinion interpreting the right to privacy does not include the right to same-sex sexual acts. For this reason, the majority opinion concluded that Mr. Hardwick did not suffer from the limitation of his fundamental right through arrest in his home during his sexual acts with another adult man. Sexual intimacy is central to an individual's development of personality, and it cannot be ignored by the state's power or regulation. In this sense, the sodomy law violates the core of individual's most intimate sphere, which should be protected as a right to privacy. Secondly, the majority opinion depended on "deeply rooted" standards,[79] which prioritized traditional values over evolving thoughts through time. Justice *White* wrote the majority opinion under the "deeply rooted" standards and tried to analyze "ancient roots" to prove a long history of criminalizing same-sex sexual acts. Nevertheless, traditional values cannot be the ground to keep the law even if the law cannot be justified according to a constitutional perspective and democratic values.

7.3.2 Further Discussions

The case of *Romer v. Evans* (1996)[80] decided that passage of Amendment 2 violated the Equal Protection Clause.[81] In 1992, voters in the state of Colorado in 1992 approved this Amendment 2,[82] which would prohibit any city, town, or country in the state from taking any legislative, executive, or judicial action to recognize male homosexuality, female homosexuality, or bisexual orientation as protected grounds. The immediate purpose of Amendment 2 is to invalidate laws, regulations, ordinances, and policies to prohibit discrimination based on sexual orientation. Furthermore, the ultimate effect of this Amendment 2 is that any state government agency is

---

[79] For the "deeply rooted standards," please see Marcus (2014), p. 17.

[80] Romer v. Evans, 517 U.S. 620 (1996), pp. 623–626.

[81] The Equal Protection Clause is located at the end of Section 1 of the Fourteenth Amendment:

> All persons born or naturalized in the United States, and subject to the jurisdiction thereof, are citizens of the United States and of the State wherein they reside. No State shall make or enforce any law which shall abridge the privileges or immunities of citizens of the United States; nor shall any State deprive any person of life, liberty, or property, without due process of law; nor deny to any person within its jurisdiction the equal protection of the laws.

[82] Passage of Amendment 2 has been stated as follows:

> Neither the State of Colorado, through any of its branches or departments, nor any of its agencies, political subdivisions, municipalities or school districts, shall enact, adopt or enforce any statute, regulation, ordinance or policy whereby homosexual, lesbian or bisexual orientation, conduct, practices or relationships shall constitute or otherwise be the basis of or entitle any person or class of persons to have or claim any minority status, quota preferences, protected status or claim of discrimination. This Section of the Constitution shall be in all respects self-executing.

not allowed to establish similar or more protective laws unless state constitutions are amended to allow such measures.

Amendment 2 imposes legal incompetence especially on sexual minorities because they are prohibited from enjoying all the protections that are enjoyable without any restrictions to others. Amendment 2 cannot pass the test of rationality under the Equal Protection Clause because it defines the identity of a person with one characteristic of "homosexual, lesbian or bisexual orientation,"[83] and it denies all the protections to people with this characteristic. Under *the principle of proportionality*, this Amendment 2 already fails in the first step of legitimate aim. It does not have any legitimate aim. It is "status-based" legislation, "classification of persons" that is not allowed under the Equal Protection Clause.[84] This Amendment 2 classifies people with "homosexual, lesbian or bisexual orientation" from other people in order not to provide protections to any discriminatory measures.

On the other hand, the dissenting opinion of the *Romer v. Evans* case claimed that the Amendment 2 has a legitimate aim of preventing the gradual decline of sexual morality that is favored by a majority of residents in the state of Colorado.[85] Furthermore, the dissenting opinion insists that the Amendment 2 is *suitable* to achieve such a legitimate aim for the following reasons: the constitution does not prohibit the criminalization of "perverting acts." If it is constitutionally allowed for a state to criminalize such "perverting acts," it is naturally constitutionally permissible to enact laws that do not favor "perverting acts" such as Amendment 2. However, such an ambiguous aim of stopping the decline of sexual morality cannot be recognized as a *legitimate aim*. Even if it can, taking away all the protections only because of their sexual orientations cannot be justified as necessary measures to attain such an objective because there should be less restrictive measures than taking away all the protections. Therefore, contrary to the dissenting opinion, Amendment 2 clearly violates the *principle of proportionality*.

Such discussions lead towards legalizing same-sex marriage cases[86] in the US. In the *U.S. v. Windsor* (2013)[87] case, it is questioned whether the concept of spouse according to the Federal Law of Defense of Marriage Act ("DOMA") includes same-sex partners or not. Windsor and her partner *Spyer*, both residents of New York, married in Toronto, Ontario under the provisions set forth in the Canadian Civil Marriage Act, after a romantic partnership of 40 years. *Spyer* died in 2009, Windsor had to pay $363,053 in federal estate taxes on her inheritance of *Spyer*'s estate, which she would not have had to pay if federal law had recognized the validity of their marriage, and unlimited spousal deduction applied. However, federal estate tax

[83] Passage of Amendment 2.

[84] Romer v. Evans, 517 U.S. 620 (1996), pp. 626–635.

[85] Ibid., pp. 638–653.

[86] The case analysis of same-sex marriage will be discussed in Chap. 8.

[87] United States v. Windsor, 570 U.S. 744 (2013).

exemption for surviving spouses was not applied to Windsor because of the definition of marriage by Section 3 of DOMA.[88] The United States Supreme Court held in this case that Section 3 of DOMA, which denied federal recognition of same-sex marriages, was a violation of the Due Process Clause of the Fifth Amendment.

The case of *Obergefell et al. v. Hodges* (2015)[89] of the US Supreme Court is worth discussing because the ECtHR quoted this specific case in the *Oliari* Case. In the case of *Obergefell*, the applicants, 14 same-sex couples and two men whose same-sex partners are deceased, claim that the respondent state officials violate the Fourteenth Amendment by denying them the right to marry or to have marriages lawfully performed in another state given full recognition. The problem in the case was that marriage is defined as a union between one man and one woman in the states of Michigan, Kentucky, Ohio, and Tennessee. The Supreme Court holds that under the Fourteenth Amendment of the US Constitution, all states must license a marriage between two people of the same sex and recognize such a marriage if it was lawfully licensed and performed in another state. The judgment states that marriage is a timeless institution. However, it has changed over time. Therefore, it is impossible to rely on history as a defense.[90] The Supreme Court provides four principles and tradition to demonstrate that the reasons why marriage is fundamental under the Constitution, and it should be applied with equal force to same-sex couples. The principles are the concepts of individual autonomy, intimate association, safeguarding children and families. Above all, marriage is a keystone of the Nation's

---

[88] Section 3. Definition of marriage in Defense of Marriage Act reads as follows:

> In determining the meaning of any Act of Congress, or of any ruling, regulation, or interpretation of the various administrative bureaus and agencies of the United States, the word "marriage" means only a legal union between one man and one woman as husband and wife, and the word "spouse" refers only to a person of the opposite sex who is a husband or a wife.

[89] Supreme Court of the United States, *James Obergefell, et al., Petitioners v. Richard Hodges, Director, Ohio Department of Health, et al.* 576 U.S. decided on June 26, 2015. (The case is not the culmination of one lawsuit, but the consolidation of six lower-court cases coming from Michigan, Ohio, Kentucky, and Tennessee. I will introduce the factual information of Michigan and Ohio here to help understanding of the Supreme Court case. (1) Michigan case of *DeBoaer v. Snyder*: April DeBoer and Jayne Rowse have lived together for ten years, own a home together, and have three children. Laws in Michigan, where they live, prevented them from jointly adopting their children, so DeBoer adopted on child on her own, while Rowse adopted the other two. This also means that Rowse cannot cover DeBoer's child on her health insurance, and vice-versa. And if one of them were to die, the other would not automatically get custody of her children. So, the two women want to get married, but they cannot, because Michigan laws specifically prohibit this. (2) Ohio case of *Obergefell v. Kasich*: In 2013, James Obergefell married John Arthur, his partner of more than twenty years, on a tarmac at an airport in Maryland, which permits same-sex marriage, where they had flown in a medically equipped plane because Arthur was battling ALS. After Arthur died a few months later, Obergefell filed a lawsuit, seeking to be recognized as Arthur's spouse by the state of Ohio, where the pair lived and he still lives, so that, for example, his name will appear on Arthur's death certificate as his spouse.)

[90] Supreme Court of the United States, *James Obergefell, et al., Petitioners v. Richard Hodges, Director, Ohio Department of Health, et al.* 576 U.S. decided on June 26, 2015, 6–10.

social order. The development of cases from non-criminalization to same-sex marriage in the US Supreme Court confirms that the protections of history or traditions cannot be claimed against the rights of sexual minorities.

7.4 Conclusion

Despite the provisions of the National Human Rights Commission Act[91] prohibiting discrimination based on sexual orientation in South Korea, prejudice against homosexuals can be considered to be worse in the closed context of the military society due to the special security situations in which North Korea and South Korean confront each other. This chapter shows that the Korean Military Criminal Law, which criminalizes homosexual activities, violates fundamental principles and rights of the Korean Constitution because its legislative objective and protected interests are vague. Furthermore, Article 92 KMCL should be abolished because this criminalization violates the principle of legality, the principle of proportionality, and the principle of non-discrimination.

The most problematic part of this criminalization concerns same-sex relations between consenting adults. Even if it is difficult to fully abolish this article immediately sexual relations between consenting adults must at least be decriminalized. If necessary, those acts should not be dealt with using military compliance measures and not with criminal punishment. To avoid ambiguous stipulations, specific cases should be more concretely stated. Firstly, sexual assaults where coercion is used can be punished under the military penal code. Secondly, sexual assaults by misused power which would not be considered as coercion should be punished as a provision separate from the military penal code. Lastly, other assaults by minor coercion which is not regarded as misused power could be dealt with using disciplinary measures. The current problem with the punishment under Korean Military Law lies with the ambiguity in such stipulation where no specific classifications depend on the existence of types of coercion. Ultimately, criminal penalties for consenting homosexual

[91] Article 2 (Definitions), paragraph 3 of the National Human Rights Commission of Korea (amended by Act No. 14027, February 3, 2016) stipulates as follows: The term “discriminatory act violating the equal right” means any of the following acts, without reasonable grounds, on the grounds of sex, religion, disability, age, social status, region of origin (referring to a place of birth, place of registration, principal area of residence before coming of age, etc.), state of origin, ethnic origin, physical condition such as features, marital status such as single, separated, divorced, widowed, remarried, married de facto, or pregnancy or childbirth, types or forms of family, race, skin color, ideology or political opinion, record of crime whose effect of punishment has been extinguished, ***sexual orientation***, academic career, medical history, etc.: Provided, That the temporary favorable treatment to a particular person (including a group of particular persons; hereafter the same shall apply in this Article) to solve the existing discrimination, the enactment and amendment of statutes and the formulation and enforcement of policy to this effect shall not be deemed a discriminatory act violating the equal right (hereinafter referred to as “discriminatory act”).

acts must be abolished as a minimum protection against discrimination based on sexual orientation in South Korea. To overcome the prejudice and various types of discrimination against sexual minorities in the context of the military, some institutional measures must be provided to help sexual minorities overcome such harm caused by discriminatory experiences.

Non-criminalization of homosexual relations is considered as the initial step towards the prohibition of discrimination based on sexual orientation. There is a certain trend towards non-criminalization of homosexual relations in many jurisdictions, which is also in line with the position of the Human Rights Committee.[92] Nevertheless, the article under the Korean Military Criminal Law still exists to punish homosexual relations between consenting adult soldiers in South Korea. Moreover, the Constitutional Court of Korea has not yet decided that this article is unconstitutional. The experiences from other countries such as Europe, India, and America on similar matters will provide a considerable positive incentive for Korea to take the positive step forward of abolishing it. Sexual minorities suffer[93] tremendously from the existence of such laws to criminalize same-sex sexual acts.

References

Barak A (2012) Proportionality: constitutional rights and their limitations (trans: Kalir D). Cambridge University Press, Cambridge

Chandra A (2018) Courting the people: public interest litigation in post-emergency India. Int J Const Law 16(2):710–718. https://doi.org/10.1093/icon/moy045. Accessed November 30, 2021.

Dipika J et al. (2019) The report of Jindal Global Law School on recent legal reforms on gender recognition: a global review, the Centre for Health Law, Ethics and Technology (CHLET) at

[92] In the case of *Toonen v. Australia*, which was submitted by individual complaint communication according to the Optional Protocol to the ICCPR, the Human Rights Committee noted that "the criminalization of homosexual practices cannot be considered as a reasonable means or proportionate measure to achieve the aim of preventing the spread of AIDS/HIV." In this case, the Committee seems to apply suitability test because the means used is not appropriate to pursue the aim mentioned. Furthermore, the Committee has stated that "statutes criminalizing homosexual activity tend to impede public health programs by driving underground many of the people at the risk of infection," rather than protecting public health (taken from Toonen v. Australia, Communication No. 488/1992, U.N. Doc CCPR/C/50/D/488/1992 (1994). University of Minnesota Human Rights Library http://hrlibrary.umn.edu/undocs/html/vws488.htm. Accessed November 30, 2021).

[93] The Korean transgender soldier *Hui-Soo Byun*, who I have introduced in Chap. 3 committed suicide on March 3, 2021. Since I have introduced her story in my work and supported her legal actions against forcible dismissal from Korean military because of her transsexuality, I feel very sad. I hope that the Constitutional Court of Korea will abolish the criminalization of same-sex sexual acts under the Korean military law because the law violates the principle of proportionality and the principle of equality. It is the beginning step towards lessening suffering of sexual minorities in South Korea. I send my sincere condolences to Ms. Byun (related article from http://www.hani.co.kr/arti/society/society_general/985309.html. Accessed November 30, 2021).

Jindal Global University. https://jgu.edu.in/cjls/centre-reports/recent-legal-reforms-on-gender-recognition-a-global-review/. Accessed November 30, 2021.
Edel F (2015) Case law of the European Court of Human Rights relating to discrimination on grounds of sexual orientation or gender identity. Council of Europe
Fredman S (2011) Discrimination law, 2nd edn. Oxford University Press, Oxford
Han E, O'Mahoney J (2014) British colonialism and the criminalization of homosexuality. Camb Rev Int Aff 27(2):268–288. https://doi.org/10.1080/09557571.2013.867298
Human Rights Watch (2008) This Alien Legacy: the origins of "Sodomy" laws in British Colonialism, 17 December 2008, available at: https://www.hrw.org/report/2008/12/17/alien-legacy/origins-sodomy-laws-british-colonialism. Accessed November 30, 2021.
International Commission of Jurists (2017) "Unnatural Offences" obstacles to justice in India based on sexual orientation and gender identity, available at: https://www.refworld.org/pdfid/58d4fc074.pdf. Accessed November 30, 2021.
Johnson P (2016) Going to Strasbourg: an oral history of sexual orientation discrimination and the European Convention on Human Rights. Oxford University Press, Oxford
Kim M-S (2011) A study on legal discrimination of sexual minorities – Constitutional Court precedents on the Article 92 of the Military Criminal Law. World Const Study 18(1): 59–89, UCI: G704-001436.2012.18.1.002
Kirk J (1997) Constitutional guarantees, characterisation and the concept of proportionality. Melb Univ Law Rev 21:1–64
Lee G-H (2008) Regarding the punishment of homosexual acts in Korean military. Public Interest Hum Rights 5(1):65–99. https://snuhumanrights.tistory.com/107. Accessed November 30, 2021.
Lee H-J (2013) Korean Military Criminal Law Art 92(6) must be abolished, Discussion in National Assembly of Korea
Lokaneeta J (2017) Debating the Indian Supreme Court: equality, liberty, and the rule of law. Law Cult Humanit 13(3):353–368. https://doi.org/10.1177/1743872115596158
Marcus NC (2014) Deeply rooted principles of equal, liberty, not "Argle Bargle": the inevitability of marriage equality after Windsor. Tul J Law Sex 23(17):25–29
Maues AM et al (2021) Judicial dialogue between National courts and the Inter-American Court of Human Rights: a comparative study of Argentina, Brazil, Colombia and Mexico. Hum Rights Law Rev:1–24. https://doi.org/10.1093/hrlr/ngaa047. Accessed November 30, 2021.
McGoldrick D (2019) Challenging the constitutionality of restrictions on same-sex sexual relations: lessons from India. Hum Rights Law Rev 19(1):173–185. https://doi.org/10.1093/hrlr/ngy041. Accessed November 30, 2021.
Mendos LR (2019) State-sponsored homophobia, 13th edition, the International Lesbian, Gay, Bisexual, Trans and Intersex Association (ILGA World), ilga. Org
Narrian A (2010) A new language of morality: from the trial of Nowshirwan to the Judgment in Naz Foundation: 84–104. http://www.commonlii.org/in/journals/INJlConLaw/2010/5.html. Accessed November 30, 2021.
Noh K-H (2009) A study on the unconstitutionality of "Sexual molestation" in the Military Criminal Law Art. 92. Const Law Study 15(2):263–300
Park C-G (2011) The problem of assault under the Korean Military Criminal Law. Han Yang Law J 22(3):73–104
Raghavan V (2013) Taking sexuality seriously: The Supreme Court and the Koushal Case – Part 1, LAW & OTHER THINGS (Dec. 14, 2013, 8:48 AM). https://lawandotherthings.blogspot.ca/2013/12/taking-sexuality-seriously-supreme.html, http://perma.cc/Y3VD-7LQ6. Accessed November 30, 2021.
Schauer F (2014) In: Huscroft G et al. (eds) Proportionality and the question of weight. Cambridge University Press, Cambridge
Thomas S (2019) 14% of those arrested under section 377 last year were minors. The Times of India, 29 September 2019. https://timesofindia.indiatimes.com/city/mumbai/14-of-those-arrested-under-section-377-last-year-were-minors/articleshow/54573741.cms. Accessed November 30, 2021.

Chapter 8
Case Analysis: Same-Sex Marriage

8.1 The Proportionality in the Same-Sex Marriage Cases of the ECtHR

Legal recognition of same-sex marriage is not sufficiently protected in the European system compared to non-criminalization of same-sex relations that was discussed in the previous chapter.[1] I will argue that the ECtHR should adopt the fully structured proportionality test to provide sufficient protection for sexual minorities including legalizing same-sex marriage in the European context. Such a structured test should include the necessity test, which is also known as Less Restrictive Means test as well as the balancing test to enhance clarity and predictability. It will definitely help the ECtHR to solve some outstanding issues regarding discrimination based on sexual orientation.

There are a number of criticisms about the proportionality arguing that it cannot enhance the clarity and foreseeability because an application by the courts of the principle of proportionality cannot provide objectively justifiable conclusions used particularly for balancing competing interests.[2] However, the fully structured proportionality test can provide an objectively justifiable answer at least in some cases such as same-sex marriage by analyzing the degree of interference, the importance of satisfying a competing principle, and an examination of the justification[3] through each of the four steps. Furthermore, the case analysis in the ECtHR and the CCK shows that the application of the structured proportionality enhances the possibility

[1] Mendos (2019).

[2] Young (2014), pp. 52–53.

[3] *R. Alexy* responds to the objection related to balancing which argues irrational and subjective with two main theses: first, balancing is based on a rational form of argument that can be made explicit by means of a "Weight Formula" and second, a constitutional review complies with the requirement of democratic legitimation to the extent that it succeeds in becoming an argumentative representation of the people in supplying this formula with arguments (taken from Alexy 2005, pp. 572–581).

H. J. Lee, *Discrimination Based on Sexual Orientation*, Interdisciplinary Studies in Human Rights 8, https://doi.org/10.1007/978-3-030-95423-9_8

of finding more violations compared to the vague expressions of "necessary in a democratic society"[4] of the ECtHR and "when necessary"[5] of the CCK.

Another criticism against the structured proportionality test is particularly related to the balancing test because it provides the judge with too wide a discretion.[6] Further criticisms claim that proportionality should not be applied as a means of restricting the democratically justifiable conclusions of the legislature.[7] My answer to this criticism is "no" for the following reasons. The institution of democracy exists for the citizens, and the protection of their human rights needs balances between the formal institution and the fundamental grounds. If we focus too much only on formal principles of democracy such as separation of powers or orderly processes, we may disregard the fundamental reason why democracy and human rights should be respected. It is also in line with *Krajewski's*[8] emphasis on a proper balance between the protection of individual human rights and the functional necessity.

As *Sieckmann*[9] proposes in his article, the principle of proportionality is not confined to negative, civil and political rights, or some specific jurisdiction. Since the principle of proportionality has universal characters, it is universally valid. In this regard, *Clérico*[10] also argues that it is important to apply the structured test of proportionality including suitability and necessity. Similarly, if the ECtHR adopts the fully structured proportionality test in the cases dealing with discrimination based on sexual orientation, it could enhance the clarity and foreseeability in the use of methodological tools.

8.1.1 Positive State Obligations in the Same-Sex Marriage Cases of the ECtHR

In the past, negative state obligation seems to have been enough and these negative rights seemed to be protected as long as states did not interfere. However, positive state obligation has become more important especially in the area of discrimination

[4]For example, in Article 8 ECHR, paragraph 2 states the elements of limitations of "necessary in a democratic society in the interests of national security, public safety or the economic well-being of the country," which the ECtHR applies in its decisions (i.e., European Court of Human Rights, *Oliari and others v. Italy*, judgment of 21 July 2015, paragraph para. 113).

[5]Article 37, paragraph 2 of the Korean Constitution states the expression of "when necessary" as "the freedoms and rights of citizens may be restricted by Act only when necessary for national security, the maintenance of law and order or for public welfare," which is applied by the Constitutional Court of Korea in deciding the constitutionality of Article 92 (5) Korean Military Criminal Law to criminalize same-sex sexual acts of soldiers.

[6]Barak (2012), p. 487.

[7]Young (2014), p. 53.

[8]Krajewski and Singer (2012), p. 34.

[9]Sieckmann (2018), pp. 3–24.

[10]Clérico (2018), pp. 25–48.

based on sexual orientation because the state must provide legal institutions instead of doing nothing. This section aims to show how the concept of positive state obligation as well as the principle of proportionality is applied particularly in the case law of same-sex marriage in the ECtHR. Using the examples of those cases, I want to show that the principle of proportionality can work effectively in matters where state positive obligation is emphasized. Same-sex marriage cases are mostly involved with state positive obligations.

First, the case of *Oliari* will be compared to *Hämäläinen*,[11] because positive state obligation was dealt with importantly in the *Oliari* case when the ECtHR found a violation. Unlike *Oliari*, the main argument was not about positive state obligation in *Hämäläinen*. Comparing these two cases is significant to determine the different position by the ECtHR in dealing with the concept of positive state obligation by analyzing these two cases. In the *Oliari* case, the ECtHR held that "the object of Article 8 is 'essentially' that of protecting the individual against arbitrary interference by the public authorities."[12] Nonetheless, according to the ECtHR, it does not only compel the state to abstain from such interference. In addition to these primarily negative obligations, there may be positive obligations inherent in an effective "respect" for family life. The essential object of Article 8 ECHR is to protect individuals against arbitrary interference by public authorities. At the same time, it may also impose certain positive obligations on a state to ensure effective respect for the rights protected by Article 8. Such positive obligations may involve the adoption of measures designed to secure respect for private or family life in the sphere of the relations of individuals between themselves.[13] These measures include the provision of legal recognition such as same-sex marriage.

As of July 2015, when the ECtHR issued the judgment, the applicants in the *Oliari* case still had no opportunity to enter into a civil union or registered partnership while marriage was not allowed in Italy.[14] It was thus for the ECtHR to determine whether Italy, at the date of the ECtHR's analysis, failed to comply with a positive obligation to ensure respect for the applicants' private and family life in 2015. To do that, the ECtHR imposed a positive obligation on the contracting state by providing a legal framework allowing applicants to have their relationship

[11] European Court of Human Rights, ***HÄMÄLÄINEN v. FINLAND*** (Application no. 37359/09), Grand Chamber judgment of 16 July 2014. (The applicant was born in 1963 and lives in Helsinki as a male, but she always felt that she was a female in a male body. In 1996, she married a woman and in 2002 they had a child. In April 2006, she was diagnosed as a transsexual, and she lived as a woman ever since then. On September 29, 2009, she underwent gender reassignment surgery, and she changed her first names and renewed her passport and driver's license. However, she could not have her identity number changed from male to female unless she divorced, which she did not want to do because of her religious conviction. The Court held that there had been no violation of Article 8, Article 14 conjunction with Article 8, and Article 12 of the Convention.)

[12] European Court of Human Rights, *Oliari and others v. Italy*, judgment of 21 July 2015, paragraph 159.

[13] Ibid., paragraph 159.

[14] Ibid., paragraph 164.

recognized and protected under Italian domestic law. The concurring opinions in *Oliari*,[15] on the other hand, find no need to assert that Article 8 imposes a positive obligation on Italy to provide a specific legal framework for the recognition and protection of same-sex unions. Instead, the concurring opinions assert that it is not necessary to invoke the pre-existence of a positive obligation, because the ECtHR can find a violation of a negative obligation by the state's intervention into the applicants' personal relations. The concurring opinions do not agree with the majority opinions because violation should be analyzed in terms of "defective state intervention," not as a failure of complying with a positive obligation. In my opinion, the matter in this case involves a positive obligation as the majority opinions argue because the state should provide a specific legal framework.

The court assessment of the alleged violation of Article 8 of the Convention in the case of *Hämäläinen* discusses whether the case involves a positive obligation or an interference with a negative obligation. The applicant wanted to have her new gender legally recognized whilst at the same time remaining married, which was not allowed under the domestic law of Finland. There were two judgments in the case of *Hämäläinen*—Chamber and Grand Chamber.[16] The Chamber examined this case as an interference with the applicant's right to respect for her private life in that she was not granted a new female identity number. However, the grand Chamber considers that the main question is whether respect for the applicant's private and family life entails a positive obligation. Thus, the state must provide an effective and accessible procedure allowing the applicant to have a new gender identity recognized whilst at the same time staying married according to her religious convictions. Therefore, the Grand Camber considers it more appropriate to analyze the applicant's complaint from the positive obligation aspect.[17] While the applicants do not have any way to legally recognize their same-sex relationships in Italy in the *Oliari* case, changing the identity number is allowed under the Transsexuals law in Finland, but with some exceptional conditions such as "not married." Despite the difference, the alleged violations in *Hämäläinen* can be interpreted as a violation of a positive obligation, as Grand Chamber argues because a specific legal framework needed to be provided to make both changing the identity number and staying married possible.

In the case of *Schalk and Kopf*,[18] the ECtHR would no longer consider that the right to marry must be limited to marriage between two persons of the opposite sex,

[15] Ibid., Concurring Opinion.

[16] On November 13, 2012, the Chamber decided unanimously to declare the complaints concerning Articles 8, 12, and 14 of the Convention admissible and held that there had been no violation of Article 8 of the Convention, no violation of Article 14 taken in conjunction with Article 8 of the Convention. On February 13, 2013, the applicant requested the case to be referred to the Grand Chamber which accepted the request on April 29, 2013. (European Court of Human Rights, *Hämäläinen v. Finland*, judgment of 16 July 2014, paragraphs 4–5.)

[17] European Court of Human Rights, *Hämäläinen v. Finland*, judgment of 16 July 2014, paragraphs 4–5.

[18] European Court of Human Rights, *Schalk and Kopf v. Austria*, judgment of 24 June 2010.

stating that it cannot be said that Article 12 (Right to marry) is inapplicable to the applicants' complaint. The question of whether to allow same-sex marriage is left to the regulations by the national law of the Contracting State. On the grounds that marriage has deep-rooted social and cultural connotations, the ECtHR considered that national authorities are best placed to assess and respond to the needs of society. Furthermore, Article 12 ECHR does not impose a positive obligation on states to grant applicants access to marriage. Hence, the ECtHR concluded that there is no violation of Article 12 in this case.[19] Even if the ECtHR has not interpreted Article 12 as imposing an obligation on the Contracting States to open marriage to same-sex couples yet,[20] it is expected to change over time since the right to same-sex marriage is evolving. The ECtHR should interpret Article 12 as requiring that all the legal effects attaching to marriage should apply equally to situations that are comparable to marriage. Furthermore, Article 12 should be interpreted to impose a positive duty on a state in the forthcoming decisions.

The case of *Vallianatos and Others v. Greece*[21] delimits the scope not to comply with any positive obligations when assessing compliance with Article 14 (Prohibition of discrimination) taken in conjunction with Article 8 (Right to respect for private and family life). The ECtHR did not elaborate whether Law No. 3719/2008 which allowed "civil union" only to different sex couples does not relate to the state's positive obligation. Instead, it only delimited the scope of the case by stating that the applicants' complaint is not about positive obligation. However, in the reasoning of the ECtHR, it is obvious that there was no legal recognition provided for same-sex relationships. The ECtHR observes that different-sex couples, unlike same-sex couples, could already have their relationship legally recognized even before the enactment of the Law in question.[22] As the Law No. 3719/2008 was primarily aimed at affording legal recognition as a new form of alternative to marriage, it is obvious

[19] Ibid., paragraph 61–64.

[20] In Chapin and Charpentier v. France (2016), the ECtHR reiterated that neither Article 12, nor Article 14 in conjunction with Article 8, which was more general in purpose and scope, could be interpreted as imposing an obligation on the Contracting States to open marriage to same-sex couples (taken from European Court of Human Rights, Guide on Article 12 of the European Convention on Human Rights – Right to marry, First edition – 31 December 2020, p. 10).

[21] European Court of Human Rights, ***CASE OF VALLIANATOS AND OTHERS v. GREECE*** (Applications nos. 29381/09 and 32684/09), Grand Chamber judgment of 7 November 2013. (The applicants live together as a couple in same-sex relationships in Athens. The first and second, third, and fourth applicants have lived together for a long time as couples in Athens. The fifth and sixth applicants are in relationship but do not live together. The sixth applicant pays the fifth applicant's social security contributions. The seventh applicant is a not-for-profit association to support gays and lesbians. On November 26, 2008, Law No. 3719/2008 "Reforms concerning the family, children and society" came into force. Under the section 1 of the Law, "civil unions" can be entered into only by two adults of "different sex." Applicants complained that the fact the civil unions were designed only for couples composed of different-sex adults infringed their right to respect for their private and family life and amounted to unjustified discrimination between different-sex and same-sex couples.)

[22] European Court of Human Rights, *Vallianatos and Others v. Greece*, judgment of 7 November 2013, paragraph 90.

that same-sex couples did not have any forms of legal recognition to their relationship in the situation where the marriage is not allowed. Therefore, the ECtHR should have dealt with a positive obligation to be imposed on the contracting state of Greece by the Convention in the *Vallianatos* case, as the state's obligation is to provide for a form of legal recognition in domestic law for same-sex couples.

The ECtHR held unanimously that there had been a violation of Article 14 (Prohibition of discrimination) taken in conjunction with Article 8 (Right to respect for private and family life) of the Convention in the case of *Pajić v. Croatia*.[23] In its judgment, the ECtHR does not clearly state whether the case concerns positive or negative obligations of the state. Nevertheless, the issue in the *Pajić* case can be interpreted to concern positive obligations of Croatia, as the majority opinions in the *Hämäläinen* case also do. A specific legal framework should be provided to allow the identity numbers to be changed as well as remaining married. Likewise, in *Pajić v. Croatia,* a temporary resident permit was provided for the purpose of family reunification to foreigners under the Aliens Act and Family Act. Nevertheless, the applicant was rejected because the family act defines an extramarital relationship as a union between an unmarried woman and man.[24] Therefore, a specific legal framework needed to apply to the applicant as a same-sex partner in order to issue a temporary resident permit.

In this section, same-sex marriage cases of the ECtHR have been discussed to involve positive obligations of the state. Some of these cases will be restructured to the steps of the proportionality in the next section. Using this restructuring, I argue that the same-sex marriage cases of the ECtHR involving positive obligations can be restructured to the proportionality test.

8.1.2 *The Principle of Proportionality in Same-Sex Marriage Cases*

The structured proportionality test is not applied to the same-sex marriage case law of the ECtHR. However, my thesis is that the principle of proportionality can

---

[23]European Court of Human Rights, ***CASE OF Pajić v. Croatia*** (Applications no. 68453/13), judgment of 23 February 2016. (The applicant was born in 1973 and lives in Bosnia and Herzegovina. On December 29, 2011, the applicant lodged a request for a residence permit in Croatia on the grounds of family reunification with her partner, Ms. D.B., who was living in Sisak, Croatia. In her request, she explained that she wanted to live with D.B. with whom she had been in a relationship for two years. On February 24, 2012, the Sisak Police Department dismissed the applicant's request, because the Aliens Act did not allow family reunification for same-sex couples, unlike different sex couples. She complained she had been discriminated against based on her sexual orientation to the Court on October 23, 2013. The Court unanimously holds that there has been a violation of Article 14 taken in conjunction with Article 8 of the Convention.)

[24]European Court of Human Rights, *Pajić v. Croatia*, judgment of 23 February 2016, paragraphs 19–21.

function as a very effective methodological tool in the same-sex marriage cases of the ECtHR. Even if the ECtHR does not explicitly apply the structured proportionality test, its reasoning can be reanalyzed according to the steps used when defining proportionality. In this sense, this section will show how the ECtHR could enhance clarity by applying the structured proportionality test particularly using examples of same-sex marriage cases of the ECtHR.

Rights stipulated in the European Convention of Human Rights[25] ("ECHR") are mostly not absolute except some rights such as the prohibition of torture (Article 3), the prohibition of slavery and forced labor (Article 4), no punishment without law (Article 7) and the "internal" dimension of freedom of religion (Article 9(1)).[26] Interference in these rights is therefore possible in principle, although any such interferences would only be acceptable as long as there was a proportionate relationship between the aims pursued by the interference and the rights of the Convention at stake. Articles 8 to 11 of the ECHR state that limitations are justifiable if they are "necessary in a democratic society." What does the ECtHR mean by this phrase? It seems that the expression is relatively nontransparent in terms of its terminology and tends to mix distinct elements of judicial review.[27]

The ECtHR interprets the phrase as assessing "whether the interference complained of corresponded to a pressing social need, whether it was proportionate to the legitimate aim pursued and whether reasons are relevant and sufficient."[28] Classic elements of the proportionality review of suitability, necessity, and balancing may be read into the formula of a pressing social need in the ECtHR, but the ECtHR has never explicitly mentioned it. Furthermore, the requirement of relevant and sufficient reasons is often not fully apparent in the court reasoning so that its concrete meaning remains opaque, which is problematic in this context because of the resulting lack of clarity as to the test and standards applied by the ECtHR in its case law.[29]

Regarding the first element of *legitimate aim*, the ECtHR requires legitimacy, in addition to legality, in order to justify the limitation on the Convention rights to be valid as the proper purpose component of the proportionality analysis. In the case of *Vallianatos*,[30] the ECtHR considers the aim of Law No. 3719/2008[31] to introduce civil unions as a form of civil partnership only to different sex couples as *legitimate.*

---

[25] It is also referred to as "European Convention" or the "Convention for the Protection of Human Rights and Fundamental Freedoms (1950)." In this work, European Convention of Human Rights ("ECHR") refers to this Convention.

[26] Brems and Lavrysen (2015), p. 140.

[27] Gerards (2008).

[28] European Court of Human Rights, *Sunday Times v. U.K.*, judgment of 26 April 1979, paragraph 62.

[29] Gerards (2013), pp. 467–468.

[30] European Court of Human Rights, *Vallianatos and Others v. Greece*, judgment of 7 November 2013.

[31] Section 1. Conclusion of a civil union in Law No. 3719/2008 states that "*A contract between two different-sex adults* governing their life as a couple ("civil union") shall be entered into by means of

The contracting state of Greece argues that the law in question is designed to strengthen the legal status of children born outside marriage and to make it easier for parents to raise their children without being obliged to marry. Therefore, civil unions could only be allowed for couples of opposite sexes, because same-sex couples cannot have biological children together. The ECtHR acknowledges its legitimacy from the standpoint of Article 8, stating that regulating the situation of children born outside of wedlock as well as indirectly strengthening the institution of marriage[32] would be accepted as a notion to protect the family in the traditional sense.[33]

The second element is *suitability*. In the case of *Schalk and Kopf*,[34] the ECtHR takes note that same-sex couples are just as capable as different sex couples of entering into stable, committed relationships. In the assessment as to whether a difference in treatment of persons in relevantly similar situations under Article 14 (Prohibition of discrimination) of the ECHR, the ECtHR had to assess whether the registered partnership ("M1") compared to marriage ("M2") would be appropriate to accomplish the aim of protecting the legal recognition of same-sex couples. Registered partnerships have been available since January 1, 2010, in Austria when the Registered Partnership Act came into force. To find out whether M1 is suitable, it is necessary to compare M1 and M2.[35] The ECtHR found that M1 is also a suitable measure to attain the aim of protecting the legal recognition of same-sex couples[36] just as M2 is. The reason is that there are only slight differences between M1 and M2 regarding material consequences.

The third element is the test of *necessity*. The ECtHR has not yet explicitly endorsed the less restrictive means test in the cases of same-sex marriage. Nevertheless, the reasoning of the case of *Vallianatos and Others v. Greece*[37] in finding a

---

a notarized instrument in the presence of the parties" (taken from European Court of Human Rights, *Vallianatos and Others v. Greece*, judgment of 7 November 2013, paragraph 16).

[32] The ECtHR accepted the government's argument of strengthening the institution of marriage, in that the Law No. 3719/2008 would promote the notion that the decision of marriage would be taken purely based on two individuals' mutual agreement, independently of outside constraints such as having children. Therefore, the law will play a role as making the institution of marriage stronger. (European Court of Human Rights, *Vallianatos and Others v. Greece*, judgment of 7 November 2013, paragraph 83.)

[33] Ibid., paragraph 82–83.

[34] European Court of Human Rights, *Schalk and Kopf v. Austria*, judgment of 24 June 2010.

[35] European Court of Human Rights, *Schalk and Kopf v. Austria*, judgment of 24 June 2010, paragraph 109.

[36] Ibid., paragraphs 109–110 (In addition, the ECtHR adapted the consensus argument as it states that the case deals with evolving rights and there is no established consensus yet. Due to the lack of consensus, the ECtHR considers a margin of appreciation to be wide where Austria could decide when it adopts legislative changes. Therefore, the majority opinion concluded there is no violation of Article 14 in conjunction with Article 8 even if there were no possibilities for legal recognition of same-sex relations before the Act of registered partnership came into force.).

[37] European Court of Human Rights, *Vallianatos and Others v. Greece*, judgment of 7 November 2013, paragraph 85.

violation of Article 14 the ECHR (Prohibition of discrimination) taken in conjunction with Article 8 (Right to respect for private and family life) can be restructured according to the less restrictive means test. The means at issue in this case was Law No. 3719/2008 as entitled "Reforms concerning the family, children and society," which came into force on November 26, 2008. This law was the first time in Greece that a provision had been made for an official form of partnership other than marriage, known as "civil unions," which only two adults of a different sex can enter into.[38] The main aim which the state argued for was to protect children born outside marriage,[39] which was considered as legitimate.[40] Nevertheless, "excluding same-sex couples" is not regarded as being a less restrictive measure than "including same-sex couples" for the following reasons. Firstly, even if the state claimed that the main aim was to protect children born outside marriage, the ECtHR considered the primary aim of the law was legal recognition of a new form of non-marital partnership.[41] To attain the aim, "including same-sex couples" is considered as less restrictive means than "excluding same-sex couples" because the primary aim is to provide legal recognition to a form of partnership other than marriage and protecting couples in a stable relationship. Secondly, even if the aim of protecting children born outside marriage is considered as the state claimed, including "some provisions dealing specifically with children born outside marriage"[42] at the same time "including same-sex couples" can be less restrictive as well as equally effective means attaining the state-claimed aim.

As *Laura Clérico* argues in her recent work on "Proportionality in Social Rights Adjudication,"[43] it is important to apply the structured test of proportionality including the sub-steps of suitability, necessity and balancing. *Clérico* suggests qualitative, quantitative and probabilistic assessments in the applicability of the alternative means test to find better alternative means. For example, to apply her assessments in the *Vallianatos* case, it is easy to find a better alternative means (including same-sex couples) than the measure in question (excluding same-sex couples). As to the qualitative aspect, alternative means will benefit same-sex couples in need of alternative legal recognition, whilst at the same time not creating additional burdens for the state; therefore, alternative means will provide better quality as a measure of non-discrimination or with no potential discrimination. In the quantitative analysis, alternative means will benefit more couples in need because it covers hetero-sexual couples as well as same-sex couples. Lastly, as a probabilistic perspective, the alternative means will adapt to the future trend of non-discrimination between same-sex couples and hetero-sexual couples. The

[38] Ibid., paragraph 9.

[39] Ibid., paragraph 80.

[40] Ibid., paragraph 83.

[41] European Court of Human Rights, *Vallianatos and Others v. Greece*, judgment of 7 November 2013, paragraph 87.

[42] Ibid., paragraph 89.

[43] Clérico (2017).

necessity test will allow the ECtHR to examine the justification of the reasonableness in the choice of means.

The last element analysis is *Proportionality in a narrow sense.* The ECtHR fails to balance between the two human rights—the right to recognition of one's gender identity and the right to maintain one's civil status in *Hämäläinen.*[44] The ECtHR regards civil partnership as an adequate option to the applicant, because a civil partnership carries almost all the same legal rights and obligations as marriage even if the two are not identical.[45] Such an assumption clearly fails to point out what the applicant really wants to choose. The applicant could not choose only one between maintaining her marriage and obtaining a female identity number because only both at the same time are important to her. Therefore, a civil partnership could not be an adequate alternative to the applicant. On the one hand, gender identity is particularly important to an individual. At the same time, the other side of civil status is also very important especially considering that the applicant and her spouse are deeply religious and expect their marriage to last for life. The balancing test done by the ECtHR was problematic because it assumed a wrong degree of interference. The interference of the applicant's right to respect for her private life was more intense than the ECtHR has assumed. The ECtHR did not seem to consider the degree of interference to be severe because there are alternative options of getting a divorce or transforming a marriage into a civil partnership. Nevertheless, these alternative options were not regarded as actual alternatives for the applicant because they only allowed the applicant the right to maintain the marriage or obtain a female identity.

As the case examples show, the issues in the cases related to recognition of same-sex relations particularly same-sex marriage in the ECtHR are considered to be associated with the positive obligations of the state. Furthermore, the reasoning of

---

[44]European Court of Human Rights, ***HÄMÄLÄINEN v. FINLAND*** (Application no. 37359/09), judgment of 16 July 2014: The applicant was born a male and married a woman, and the couple had a child in 2002. In 2009 the applicant underwent gender re-assignment surgery from male to female. Nevertheless, she could not have her identity number changed to a female one after she changed her first names. To change the identity number, her wife consented to the transformation of their marriage into a civil partnership or the couple had to divorce. The couple wanted to remain married because of their religious convictions and considered that a civil partnership did not provide the same protection as marriage for their family. Chamber judgment applied the law of balancing between the two competing rights. On one hand, the applicant's right to respect for her private life is interfered with because she could not obtain a new identity number as a woman. On the other hand, the State's interest is to maintain the traditional institution of marriage between different sexes only. Chamber and grand chamber judgment consider that there has been no violation of Article 8 because the applicant has options of receiving the consent from the spouse to obtain a registered partnership or divorcing (para. 38, 40, 88, 89). Chamber and Grand chamber found it unnecessary to examine the case separately under Article 12 (Right to marry) (para. 92, 97). Furthermore, Article 14 taken in conjunction with Article 8 does not impose states to grant same-sex couples a right (what is the sense of the previous words, especially "impose"? "does not allow States to grant same-sex couples a right" would make sense, I think, is this what it meant? to remain married, there has been no violation of Article 14 in conjunction with Article 8 (para. 102, 113).

[45]European Court of Human Rights, *Hämäläinen v. Finland*, judgment of 16 July 2014, dissenting opinion paragraph 5.

these cases can be restructured according to the steps of the proportionality. This shows that the structured proportionality can function as a positive methodological tool in finding a violation in the cases of positive obligations.

8.2 Discussions of Same-Sex Marriage in Korea

Same-sex marriage is not yet legally recognized in South Korea. However, there is no specific stipulation to prohibit same-sex marriage in South Korean laws. Unlike other parts of the world such as Europe or the United States of America, the discussion started relatively recently in the late 1990s. Society at large has only been interested in it since the early 2000s. Due to the Supreme Court[46] decision in 2011, the topic of same-sex marriage attracted discussions as to whether the identity number must be allowed when a different gender from that at birth was already recognized. Nevertheless, discussions have developed slowly because sexual minorities in South Korea are considered as one of the most vulnerable groups. For example, in the United States, there are considerable numbers of same-sex couples who could affect the election results, whereas there are few same-sex couples in South Korea and thus politicians do not really have any interests in protecting their rights.

8.2.1 General Discussion of Same-Sex Marriage

The Constitution of the Republic of Korea has no provision to define the legal concept of marriage. Generally, Article 36, Paragraph 1[47] of the Constitution is accepted in the Korean Constitution as a basis for rejecting same-sex marriage. The provisions of "equality of both sexes" is an expression of the legislature's will to

[46] Supreme Court of Korea, 2009 Su-I 117, Grand Chamber Decision of September 2, 2011: Just like *Hämäläinen* in the HÄMÄLÄINEN v. FINLAND (Application no. 37359/09, 2014) case, the applicant was born male, married a woman, had a child. Nevertheless, the applicant always felt that she was a female in a male body. The applicant divorced, underwent gender reassignment surgery, and lived as a woman. The applicant applied for the change of legal gender from male to female, which was rejected by the Supreme Court decision on the ground that she has a child from the previous marriage. The applicant is in even worse situation than Hämäläinen because she could not change her legal gender even if she had already divorced, which was the condition for Hämäläinen to change her identity number.

[47] Article 36, paragraph 1 of the Korean Constitution reads as follows:

> Marriage and family life shall be entered into and sustained on the basis of individual dignity and equality of the both sexes, and the State shall do everything in its power to achieve that goal.: Some scholars in Korea interpret the expression of "equality of both sexes" mean the marriage is only possible between both sexes of men and women and this is the reason why same-sex marriage is not permitted in Korea.

regard marriage only as the union between men and women. Such an interpretation is nothing less than a paradoxical situation in which the provisions of gender equality serve as grounds for rejecting same-sex marriages. This situation has created a need to interpret the will of the legislators. Otherwise, the question arises as to whether the basis can only be provided for recognizing same-sex marriage if the constitution is amended.

As stated briefly above, the Korean Constitution does not explicitly define the legal concept of marriage. Of course, this can be regarded as an omission because of the natural premise of marriage as a bond between men and women. However, it serves instead as a basis for not rejecting same-sex marriage because there is no specific provision in the constitution at all.[48] In the more recent report,[49] seven judges among nine judges in the Constitutional Court of Korea have stated that they recognize homosexuality as an individual's sexual orientation; however, so far, only one judge has publicly expressed his opinion to support same-sex marriages. In the current Korean situation where there is no explicit stipulation to define legal marriage, constitutional interpretations are considered important in the question of same-sex marriage.

Regarding a constitutional interpretation, no specific methodology is prescribed in the Korean Constitution. *Winfried Brugger*[50] cited the following as measures of constitutional interpretation recognized as methods of practice in the United States: (1) Constitutional texts, historical intention, constitutional theory, precedent argumentations for moral, political, and social values, (2) Dogmatic prudence arguments ("Klugheitsargumente" in German), analysis of constitutional texts such as objective arguments, history, and structure. According to *Brugger*,[51] literary or textual interpretation ("die gramatische"), logical interpretation ("die logische"), historical interpretation ("die historische"), systematic interpretation ("die systematische") and teleological interpretation ("die teleologische") are regarded as constitutional interpretative methods in Germany.

One of the most important factors to consider when interpreting a constitutional clause is the intent of those who drafted the Constitution, and another important factor is an obligation to reinterpret articles to fulfill the level of progressively developed human dignity. When the Constitutional provisions are not clearly defined, it is necessary to faithfully interpret and indicate the intentions of the drafters who originally created the provisions. At the same time, instead of sticking solely to the original intention of the drafters of the Constitution, one should also examine whether the constitution corresponds to changed circumstances of the

---

[48] Han (2015).

[49] "7 judges of the Constitutional Court of Korea to recognize homosexuality as a sexual orientation, but why does only one judge support same sex marriage?" Column in Joonang Daily Newspaper, published on April 19, 2019. https://news.joins.com/article/23445289. Accessed November 30, 2021.

[50] Brugger (1994), p. 575.

[51] Park (2003), p. 102.

situation of human rights in modern society. Direct interpretation of articles in the Constitution or sticking only to the drafters' original intentions could result in the changes in circumstances being ignored. As *P. Łącki* argues, the dynamic interpretation is not a matter of setting a completely new standard, but of better understanding the importance of the rights protected.[52] Likewise, the duty of the judge is to face the issues that the article poses reflecting the societal views that are currently dominant.

Article 20 Paragraph 3 of the German Basic Law[53] aims at both the formal as well as substantive elements of constitutionalism by stipulating that judges are bound by law and justice ("Recht und Gesetz" in German). Judges are strictly obliged to protect people's rights even when the law does not explicitly prescribe it. For this reason, the demand for legal positivism ("Gesetzespostivismus")[54] cannot be generally accepted. The law is incomplete because it cannot prescribe every detail in its stipulations. This is why constitutional interpretation is needed. For these reasons, judges are bound by the law. This implies that Constitutional interpretation, should not only be tied to texts, but should consider the intent of the drafters as well as historical contexts of the Constitution. Dynamic and evolutionary interpretations are particularly needed to fill the gap in the stipulations of law and order so that they could adapt to the "attitudes" or "ideas prevailing in democratic States" to "the common axiological standard"[55] as of today.

No constitutional cases on same-sex marriage in the Constitutional Court of Korea have occurred yet. Therefore, the view of Korean courts can be inferred from a decision of the first district court decision about same-sex marriage. In this case, the district court dismissed the claim by the same-sex couple *Kim Cho Gwangsoo* and *Kim Seung-Hwan* who had public wedding celebrations in 2013. They submitted a marriage registration, which was rejected by the *Seoul Seodaemun District Office* in Korea. The *Seoul Seo-Bu District Court* decided in this case as follows:

> The applicants, who were male same-sex couples, tried to register their marriage legally, but the District office refused to allow it. In this case where the applicants filed a complaint against this same-sex marriage ban, the Court clarified its position about the marriage system in Korea. The marriage system has changed in various ways. However, the essence of the marriage system, which is the union of a man and a woman, does not seem to have changed considerably. The general public's perception about this has not changed either. Considering all these circumstances, the Court can interpret "marriage" as stipulated in the Constitution, the Civil Code, and the Act on Registration of Family Relations referring to the "union aimed at living together for a long life based on the affection of men and women as justified

---

[52] Łącki (2021), p. 200.

[53] Article 20, paragraph 3 of Basic Law for the Federal Republic of Germany reads as follows:

> The legislature shall be bound by the constitutional order, the executive and the judiciary *by law and justice*.
>
> (In German: Die Gesetzgebung ist an die verfassungsmäßige Ordung, die vollziehende Gewalt und die Rechtsprechung sind an *Gesetz und Recht* gebunden.).

[54] M. Jachmann, Maunz/Dürig, *Grundgesetz-Kommentar IX*, Article 95 Rn. 13.

[55] Łącki (2021), p. 190.

> morally as well as by custom." Beyond such a common textual interpretation of the current law, it cannot be interpreted as an extension to "union for the purpose of a shared life based on the affection of two people regardless of their genders." For this reason, with the common interpretation of the Court, the applicants' consents cannot be regarded as a legally proper consent to marry; therefore, their marriage registrations cannot be recognized as legal registrations of marriage.[56]

As noted above, The *Seoul Seo-Bu District Court* referred to the provisions of Article 36 (1) of the Constitution of the Republic of Korea as grounds for limiting marriage to the union between men and women. In addition, the District Court also introduced some Supreme Court decision as well as the interpretation by the Constitutional Court of Korea in other related decisions. The Supreme Court's interpretation on marriage is that "marriage is based on the affection of men and women, morally justified integration for the purpose of life time co-habitations."[57] Although there are no specific legal articles to define the marriage in the Korean law system, there are interpretations on this matter by the Supreme Court of Korea as well as the Constitutional Court of Korea. As there is no same-sex marriage case in the Constitutional Court of Korea yet, the interpretations come from other cases.

The *Seoul Seo-Bu District Court* cited the interpretation of marriage from the Supreme Court decision.[58] In this decision, the Supreme Court of Korea decided that "Article 36, Paragraph 1 of the Korean Constitution stipulates that marriages and family lives have to be performed and maintained on the basis of individual dignity as well as the equality of the two sexes, and the state has to guarantee this. In this sense, marriage is established through physical and mental integration between men and women. It is interpreted that the Korean civil law system allows marriage

---

[56] Seoul Seo-Bu District Court, 2014 Ho-Pa 1842 Decision, May 25, 2016 (translated and commented by myself).

[57] Supreme Court of Korea, 82 Mu-I 4 Decision, July 13, 1982. (Actually, this is a divorce case to decide whether divorce can be claimed with some specific circumstances where the relation of married couple becomes problematic due to temporary hazards or obstacles. In this case, the Supreme Court of Korea defines marriage as the union between men and women.); Supreme Court of Korea, 97 Mu-I 612 Decision, February 12, 1999. (This is also the case of divorce and alimony. This case defines marriage as the union based on the affections of men and women, citing Article 826, paragraph 1 of Civil Act of Korea. However, Article 826 (1) does not define marriage as the union of different sexes.)

Article 826 (Duties of Husband and Wife), paragraph 1, Korean Civil Act reads as follows:

> Husband and wife shall live together, and shall support, and aid each other: *Provided*, that both parties must tolerate (this verb needs an object), if they do not live together temporarily for a particular reason.

[58] Supreme Court of Korea, 2009 Su-I 117, September 2, 2011, Grand Chamber Decision. (This case is about whether registration to change gender is allowed or not. The applicant and his wife were legally married and had one child. During their marriage, the applicant had surgery to change the gender from male to female and applied to change the gender in the family registry. In this case, the applicant's claim had been refused. However, in this case, there were dissenting opinions to argue that such a refusal could harm the welfare of the child.)

between different sexes only. Same-sex marriages are not permitted in the Korean civil law system."[59] The Constitutional Court of Korea has interpreted marriage as "physical and mental integration of one male and one female and there is no change with this concept,"[60] or "marriage fundamentally means the union of male and female based on mutual love and trust."[61] Nevertheless, such interpretations of Korean courts are not considered dynamic interpretations, which consider the importance of the rights of sexual minorities and evolving societal views.

8.2.2 Legal Recognition of Same-Sex Marriage in Korea

When looking into some specific law articles, Article 10 of the Korean constitutional law stipulates the right of individuals to pursue happiness. The CCK interprets the scope of protection with this Article 10 to include the general freedom to behave, the freedom to express individuals' personality and characteristics, and the right to sexual self-determination.[62] Since there is no article to stipulate the right to marry specifically, same-sex couples should claim their right to marry based on the interpretation of the CCK. One possibility is to claim Article 10 of the right to pursue individual happiness based on the interpretation by the CCK above. Another possibility is to claim based on Article 17[63] (the privacy of the citizen) since this article can be compatible with Article 8 (Right to respect for private and family life) ECHR. Unlike Article 8 ECHR, the Constitution of Korea does not stipulate private life and family life together as one article. Therefore, Article 36 (1)[64] (Marriage and family life) of the Korean Constitution can also provide a legal basis to claim the right to same-sex marriage.

To discuss same-sex marriage in the Korean context, it must be remembered how the CCK interprets marriage, namely as "physical and mental integration of man and woman."[65] This interpretation did not come from the case of same-sex marriage, but

---

[59] Supreme Court of Korea, 2009 Su-I 117, September 2, 2011, Grand Chamber Decision (translated and commented by myself).

[60] The Constitutional Court of Korea, 95 Hun-Ga 6, July 16, 1997, Grand Chamber Decision. (This case is the prohibition of marriage between same surnames and same origins. The details of this case are dealt with in Chap. 2.)

[61] The Constitutional Court of Korea, 2009 Hun-Ba 146, November 24, 2011, Grand Chamber Decision. (This case is to decide whether to pay more taxes when owning more assets because of marriage discrimination based on marriage or not. In this case, such a tax imposing violates non-discrimination principle based on marriage and violates the freedom to marry.)

[62] The Constitutional Court of Korea, 2004 Hun-Ba 65, decided on April 28, 2005.

[63] Article 17 of the Korean Constitution reads as follows: The privacy of no citizen shall be infringed.

[64] Article 36, paragraph 1 of the Korean Constitution reads as follows: Marriage and family life shall be entered into and sustained on the basis of individual dignity and equality of the sexes, and the State shall do everything in its power to achieve that goal.

[65] The Constitutional Court of Korea, 1995 Hun-Ga 6, decided on July 16, 1997.

from the case dealing with the constitutionality of Civil Law Article 809 (1). The article stipulated the prohibition of a marriage between two persons with the same family name and family origin.

South Korean courts are still reluctant to legalize same-sex marriage because they feel it is against the wishes of the people.[66] The first court case[67] dealing with same-sex marriage in Korea was on May 25, 2016. The Korean legal newspaper, Law Times, reported that Seoul Seo-Bu District Court did not accept admissibility of the same-sex couple's claim to approve marriage ban. The applicants are two Korean males, who had had a stable relationship for many years and had a wedding ceremony in September 2013. The Seoul District Court stated that legal marriage is interpreted to be allowed only among opposite sex couples in the current Korean legal system. Furthermore, in the decision the District Court referred to the fact that most Korean people's sentiment is still against same-sex marriage. The Appeal Court also agreed with the decision by the District Court, when saying that the decision by Seoul Western District Court could be sufficiently justified, in that the marriage should be allowed only among "opposite sex couples" under the current Korean legal context.[68] The Appeal court dismissed the applicants' appeal on 6 December, 2016.[69] The Appeal court decided that the right to same-sex marriage cannot be recognized based on the interpretation of the CCK regarding marriage as the integration of man and woman.

Despite the court decisions mentioned above, same-sex marriage must be recognized in Korea from a legal perspective. Firstly, Korean laws never prohibited same marriage explicitly through their stipulations. According to Korean family law,[70]

---

[66] Brief introduction of progress of same-sex marriage issue in Korean courts: Regarding the people's sentiment about same-sex marriage in Korea, recent statistics show that about 58% of the people are against legal recognition of same-sex marriage (referenced by the survey on "same sex marriage" by Gallop Korea, available at: http://m.post.naver.com/viewer/postView.nhn?volumeNo=1835954&memberNo=10005291&vType=VERTICAL, Accessed November 30, 2021). Comparing the percentage on the results of the survey between 2001 and 2014, the percentage of supporting same-sex marriage has increased from 17% to 35% while the opposing percentage has dropped from 67% to 56%. Looking at the difference among age groups, 66% in 20s, 50% in 30s, 35% in 40s, 19% in 50s, and 13% in 60s think that same-sex marriage should be allowed in the Korean legal system. The younger the age groups are, the more positive they are about same-sex marriage.

[67] http://news.heraldcorp.com/view.php?ud=20161206000799. Accessed November 30, 2021.

[68] The Korean News Article, *The Court decision on the first same sex marriage case*, May 25, 2016, available at: https://www.lawtimes.co.kr/Legal-News/Legal-News-View?serial=100762&kind=&key=%ED%8C%90%EA%B2%B0&page=1. Accessed November 30, 2021.

[69] Seoul Seo-Bu District Court, 2014 Ho-pa 1842, December 6, 2016.

[70] Korean Civil Law **Article 812 (Formation of Marriage)** (1) A marriage shall take effect by reporting in accordance with the provisions of the Act on the Registration, etc. of Family Relationship. <Amended by Act No. 8435, May 17, 2007>.

(2) The report mentioned in paragraph (1) shall be submitted in writing with co-signatures of both parties and two adult witnesses.

marriage is accomplished through the consent of the two persons above 18 years old.[71] There are no other law articles to stipulate that marriage must be only contracted between a man and a woman. Furthermore, the fact that there is no explicit recognition cannot be interpreted as absolute prohibition considering the general principle of protecting constitutional rights. Constitutional rights and freedom must be fully guaranteed in principle, and they will be limited only in necessary cases.[72] In conclusion, same-sex marriage must be recognized according to the principle of constitutional rights to be fully guaranteed and can be limited when the limitation is necessary according to the principle of proportionality. A complete ban on same-sex marriage in the current Korean situation is not considered as a necessary limitation because the state will not have sufficient reasoning to balance a serious interference to same-sex couples caused by a complete ban.

Some legal scholars in Korea claim[73] that Article 36 of the Korean constitutional law can be grounds for prohibiting same-sex marriage. Article 36, paragraph 1 stipulates that "Marriage and family life shall be entered into and sustained on the basis of individual dignity and equality of the two sexes." The scholars think "the sexes" mean two different sexes due to the "plural" form; therefore, same-sex marriage is not included to the concept of legal marriage because it is not based on the two sexes. However, this cannot be used as grounds to prohibit same-sex marriage in Korea considering the intention of the stipulators.[74] This article is stipulated to eliminate the inequality that existed between men and women. In any case, it is not the article stipulating that marriage must be contracted only between a man and a woman.

Article 10[75] of the Korean Constitution guarantees that all citizens shall be assured of human worth and dignity and have the right to pursue happiness. It shall be the duty of the state to confirm and guarantee the fundamental and inviolable human rights of individuals. Article 10 can be the grounds for protecting the freedom for general behavior, the right to free expression of individual's character and the

[71] Korean Civil Law **Article 800 (Freedom of Matrimonial Engagement)** Any adult person may freely enter into a matrimonial engagement.

Korean Civil Law Article 801 (Eligible Age for Matrimonial Engagement)

Any person who has attained the age of 18 may enter into a matrimonial engagement upon the consent of his/her parents or adult guardian. Article 808 shall apply mutatis mutandis to such cases.

[This Article Wholly Amended by Act No. 10429, 7 Mar. 2011].

[72] **The Korean Constitutional Law Article 37**(1) Freedoms and rights of citizens shall not be neglected on the grounds that they are not enumerated in the Constitution. (2) The freedoms and rights of citizens may be restricted by Act only when necessary for national security, the maintenance of law and order or for public welfare. Even when such restriction is imposed, no essential aspect of the freedom or right shall be violated.

[73] Lee (2016), p. 74.

[74] http://h21.hani.co.kr/arti/PRINT/35264.html. Accessed November 30, 2021.

[75] **The Korean Constitutional Law,** Article 10: All citizens shall be assured of human worth and dignity and have the right to pursuit of happiness. It shall be the duty of the State to confirm and guarantee the fundamental and inviolable human rights of individuals.

right to self-determination.[76] Therefore, Article 10 could provide legal grounds to guarantee the right to marry for same-sex couples. In addition, Article 10 of the Constitution can be considered as legal grounds of same-sex marriage in the absence of specific legal stipulations about it.

Furthermore, in a modern society, reproductive capacity is no longer a condition of marriage. In the same sense, reproductive capacity cannot be used as grounds to prohibit same-sex marriage or discrimination based on sexual orientation. In this case, such arbitrary reasons cannot be justified as the grounds for prohibition. The right to same-sex marriage should be protected as an individual life plan, and lifestyles including marriage or childbirth are respected.[77] Democracy to protect diversity should recognize a diversified form of the family.[78] In respecting diversity, same-sex marriage should also be recognized as minority protection of human rights.

8.3 Legalizing Same-Sex Marriage in Taiwan

As recently as May 24, 2017, the Constitutional Court of China (Taiwan) ("CCT") made a decision to legalize same-sex marriage for the first time in Asia.[79] Ten out of 14 judges in the decision decided that it is against the freedom to marry as stipulated in the Article 22 of the Taiwanese Constitution as well as the non-discrimination principle of Article 7 of the Constitution that the Civil Law article prohibits same-sex couples from marrying. Through their judgment, the Taiwan Constitutional Court legally recognized the marriage of same-sex couples, even if the Parliament did not make adequate legislations regarding this. The judges pointed out that it is an unreasonable discrimination for same-sex couples not to be allowed to marry, on the grounds that they cannot biologically have babies of their own. The CCT stated that there are no Taiwanese local law articles imposing any obligations of bearing and raising children to any married couples including different-sex couples. Furthermore, different-sex couples had not had any disadvantages up to that point on the grounds that they do not have children themselves. Thus, if same-sex couples are not allowed to marry because of their inability to have biological babies, it is discrimination against their sexual orientation because they are treated less favorably compared to different-sex couples who do not have children themselves.

Taiwan's same-sex marriage case[80] will be introduced in this section. Compared to Europe, Taiwan shares many cultural similarities with South Korea, therefore, this case could have positive implications for future same-sex marriage cases in Korea.

---

[76]The Constitutional Court of Korea, 2004 Hun-Ba 65, decided on April 28, 2005.

[77]Ryu (2013), p. 94.

[78]Cho (2007), pp. 221–241.

[79]Kuo and Chen (2017).

[80]The Constitutional Court of Republic of China (Taiwan), The consolidated petitions of Huei-Tai-12674 filed by Chia-Wei and Huei-Tai-12771 filed by the Taipei City Government, regarding the

After this landmark decision in Taiwan where same-sex marriage legislation was passed, lawmakers in Taiwan finally approved a bill legalizing same-sex marriage. In the constitutional decision, the CCT gave the lawmakers two years to amend the existing law or enact new laws. On May 17, 2019, which was only a week before this two-year deadline, the Taiwanese Parliament passed a bill to make same-sex marriage possible, which went into effect on May 24, 2019.[81] This accomplishment in Taiwan was achieved only after a long struggle. In 2015, *Chi Chia-wie*, who is known as veteran gay rights activist filed a request to the CCT regarding the constitutionality of the civil code stating that marriage is only between a man and a woman. In the same year, Taipei city government filed a similar request after three same-sex couples started an administrative lawsuit against the government when their registrations for marriage were rejected. These requests finally led to a ruling of the CCT deciding that the corresponding civil code violated the Constitution of Taiwan.[82]

8.3.1 The Decision of the Constitutional Court of China (Taiwan)

The issue of the same-sex marriage case in Taiwan (Case No. 748) is the constitutionality of the provisions of Chapter 2 on Marriage of Part IV Family of the Civil Code,[83] because these provisions do not allow two persons of the same-sex to create a permanent union of intimate and exclusive nature for the purpose of living a common life. The main issue is to decide whether such prohibition violates the constitution's guarantees of freedom of marriage (Article 22[84]) and right to equality (Article 7[85]). The CCT decided that the authorities concerned shall amend or enact the laws as appropriate, in accordance with the ruling of its interpretation, within two

constitutionality of same-sex marriage, the Constitutional Court announces the J.Y. Interpretation No. 748 at 4 PM on 24 May 2017.

[81] CNN, May 17, 2019, "Taiwan legalizes same-sex marriage in historic first for Asia." https://edition.cnn.com/2019/05/17/asia/taiwan-same-sex-marriage-intl/index.html. Accessed November 30, 2021.

[82] Ibid. Last accessed on December 10, 2019.

[83] Article 972 of Section 1 – Betrothal (Articles 972–979), Chapter II, Marriage in the civil code of Taiwan stipulates that "An agreement to marry shall be made by the male and the female parties in their own concord."

[84] There is no specific article to guarantee freedom of marriage in Constitution of the Republic of China (Taiwan). The Constitutional Court of Taiwan interpreted that freedom of marriage is protected under the Article 22 of the Constitution to reads as follows: Article 22 All other freedoms and rights of the people that are not detrimental to social order or public welfare shall be guaranteed under the Constitution.

[85] Article 7 of the Constitution of the Republic of China (Taiwan) states that "All citizens of the Republic of China, irrespective of sex, religion, race, class, or party affiliation, shall be equal before the law."

years from the announcement of this interpretation. The decision mentioned that it is within the discretion of the authorities concerned "to determine the formality for achieving the equal protection of the freedom of marriage."[86] Furthermore, the CCT stated that "two persons of the same-sex who intend to create the said permanent union shall be allowed to have their marriage registration effectuated at the authorities in charge of household registration, by submitting a written document signed by two or more witnesses in accordance with the said Marriage Chapter."[87]

As the main reasons for the interpretation, the Constitutional Court of China (Taiwan) ("CCT") mentioned the duty of the court, the freedom to marry, the legislative flaw, and the equality in the sense of protecting minorities. These main reasons of the CCT can be analyzed from different aspects, particularly formal, negative, and material ones.

First, in terms of the formal aspect, the CCT stated that the duty of the court in the decision was one of the main reasons for the interpretation. According to the CCT, the duty of the representative body is to enact or revise the relevant laws in due time. However, the CCT considers that the timetable for such a legislative solution is hardly predictable while these petitions are involved with the protection of people's fundamental rights. At this point, the CCT justifies the positive and active role of the court by mentioning that "it is the constitutional duty of this Court to render a binding judicial decision, in time, on issues concerning the safeguarding of constitutional basic values such as the protection of people's constitutional rights and the free democratic constitutional order."[88] These positive duties of the court should not be regarded as being opposed to democracy, but should be reiterated in terms of the importance of positive duties when realizing all the rights in the constitution.[89] As the right to marry of same-sex couples is protected as a constitutional right, the positive duty of the CCT should also be considered as a democratic role for the court to ensure human dignity, freedom, and equality.[90]

A second negative aspect is that the CCT considers the prohibition of same-sex marriage to be a gross legislative flaw for the following reasons. Even if same-sex marriage is allowed for same-sex couples, it will not affect the application of the Marriage Chapter to the union of two persons of the opposite sex at all. Usually, a majority group of people do not welcome the idea of granting the same right to a minority, because the majority group may fear that their rights will be negatively affected by doing so. However, this is not the case regarding same-sex marriage because it does not have any influence on the existing institution of marriage between opposite sexes. Moreover, same-sex marriage will not alter any social

[86] The Constitutional Court Republic of China (Taiwan), Press Release On the Same-Sex Marriage Case, released on May 24, 2017, p. 1.

[87] Ibid., p. 1.

[88] The Constitutional Court Republic of China (Taiwan), Press Release On the Same-Sex Marriage Case, released on May 24, 2017, p. 2.

[89] Fredman (2008), p. 117.

[90] Ibid., p. 117.

order which is already established upon the existing opposite sex marriage. Same-sex marriage is not put in the position of being opposed to marriage between men and women. The CCT continuously argues that the freedom to marry for same-sex couples will constitute the collective basis, together with opposite sex marriage to stabilize society by institutionalizing marriage system for all. Lastly, the CCT mentions that "the need, capability, willingness and longing, in both physical and psychological senses, for creating such permanent unions of an intimate and exclusive nature are equally essential to homosexuals and heterosexuals."[91] By emphasizing the important nature of legislating same-sex marriage, the CCT seemed to justify the need to fill this legislative flaw through the Constitutional decision.

Thirdly, employing a material aspect to emphasize freedom, the CCT highlights people's freedom to marry in its interpretation. As to the freedom to marry, the CCT clarifies that all the single persons eligible to marry shall have their freedom to marry regardless of their sexual orientation. Furthermore, this freedom to marry includes the freedom to decide not only "whether to marry or not" but also "whom to marry." The CCT interprets that "decisional autonomy"[92] is included in the scope of protection under the freedom to marry. The CCT has reasoned that such decisional autonomy is very important for the sound development of the individual's personality as well as for safeguarding human dignity. For this reason, freedom to marry is a fundamental right which must be protected under Article 22[93] of the Constitution of Taiwan even if there is no separate article stipulating the freedom to marry in the Constitution.

Fourthly, from another material aspect of equality, the CCT argued that different treatment based on other classifications, such as disability or sexual orientation, shall also be governed by the right to equality under Article 7[94] of the Constitution. Even if Article 7 of the Constitution does not specifically mention disability or sexual orientation, the CCT has interpreted that both disability and sexual orientation must be included as the grounds for preventing discrimination. The CCT particularly mentioned disability and sexual orientation, which should be protected even if they are not explicitly stated in Article 7 as emphasizing both an immutable characteristic that is resistant to change and attained regardless of an individual's personal choices. Another reason is that the principle of equality comes from the purpose of protecting

[91] The Constitutional Court Republic of China (Taiwan), Press Release On the Same-Sex Marriage Case, released on May 24, 2017, p. 2.

[92] The Constitutional Court Republic of China (Taiwan), Press Release On the Same-Sex Marriage Case, released on May 24, 2017, p. 2.

[93] Article 22 of the Constitution of the Republic of China (Taiwan) reads as follows: All other freedoms and rights enumerated in the preceding Articles shall not be restricted by law except by such as may be necessary to prevent infringement upon the freedoms of other persons, to avert an imminent crisis, to maintain social order or to advance public welfare.

[94] Article 7 of the Constitution of the Republic of China (Taiwan) reads as follows: All citizens of the Republic of China, irrespective of sex, religion, race, class, or party affiliation, shall be equal before the law.

minorities including sexual minorities because they lack political power, have been isolated, and have suffered various forms of exclusion or discrimination.

In finding discrimination, the CCT has specifically analyzed two important arguments of procreation and ethical order, which are commonly referred to as the arguments against same-sex marriage. People who are against same-sex marriage often argue that two persons of the same-sex are incapable of natural procreation, which differentiates them from opposite sex couples. However, the CCT argued that such an incapability of the same-sex couple is no different from different sex couple who are unable or unwilling to have their own children. No one will easily agree on the prohibition of marriage of different sex couples by applying the reasons of procreation. Therefore, not allowing same-sex couples to marry because of their inability to reproduce is a different treatment between same-sex couples and opposite sex couples without an apparent rational ground. To the counterargument of ethical orders, the CCT reaffirms that the existing basic ethical orders based on the existing marriage institution will remain the same, even after same-sex marriage is legally recognized. In this regard, if same-sex marriage is not allowed for the sake of safeguarding basic ethical orders, it is also a different treatment without reasonable grounds.

8.3.2 Explication of the Decision

Some important methodological tools have been applied in the Taiwanese case. The first one is the *law of balancing*. In the reasoning, the Constitutional Court of Taiwan applied the *law of balancing* when it assesses the violation of the non-discrimination principle. As briefly mentioned above, the CCT has regarded the prohibition of same-sex marriage as a violation of equal treatment in terms of protecting sexual minorities. Homosexuals are a minority which has been discriminated against based on their sexual orientation regarded as an immutable characteristic regardless of the will of an individual. For this reason, the CCT affirmed that a heightened standard shall be applied in determining the constitutionality of different treatment based on sexual orientation.

As such, the *principle of proportionality* and the *law of balancing* were also very important tools applied in the main reasons of the interpretation by the CCT. In the judgment, the CCT stated that the prohibition fails the review under the principle of proportionality as required by Article 23[95] of the Constitution. Excluding same-sex couples from marriage is not substantially related to the furthering of an important public interest. From there, it is clearly seen that the CCT has applied the basic

[95] Article 23 of the Constitution of the Republic of China (Taiwan) states that "All the freedoms and rights enumerated in the preceding Articles shall not be restricted by law except by such as may be necessary to prevent infringement upon the freedoms of other persons, to avert an imminent crisis, to maintain social order or to advance public welfare."

principle of proportionality as well as the law of balancing with a heightened standard in the reasoning although the structured proportionality with three concrete steps has not been explicitly applied.

In conclusion, this Taiwanese case is relevant to the same-sex marriage in South Korea because the two countries are similar in terms of their cultural background. The Constitutional Court of Korea has not yet dealt with the issue of whether two persons of the same sex are allowed to marry just like the Taiwanese Constitutional Court before this case. It could be easier for the Constitutional Court of Korea to legalize same-sex marriage because there is no provision expressly mandating that the two parties of a marriage are one male and one female in the Korean civil code, unlike the Taiwanese Civil Code. Since there is no specific provision to define marriage as a contract only between different sexes, the CCK could legalize same-sex marriage by interpretation. For the interpretation methodologies, a dynamic interpretation should be adopted to reflect on the currently evolving situation to provide legal recognitions for same-sex couples in constitutional courts over the world including the CCT. The Constitutional Court of Korea can refer to the interpretation by the Taiwanese Constitutional Court to legalize same-sex marriage.

8.4 Case Analysis: Inter-American Court of Human Rights

In this section, leading cases related to discrimination based on sexual orientation[96] in the Inter-American Court of Human Rights ("IACtHR") will be introduced. The reason why learning from the IACtHR are important is that the IACtHR shows a more progressive tendency in applying clearer methods of adjudication in the cases of discrimination based on sexual orientation compared to the ECtHR: it applies a more structured proportionality test, and it decides in favor of protecting sexual minorities despite of lack of consensus.

In the case of *Aldeguer Tomás vs. Spain,*[97] the ECtHR refers to the Inter-American case of *Angel Alberto Duque v. Columbia*[98] cited in the Inter-American

[96] Even if the main topic of case analysis in this chapter is same-sex marriage, the cases of the Inter-American Court of Human Rights ("IACtHR") are not confined to the cases of same-sex marriage. It is because the aim of this section is to show the standards and the methods of adjudication applied by the IACtHR in the cases dealing with the discrimination based on sexual orientation. Therefore, the cases of the IACtHR introduced in this section does not specifically deal with same-sex marriage but more comprehensively the cases of discrimination based on sexual orientation.

[97] European Court of Human Rights, *Aldeguer Tomás vs. Spain*, judgment of 14 June 2015, paragraphs 54–55.

[98] CASE OF *Angel Alberto Duque v. Columbia*, Case 123-05, Report No. 150/11, The Inter-American Court of Human Rights (2011): On February 8, 2005, the Inter-American Commission on Human Rights ("the Commission") received a petition presented by the Comision Colombiana de Juristas and German Humberto Rincon Perfetti ("the petitioners") alleging the responsibility of the Republic of Colombia ("Colombia") for the inability of Duque to benefit from the survivor's pension of his deceased partner, considering that the norms that regulate the right to social security

Commission on Human Rights Report. As this case deals with the complaint by the applicant that he was denied a survivor's pension based on his sexual orientation, the proportionality analysis used is comparable to the case law of the European Court of Human Rights. The applicant, Mr. *Duque* was denied a survivor's pension because he and his late permanent partner could not marry because they were in a same-sex relationship.

The Commission maintains that it is *legitimate* to exclude same-sex couples from the survivor's pension to protect the family and the family in this sense is understood as being "formed by the union of a man and a woman, the only union capable of preserving the species through procreation."[99] For the test of *suitability*, the Inter-American Court has established that "the American Convention does not define a limited concept of family, nor does it only protect a 'traditional' model of the family."[100] Hence, the Commission considers that there is no causal relationship between the means of arbitrarily excluding diverse forms of families such as those formed by same-sex couples and the means of protecting families.

Article 1 of American Convention states that all the State Parties of the Convention should respect, ensure and protect the rights contained in the convention—without any discrimination for reasons of race, color, sex, language, religion, political or other opinion, national or social origin, economic status, birth, or any other social condition: sexual orientation can be interpreted as being included on the grounds of sex or any other social condition. Another landmark IAtHR case, *Atala Riffo and Daughters v. Chile*[101] is referred to the ECtHR's ruling in the case of *E. B. v. France*.[102] However, the IACtHR establishes a lower threshold meaning that discriminatory treatment does not need to be fundamentally and solely based on sexual orientation but it is enough to prove that to a certain extent this ground has been considered.[103] Such an interpretation of the IACtHR is considered as much more progressive in finding discrimination based on sexual orientation than the ECtHR, which requires that the influence of homosexuality has to be a "decisive factor."[104]

---

excluded same-sex couples from that benefit. (Case summary from University of Minnesota Human Rights Library, available at http://hrlibrary.umn.edu/cases/150-11.html. Accessed November 30, 2021.)

[99] The Report No. 5/14 by the Inter-American Commission on Human Rights. April 2, 2014 (Case 12.841 *Angel Alberto Duque v. Colombia*).

[100] Ibid.

[101] Atala Riffo and Daughters v. Chile, Inter-American Court of Human Rights (ser. C) No. 254, ¶ 30 (February 24, 2012): This is the case of a lesbian woman who was denied the custody of her three daughters on the basis that her sexual orientation had adverse effects on them. The IACtHR decides that the sexual orientation of persons is a category protected by the American Convention, therefore, any regulation, act, practice considered as discriminatory based on a person's sexual orientation is prohibited.

[102] European Court of Human Rights, ***E.B. v. FRANCE*** (Applications no. 43546/02), Grand Chamber judgment of 22 January 2008.

[103] Abrusci (2017), p. 253.

[104] European Court of Human Rights, *E.B. v. France*, decided on January 22, 2008, paragraph 89.

More recently, the IACtHR set new standards through the case of *Azul Rojas Marin and another v. Peru*,[105] which provides the potential to reduce the levels of violence suffered by the group of LGBTI persons both within and beyond the Americas.[106] The applicant *Azul*, a transgender woman, was arbitrary kept by members of the Peruvian police for almost six hours—stripped naked, beaten, and raped. The IACtHR played a positive role in assessing various pieces of evidence including the applicant's statements, medical examinations as well as the forensic examination of the clothes which the applicant wore at the time of detention. This case is evaluated as "the first case decided by an international tribunal to conclude that torture can take place with the specific purpose of discriminating against a person because of sexual orientation."[107] As such, the IACtHR is very progressive in tackling discrimination based on sexual orientation including recognizing same-sex marriages.

8.5 Conclusion

This chapter began with the question of how Korean courts can learn from Europe, from Taiwan, and from the cases of IACtHR in legalizing same-sex marriage. However, unlike the non-criminalization of homosexual relations, the standard of protection is not sufficient in the European system. The ECtHR can improve its

---

[105] Inter-American Court of Human Rights, ***CASE OF AZUL ROJAS MARÍN ET AL. V. PERU***, judgment of 12 March 2020: The applicant, Azul Rojas Marín, identified herself as a gay man at the time of her arrest on February 25, 2008. On February 25, 2008, at 00:30 hours, the applicant was walking home along when a police car approached her and searched her, they hit her, and they made her get into the police car while they shouted "queer, motherfucker." During her detention, they continued to insult her referring to her sexual orientation. She was taken to the Casa Grande Police Station where she was forcibly undressed, beaten, tortured, raped because the state agents twice introduced a police baton in her anus. The applicant remained at the police station until 6 a.m. without her arrest being recorded. Upon filing a complaint by the applicant, the prosecution service ordered that a formal preliminary investigation be opened for the offenses of rape and abuse of authority against three police officers. The applicant requested the expansion of the complaint and the investigation to include the crime of torture, which was rejected by the prosecutor. The prosecutor requested the dismissal of the proceedings against the three police officers, and the court dismissed the proceedings on January 9, 2009. On November 20, 2018, Inter-American Commission on Human Rights made recommendation and in accordance with this, the prosecutor ordered the re-opening of the investigation. But on January 16, 2019, the prosecutor asked the criminal judge to annul all the actions in the proceeding against the three police officers and the court declared the request for annulment inadmissible. The Inter-American Court of Human Rights stated that Peru violated the right to personal liberty, the right to personal integrity and privacy, the rights to judicial guarantees and judicial protection of the applicant, and the right to personal integrity of the applicant's mother (taken from "Official Summary Issued by the Inter-American Court of CASE OF AZUL ROJAS MARÍN ET AL. V. PERU," https://www.corteidh.or.cr/docs/casos/articulos/resumen_402_ing.pdf. Accessed November 30, 2021).

[106] Esdaile et al. (2020).

[107] Esdaile et al. (2020).

standard of protection in the cases of same-sex marriage with a fully structured proportionality test. Most of the Convention rights can be limited with certain conditions, except a few absolute rights. Such limitations or interferences are only justified when there is a proportionate relationship between the aims and the rights at stake. The ECtHR does not explicitly adopt the structured test of proportionality, consisting of legitimacy, suitability, necessity, and balancing. In the beginning of this chapter there was an analysis as to whether it is possible to reconstruct the case law of same-sex marriage according to a structured proportionality test. As we have looked at the examples of the specific cases, the answer is yes. It is possible to reconstruct the sexual orientation case law of the ECtHR with a structured proportionality test. Moreover, the ECtHR should adopt the fully structured proportionality test to enhance its clarity in its methodological use of the principle of proportionality, as well as to protect the human rights of sexual minorities by finding violations with the full analysis of proportionality.

In addition, there are good lessons that Korea can learn from the first legal recognition of same-sex marriage in Taiwan. Particularly, unlike Europe, Taiwan shares many cultural and social similarities with Korea so that the Taiwanese decision will provide many progressive stimuli to the Korean court when deciding the case of same-sex marriage in the near future. This chapter ends with an introduction of some landmark cases of the IACtHR on discrimination based on sexual orientation. The IACtHR is very active in protecting the rights of sexual minorities when applying methods of adjudication such as the structured proportionality test as well as the consensus argument, ordering holistic forms of reparation, and making progressive interpretation. This will provide progressive and inspiring sources to courts in other parts of the world, including South Korea where court decisions do not sufficiently protect sexual minorities.

References

Abrusci E (2017) A tale of convergence? Discrimination based on sexual orientation in regional human rights bodies and the Human Rights Committee. Nord J Hum Rights 35(3):240–257. https://doi.org/10.1080/18918131.2017.1355434. Accessed November 30, 2021.

Alexy R (2005) Balancing, constitutional review, and representation. Int J Const Law 3(4): 572–581. https://doi.org/10.1093/icon/moi040. Accessed November 30, 2021.

Barak A (2012) Proportionality: constitutional rights and their limitations (trans: Kalir D). Cambridge University Press, Cambridge

Brems E, Lavrysen L (2015) 'Don't use a sledgehammer to crack a nut': less restrictive means in the case law of the European Court of Human Rights. Hum Rights Law Rev 15(1):139–168. https://doi.org/10.1093/hrlr/ngu040. Accessed November 30, 2021.

Brugger W (1994) Verfassungsinterpretation in den Vereinigten Staaten von Amerika. JöR 42, S. 571 ff

Cho H-S (2007) New model of 'Family': constitutional possibility and limit. Public Law J 8(4): 221–241

Clérico L (2017) Proportionality and balancing. In: Mendes CH, Gargarella R (eds) Oxford handbook of constitutional law in Latin America. Oxford University Press, Oxford

Clérico L (2018) Proportionality in social rights adjudication: making it workable. In: Duarte D, Sampais JS (eds) Proportionality in law. Springer, Heidelberg, pp 25–48

Esdaile C et al. (2020) Discriminatory torture of an LGBTI person: landmark precedent set by the Inter-American Court (Azel Rojas Marin and Another v. Peru), https://www.ejiltalk.org/discriminatory-torture-of-an-lgbti-person-landmark-precedent-set-by-the-inter-american-court-azul-rojas-marin-and-another-v-peru/?utm_source=mailpoet&utm_medium=email&utm_campaign=ejil-talk-newsletter-post-title_2. Accessed November 30, 2021.

Fredman S (2008) Human rights transformed: positive rights and positive duties. Oxford University Press, Oxford

Gerards J (2008) Judicial deliberations in the European Court of Human Rights. In: Huls N, Adams M, Bomhoff J (eds) The legitimacy of highest court's rulings. T.M.C. Asser Institute, The Hague

Gerards J (2013) How to improve the necessity test of the European Court of Human Rights. Int J Const Law 11(2):466–490. https://doi.org/10.1093/icon/mot004

Han S-H (2015) Should same sex marriage be legalized?: Same sex marriage is originally legitimate. Column in Joon-Ang Daily Newspaper, published on July 31, 2015. https://news.joins.com/article/18358135. Accessed November 30, 2021.

Jachmann M, Maunz/Dürig, Grundgesetz-Kommentar IX, Art. 95 Rn. 13

Krajewski M, Singer C (2012) Should judges be front-runners? The ICJ, state immunity and the protection of fundamental human rights. In: Bogdandy, Wolfrum R (eds) Max Planck Yearbook of United Nations Law, vol 16, pp. 1–34. https://www.mpil.de/files/pdf3/mpunyb_01_krajewski_neu.pdf. Accessed November 30, 2021.

Kuo M-S, Chen H-W (2017) Responsibility and judgment in a muted 3-D dialogue: a primer on the same-sex marriage case in Taiwan. Int'l J. Const. L. Blog, May 26, 2017, at: http://www.iconnectblog.com/2017/05/responsibility-and-judgment-in-a-muted-3-d-dialogue-a-primer-on-the-same-sex-marriage-case-in-taiwan/. Accessed November 30, 2021.

Łącki P (2021) Consensus as a basis for dynamic interpretation of the ECHR – a critical assessment. Hum Rights Law Rev 21(1):186–202. https://doi.org/10.1093/hrlr/ngaa042. Accessed November 30, 2021.

Lee J-H (2016) A study of same-sex marriage in South Korea and Germany's Act on registered life partnerships. Won Kwang Law J 32(2)

Mendos LR (2019) State-sponsored homophobia, 13th edition, the International Lesbian, Gay, Bisexual, Trans and Intersex Association (ILGA World), ilga. Org

Park Z-W (2003) Constitutional interpretation and judicial review. Korean Public Law Assoc 32(1)

Ryu S-J (2013) US Supreme Court's recent decisions about homosexuality: analysis and meaning of US V. Windsor case. Public Law Study 14(4):87–114. https://doi.org/10.31779/PLJ.14.4.201311.004

Sieckmann J (2018) Proportionality as a universal human rights principle. In: Duarte D, Sampaio JS (eds) Proportionality in law. Springer, Heidelberg

Young AI (2014) Proportionality is dead: long live proportionality! In: Huscroft G, Miller BW, Webber G (eds) Proportionality and the rule of law. Cambridge University Press, Cambridge

Chapter 9
General Conclusion

This chapter consists of a summary of findings, suggestions for further research, personal reflection, and the last comment on "towards protection of sexual minorities in Korea." The purpose of this chapter is to show my findings from case analyses as well as from a review of the literature and to suggest what has to be done in future research because some important issues have not been dealt with deeply in this work although they are related to the issues concerning prohibition of discrimination based on sexual orientation. The last comment is to provide suggestions to prohibit discrimination based on sexual orientation in South Korea.

9.1 Summary of Findings

This work has three central aims which are analytical, critical, and normative. Firstly, the analytical aim is to better understand the principles and theories applied in the jurisprudence of the ECtHR and the Constitutional Court of Korea in the case law of discrimination based on sexual orientation. To achieve this aim, I have analyzed the principle of non-discrimination in Chap. 4, the principle of proportionality in Chap. 5, and other relevant theories and concepts in Chap. 6. This study starts from understanding the enforcement of morality, recognizing the problem of underdeveloped protection of sexual minorities in South Korea, and comparing it with the European context. To better understand the principles and theories, a comparative analysis has been done from other jurisdictions on the common topic including the ECtHR and the CCK cases. A lack of clarity is found in the legal reasoning of the ECtHR. Looking at the sexual orientation case law of the ECtHR, the basic structure of the proportionality test serves as an analytical tool to reconstruct a decision, although the ECtHR did not opt for the formal adoption of the proportionality test. Including the principle of proportionality, relevant concepts such as positive state obligations, the margin of appreciation doctrine, the core right argument, and the European consensus argument have been applied in the decisions of the ECtHR

H. J. Lee, *Discrimination Based on Sexual Orientation*, Interdisciplinary Studies in Human Rights 8, https://doi.org/10.1007/978-3-030-95423-9_9

cases related to discrimination based on sexual orientation. Applying the structured proportionality test could also serve an important role in future cases of the CCK and enhance clarity as well as foreseeability in its upcoming cases related to discrimination based on sexual orientation.

Secondly, the critical aim is to examine the jurisprudence of the ECtHR and the Constitutional Court of Korea from a critical perspective with a view to making the prohibition of discrimination based on sexual orientation workable. To achieve this, I have focused on examining the case law of non-criminalization of same-sex relations in Chap. 7 and the same-sex marriage in Chap. 8. Among various topics of the jurisprudence, these two topics were chosen because non-criminalization of same-sex relations is the beginning of a discussion in which the CCK is expected to challenge the existing jurisprudence in the near future. Furthermore, same-sex marriage is still regarded as a topic of a difficult case without European consensus in the jurisprudence of the ECtHR, and only the Taiwanese Court has legalized same-sex marriage in Asia.

Thirdly, the normative aim is to contribute to a better development of the legal methodology in discrimination based on sexual orientation. Specifically, I have suggested not only applying the principle of non-discrimination and the principle of proportionality but also understanding positive state obligations, the margin of appreciation doctrine, the core right argument, and the consensus argument. My primary suggestion is that courts should enhance clarity in the application of these legal methodologies. Furthermore, courts should clarify standards concerning rights where each methodological tool is consistently applied to protect the rights of sexual minorities. The state's positive obligation involves the adoption of measures that provide a legal framework to allow same-sex couples to have their relationship recognized under domestic law. The state's positive obligation is related to the doctrine of the margin of appreciation, which grants national authorities some leeway in fulfilling the state's obligations. The margin is decided with many factors including the positive state obligation, the core right argument, and the consensus argument.

In the first chapter, I raised a number of research questions, including how Korea can overcome the current situations of discriminatory acts based on sexual orientation. I wondered why people's hatred of sexual minorities is particularly strong compared to other groups such as disabled, or elderly, or women. I have looked for the grounds in the sense that sexual orientation is regarded as an issue between law and morality. To discuss this issue, I have discussed the enforcement of morality in the second chapter. In this second chapter, I introduced the two Korean Constitutional cases of adultery and prohibition of marriage between same surnames and same places. With these decisions, the two issues which have faced strong resistance because they are seen as offending against their sense of morality have been solved as legal entitlements. Particularly, I have showed that reasoning for non-criminalization of adultery could be applied to the reasoning of non-criminalization of same-sex relations according to the Military Criminal Law in Korea. In addition, the constitutional decision to abolish the marriage ban between people with the same surnames and the same place of origin clearly showed that the marriage ban between same-sex couples could be abolished.

The third chapter provided an overview of legal recognition of same-sex relationships in Korea and Europe, which could be the answer to another research question of why it is important to deal with discrimination based on sexual orientation. I have informed readers why sexual orientation should be regarded as a ground not to discriminate concerning current discriminatory situations in Europe and South Korea. Furthermore, I emphasized the importance of a dynamic interpretation to provide sexual minorities with effective protection.

The fourth chapter provided a comparative perspective by applying the principle of non-discrimination and the anti-discrimination law in different jurisdictions. My suggestion to prohibit discrimination based on sexual orientation is that courts should apply the standards of equality clearly, consistently, and in a foreseeable way. To show the importance of standards of equality, I have introduced discussion on similar issues in different jurisdictions, particularly including the U.S. and Germany because these two have been introduced in Korea, and influenced on developing standards of equality in Korean courts. Another suggestion is to legislate for a comprehensive anti-discrimination law to protect sexual minorities from discrimination. Using the EU Anti-discrimination law, German equality law, and British equality law, I have successfully showed that the legislation of a general anti-discrimination law has positively worked to protect the rights of vulnerable groups. At the same time, I have pointed out the challenges facing future improvement of these legislations.

The fifth chapter discussed the principle of proportionality in the case law of the ECtHR related to sexual orientation. This chapter successfully showed that applying the structured proportionality could enhance clarity in applying methodological tools of the ECtHR particularly in the cases of discrimination based on sexual orientation. The fifth chapter showed that the reasoning of the ECtHR could be restructured according to the steps of the proportionality in the jurisprudence of Articles 8, 10, and 11 of the ECHR. Furthermore, the analysis showed that applying the structured proportionality could have found more violations even in the cases where no violation has been found.

In the sixth chapter, I have provided an in-depth analysis of the relevant concepts of positive state obligation, the margin of appreciation doctrine, the core right argument, and the consensus argument in the case law of the ECtHR. I have pointed out the problem with the applications of these concepts of the ECtHR, which is unclear and inconsistent. For example, in the same case, the chamber judgment understood the issue as negative obligations, and the grand chamber judgment regarded it as positive obligations, which led to different reasonings. Another problem is that the ECtHR used the consensus argument as an excuse not to recognize the rights of sexual minorities.

The seventh chapter is dedicated to analyzing the cases of different jurisdiction on the same topic of non-criminalization of same-sex relations. I have criticized the case of the Constitutional Court of Korea when regarding criminalization of same-sex relations according to the Military Criminal Law as constitutional. To support my claim that the Article of the Law to criminally punish same-sex relations should be abolished, I have comparatively analyzed cases from different jurisdictions including the ECtHR, India, and the United States. I have particularly selected these jurisdictions because the ECtHR provides sufficient protection in non-criminalization of same-sex relations, for instance, India has recently decriminalized same-sex relations through its Supreme Court decision, and the United States decisions have been the object of comparative research in the Korean Constitutional Court. The case analysis in this chapter showed that criminalization of same-sex relations violates the principle of proportionality as well as the principle of non-discrimination.

The eighth chapter focused on analyzing the case of same-sex marriage. I selected same-sex marriage cases because the right is evolving and there is recent development in the legal recognition of same-sex relations. In this chapter, I first analyzed the case law of the ECtHR and proved the reasoning of the cases could be restructured according to the steps of the proportionality, which could also be applied in the issue of positive state obligations as well as negative state obligations. Then, I suggested the possibility of allowing same-sex marriage under the Korean legal system in situations where there has been no constitutional case. Next, I analyzed the reasoning of the recent decision of the Constitutional Court of China (Taiwan) to make Taiwan the first Asian country to legalize same-sex marriage. Lastly, the cases of Inter-American Court of Human Rights were introduced, which have positive implications particularly with applying the structured proportionality, and the application of Consensus argument in favor of the victims.

The objective of this book is to urge the ECtHR as well as the Constitutional Court of Korea to adopt the fully structured proportionality test including the less restrictive means test and the law of balancing, so as to enhance clarity and foreseeability in the jurisprudence of discrimination based on sexual orientation. With the exception of some absolute rights, rights could be interfered with, yet such interference is only justified as long as there is a proportionate relationship between the aims and the right at stake. Providing that there is a legitimate aim behind a law or measure, the subtest of proportionality asks whether the measure is suitable, if there are other less restrictive measures, and if it is proportional in the narrow sense relating to the intensity of interference to the importance of the state objective.

Besides the experiences of the ECtHR, discussions in other jurisdictions including Germany as well as the United States have been introduced particularly in relation to the principle of non-discrimination. This comparative analysis, where the principles and standards are examined from the experiences of different jurisdictions, will certainly provide positive stimuli for Korean courts, where the protection of sexual minorities is considerably underdeveloped. One of the positive implications is to legislate for a comprehensive anti-discrimination law. Such a general and comprehensive anti-discrimination law will help to protect sexual minorities in Korea. The second of the positive implications is to accomplish non-criminalization of homosexual relations. The current constitutional decision to regard the criminalization of same-sex relations in the military as constitutional was criticized according to the principle of proportionality. The recent experience of India to abolish the criminalization of homosexual relations could inspire the Korean court to move forward into non-criminalization. The third of the positive implications is to legalize same-sex marriage. Taiwanese legalization of same-sex marriage and the process of evolving case law of the ECtHR can be used as inspirational legal sources for the Korean courts.

It is particularly difficult to enhance the rights of sexual minorities in South Korea because the issue is mostly regarded as a moral matter. In the absence of a same-sex marriage decision in the Constitutional Court of Korea, the previous cases that have been regarded as dealing with moral matters could have positive implications. The first case is non-criminalization of adultery. The process whereby the criminal punishment of adultery was abolished can have such positive implications for how the Constitutional Court of Korea should decriminalize same-sex relations under the Military Criminal Court in future decisions. The second case is the prohibition on marriage between people with the same surnames and the same places of origin, which was introduced in Chap. 2 of this book. This case can be a good example of the decision to legalize same-sex marriage by the Constitutional Court of Korea. Furthermore, the legislation of comprehensive anti-discrimination law (Chap. 4) and the application of the structure proportionality test (Chap. 5) are needed to make prohibition of discrimination based on sexual orientation workable in South Korea.

9.2 Suggestions for Further Research

In this section, further research suggestions are introduced. The first suggestion concerns case laws of discrimination based on sexual orientation in other jurisdictions. The main object of this work has been the case law of the ECtHR and the Constitutional Court of Korea. Recently the Zimbabwe High Court[1] has decided on the unlawful and malicious arrest of a transgender woman as constituting inhuman and degrading treatment, and it made reference to the Indian Supreme Court Case *Navtej in Singh Johar &Others v. Union of India &Others*, which was introduced in

[1]Zimbabwe High Court Decision, Nathanson v Mteliso and Ors. (HB 176/19, HC 1873/14) [2019] ZWBHC 135 Judgment of 14 November 2019: The Plaintiff, a transgender woman, awaited a business client at the Palace Hotel bar when the first Respondent called her over to his table where he sat with a male companion. The 1st Respondent told the Plaintiff for 20 dollars to let her go, which she declined. Her refusal enraged the 1st Respondent. When the Plaintiff attempted to leave the hotel, she was prevented by the first defendant and his friend as threatened and subsequently detained for forty minutes until the arrival of the police. She was arrested at the Hotel by six armed Police officers, and transported in an open truck to the Bulawayo Central Police Station. At the police station, the Plaintiff was ordered to take off her shoes and sit down on the floor, and curious members of the public and the media took photographs of her. Five male officers asked her to lower her trousers, and the officers laughed, jeered and taunted her. And then she was taken to the charge room where she found the first Respondent giving an animated statement in support of her arrest. The plaintiff was detained for two nights at the police station. In this case, the High Court concluded that the Plaintiff was entitled to an award of damages for the abuse she suffered from the police relating to her unlawful arrest, violation of her rights while being detained and for malicious prosecution as her constitutional rights were significantly violated (taken from Phele (2021)).

Chap. 7 of this work. Likewise, it is important to research cases in other jurisdictions because they affect each other through judicial references and judicial dialogues.

As *Zago* states in his writing about the *Oliari* case, the judges in the ECtHR are "sensible to new developments at the global level."[2] This is particularly important in dealing with cases such as same-sex marriages because these cases are sensitive to international trends. Another point is that inter-institutional interaction or communication plays an important role in fulfilling a common mission[3] such as prohibiting discrimination. In this sense, it is also important to know how other jurisdictions or countries are dealing with cases of discrimination based on sexual orientation. Some discussions regarding the principle of equality in other jurisdictions such as Germany, U.S., and Britain have been briefly introduced in this work. However, when focusing on the ECtHR cases, it was not possible to analyze cases in other jurisdictions deeply. Besides India and Taiwan, the analysis of recent case laws of other Asian countries will definitely provide very helpful insights to Korean courts since Asian countries may share common cultural and social backgrounds. Particularly, the case analysis from the IACtHR will be necessary to enhance protection of sexual minorities because the IACtHR works very progressively in terms of the rights of sexual minorities through legal interpretations as well as holistic forms of reparations. This research will definitely help prohibit discrimination based on sexual orientation in South Korea.

The second suggestion is based on the discussion between democracy and courts. The role of court and judicial review are particularly important topics in relation to the applicability of the Principle of Proportionality, which needs to be discussed in depth. The applicability of structured proportionality related to the discussion of the role of judicature and the scope of judicial review: in applying the test of *necessity*, the discussion often addresses whether the ECtHR has the power to look for other less restrictive alternatives even when the applicants do not submit or present them. As the dissenting opinion of the case of *Genderdoc-M v. Moldova* argues, it is questionable whether the ECtHR should compare "other possible assemblies that were or were not allowed for the same reasons of public order"[4] in an assessment of the proportionality. Such a positive role of the judicature is often criticized regarding expressions of "the expansive scope of judicial review defended by proponents of proportionality."[5] In the application of the structured test of the proportionality,

[2] Zago (2015).

[3] Maues et al. (2021), p. 2: in this article, the authors discusses the dialogue between the Supreme Courts of Argentina, Brazil and Mexico and the Constitutional Court of Colombia with the Inter-American Court of Human Rights particularly regarding the common patterns in these four countries' relations with the Inter-American Court of Human Rights. As the authors stated, a different type of communication between international and domestic courts became widespread, judicial communications are worth studying especially when dealing with the common evolving topic such as the jurisprudence of discrimination based on sexual orientation.

[4] European Court of Human Rights, *Genderdoc-M v. Moldova,* judgment of 12 September 2012. Dissenting opinion, paragraph 4.

[5] Webber (2018), p. 95.

particularly the less restrictive means test and the balancing test are criticized. The criticisms are related to the role of the judicature—how far the courts could decide. And the issue of intensity of judicial review is discussed in relation to the application of proportionality, because different degrees of judicial review are applied with the principle of proportionality by courts. In this sense, further research on the role of the judicature and the principle of proportionality is needed.

Another important topic for further research is to study the principle of proportionality as a universal human rights principle, as *Jan Sieckmann*[6] proposes in his article. The principle of proportionality is not confined to negative, civil and political rights, or some specific jurisdiction. As the principle of proportionality has universal characters, it is universally valid. *Sieckmann* suggests the following as the universal character of the principle of proportionality, (1) *A Priori-Validity* means that norms are universally valid as far as their application is a necessary condition for any substantive normative justification, because such normative justification requires balancing and balancing requires proportionality. (2) *Necessary Validity in Each Legal System* because a norm is universally valid if it must be recognized as legally valid by each legal system. *Sieckmann* concludes that the principle of proportionality is at least universally valid as a necessary condition of any normative justification due to the intrinsic relation between balancing and proportionality. Considering the important role of the principle of proportionality, analysis on applicability in other rights other than the case law related to discrimination based on sexual orientation is needed to protect rights of other vulnerable minorities and finally to fulfill the non-discrimination principle in the area of other rights.

The role of the judicature in relation to the principle of proportionality is also a topic which needs to be further researched. As discussed in earlier chapters, it is problematic that the ECtHR does not have sufficient clarity as to the test and standards especially in the case law of same-sex marriage. To raise the level of clarity and transparency in the uses of methodological tools, it is important for the Court to use a more structured proportionality test, especially including the test of suitability, necessity, and the proportionality in the strict sense. To improve the test of necessity, whether the Court itself has the power to assess necessary or useful means or other less restrictive measures is often discussed. *Gerards*[7] introduced the notion that these potential problems could be solved if the Court assessed alternatives which the applicant has presented with evidence, or took a pragmatic approach by limiting itself to mentioning a few examples put forward by the parties.

Among the steps of the German tradition-like structured proportionality test, the sub-test of suitability asks whether the right-restricting measure can attain its objective. In addition, the sub-test of necessity assesses whether the measure is necessary or if there are less restrictive measures available to accomplish the same end. While

[6] Sieckmann (2018).

[7] Gerards (2013), pp. 486–488.

the test of suitability has been applied, the less restrictive measure test[8] in particular has hardly been used in the case law of ECtHR. By integrating less restrictive measures into the proportionality analysis, as *Brems* and *Lavrysen* discuss, the Court could be equipped with an effective and rationally coherent basis for judicial review. The Court could unburden the balancing exercise by introducing a more structured three-tiered proportionality analysis including the Less Restrictive Measure (LRM) test.[9] However, criticism often points out that the LRM test empowers a court to make difficult decisions about the relationship between means and ends. *Katharine Young* also criticizes the LRM test, arguing that the sub-test of proportionality encounters the problem of separation of powers because "too little deference causes the court to usurp the democratically elected branches."[10] However, such a criticism is not clear enough, in that the problem is not limited to only positive obligations, and the problem with the separation of powers does not make the LRM test useless. Considering the importance of the principle of proportionality as a methodological tool, the applicability of the principle of proportionality in the cases other than discrimination based on sexual orientation should be continuously researched and discussed.

9.3 Personal Reflection

Considering the current Korean situation where non-criminalization of same-sex relations has not been accomplished, discussing same-sex marriage seems to be hopeless. Nevertheless, the decision of the Taiwanese Constitutional Court to legalize same-sex marriage gave me some hope. Although my home country, South Korea, has not yet held a mature discussion of same-sex marriage,[11] I came to have a positive impression that it may happen in the near future. Many

[8]Gerards differentiates the necessity test from the least intrusive/restrictive means in that necessity can also be determined on its own, by examining whether the intended results could not or could less easily have been achieved, and necessity means that the instrument must generally be shown to be useful or worthwhile, rather than being the "least intrusive" means (taken from Gerards (2013), pp. 481–482). I also agree with her to differentiate the necessity test from the least intrusive means test as I also could not find any case law of ECtHR with same-sex marriage to apply or to be implied to apply the less restrictive means test. Nevertheless, I was able to reconstruct some cases to be inferred from using the test of necessity in this work.

[9]Brems and Lavrysen (2015), pp. 145–147.

[10]Young (2017), p. 24.

[11]I feel as if the foundations for a discussion about same-sex marriage are still not available, because Korean people still do not want to discuss same-sex couples. In the last discussion among president candidates in April 2017, legal recognition of same-sex relationship was an important question. Except only one candidate from the progressive party, all the candidates including the current Korean president expressed their opinion against the legal recognition of same-sex relationship. It was ironic that the current president is against same-sex marriage while expressing his opinion against any discrimination based on sexual orientation. The first step is decriminalizing same-sex

Constitutional Courts in Asia including the Constitutional Court of Korea are reluctant to make a decision regarding same-sex marriage because they believe that it is not the court but the National Assembly which legalizes or makes a legal recognition. I think such reluctance come from misunderstanding about the role of courts. The court misunderstands that the right to same-sex marriage is not recognized as a fundamental or core constitutional right although in fact it is. Although the Constitutional courts make decisions on the alleged violation of fundamental human rights through the constitutional lawsuits, at the same time they are making excuses as if constantly violating fundamental rights were not their fault, but that of the legislature's. Perhaps such an excuse is that the Constitutional court, especially that of Korea, acknowledges itself that the court has a functional limitation resulting from its own logic. Of course, the legislature primarily takes responsibility if there is a lack of legal provisions to set up such a system. However, if some fundamental rights are violated by the absence of legislation or even wrongful legislation, courts should not leave these rights to be continuously violated.

The other problems with the Constitutional Court of Korea, as I pointed out from the ECtHR case law, is that it does not properly apply the structured test of proportionality test. For example, adultery was previously a crime in Korea. The Constitutional Court of Korea constantly regarded a criminal punishment as constitutional from the year 1990 up to 2008. The CCK did not properly apply each sub-test of the proportionality test in its decision, but only applied it vaguely, thereby putting considerable energy on explaining its conservative Confucianism culture and the consensus of the people. Finally, the CCK decided that it is unconstitutional to punish adultery criminally and the law was abolished. Conscientious objection to military service has been criminally punished in South Korea until the law has been amended after the CCK decision in 2018. If the CCK properly applies the structured proportionality test in the legal reasoning of its decision, it is an open question as to how many problematic laws would still remain after the test of suitability, necessity, and balancing. I am sure that it should not be the least restrictive measure that conscientious objectors are criminally punished and put in jail for an average period of 1 year and 6 months without being provided with any alternative service.

In Asia, especially in South Korea, social debate on same-sex marriage is still at a very early stage. I personally believe that the CCK needs to refer to the Taiwanese ruling on the same-sex marriage, considering the role of judicature and applying the structured principle of proportionality. Marriage is a right, not an obligation. In other words, it is not an area to be enforced or punished by legislation in the country but an area where the individuals in society should conduct an ongoing debate and reach agreement. The issue should also be dealt with from a point of view which sees it as discrimination based on sexual orientation. Furthermore, sexual minorities are considered as being the most vulnerable minorities in the Korean society. How to deal with same-sex marriage is a problem related to the customs of the society, but at

---

relationship in the military according to Korean military law. The next step is the legal recognition of same-sex relations including legalizing same-sex marriage.

the same time, as we all agree, we should not leave it as it is since it is a violation of the fundamental rights of minorities. I believe that the structured test of proportionality as well as the role of the judicature will help to prohibit further discrimination and violation of a very important fundamental human right.

Recent tragic news from Korea is the suicide of Ms. *Byun Hui-Soo*, who first revealed her transsexuality in public. She did not violate any laws, and therefore there was no reason for her to be forcibly dismissed from the army. Nevertheless, the Korean military forcibly dismissed her because of her sexual orientation and ignored the recommendation from the Korean Human Rights Committee not to do this. Following her death the Korean military did not express any condolences because she was no longer a soldier.[12] "Representation of the world, like the world itself, is the work of men; they describe it from their own point of view, which they confuse with the absolute truth." This is the quotation from the preface of the bestselling book "invisible women"[13] which was an eye-opener for many women including myself. Invisibility leads to minorities being discriminated against, ignored, and hated. Sexual minorities are the most invisible group in Korean society, and the first brave female who revealed her transsexuality was ultimately not able to fight against all those prejudices. While reading the hateful comments following the news article about the death of *Byun*, I wondered whether these people think that discrimination is their right. What if the right not to be discriminated against is "the commons" everyone has ownership to? Even if the tragedy of the commons is discussed from the economic perspective, vulnerable minorities in society do not deserve "the least care" as Aristotle states: "what is common to the greatest number has the least care bestowed upon it. Everyone thinks chiefly of his own, hardly at all of the common interest."[14] Discrimination against sexual minorities is so harsh that this "the least care" is not bestowed. If majorities realize that they do not have right to discriminate against others and sexual minorities also have the right not to be discriminated against, sexual minorities will no longer invisible.

9.4 Towards the Protection of Sexual Minorities in Korea

The very evidence for how sexual minorities suffer in South Korea illustrates that they are invisible in society. There are those who hate, abuse and curse them throughout the society, forcing them to hide. Korea's success in controlling the Covid-19 virus was seen positively, yet there are human rights violations behind the

[12] The Hankyoreh (March 4, 2021), *Social murder by discrimination and hate*, http://www.hani.co.kr/arti/opinion/editorial/985499.html. Accessed November 30, 2021.

[13] Perez (2019), Preface.

[14] Ostrom (2018), p. 2.

effectiveness. All the personal information of those infected with Covid-19 is shared via the media with the public. Unexpectedly, one of the infected has visited the five clubs where sexual minorities usually gather in downtown Seoul. After such information was released, the mass media excessively focused on the sexual orientation of the infected. Typically reflecting the atmosphere where homosexuality is abhorred, many people argue that all those bars and clubs for gay people have to be closed by the authorities.[15] Such an ambience leads to increasingly less room for sexual minorities in Korea in the public sphere.

The controversy over non-discrimination based on sexual orientation and equality of sexual minorities affects not only the basic rights of homosexuals in Korean society, but also the general issue of minority discrimination. As discussed in the earlier chapters, the absence of a general anti-discrimination law only exposes the limits of guarantees under individual laws, and even has the effect of preventing recognition of discrimination among society as a whole. If a general non-discrimination law is enacted, the ripple effect will be much greater than we think. However, while considering many realities where there are considerable numbers of scholars who have a skeptical perspective on the legislation of a comprehensive anti-discrimination law, further discussions are needed to present the reasons to persuade them otherwise.

Article 11 of the Korean Constitution stipulates the following: "Paragraph 1. All citizens shall be equal before the law, and there shall be no discrimination in political, economic, social or cultural life on account of sex, religion or social status. 2. No privileged caste shall be recognized or ever established in any form. 3. The awarding of decorations or distinctions of honor in any form shall be effective only for recipients, and no privileges shall thereby ensue." Other grounds such as disability, age, and sexual orientation are not explicitly stated in the grounds for discrimination. In addition, there is no indication of direct or indirect discrimination. These provisions do not seem to reflect the changing times. It is also true that it does not reflect cultural changes.

Prohibiting discrimination based on sexual orientation, as some argue, does not generally promote homosexuality or destroy the values traditionally protected. It literally includes the prohibition of discrimination as well as protecting the rights of sexual minorities. It took South Korea decades for the crime of adultery and the prohibition of marriage between the same surnames and same origins to be abolished. The debate before the abolition was not meaningless, but there were many victims under the provisions of this criminal code before their abolition. The prohibition of discrimination based on sexual orientation also has its significance in preventing the justification of closedness and repression of society in the name of tradition and culture, ultimately through criminal punishment. The public opinion

[15] Yonhap news (2020), *Korean Itaewon Club corona confirmed: discrimination of sexual minorities concerned*, https://www.yna.co.kr/view/AKR20200510005351009?input=1195m. Accessed November 30, 2021.

forum of civil society is already open. However, discussions on legislation are proceeding too slowly.

In modern society, it is difficult to completely separate the private and the public sphere, and it is difficult to form a free relationship between individuals beyond the dimension that protects individual rights from national repression. These changes have led states to intervene in discrimination and inequality that exist in the private realm. Thus, private autonomy no longer justifies discrimination between individuals, but it has to be formally established through legislative debates. Legislating for general and comprehensive anti-discrimination laws not only prevents discrimination that exists in personal relationships, but also contributes to changing public awareness of individuals who suffer from discrimination. It can be said that the dislike of homosexuality, which the Constitutional Court and the Supreme Court showed in the case of the Korean military criminal law to criminalize homosexual relations between consenting adults, was revealed in the absence of a non-discrimination law.

Furthermore, the logic that the state must insist on strict neutrality is a leap of logic for individuals who suffer from discrimination. It is more appropriate to understand the principle of a state's neutrality, not the neutrality of results, but the neutrality of reasoning and neutralization of justification. The principle of a state's neutrality should be understood as a derivative principle which serves to establish equal respect for human dignity, rather than the principle to guide state's actions.[16] In other words, the state should intervene on matters between individuals for the purpose of establishing human dignity. The principle of private autonomy cannot exist over the prohibition of discrimination, which is enacted on unreasonable grounds.

Moreover, in connection with the implementation of same-sex marriage in Korea, I think the following suggestions are suitable. The term "the sexes" used in Article 36 (1) of the Constitution[17] is based on the concept of marriage at the time the Constitution was enacted. Moreover, such a concept of marriage may have been different from our understanding of marriage today, but in no way does it prohibit same-sex marriage. The most desirable way is to define marriage as "a bond between two people" so that heterosexual and same-sex couples are treated in the same way in all respects, and such terms as "the sexes" or "married couple" used in other Korean laws can be newly defined accordingly.[18] A decision of legal marriage is entirely a national administrative function and also a legislative function. Therefore, if only heterosexual couples are granted the right to marry, the state is discriminating against same-sex couples because it deprives them of the right to marry based on their sexual

[16] Kim (2015), p. 70.

[17] Article 36, The Constitution of the Republic of Korea

Paragraph 1. Marriage and family life shall be entered into and sustained on the basis of individual dignity and equality of *the sexes*, and the State shall do everything in its power to achieve that goal.

[18] Oh (2015), p. 344.

orientation.[19] Therefore, the excuse that society is not yet ready to accept same-sex marriage is not valid as a reason to justify such discrimination. Society has almost never been ready to accept minority issues because of prejudice and stereotypes. However, it is the function of the Constitutional Court to make many of those who try to maintain such inequalities realize the importance of equality, which is the foundation of fundamental rights.[20]

I have discussed discrimination based on sexual orientation in over 200 pages ultimately to seek some alternatives to prohibit discrimination. It is not easy to suggest alternatives given the long history of discrimination against sexual minorities. Nevertheless, I want to finish this long journey with some humble alternatives of mine. Firstly, the courts should apply a clear, consistent, foreseeable methodology in their reasoning process including the fully structured proportionality test. Secondly, constitutional courts should take a positive role to protect the human rights of vulnerable minorities in society instead of leaving the existing legislative gaps or flaws. Thirdly, it is important to legislate for a comprehensive anti-discrimination law. Fourthly, strategic litigation working together with human rights organizations can help the future development of an anti-discrimination law. The tasks involved in working towards the prohibition of discrimination based on sexual orientation have often produced incomplete solutions, nevertheless, progress has been evident, and ultimately deeply rewarding[21] and now is certainly not the time to give up.

References

Brems E, Lavrysen L (2015) 'Don't use a sledgehammer to crack a nut': less restrictive means in the case law of the European Court of Human Rights. Hum Rights Law Rev 15(1):139–168. https://doi.org/10.1093/hrlr/ngu040. Accessed November 30, 2021.

Fredman S (2011) Discrimination law, 2nd edn. Oxford University Press, Oxford

Gerards J (2013) How to improve the necessity test of the European Court of Human Rights. Int J Constit Law 11(2):466–490. https://doi.org/10.1093/icon/mot004. Accessed November 30, 2021.

Kim D-K (2015) The principle of state neutrality as equal respect, research on legal philosophy. Korean Acad Leg Philos 18(3):41–72. UCI: G704-001303.2015.18.3.007

Maues AM et al (2021) Judicial dialogue between National courts and the Inter-American Court of Human Rights: a comparative study of Argentina, Brazil, Colombia and Mexico. Hum Rights Law Rev 00:1–24. https://doi.org/10.1093/hrlr/ngaa047

Oh S-J (2015) The right to same-sex marriage - analyses of U.S. cases and trends of international human rights law. Dankook Law Rev 39(3):325–347. https://doi.org/10.17252/dlr.2015.39.3.011

Ostrom E (2018) Governing the commons. Cambridge University Press, Cambridge

Perez CC (2019) Invisible women. Vintage, Penguin Random House UK, London

[19] *Young v. Australia*, Communication No. 941/2000, U.N. Do. (CCPR/C/78/D/941/2000).

[20] The Constitutional Court of Korea, 88 Hun-Ga 7, decided on January 25, 1989.

[21] Fredman (2011), p. 335.

Phele K (2021) Zimbabwe: High Court upholds Transgender persons' constitutional rights, Case comment for Legal Grounds III: Reproductive and Sexual Rights in Sub-Saharan Africa, Reprohealthlaw Blog Commentaries, February 16, 2021, https://africlaw.com/2021/02/19/zimbabwe-high-court-upholds-transgender-persons-constitutional-rights/. Accessed November 30, 2021.

Sieckmann J (2018) Proportionality as a universal human rights principle. In: Duarte D, Sampaio JS (eds) Proportionality in law. Springer, Heidelberg

Webber G (2018) Proportionality and absolute rights. In: Jackson V, Tushment M (eds) Proportionality, new frontiers, new challenges. Cambridge University Press, Cambridge

Young KG (2017) Proportionality, reasonableness, and economic and social rights. In: Jackson V, Tushnet M (eds) Proportionality: new frontiers, new challenges (comparative constitutional law and policy). Cambridge University Press, Cambridge, pp 221–247. https://doi.org/10.1017/9781316691724.012

Zago G (2015) A victory for Italian same-sex couples, a victory for European homosexuals? A commentary on Oliari v. Italy. Article 29, August 21, 2015. Available at SSRN: https://ssrn.com/abstract=2689060. Accessed November 30, 2021.

The manufacturer's authorised representative in the EU is Springer Nature Customer Service Centre GmbH, Europaplatz 3, 69115 Heidelberg, Germany. If you have any concerns regarding our products, please contact ProductSafety@springernature.com

Printed and bound by CPI Group (UK) Ltd, Croydon, CR0 4YY
30/09/2026
02225460-0017